DANCES IN DEEP SHADOWS

DANCES IN DEEP SHADOWS

The Clandestine War in Russia, 1917–20

Michael Occleshaw

CARROLL & GRAF PUBLISHERS
New York

Carroll & Graf Publishers
An imprint of Avalon Publishing Group, Inc.
245 W. 17th Street
11th Floor
New York, NY 10011–5300
www.carrollandgraf.com

AVALON
publishing group incorporated

First published in the UK by Constable,
an imprint of Constable & Robinson Ltd, 2006

First Carroll & Graf edition 2006

ISBN-13: 978–0–78671–789–7
ISBN-10: 0–7867–1789–0

Printed and bound in the EU

Contents

◄○►

CONTENTS

List of Illustrations

◄○►

Major Terence Keyes with pony and dog, Turbar-i-hind, India.
(*Courtesy of the British Library, PHOTO 851/3 (39)*)

General Alexei Maximovich Kaledin.
(*Courtesy of RIA-Novosti*)

Felix Edmundovich Dzerzhinsky.
(*Courtesy of the Mary Evans Picture Library*)

Lord Robert Cecil.
(*Courtesy of the Mary Evans Picture Library*)

Count Ernst von Brockdorff-Rantzau.
(*Courtesy of the Deutsches Historisches Museum, Berlin*)

General Pustovoytenko, Nicholas II and General Alexeyev.
(*Courtesy of RIA-Novosti*)

Générals Lavergne and Niessel and Ambassador Noulens.
(*Courtesy of Getty Images*)

Count Wilhem von Mirbach.
(*Courtesy of EarthStation1.com*)

Boris Viktorovich Savinkov.
(*Courtesy of Getty Images*)

Caricature of Admiral Sir William Hall.
(Courtesy of the National Archives)

Captain Proctor's alarmist submission.
(Courtesy of the National Archives)

Captain Francis Cromie.
(Courtesy of the RN Submarine Museum (RNSM))

Consul Douglas Young and Mrs Young.
(Courtesy of the British Library, ADD 61855 No.2)

Dramatis Personae

◄o►

Where ranks or titles altered during the years covered by this history or afterwards, the later rank or title is given in parentheses.

Alexeyev, General Mikhail Vasilievich: Former Chief of Staff to Tsar Nicholas II. Leader of the Volunteer Army.

Balfour, (Lord) Arthur: British Foreign Secretary.

Boyce, Commander Ernest: Head of the British Secret Service's Moscow station.

Brockdorff-Rantzau, Count Ernst von: German Ambassador to the Kingdom of Sweden. In 1919 he was German Plenipotentiary at the Versailles Peace Conference.

'C': *See* Smith Cumming.

Cecil, Lord Robert: British Minister of Blockade and Assistant Foreign Secretary. He was an avid advocate of intervention.

Chaplin, Grigori: (*alias Captain Thomson RN*) Russian Naval officer and friend of Captain Cromie. Instrumental in preparing intended *coup* at Archangel with Captain McGrath.

Chicherin, George: People's Commissar for Foreign Affairs after the resignation of Trotsky.

Churchill, Winston Leonard Spencer: Minister of Munitions in 1918, then Minister for War. He was a confirmed imperialist and interventionist.

Cromie, Captain Francis Newton Allen: British Naval Attaché, Petrograd.

De Verthamon, Martial-Marie-Henri: French agent and saboteur.

Dukes, (Sir) Paul: British Secret Service agent S.T.25.

Dunsterville, Major-General, Lionel: Led a British expedition to secure control of Transcaucasia.

Dzerzhinsky, Felix Edmundovich: First head of the Cheka.

Fetterlein, Ernest Constantinovich:	Tsarist code breaker *par excellence*. Fled to Britain in 1918 and joined Room 40.
Goldsmith, Major G.M.:	British Intelligence officer in Transcaucasia.
Grenard, Joseph Ferdinand	French Consul-General in Moscow. Heavily involved in clandestine activity.
Guinet, Commandant Alfonse:	French officer responsible for coordinating the activities of the Czechoslovaks and Whites in Siberia.
Hall, Admiral (Sir) William Reginald 'Blinker':	British Director of Naval Intelligence. One of few commanders in the First World War worthy of the term 'genius'. A determined opponent of Bolshevism.
Helphand, Alexander Israel:	Russian-German Revolutionary theorist and practitioner who collaborated with the Germans and inspired them to seek to subvert the Russian Empire. Instrumental in persuading the Germans to turn to Lenin.
Hill, Captain George:	Officer in the RAF, attached to Rusplycom and then the British Secret Service.
Kalamatiano, Xenophon B.:	Main American Secret Intelligence operative.
Kaledin, General Alexei Maximovich:	Ataman of the Don Cossacks and leader of the South Eastern Confederacy (or Federation).
Karachan, Leo:	Deputy to, firstly, Trotsky, then Chicherin in the People's Commissariat for Foreign Affairs.
Keyes, Major (later Colonel) Terence:	Political Officer attached to the British Embassy in Russia. Responsible for the first two phases of the Banking Scheme.
Knox, Major-General (Sir) Alfred:	Formerly British Military Attaché in Russia. One of the main proponents of intervention in Russia. He became Military Attaché to the Kolchak regime.
Krivoshein, Alexander:	Leader of one of the most powerful Monarchist factions in Russia. Involved in the first Banking Scheme.
Lavergne, Général:	French General on the staff of the French Ambassador to Russia. Involved in espionage.
Le Page, Commander George Wilfred:	Captain Cromie's deputy.
Lindley, (Sir) Francis:	Counsellor to the British Embassy in Russia. Later British High Commissioner at Vologda.
Litch (Christian name unknown):	British agent responsible for financing opposition to Germany in Ukraine and the occupied territories.

Lockhart, (Sir) Robert Bruce Hamilton:	British diplomatic agent in Moscow, 1918. More closely engaged in clandestine activity than is normally considered to be the case. Sentenced to death *in absentia* by the Soviet regime.
McAlpine, Major R.:	Originally a civil servant. General Poole's deputy in Russia.
MacDonell, Ranald:	Formerly British Vice-Consul at Baku. Heavily involved in espionage.
Macdonogh, Lt.-Gen George Mark Watson:	British Director of Military Intelligence.
McGrath, Captain W.M.A.:	British Secret Service officer active in north Russia and Petrograd.
Marchand, René:	French journalist. Disillusioned with his country's attitude to the Bolsheviks, he revealed the Allied plot of August 1918 to the Bolsheviks.
Milner, Viscount Alfred:	Senior British administrator and member of the War Cabinet. An imperialist who favoured intervention.
Mirbach, Count Wilhelm von:	German Ambassador to Russia, April–July 1918.
Nikitine, Colonel Boris Vladimirovich:	Head of Russian counter-espionage under the Provisional Government.
Noel, Captain Edward:	British Political Officer.
Noulens, Joseph:	French Ambassador to Russia. Strong advocate of intervention and an important influence behind Allied attempts to subvert Soviet Russia.
Parvus:	*See* Helphand, Alexander.
Poole, De Witt C.:	United States' Consul-General in Moscow. Ultimately responsible for American clandestine activity there.
Poole, General Frederick:	Originally head of BMES, then Rusplycom. His conversion to the interventionist cause in the spring of 1918 was influential in bringing about intervention. Commanded Allied interventionist forces in north Russia.
Reilly, Sydney George:	Officially an officer in the RAF, in fact agent S.T.1 of the British Secret Service. He used several aliases including Mr Constantine, Konstantin Markovich Massino and Sigmund Rellinsky.

Riezler, Kurt: German career diplomat, originally from Bavaria. In 1918 he was Counsellor with the German Embassy in Moscow.

Rodzianko, Mikhail: Chairman of the Duma. A leader of the 'Party of Collection' in south Russia.

Savinkov, Boris Viktorovich: A professional revolutionary but a Russian patriot. He had an unfortunate knack of making enemies out of friends and associates.

Scale, Captain (later Major) John: British Secret Service officer.

Semenoff, Grigori: Self-styled 'Ataman' and 'General'. Led ostensibly anti-Bolshevik and anti-German band in Siberia. In reality little more than a bandit.

Skoropis-Yoltukhovsky, A: Chairman of the Union for the Liberty of the Ukraine.

Smith Cumming, Captain (Sir) Mansfield: Head of MI1(c), the British Secret Service. Known as 'C'.

Steel, Lt.-Colonel Richard Alexander: Officer in the 17th Cavalry, Indian Army. Appointed head of MIO and, later, MO5.

Teague-Jones, Captain Reginald: British Political Officer in Transcaspia.

Trotsky, Leon Davidovich: People's Commissar for Foreign Affairs, then People's Commissar for War. One of the main Bolshevik leaders.

Wangenheim, Baron von: German Ambassador in Constantinople.

Wardrop, (Sir) Oliver: British Consul-General in Moscow, 1918. Engaged in espionage.

Wilson, General (Field-Marshal) Sir Henry Hughes: British Chief of the Imperial General Staff. Confirmed supporter of intervention.

Woodhouse, Arthur: British Consul-General at Petrograd.

Yaroshinsky, Karol: Ukrainian banker and financier, the mainstay of the Banking Scheme.

Yermolenko, Ensign: Russian prisoner of the Germans, used by the Germans to spread subversive propaganda. His testimony was used to label Lenin as a German spy.

Young, Douglas: British Consul at Archangel. He warned the British Government against intervention.

Zimmermann, Arthur: German Under Secretary of State, 1917. He was effectively the German Foreign Minister.

Zinoviev, Grigory: One of the leading Bolsheviks of 1917. Regarded as a key figure by Parvus and a companion of Lenin.

Preface

—◄o►—

There is nothing in this book that has been invented. All of the people who populate its pages were real people. Everything that I have reported them saying and doing is based on documentary evidence. It is certain that the evidence remains incomplete. Some has not been released, even under the Freedom of Information Act; some has been destroyed, including material lost through enemy action at the Arnside Record Repository in 1940; doubtless more remains to be discovered. To that extent this book is a contribution to the history of the events of 1917–20 and all that they meant for the world in the following years.

Since the attack by the Allied Intelligence Services on Soviet Russia was both so far-reaching and all pervasive, it can be cogently argued that a book of this nature is sorely needed, one that considers the clandestine war as a whole, rather than concentrating on particular aspects of it. Spies there are, but they represent only part of the story. While studies of particular parts of this great enterprise have an obvious value, it is the cumulative effect of the whole that shaped the history, or life, of the peoples of the twentieth century.

More material is available in the British National Archives than might initially appear to be the case. However, it is scattered among many different classes and departments of government. Pulling that into a coherent whole has been a major effort and a book of this size necessarily means that much of interest, but remaining marginal to the main thrust of the history, has necessarily been omitted.

Several salient factors emerged in the course of working on this history. One is the role of a section in the British War Office that few appear to have heard of. The part played by MIO under Lieutenant-Colonel Richard Steel has attracted little attention. It is ignored in virtually every history of the First World War. The disappearance of its papers, either by accident or design, represents a lamentable loss. MIO was largely responsible for the British element in the clandestine war in Russia from its outset. It was the waging of this war that led to the recognition that the aim of the Western Allies was to bring about the downfall of the Bolshevik regime by civil war much earlier than conventional histories would have us believe. Civil War was both implicit and inherent in its strategy from the very beginning.

In turn this led to the unveiling of a whole diplomatic underworld that worked in harness with formal diplomacy. Much of this secret world remains hidden, as it is doubtless intended that it should. Its existence and conduct belie the attitude that is so often struck by Western governments, their diplomatic representatives and historians, that their hands are always clean, and it is solely the object of their enmity that has a monopoly on double dealing and underhand methods.

Every effort has been made to trace the holders of copyright in the original material quoted in this work. There may be a very few where the effort has proved forlorn. Any of the copyright-holders whose material has been included but where it has not been possible to contact them, are cordially invited to contact me.

Acknowledgements

─◄o►─

I would like to offer my profound thanks to the members of staff of the British Library, particularly the Oriental and India Office; extracts from documents held by the British Library are quoted by permission of the British Library. My thanks are no less due to the House of Lords Record Office; the Department of Documents at the Imperial War Museum; the National Archives (formerly the Public Record Office), Kew, Surrey; the National Archives of Scotland, Edinburgh; the Royal Naval Submarine Museum, Gosport, and the Service Historique de l'Armée de Terre at the Chateau de Vincennes.

My thanks for permission to quote material from the Hankey Papers are due to the Master and Fellows of Churchill College, Cambridge, and they are equally due to the Trustees of the Liddell Hart Centre for Military Archives, King's College, London, for permission to quote from the papers of General Sir Frederick Poole.

The assistance of Tessa Stirling and the staff at the Cabinet Office deserve special mention for their valuable assistance with so many subjects, as does that of my MP, Mr Michael Foster, who helped unlock one particular door.

I would also like to thank Peter Hofschroer and Franciska Laursen for their valued work in translating some of the longer and trickier German passages.

That noble body, the Authors' Foundation, deserves every credit for their particularly valuable assistance at critical junctures.

My literary agent Anne Harrel, the granddaughter of a Naval Intelligence Officer of the First World War, has as ever been a stalwart. I would like to record my especially warm appreciation for her support, help and encouragement despite the most trying personal circumstances.

My friends Brian McCarter and Michael Kingscote are thanked for their interest, encouragement and unfailing good humour throughout the long months of research and writing. They have, perhaps, little idea of how important their company has been in providing very welcome breaks and light relief.

Most of all I would like to thank in the warmest possible terms my wife Elizabeth. I appreciate how trying it must have been living with someone who was so often wrapped up in work that, at times, it provided her with little positive company. My appreciation of her continual support, encouragement and assistance in so many respects is difficult to put into words; the English language cannot do adequate justice to it.English language cannot do adequate justice to it.

Notes on the Text

◄o►

Russian dates

Russia used the Julian calendar until midnight on 31 January 1918, when the Bolshevik Government decreed that the Gregorian calendar that was in use in Western Europe and the United States was to be adopted. Thus within Russia the date following 31 January 1918 became 14 February 1918. All dates relating to events within Russia prior to 31 January 1918 are given in accordance with the Julian calendar and identified by the suffix [OS]. Events elsewhere in Europe are invariably given in accordance with the Gregorian calendar.

Quotations

All quotations are rendered as in the original. Words or groups of words that have proved difficult or impossible to decipher in official documents are indicated with question marks within brackets.

The Germans never accepted the change in name of Russia's western capital city from St Petersburg to Petrograd, hence German official documents quoted refer to the city as St Petersburg.

List of Commonly Used Abbreviations

◄o►

2ème Bureau	Second Section of the French General Staff, responsible for espionage and counter-espionage.
ADM	Admiralty (British).
'C'	Captain Mansfield Smith Cumming RN, head of the British Secret Service.
Cadets	Constitutional Democratic Party, a centre-right Russian political party.
Cheka	All-Russian Extraordinary Commission for Combating Counter-Revolution and Sabotage. Essentially the Bolsheviks' political police. (*Successor organizations with the same function were* GPU, OGPU, NKVD & KGB.)
CIGS	Chief of the Imperial General Staff (British).
DMI	Director of Military Intelligence (British).
DNI	Director of Naval Intelligence (British).
FO	Foreign Office (British).
GC & CS	Government Code & Cipher School (British).
Krug	Cossack assembly.
MI1(c)	British Secret Service (later MI6).
MI2(c)	Military Intelligence, section 2, subsection c.
MI2(d)	Military Intelligence, section 2, subsection d.
MIO	Military Intelligence Operations.
MIR	Military Intelligence Russia – section of the War Office charged with directing Intelligence in Soviet Russia and adjacent territories.
MO2	Military Operations, section 2.

MO5	Military Operations, section 5 – section of the British War Office charged with directing military operations in Soviet Russia and adjacent territories.
NCO (nco)	Non-commissioned officer.
OHL	*Oberste Heeres Leitung* (Supreme Military Leadership) (German).
RAF	Royal Air Force (British).
RFC	Royal Flying Corps (British).
RN	Royal Navy (British).
Rusplycom	Committee on Russian Supplies.
SR	Social Revolutionary Party, a Russian political party with a focus mainly on reform of land ownership. They split into two factions in 1918: LSR: Left Social Revolutionary (Party), a radical section of the Social Revolutionary Party that shared much common ground with the Bolsheviks. RSR: Right Social Revolutionary (Party), the majority of the essentially peasant-based Social Revolutionary Party.
Sovnarkom	Soviet of People's Commissars.
WO	War Office (British).

Russia, 1918.

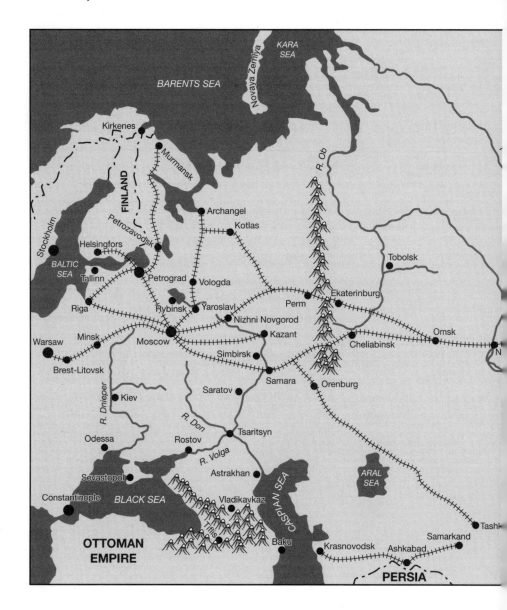

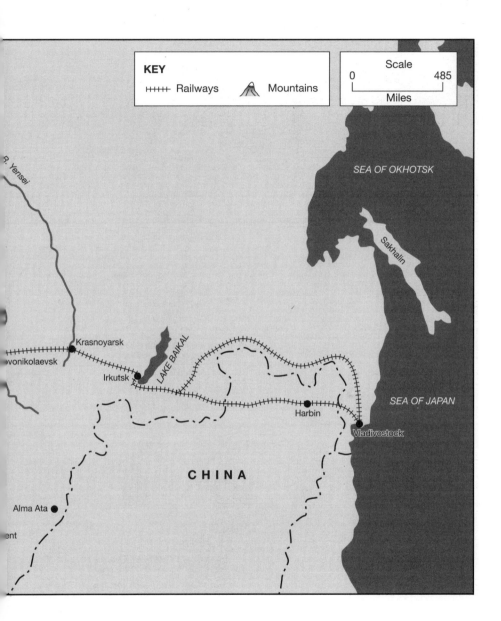

KEY

╫╫╫ Railways   🏔 Mountains

Scale

0 _____ 485

Miles

R. Yensei

SEA OF OKHOTSK

Sakhalin

Krasnoyarsk

LAKE BAIKAL

vonikolaevsk

Irkutsk

SEA OF JAPAN

Harbin

Vladivostock

C H I N A

Alma Ata

ent

Transcaucasia and Transcaspia, including Afghanistan and India, 1918.

RUSSIAN

R. Volga

Astrakhan

BLACK SEA

Vladikavkaz

Grozny

CASPIAN SEA

Poti

Batum

Tiflis

Trebizond

GEORGIA

Kars

Erzerum

ARMENIA

AZERBAIJAN

Baku

Krasnovodsk

OTTOMAN

Yerevan

EMPIRE

Enzeli

Resht

Tehran

Van

Qazvin

Mus

R. Tigris

Tabriz

Mosul

Kirkuk

Hamadan

Kermanshah

R. Euphrates

Baghdad

Isfahan

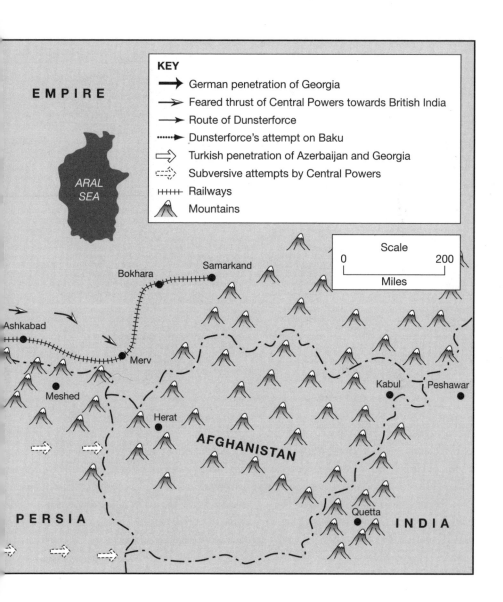

KEY

→ German penetration of Georgia

→ Feared thrust of Central Powers towards British India

→ Route of Dunsterforce

····► Dunsterforce's attempt on Baku

⇨ Turkish penetration of Azerbaijan and Georgia

⊏⇾ Subversive attempts by Central Powers

+++++ Railways

🌋 Mountains

EMPIRE

ARAL SEA

Scale
0   200
Miles

Ashkabad

Bokhara   Samarkand

Merv

Meshed

Herat

AFGHANISTAN

Kabul   Peshawar

PERSIA

Quetta   INDIA

I

Insidious and Effective

To Autumn 1917

◄o►

On 26 February [OS] 1917, soldiers sent to stamp out popular disturbances in the Russian capital, Petrograd, joined forces with the mob.
The State Duma, Russia's parliament, was invaded, with the mob occupying
the left side of it, while the soldiers occupied the right. The hastily convened
Temporary Committee of the State Duma huddled together in two rooms
and tried to extract order out of chaos.[1]

This Revolution owed little to German inspiration, despite the Germans'
efforts to bring about just such chaos in Russia over the previous two years.
Indeed, news of the revolutionary outbreak was received with as much
surprise in Berlin as in every other capital of the world. There had been
numerous plots and most governments had been anticipating some sort of
coup from the wide range of Russian society that was thoroughly disen-
chanted with the corrupt and inefficient conduct of the First World War by
the Tsar's government. That there would or could be a spontaneous rising
seems not to have entered anyone's calculations.

What the first Russian Revolution of 1917 did for the Germans was to
break open the door for a more insidious and effective propaganda than any
that they had tried hitherto. The reason for such tactics was simple enough –
Germany was faced with a war on two fronts, a war that had reached crisis
point in 1916 when, engaged in her own offensive at Verdun, she was hit in
quick succession by a major offensive from the Western Allies on the
Somme, then by the Brusilov offensive on the Eastern front. Although the
German lines had held, the strain this concatenation of events had imposed
led to the replacement of the Chief of General Staff, General Erich von
Falkenhayn, by the duo already famous through their victories in the east,
Paul von Hindenburg and Erich Ludendorff.

Yet it was Falkenhayn who had put his finger on the key to the problem facing Germany as early as November 1914, when he assumed command. In a memorandum dated 27 November, he had stated that Germany needed to transform the war into a one-front engagement and advocated a foreign policy designed to isolate one of the hostile powers and conclude a separate peace with it.[2] Sound as this reasoning was, it was a difficult policy to achieve in practice.

In 1914 and 1915 no 'civilized' Western government would have thought in terms of inspiring something as dangerously radical as a socialist revolution in the ranks of its enemies. The Germans and their Austrian allies were instead seeking to promote unrest among the subject nationalities of the Russian Empire, as with the Irish in 1916, and among the subject nationalities and religions of the British Empire throughout the war. Blandishments were extended to the Poles, who were to form a Polish Legion that fought against Russia alongside the Austro-Hungarian armies, but a major investment was also made in Ukrainian nationalism. The Central Powers forged links with the Union for the Liberty of the Ukraine and provided it with considerable sums of money. However, they also placed it under the control of the Foreign Ministry in Vienna – a considerable mistake since so obvious an association with a declared enemy discouraged much of the support they hoped to win.

However, these activities first drew the attention of the Germans to one of history's most astonishing characters, Alexander Israel Helphand, better known as Parvus. A dedicated professional revolutionary, like Lenin, he saw the war as the crisis of capitalism that had to be exploited for the sake of a socialist revolution. According to both men, this was the proper task of socialist policy in the war. One of several respects in which he differed from Lenin was in his view that revolution in Russia was *the* major objective of his thinking about the war, but like Lenin no price was too high to pay for the attainment of the objective.[3]

Parvus put his house in Constantinople at the disposal of the Union and aided them through his contacts and personal fortune. This led to liaison with the vigorous German Ambassador to the Porte, Baron von Wangenheim, who drew Berlin's attention to Parvus' plans to incite a revolution in one of Germany's most powerful enemies. In February 1915 Parvus

2

was summoned to Berlin to meet the German Under Secretary of State, in effect the Foreign Minister, Gottlieb von Jagow, and a career diplomat, Kurt Riezler, then serving as liaison officer with the German High Command. There, Parvus presented a plan on a vast scale for the subversion of the Tsarist Empire in a document called 'Germany and the Revolution in Russia'.

At this stage his listeners were unprepared to make such a radical leap, preferring instead to rely on the dynastic ties between the Houses of Hesse and Romanov (the Tsarina was a daughter of a Grand Duke of Hesse). When these hopes proved fond – for whatever else the Tsarina could be accused of, treachery was certainly not among them – the Germans were more inclined to reconsider. The situation presented them with a choice between a peace with the existing Russian government, or to help engineer a revolution in Russia and hope to make peace with whatever government then came to power. As the Tsar's government would not make a separate peace with Germany, the choice was effectively made for them.

This should not surprise us. The great Greek historian Thucydides said:

> In times of peace and prosperity cities and individuals alike follow higher standards, because they are not forced into a situation where they have to do what they do not want to do. But war is a stern teacher; in depriving them of the power of easily satisfying their daily wants, it brings most people's minds down to the level of their actual circumstances.[4]

Parvus made his way to Stockholm where he made contact with the German Ambassador, Count Ernst von Brockdorff-Rantzau, someone with no illusions about the dynastic ties between Germany and Russia, nor any sentimentality for the lengthy friendship between the Hohenzollern and Romanov dynasties. In his eyes the Tsar had 'assumed a frightful historical guilt and forfeited the right to any leniency from us' and, 'under the influence of mystic flagellants dreams of victory over an enemy who never wanted to start hostilities against him'.[5] Brockdorff-Rantzau engineered for Parvus to be recalled to Berlin, whence he came away with the promise of one million roubles for propaganda aimed against the Russian Army.

January 1916 saw major strikes at the naval factory in Nikolaev, where the strikers presented absurdly high wage demands that the management could never hope to meet, and one major strike at the massive Putilov works in Petrograd. These can generally be attributed to Parvus' propaganda but they were clearly insufficient to cripple the Russian war effort or lead to revolution. Parvus himself knew that Lenin and the Bolsheviks were the keys to inciting revolution in Russia.

Lenin was then an exile in Switzerland and Parvus had travelled to meet him there in May 1915. The two men could not agree since their strategies were fundamentally irreconcilable. Lenin saw the road to revolution being created by a hard core of professional revolutionaries, the point over which the Russian Social Democrat Party had split into Bolsheviks (Maximalists, or the majority) and Mensheviks (the minority), with the latter advocating a slower, more broadly based transition to a socialist state, if necessary in alliance with bourgeois liberal parties. Parvus broadly favoured the Menshevik approach and sought in vain to heal the rift between the two.

The Revolution of February 1917 then transformed the theatre in which the subversive campaign would be fought. There were in reality two governments in Russia following it. The Temporary Committee of the State Duma rapidly evolved into the Provisional Government, a body that hoped to control the unstable situation and lead Russia on to a path of essentially bourgeois reform. The Petrograd Soviet (Council) was an alternative power base and the aims of the two bodies sometimes conflicted. One of the most serious problems the Provisional Government faced was that it had little ability to enforce its will. The police force had effectively disappeared, many of its members in Petrograd having been killed by the enraged mob after they came under fire from policemen trying to stamp on the excesses of the mob, while the rest had fled.

Worse still, on 1 March, the Petrograd Soviet published Order No. 1 that effectively undermined military discipline, reducing the Russian Army to little more than a mob of dangerous armed men. The order subordinated military authority to the Soviet and ruled that the orders of the Military Commission of the State Duma should be executed only in such cases as did not conflict with the orders and resolution of the Soviet.[6] The order meant that the Provisional Government had no prospect of enforcing its laws unless it secured the prior agreement of the Soviet. As criticism of the order grew from both officers and members of the government, the Soviet tried to absolve itself by pointing out that the order was addressed exclusively to the Petrograd garrison. However, it was unrealistic to expect that its influence would be restricted to such a body when the events in Petrograd were followed throughout Russia.

The Executive Committee of the Soviet also argued that the order had been issued in agreement with the Temporary Committee of the State Duma and thus could not be considered as an order competing with the authority of the government.[7] This version was disputed by Mikhail Rodzianko, the chairman of the State Duma, and it is true that there is no reference to the agreement of the Duma in the document, which was issued in the name of the Petrograd Soviet of Workers' and Soldiers' Deputies alone.

Many have claimed that the worst error the Provisional Government made was to decide to continue the war against the Central Powers: with a peace in 1917 that was not too onerous, they would have won time to consolidate their position and drawn the sting from the propaganda of their worst internal enemies. However, it was not that simple. Russia would undoubtedly have forfeited the goodwill of her Western Allies, who provided the financial backing for the state. More important, perhaps, was the fear that Imperial Germany would crush the Western Allies and then, flushed with victory, turn her full might against a Russia still in the process of reconstruction. While much of the anger was directed against the Tsarist regime for its obvious mishandling of the war effort, that was an entirely different matter to wanting peace at any price. There were still many Russians who were prepared to fight on.

After winning Brockdorff-Rantzau's support for the Bolsheviks, by the expedient of assuring him that they would unfailingly increase anarchy in Russia and exploit the revolution so that the Russian war effort would be crippled, Parvus began preparing the way for the Bolshevik leaders to cross Germany and return to Russia. In concert with the German General Staff, he arranged for Lenin and Zinoviev alone to travel through Germany. Using one of his revolutionary contacts, Hanecki (who used the pseudonym Furstenberg), who was also a friend of Lenin, he let Lenin know that transit through Germany had been arranged. Another contact, Georg Sklarz, hastened to Zurich to accompany the two revolutionaries across Germany.

Lenin was suspicious. He demanded that Hanecki should provide more details about the arrangements and bluntly told him on 24 March, 'Official transit for individuals unacceptable.' When Sklarz arrived and sought to overcome the difficulties by offering to pay the two revolutionaries' fares, Lenin immediately broke off negotiations.

He had good reasons for doing so. If anyone thought that Lenin was the tool of the Germans, he would inevitably have been discredited in the eyes of both the Russians and his fellow Bolsheviks. When the German Foreign Ministry pressed the German Ambassador to Switzerland to hasten the move of Lenin and his party, he replied that nothing had been heard from the Bolsheviks as yet, since they were anxious to avoid compromising themselves by association with the Germans.[8]

Parvus hastened to make amends via Diego von Bergen, an official in the Foreign Ministry, who agreed to transport not only Lenin but the majority of his Bolshevik associates. They travelled across Germany in the infamous sealed train, granted extraterritorial rights in order to invalidate any claims that they had been open to German influence.

The Emperor Karl of Austria-Hungary knew of the German intention to grant passage across Germany to the Bolshevik leadership. That indicates that it was a policy that had been decided at the highest levels; it was certainly a policy with which the young Emperor profoundly disagreed. He pleaded with both the Kaiser and his chancellor to abort the project on the grounds that Lenin was a threat to all empires, not merely the Russian Empire. Moreover, he promptly dismissed the German proposal that the sealed train carrying the Bolshevik leadership should go to Russia via Austrian territory.

When Lenin reached Russia, there occurred one of those ironies of history that demonstrate how much depends on the actions of men rather than on impersonal movements. The Allies had established a counter-espionage system in Russia whereby British Military Control Officers, many of them young and inexperienced, endeavoured to prevent the movement of hostile individuals into the country. The system mirrored that used to control entry and exit from France, which had generally operated with success. Lenin and most of his party were permitted to enter Russia from Sweden, but a British officer stopped Fritz Platten, who was known to have links with the Germans, and Karl Radek, who was both an Austrian subject and a member of the German Social Democratic Party, at the frontier and cancelled their entry visas.[9] Thus were small minnows caught and a large shark allowed to escape.

William Gerhardie, then on the staff of the British Embassy in Petrograd, left a rather petty account of the incident in his autobiography. Although Gerhardie concedes that the officer acted on instructions 'from the liberal-minded Kerensky' when he let the rest through, it did not save him from childish ragging at the hands of his countrymen in Russia:

> The same young officer served with me later, on the British Military Mission in Siberia, and we, the intelligentsia of the mission, twitted him for ever after: 'You're a bright lad, locking the stable door when the horse was out, or, rather, in.' He felt the responsibility of having caused the Soviet revolution acutely. Were he a Japanese he would have committed hari-kiri.[10]

The episode underlines one of the weaknesses that dogged the Provisional Government. Essentially a bourgeois liberal authority, it was utterly dependent on the support of a variety of leftwing parties, notably the Mensheviks and Social Revolutionaries. In the euphoria that followed the Revolution one totem that all were united in clinging to was the doctrine that there were no enemies on the left. Thus it mattered little what radical, unreasonable or treacherous policies a party might pursue, as long as it belonged to the left of the political spectrum it could do no wrong. Some members of the Provisional Government awaited Lenin's arrival with trepidation, or so we may judge from Kerensky's exclamation when, faced with the dithering of his colleagues, he yelled in frustration, 'Just you wait, Lenin himself is coming, and then the real thing will begin'.[11] Lenin and his followers were allowed into Russia, and Trotsky, then a Menshevik, was released from British custody in Canada as a result of pressure that Kerensky and Miliukov brought to bear.

Lenin enjoyed a rapturous reception on his return to Petrograd, but once he began work there is little doubt that his links with the Germans grew stronger. For his stirring words to reach the masses, money had to be spent. As the German State Secretary told the Foreign Ministry Liaison Officer at General Headquarters on 29 September 1917:

We have now been engaged in these activities for some time, and in complete agreement with the Political Section of the General Staff in Berlin (Capt. Von Hulsen). Our work together has shown tangible results. The Bolshevik movement could never have attained the scale or the influence which it has today without our continual support. [12]

This is what enabled the widespread distribution of the Bolshevik newspapers *Pravda* and *Izvestia*, both of which criticized the Provisional Government and spread every type of story that would undermine any inclination to fight the war.

On its own, propaganda of this sort could never have destroyed either the Provisional Government or the Russian war effort. What the propaganda, skilfully arguing the case for a swift peace and for dispossessing the landlords and capitalists in favour of the toiling masses, did do was draw more people to the Bolsheviks. This was especially the case in the major cities of Moscow and Petrograd, the political hearts of the country. There, reflecting the truth of Thucydides' words, it was becoming increasingly difficult for many among the cities' poorer inhabitants to satisfy their daily needs. After the entry of moderate socialists into the government, the discontented turned to the only political party that refused to join this 'bourgeois' government, the Bolsheviks. After April, the party's strength grew and it gained victories in elections held for factory, soldiers' and neighbourhood soviets.

On 3 and 4 July [OS] 1917, mobs poured on to the streets of Petrograd at the Bolsheviks' behest. The mob, led by a machine-gun regiment that was part of the Petrograd garrison, demanded the overthrow of the Provisional Government and that all state power should pass to the Soviets. Over 400 people were killed. There was destruction and looting of flats and shops. Fortunately for the Provisional Government, the behaviour of the Bolshevik leadership was indecisive and enough troops remained loyal so the unrest was speedily quelled.

It was decided to arrest Lenin and Zinoviev, who had gone into hiding after the Provisional Government regained control. Lenin, in fact, had cautioned his followers not to move too soon at a Conference of the Bolshevik Military Organizations on 20 June [OS]. However, he lost control of the situation when he fell ill on 29 June [OS] and more radical lieutenants cast caution to the winds. They were tipped off about their impending arrest by N.S. Karinskii, who worked on the staff of the Minister of Justice, P.N. Perevertzev, and fled. On 9 July [OS] Lenin slipped away in disguise to Finland, where he had the opportunity to write *The State and Revolution*.

At the behest of the Bolsheviks, the mob had tried to seize the Counter-Espionage Bureau where all the information on German espionage was kept. A reason for this can be found in the events that followed. In the course of the 'July Days', as these events became known, two Russians, G. Alexinsky and V. Pankratov, published a letter accusing Lenin and the Bolsheviks of treason, maintaining they were German agents. This was the last thing the Bolsheviks wanted or needed and we have seen that they had been to some trouble to avoid any sort of visible link to the Germans. There was a strong and immediate reaction. Many who had backed the Bolsheviks or flirted with them now abandoned them and where mud is thrown, it sticks. In spite of frequent strong denials, the accusation clung to them for years.

Alexinsky and Pankratov cited the testimony of one Ensign Yermolenko of the 16th Siberian Infantry Regiment, who had been arrested and told the Investigating Division of the General Staff that he had been a prisoner-of-war of the Germans, who had sent him behind Russian lines to spread anti-war propaganda. He had been told by two officers of the German General Staff that similar propaganda was being carried on in Russia by the chairman of the Union for the Liberty of the Ukraine, A. Skoropis-Yoltukhovsky, and by Lenin. The latter had been commissioned 'to use every means in his power to undermine the confidence of the Russian people in the Provisional Government'.[13] Yermolenko also stated that money for the propaganda was passed through the German Embassy in Stockholm and forwarded to Russia by 'trusted persons': Jacob Furstenberg (Hanecki) and Parvus. The money was initially transferred to Sweden from the German Diskonto-Gesellschaft Bank, to a Swedish bank that Yermolenko identified as the 'Via Bank'. It has since emerged that the Swedish Nya Banken under Olof Aschberg was the bank that was, without question, involved in these transactions and Aschberg was, by his own admission, the 'Bolshevik Banker'.[14] Yermolenko's term 'Via Bank' is quite obviously a corruption of what he was told or what he had said.

The Provisional Government saw its chance, but instead of striking immediately and capitalizing on the opportunity it ran true to character and established a commission to investigate the charges. The commission's hearings meandered on until, typically, its conclusions had lost any force. Yet the preliminary views expressed by the government ministers most intimately associated with the hearings – Tereschenko, Nekrasov and Kerensky – stated plainly:

> The data of the preliminary investigation point directly to Lenin as a German agent and indicate that, after entering into an agreement with Germany on action designed to aid Germany in her war with Russia, he arrived in Petrograd. Here, with financial assistance from Germany, he began to act to achieve this aim.[15]

Although links were discovered that pointed to cooperation between the Bolsheviks and the Germans, there was not a shred of reliable evidence for any agreement between the two. The Minister of Justice gave an interview to the newspaper *Vechernee Vremia* that was reported in *Novoe Vremia* on 7 July 1917, when he resigned from the Provisional Government. He told the reporter:

> Personally, I have been convinced for a long time that Lenin has been working for German money. I am just as deeply convinced – and I have expressed it openly – that I consider him incapable of taking the money for himself personally. I still hold this conviction, but Lenin is an almost mad fanatic who has never been and is not now interested in knowing from what sources he receives offers of funds for the struggle on behalf of his ideals.[16]

It inevitably raises the question of whether or not Lenin was indeed a German agent, as many in the Provisional Government, the British and French Governments and, later, all of the White 'movement' believed or wanted to believe. The proposition has been denied vociferously down the years. First off the mark was *Listock Pravdy*, a two-page paper that appeared on 6 July in place of the Bolshevik's own organ, *Pravda*, the offices of which had been ransacked by a large body of military cadets acting on the orders of the Minister of Justice himself. *Listock Pravdy* denounced Alexinsky as 'a notorious slanderer' and described the charge that Lenin had been receiving money from the Germans as 'this monstrous slander'. It is open to debate whether the author of this diatribe wrote out of ignorance or was lying, for there is no doubt that Lenin was receiving money from the Germans.

Orlando Figes describes Yermolenko's statement as 'dubious testimony',[17] since he claimed to have been told about Lenin's involvement with the Germans by the Germans. So he had, but Figes' view omits the fact that Yermolenko had been sent behind Russian lines to do the same job himself and had not simply been told this as a matter of idle gossip. Moreover, he also revealed the Germans' use of Ukrainian nationalism, as well as the information about the involvement of Furstenberg, Parvus and the use of the Swedish bank. This much suggests that his evidence should not be so readily dismissed.

Few outside the Russian Counter-Espionage Bureau knew this supporting evidence at the time. The head of that service was Colonel Boris Vladimirovich Nikitine, an officer from the front who was on a short leave in Petrograd when the Revolution broke out. Much against his wishes he was pressed to stay and lead the new Counter-Espionage Bureau, and in later years wrote his memoirs of the months he spent in that service. Largely forgotten now, they shed vital light on the conditions in Russia in 1917 as well as the thinking that informed the activities of his service. Significantly it was not the Counter-Espionage Bureau that gave Alexinsky and Pankratov Yermolenko's testimony:

> Incidentally the Petrograd Counter-Espionage Bureau had no knowledge whatever of Yermolenko. More than that, we did not even possess a Yermolenko dossier. I only heard his name once before the July Rising, from Perevertzev, and only learned the details of the statement he made at the Headquarters of the Sixth Army from Yermolenko himself after the Rising, when he was sent to me by Grand Headquarters on the 21st July. I was never told why his statement was not communicated to us earlier or of what use they made of it there.[18]

On their own, Yermolenko's claims might reasonably have been regarded with a degree of scepticism, but Nikitine's officers were able to intercept a courier named Lourier at the frontier post of Beloostrov and discovered letters from Lenin to Parvus, requesting him to despatch as much 'material' – that is, money – as possible. Nor did the incriminating evidence stop there.

Captain Pierre Laurent of the French Military Mission handed Nikitine copies of a series of intercepted telegrams exchanged between Lenin and four individuals including Hanecki, alias Furstenberg, and a Madame Ev'genia Mavrikievna Sumenson. Hanecki was Lenin's go-between with Parvus, who in turn was the go-between with the Germans, thus avoiding any direct contact between Lenin and the Germans.

The telegrams were worth more than their face value. They revealed the identities of several of the plotters, the most important of whom was Madame Sumenson. Described by Nikitine as a *demi-mondaine*, the telegrams revealed she was a customer of the Siberian Bank. Nikitine sent Alexandrov, one of his top agents, to the bank accompanied by a financial expert. They discovered that in the few months before July, Sumenson had withdrawn about 800,000 roubles and there were still 180,000 in her account. The money had come from Hanecki by way of the Nya Banken and was used by the Bolsheviks to destabilize Russia.

Sumenson was arrested during the 'July Days' and, according to Nikitine, 'made a full and frank confession to the officials of the Bureau who questioned her in my presence'.[19] There was enough evidence here without Yermolenko's testimony to show why the Bolsheviks attacked the offices of the Counter-Espionage Bureau and confirm that Lenin and some of his closest associates were in closer touch with the Germans than Soviet apologists would have us believe. Under wartime conditions, it was more than enough to have the leading Bolsheviks hanged for treason. Lenin himself had fled and was in hiding, but other members of the Bolshevik hierarchy were seized. Among them was Trotsky, who had switched his allegiance from the Mensheviks to the Bolsheviks that month. However, the doctrine of 'no enemies on the left' prevailed and most of them were released without trial as the Mensheviks and Social Revolutionaries fell over themselves to mend fences with the Bolsheviks.

The Germans were using – exploiting might be a better word – Lenin and the Bolsheviks for their own ends. Equally, Lenin and the Bolsheviks were using the Germans for their own. The aims of the two parties to this alliance coincided in the short term, but both were basing that alliance on pure expediency and neither had any intention of maintaining their collaboration for a moment longer than they had to. From September 1915 the Germans had been fully aware of the Bolshevik agenda, created without any input from themselves. The German Intelligence Service in Switzerland, under its chief agent Steinwachs, had formed links with Aleksander Keskula, a member of the Estonian Nationalist Committee, a body working for independence from Russia. Keskula had links with the Russian revolutionaries in Switzerland and was able to report on Lenin's programme for peace with Germany: the establishment of a republic, the confiscation of large land-holdings, an eight-hour working day, full autonomy for all nationalities and an offer of peace to Germany without consideration for France, provided Germany would renounce all annexations and indemnities. Further prospects to entice the Germans were a withdrawal of Russian troops from Turkey and renunciation of Imperial Russia's claim to the Dardanelles and Constantinople, and the advance of Russian troops into India.[20]

The great Prussian military theorist, Carl von Clausewitz, made the point that war builds up a momentum of its own, by which he meant that irrespective of what plans had been made, or what aims initially governed the conflict, the course of the war would carry the opposing governments along courses they had not envisaged. In short, it would add fuel to the blaze. This is what happened with every European state in the First World War. The history of the clandestine war in Russia emphasizes the point. We will see that the contacts between the Germans and the Bolsheviks went deeper than either party had envisaged and mutual expediency forced both to deepen them as events swept them both along like corks in a millstream.

13

II

'Support Any Responsible Body...'

Autumn 1917

◄o►

As 1917 progressed, Russia fell into increasing disarray. The Provisional Government's promises to regulate economic life 'on the model of the other belligerent states', to prepare for the transfer of land to the peasants in an orderly fashion and to create a new system of local government proved to be stillborn, largely because the government took few practical and determined steps to implement these policies.

The problems that had begun to surface before the 'July Days' grew apace as returning soldiers, many of them deserters, poured back into the rural districts of Russia. It is hard to underestimate the powerful influence that the prospect of a redistribution of land exercised on the men of the Russian Army. Most of them were peasants and many of them wanted, above all else, to be on hand to seize the land, whether it became available legally or not. Whether one looks at the army, the town or the village, the picture is the same. It is one of increasing restiveness and hardship, spiralling into what seems an inevitable recourse to violence.

Seizures of land, or produce, by the peasants was a growing menace, though its incidence and severity varied from area to area, but it is safe to say that by the late summer of 1917 every important district of rural Russia had experienced significant disturbances. They began in the Kursk, Tula, Ryazan and Tambov governments in the spring and then spread by July north-eastwards to Kazan, southwards to Voronezh and the Ukraine, and then westwards to Belorussia. The Commissar of Kazan Guberniya reported on 31 July:

> The agrarian movement continues. In Kazan' *uezd*, according to the statement of
> peasants from the village of Tarlashei on the Volga island of Bekachie, peasants

14

who owned no meadows seized the hay mowings. In Laishev *uezd* the landowner Bel'kovich reports plundering of grain harvested on his estate adjoining the village of Nadezhdina. On the estate of Shcherbakova in the same *uezd*, according to her statement, property was looted from trunks by using skeleton keys. Fruit was stolen from the garden.[1]

After recording many other such instances, the commissar reported how industrial and commercial life was deteriorating 'steadily' and that the shortage of foodstuffs had become acute. The Germans, who also observed the steps taken to try and avert its complete breakdown, monitored the disruption of the Russian economy:

> According to the most recent reports received here, the situation in Russia is that the country, whose economic life has been shattered, and which is only just being held together by English agents, could be expected to collapse as a result of any further, fairly powerful shock. The very knowledgeable specialist in Russian affairs at the Swedish Foreign Ministry has said that the English influence depends on the rail connexion between Petrograd and Haparanda, which is only capable of carrying passenger traffic and mail.[2]

By October, the newspaper *Novoe Vremia* declared:

> Not a day goes by that news does not appear in the press about the atrocious pogroms which take place in the village. In the spirit of anarchy, the propaganda inspired masses are not satisfied to seize the lands of the private owners. They also remove the workers from properties, fell forests, and destroy crops.

Placing part of the responsibility on the Bolsheviks with their formula of peace at the front and war in the rear, and part on the lack of forceful measures by the Provisional Government, the paper regarded the situation as a civil war.[3]

It is commonly argued that the biggest mistake the Provisional Government made was its failure to make peace. This argument ignores the peace moves that were actually made. There were a number of informal peace approaches by the Germans, but they foundered because they were too obviously designed to remove Russia from the ranks of their enemies so that Germany's full military might could be directed at the Western Allies –

a step too far for the Provisional Government. However, there were distinct possibilities of Russia making a separate peace with Germany's allies. The first initiative came from D. Rizov, the Bulgarian Minister in Berlin. The famous dramatist and influential Bolshevik journalist Maxim Gorky received it on 15 May 1917, and forwarded it to the Foreign Ministry with damning comment on the motivation and character of the writer. Nevertheless, a separate peace between Russia and Bulgaria was a possibility that could not be discounted. It is recorded that when Tsar Ferdinand of Bulgaria learnt about the planned announcement by the Germans of a resumption of unrestricted submarine warfare at the end of 1916, he was deeply disturbed because he expected it to bring the United States into the war. He expressed the opinion that it would be far better if peace could be hastened with concessions over Alsace-Lorraine.[4]

Rizov's approaches began at the beginning of 1917, at least as early as February. Indeed, they were then described as 'Rizov's persistent appeals' to the Russian ambassadors in Stockholm, and Christiania [Oslo]. The British Foreign Office records reveal that the Russians did communicate these approaches to the Allies and hopes were seriously raised that Bulgaria would not only desert Germany, but also join the Allies. When news of this démarche reached the British Government, their reaction, although cautious, clearly kept the door open:

> HM Government have carefully considered the telegram from the Russian Minister for Foreign Affairs communicated to them on the 12th instant by the Russian Chargé d'Affaires, and the Secretary of State for Foreign Affairs has the honour to state in reply that so far as HM Government are concerned they have no objection to M. Rizoff [sic] being approached in a manner proposed. HM Government assume that the Russian Government will separately consult the Governments of France and Italy.[5]

The Russian Government did consult the French and the Italians and it was Baron Sonnino, the Italian Foreign Minister, who damned the approach as evidence of Bulgaria's 'close connection with Germany' arguing that 'any reply we would give to Rizov would immediately be communicated to Germany and that the latter would use it as a weapon against us, her Allies and with neutrals.' Moreover, 'the mere fact that this step has been entrusted

16

to the Bulgarian Minister in Berlin seems to him a clear indication that it is directed by Germany ... As regards Rizov's personality, Baron Sonnino said he was well known in Rome as entirely untrustworthy and devoid of any good qualities.'[6]

If the Allies had their doubts about the semi-official approaches from Bulgaria, they looked more favourably on those that came from Bulgarian opposition groups. It is a time-honoured stratagem to exploit divisions in the enemy camp and provide support to those who wish to overthrow the existing government with whom one is at war. The reasons for this are obvious enough – no government can successfully wage war when a significant part of its population is in outright rebellion or undermining the war effort on a large scale. The role of subversion is a common but often overlooked theme in the First World War. Just as the Germans used the Bolsheviks and Ukrainians to undermine the Russian Empire, so equally the Allies sought with success to subvert the subject races of the Austro-Hungarian and Ottoman Empires, and play upon the radical movements in Germany for the same purpose.[7]

From July 1917, the British and French were in touch with a group calling itself the Bulgarian Committee of National Defence that wished to negotiate with them for the purpose of overthrowing the Bulgarian Government and then making a reasonable peace with the Entente. Negotiations were conducted in secrecy in Switzerland with Mr Tzokoff, the former Bulgarian Minister in London speaking for the Committee, while Captain Heard, 'attached to the Vice-Consulate at Lausanne', but in fact an officer in the British Secret Service, represented Britain. The British Secret Service officer in Montreux commented, 'In my personal opinion this proposed attempt at producing a political upheaval in Bulgaria is worthy of serious attention.'[8] It was because they feared the necessary secrecy might be imperilled, that the British opened and hoped to exploit the link through their Secret Service rather than diplomatic channels. The earliest indication of this new approach is to be found on 2 August 1917, when Lord Robert Cecil, Minister of Blockade and Assistant Foreign Secretary, wrote:

> This is from a secret agent in charge of Bulgarian matters, one of our consular officers lent to the Secret Service who knows Bulgaria well.

17

It seems important as being the first indication of anything like an organised opposition movement against the present regime in Bulgaria. How far M. Bagaroff is connected with this movement is not clear. If he is connected with it the desire for funds, communicated by M4 has to a large extent been met.

I would respectfully suggest that I might be authorised to tell the Chief of the Secret Service that he may instruct his agent to tell M4 that if Bulgaria were to secede from the Central Powers her legitimate aspirations would receive very favourable consideration and that if the opposition elements have any definite proposals to make through M. Tzokoff they can count on their being sympathetically received.[9]

The 'secret agent in charge of Bulgarian matters' was Mr Kouyoumdjian, who had been British Consular Agent at Philippopolis, while M4 was Mr Oustabashieff, the Secretary of the Committee of National Defence.

The negotiations rapidly turned into an attempt to turn the Bulgarian initiative into a tool to promote the overthrow of the Bulgarian Government. The key to this lay in the final paragraph by the Secret Service officer, who wrote:

…it must be remembered that the essence of success for any revolutionary movement lies in profound secrecy, for which Bulgarian conspirators are naturally adapted by nature, and that any indication of what is going on in revolutionary circles would not appear on the surface.[10]

Negotiations stalled as the Committee demanded guarantees from the Entente, while the British sought to determine precisely how strong and organized the Committee was, and whether their plans were realistic. Neither was prepared to make the first move.

By 21 August copies of reports from Captain Heard were forwarded to 'C'. The covering letter, addressed to 'Captain Spencer', which was an alias frequently assumed by officers of the Secret Service, came from the Service's station chief in Paris. It dwelt on relations with the French who had requested that the handling of M4 should be transferred to them, but then changed their minds and wished Captain Heard to continue dealing with him.[11]

By late August, the Committee were clearly becoming anxious to increase the momentum of the negotiations and there is the likelihood they knew that further delay would inevitably increase the risk of discovery by the Bulgarian authorities. Thus Sir Horace Rumbold, the British Minister in Berne, telegraphed the Foreign Office on 26 August to report

> ... that Mr. Heard saw Oustabashieff at Geneva on the 24th instant. Oustabashieff stated that it had been decided to cause His Majesty's Government to be informed of all the details of his scheme through the channel of a Power which was already *au courant* with the whole plot. We assume that this means Russia.[12]

Fears of discovery proved to be well founded when a fire broke out in a house in Karnobat, near Bourgas. In its aftermath the Bulgarian police discovered a trunk full of documents that revealed some details of the plot and the names of some of the plotters. Some two dozen Bulgarian officers and between 100 and 150 civilians were seized. The link with Switzerland was revealed and the Bulgarian Government promptly restricted its citizens from travelling there. Worse was to follow when documents were seized at the house of a merchant in Sofia. They revealed sixteen pseudonyms of Bulgarians in Switzerland who were involved in the conspiracy. It meant the end of the secret manoeuvres by the British and the Bulgarians.

Rumbold's message showed that the Committee had approached another Entente power other than Britain, and his assumption that this was Russia was correct. A report from Switzerland by Captain Heard makes this clear. Heard had felt that something was being held back from both himself and Tzokoff. He was told by M4, Oustabashieff, that

> ...there is a Russian, now in Switzerland, officially delegated by his Government to negotiate with the Committee, and I understand that he has been let much deeper into the secrets of the conspiracy. It will be recollected that M4 had always implied that Russia had been already approached, and that things had gone much further with her than with the Entente.[13]

The Russians were more deeply involved with the Bulgarians than either the British or the French. Indeed, the British seem to have had only the haziest idea about these negotiations. Besides the negotiations with the Committee of National Defence, there were also negotiations in Stockholm between the

19

Russians and a representative of the Bulgarian Prime Minister, Radoslavoff. Regrettably there is very little documentary evidence on which to assess whether they amounted to anything worthwhile.

An even more startling picture emerges regarding negotiations between Russia and Austria-Hungary. The Emperor Karl of Austria-Hungary had sought peace with the Allies through secret negotiations conducted by his brother-in-law, Prince Sixtus of Bourbon-Parma. What concerns us is whether there was any realistic prospect for a separate peace with Russia in 1917.

As early as 16 April 1917 – barely a month after the Tsar was overthrown – Sir Horace Rumbold was informing the British Government:

> Austrians do not seem to have any clear idea as to how the war is going to end for them. They trust in Germany to pull them through and are pinning their faith in making Peace with Russia. Negotiations with the Russians to this end are stated to have been in progress at Cracow for a month past.[14]

In June Tereshchenko, the Russian Minister for Foreign Affairs, told Sir George Buchanan, the British Ambassador, that Austria-Hungary would be willing to make a separate peace with concessions to Serbia and Italy, and to reconstitute Poland.[15] These proposals were hardly to the taste of some of the component nationalities of the Dual Monarchy who were working with the Allies in order to achieve independence from Austrian rule and thus the fragmentation of Austria-Hungary. The Yugoslavs had already got wind of the negotiations as early as April, for the Yugoslav Committee in London wrote to the Provisional Government via the British Foreign Secretary, Arthur Balfour, asking them to reject the peace offer made by the Austrians.[16]

The Russians kept what appears to be a considerable proportion of the negotiations secret from their allies; the British were reluctant to give them backing without the support of the French and the bodies representing the subject nationalities of the Austro-Hungarian Empire, and were at the same time trying to exploit the Bulgarian situation by clandestine means. The Bulgarians and the Austrians for their part were constricted by their fear of and dependence upon the German Empire. Each state was a prisoner of its alliances, which none felt it could afford to break.

There was still another twist to the story, one with powerful implications for German-Bolshevik relations – if it is true. This is Kerensky's claim that on the eve of the Bolshevik seizure of power the Austro-Hungarian Government

> ...addressed to the Provisional Government a request for a separate peace. The move was made without knowledge of Berlin. It was particularly significant because Foreign Minister Tereshchenko had long been preparing, with the co-operation of the diplomatic representatives in Bulgaria and Turkey, a plan for negotiations that would have meant the exit of Bulgaria and Turkey from the war. There could be no doubt, with Austria's example before them, that similar peace proposals would have followed soon from Sofia and Constantinople.[17]

Colonel Nikitine suggests that the timing of the Bolshevik coup, or 'Revolution' as they were pleased to call it, might not have been altogether divorced from this initiative. He observed:

> Bolshevik writers and others credit Lenin with having timed the rising correctly, although Trotsky deferred it to the 7th September, but in point of fact its actual date had been fixed by the German General Staff beforehand – and it was known to the members of the Provisional Government. In July the outbreak occurred by their instructions and against the wishes of Lenin, whereas in October he fully concurred in it.[18]

If the German General Staff directed the timing of both the 'July Days' and the October Revolution, then the links between the Bolsheviks and the Germans were much closer than those indicated by left-wing apologists. Nikitine's claim, if true, would make the Bolshevik leadership the tools of the Germans even if it did not go so far as to establish them as German agents. The timing of both the 'July Days' and the October Revolution appears to lend circumstantial support to the claim. Certainly the 'July Days' coincided with the so-called Kerensky Offensive, when the Russian Army launched what was to be its last major attack of the war on the Eastern front. The October Revolution was perfectly timed to scotch any hope of peace negotiations bearing fruit and Germany being left isolated through the desertion of her allies.

Had that happened the Germans would have been faced with the worst of all nightmares, a war on two fronts without allies to stretch enemy forces on the Eastern front. Moreover, successful peace negotiations would have

21

delivered a terrific boost to Russian morale and undermined the position of the Bolsheviks with their demand for peace. It would then have been an inescapable fact that Germany would be beaten and the Germans would have known it. As it was, even with allies, the Germans had difficulty with a war on two fronts and their support of the Bolsheviks was predicated upon removing that obstacle.

However, we would need more than Nikitine's view to substantiate an argument of such weight, even with the circumstantial evidence of the timing of the 'July Days' and the October Revolution appearing to lend it credence. One flaw in the argument is immediately apparent – Nikitine was no longer at the head of the Counter-Espionage Bureau, but back serving at the front and so would not have been privy to the information in the hands of the Bureau. This makes his view rather smack of what he (and many others) wanted to believe and, without strong additional documentary evidence to support it, it should be treated with considerable circumspection.

The Bolsheviks seized power in Petrograd on 7 November 1917. Kerensky managed to flee the city in an American motor car and sought to rally loyal troops in a bid to regain control. He was to be disappointed. Few now trusted him and many troops were more or less sympathetic to the Bolsheviks. Although Kerensky's forces made some initial progress towards Petrograd, his counter-offensive soon petered out and finally came to grief five days later, leaving him with no other realistic choice than to escape from Russia.

The Bolshevik seizure of power was promptly followed by proclamations on land and on peace. The death penalty, originally abolished immediately after the February Revolution but restored at the front after the 'July Days', was once more abolished. On 26 November Trotsky formally applied to *Oberost*, the German High Command on the Eastern front, for an immediate armistice as a precursor to negotiations leading to a 'democratic' peace without annexations or indemnities. Two days later, the move gained new impetus when the Bolsheviks' new Commander-in-Chief of the Russian Army, Krylenko, ordered a ceasefire and fraternization to begin on all fronts. Formal conversations for the armistice began on 2 December.

The Germans came to the armistice discussions well prepared. The terms they were to offer the Russians had been drawn up the previous May, when hopes of reaching a separate peace with the Provisional Government were still high. They were lenient, designed to stop the war on the Eastern front so the German Army could concentrate against the Allies on the Western front. Both the Russians and the Central Powers were to hold their present positions; in this way, it was hoped, the Russians could accept the terms without loss of face or without appearing to buckle before unjust terms.

Now the Bolshevik spokesman, Adolf Abramovich Joffe, proposed that no German troops were to be transferred from the Eastern front to other fronts, or even to be withdrawn to rest. This was a condition that was of the utmost importance to the Western Allies, who envisaged numerous German divisions being thrown into the struggle against them on the Western front.

It is worth dwelling on this for a moment, since this fact was to determine both the policies and the strategy employed by the Allies in the months to come. Arthur Balfour concisely expressed the supremely important place Russia held in Allied strategy in 1914: 'The war cannot possibly be conclusive in our favour unless the Western Allies have Russia wholeheartedly on their side till the end.'[19]

In 1914 both the British and French had been enamoured of the idea of 'the Russian steamroller', a concept that saw Russia's apparently limitless supplies of men overwhelming the Central Powers. Her withdrawal would mean the Allies would become ultimately dependent upon the as yet untapped manpower of the United States. At the end of 1917 the Americans had only four divisions in France and more would take time to come and be trained; the political consequences would thus have been tremendous. It would have meant that the principal Allies would have been reduced to political dependence on the President of the United States, who could then dictate his own terms to the world.

More than this, it would mean that choices of strategy would be severely circumscribed. Every available man and gun would have to be concentrated on the Western front to face the German offensive that could be expected, and opportunities to strike the Turks would vanish. In short it would paralyse all freedom of action of both Britain and France.

As if this was not bad enough, there was a further horror that cast its shadow over Allied deliberations. If Russia left the war it would mean the end of the British blockade of Germany. There is considerable evidence

23

revealing the hope of the German leadership that the collapse of Russia would open the gates of plenty for Germany and her allies. Besides the food-stuffs, particularly cereals and fats, that the Central Powers counted on gaining access to, there would be a huge amount of raw materials that their war effort had been deprived of during the war. Oil, minerals such as copper, manganese and platinum, textiles, including cotton and flax – all necessary for the conduct of modern war – would theoretically be available to the Germans through either trade or seizure. This was to be a genuine concern for the Allies in the coming months.

The German General Staff had, with its customary efficiency, already anticipated Joffe's proposal. General Hoffmann, the Chief of Staff at *Oberost*, advanced the counter-proposal that during the armistice the Germans would not send away any troops from the Eastern front except those that were either already being moved, or that had already received orders to go. It was a skilful ploy, for the Bolsheviks could hardly disagree and, in fact, the Germans had already issued orders for the transfer of the bulk of their army on the Eastern front to the Western front. The agreement reached thus did not affect German plans in the slightest.

On 5 December the Soviet delegation announced that they were 'treating for an armistice on all fronts with the view to the conclusion of a general peace on the basis already established by the All-Russian Congress of Soviets.' In other words, they had come to seek a general peace, not a separate one. This policy was entirely in keeping with Lenin's pamphlet, *The Aims of the Revolution*, distributed in September 1917:

> The Soviet government must *immediately* make proposals to all the belligerent nations (i.e. simultaneously both to their governments and to the masses of workers and peasants) for the conclusion without delay of a general peace on democratic conditions, and an immediate armistice (at least for three months).
>
> The chief condition for a democratic peace is the renunciation of annexa-tions – not in the mistaken sense that all the powers are to receive back what they have lost, but in the only correct sense that *every* nationality, without a single exception, both in Europe and in the colonies, shall obtain the freedom and the possibility of deciding for itself whether it shall become a *separate* state or whether it shall form part of another state....Such conditions of peace will not be favourably received by the capitalists; but they will be

received by all the peoples with such tremendous sympathy, they will cause such a great, world-historic outburst of enthusiasm and such general indignation against the dragging out of this predatory war, that it is most probable that we shall at once obtain an armistice and consent to the commencement of peace negotiations. For the workers' revolution against the war is irresistibly growing everywhere...[20]

The Bolsheviks began to publish the secret treaties between Russia and the Western Allies. These disclosed that Allied war aims were as annexationist and imperialistic as those of Imperial Germany. Under these treaties, Russia was to have annexed Constantinople and the Straits, while Britain and France carved up the rest of the Ottoman Empire between them. On mainland Europe, the French and Russians were both have a free hand in defining their respective frontiers with Germany, and Russia was free to do what she would with a common frontier with the Austro-Hungarian Empire. Equally damning were the revelations of the territorial promises made to Italy at the expense of the Austro-Hungarian Empire. Allied propaganda had continually harped on Germany's aggressive and annexationist war aims, particularly since the discovery of her plans for *Mitteleuropa* and *Mittelafrika*. The high moral stance taken by Allies now looked to be somewhat hypocritical.

In Britain this led to questions in Parliament by Mr Robert Outhwaite on 28 November, and Mr Richard Lambert the following day. The Assistant Foreign Secretary, Lord Robert Cecil, declined to make any statement on the subject. The minutes of the documents in the Foreign Office files in the National Archives betray the double standards and dishonesty of British officials and politicians. On 3 December, one civil servant wrote, 'We have not yet received the full text of what has been published, but so far the Italian, Romanian and Sykes-Picot agreements have *not* come out.' Just days later Mr Oliphant, a senior civil servant, wrote, 'The Dft [draft] reply implies, I think rather unnecessarily clearly, that we wish to see to what extent we have been given away, before we admit it.'[21]

The Bolsheviks had issued their call for an armistice in the name of all the belligerents, but found themselves forced to admit that they did not have any authority to negotiate on behalf of the Allied Powers. However, the call for an armistice had severely rattled the Western Allies and in London the War Cabinet considered whether any action could be taken against the Bolsheviks. On 22 November it considered that any openly official step might only strengthen the Bolsheviks' determination to make peace and it would be used to inflame anti-Allied feeling in Russia, 'and so defeat the very object we were aiming at'.[22] The inescapable implication was that covert means alone could be applied to change the position.

When Joffe returned to Petrograd after the signing of the armistice between Russia and the Central Powers on 15 December, Trotsky, the Soviet Commissar for Foreign Affairs, or Foreign Minister, addressed an appeal to the Allied governments 'describing the course of events and begging them not to "sabotage the course of a general peace".' He argued that since the Central Powers had accepted the Soviet formula, that acceptance entailed their agreeing to evacuate the conquered territories of Belgium, northern France, Romania, Serbia, Montenegro, Poland, Lithuania and Courland. Thus the Allies could no longer realistically claim to be fighting for the liberation of these territories.

Trotsky may have been naive to believe this, or he may have been insincere and, as some were to claim, working for the Germans, but he was certainly naive in his next step, which was to try to force the Allies' hands. He warned them that their non-participation would result in a separate peace between Russia and Germany, which 'would no doubt be a heavy blow to the Allied countries, especially France and Italy'. Worse still, he informed the Allied Military Attachés that he would appeal over the heads of their governments to their peoples:

> The question of compelling their own Governments immediately to present their peace programmes and to participate on the basis of them in the negotiations now becomes a question of national self-preservation for the Allied peoples.... If the Allied Governments, in the blind stubbornness which characterises decadent and perishing classes, once more refuse to participate in the negotiations, then the working-class will be confronted by the iron necessity of taking the power out of the hands of those who cannot or will not give the people peace.[23]

The Allied governments did not respond directly to what Sir George Buchanan considered an 'insolent communication',[24] but the British Prime

Minister, David Lloyd George, told an audience of British labour leaders a few days later, 'If the present rulers of Russia take action, which is independent of their Allies we have no means of intervening to avert the catastrophe which is assuredly befalling their country. Russia can only be saved by her own people.'[25]

The War Cabinet then began to consider the possibility of backing forces in Russia that were prepared to continue the war on the Eastern front. The foremost place among these forces was the South Eastern Confederation, which at this stage was an alliance of the four major Cossack hosts – the Don, Kuban, Terek and Astrakhan – under the leadership of the Don Cossacks' Ataman, General Kaledin, together with the Kalmuks, the peasants of the Stavropol Government, the mountaineers of the Caucasus and a motley collection of politicians and officials from the Tsarist and Provisional Governments. The Cossacks resented diktats from the Bolsheviks in Moscow as this trampled on their traditional rights and liberties. Their territory was one of the richest grain-producing areas in Europe; the populations of the Central Powers were starving as a consequence of the naval blockade, and starvation was nearly always the harbinger of revolution. For the Allies, people willing to fight Germany and, if necessary, the Bolsheviks, who also controlled such a vital strategic resource, were doubly appealing.

The Prime Minister would have known about these considerations before he gave his speech in which he said that Britain had no means of intervening to avert the catastrophe that he and the War Cabinet believed was about to fall on the Russian people. Just days later, on 3 December, the policy of intervention picked up pace when the War Cabinet decided that south Russia, with its bountiful resources of grain and strategic minerals, needed to remain in Allied hands. They also received news from C. Nabokoff, the Russian Chargé d'Affaires in London, via Andrew Bonar Law, the leader of the Conservative Party and member of the War Cabinet, that the Russian Army in the Caucasus was remaining loyal to the Provisional Government.

Nabokoff had also informed Bonar Law that the Georgians, Armenians and Tartars in the same region were determined to continue the war against the Central Powers and were raising an army. Nabokoff had added that in order for this loyal movement to progress it needed to be adequately funded, and the Commander-in-Chief of the Caucasus Army had informed him that a loan of 300 million roubles was needed, of which 70 million were required forthwith.

The minutes of the discussion at the War Cabinet went on to record that Sir Charles Marling, the British Minister in Tehran, had informed the Foreign Office on 30 November that he considered 'that it would be politic to finance the Persian Cossacks Division, who were cut off from supplies of money.'[26]

There is no record of any discussion about the implications that support of these different movements might entail, or of any disagreement. On the surface it looks like these baits were enough to make the British fish bite, but a moment's reflection will soon put this in perspective. Fear of what the collapse of the Eastern front would mean for Britain and France drove the War Cabinet to take the next, profound, step. It desired

> The Acting Secretary of State for Foreign Affairs to inform the British Ambassador at Petrograd of the action taken and to acquaint him, with reference to his telegram No. 1886, of the 28th November 1917, that the policy of the British Government was to support any responsible body in Russia that would actively oppose the Maximalist movement, and at the same time give money freely, within reason, to such bodies as were prepared to help the Allied cause; and that the detailed arrangements as to the establishment of Ukraine, Cossack, Armenian and Polish banks were left to the discretion of Sir George Buchanan.[27]

The War Cabinet had chosen to intervene indirectly in Russia and money was to be the spearhead of intervention. The war on the Eastern front was now going to be fought by proxy, using Russian forces as surrogates to achieve British aims. It was to fall to the lot of the Intelligence Services to guide this financial spearhead to its target.

III

Forging an Instrument

Winter 1917–18 (I)

—◄O►—

The man charged with putting this policy into practice was the Director of Military Intelligence (hereafter DMI), Lieutenant-General George Mark Watson Macdonogh. Born in 1865, he was the son of a Deputy Inspector of Royal Naval Hospitals, and was commissioned in the Royal Engineers in 1884. He was a retiring and diffident man who shrank from argument with more aggressive characters. This diffidence concealed an iron will and a superbly analytical and penetrating mind.

As a captain he went to Staff College, where his fellow students included the future Official Historian of the war, James Edmonds, another Royal Engineer who was to be closely involved with the creation of an efficient, professional Intelligence Service. Others included the future Field-Marshals Haig and Allenby. Macdonogh was also a keen student of law, combining this successfully with his military career, and being called to the Bar at Lincoln's Inn in 1897. In each sphere discipline, attention to detail, analytical ability, a calculating mind and the study of hard evidence are required, so Macdonogh's early career was a sound foundation for his work in Intelligence.

He had few close friends and those he had were all killed during the war, after which he set his face against letting people get too close to him, though he was universally respected and liked. His family were converts to Roman Catholicism from the Methodist Church and, in 1918, after Macdonogh had become Adjutant-General and was within striking distance of the highest ranks in the army, pressure was put on him to change his religion. Sincere in his beliefs, he refused, and thereby blighted his chances of further promotion, to his country's great loss.

His marriage to Aline Borgström, a Finn, endowed him with a love of Scandinavia and stimulated him to study Swedish and Finnish; he became proficient in both languages. In later life, he chose to represent Finnish interests, numbering among his many legal and commercial activities Presidency of the Anglo-Finnish Society, the Vice-Presidency of the Finland Fund and membership of the Finnish Aid Bureau. Their only son died in 1915, which led to Macdonogh spending some considerable time away from the front. Even under the burden of his great grief, however, he still maintained the same stolid, unflinching, capable exterior.

Macdonogh did not operate in isolation. Following the War Cabinet's decision of 3 December, the Secretary of State for Foreign Affairs was authorized to render suitable help to the Armenians through 'channels chosen by himself in consultation with the Director of Military Intelligence'.[1] The Foreign Secretary was Arthur Balfour. A son-in-law of the second Marquess of Salisbury, he was an astute philosopher and also a Spiritualist. He was tall and was widely known as 'Lofty', but less for his size than for his mind, which appeared to soar beyond the ken of lesser mortals. He had adopted a languid and deceptively sleepy pose, which masked a will of steel. His passion for philosophy marked him out from his contemporaries; his wide-ranging mind embraced science and aesthetics, metaphysics and lawn tennis, golf, social celebrity and sports cars.

His languid demeanour was attractive to many women, but he never married. Most people found him a highly agreeable and charming companion, even if they might be occasionally exasperated by what a French friend once called his 'seraphic equanimity'. Now elderly, he still retained a sharpness of intellect that would have put men many years his junior to shame.

He was faced with an additional challenge, one that excited fear and anger among those in the British elite with an imperialistic outlook – and that was most of them. The newly established Sovnarkom in Russia, under the leadership of Stalin, had urged the subject peoples of Asia to overthrow their European leaders, singling out British India for particular attention. Now the Bolsheviks were attacking the British Empire in the East; it was ammunition for those who believed the Bolsheviks were German agents.

Balfour took a broader and more relaxed view of the situation than some of his Cabinet colleagues. He submitted a paper to the War Cabinet that, with the advantage of hindsight, can be seen as notably percipient:

If they [the Bolsheviks] summon the Mohammedans of India to revolt, they are still more desirous of engineering a revolution in Germany. They are dangerous dreamers, whose power, be it great or small, transitory or permanent, depends partly on German gold, partly on the determination of the Russian army to fight no more; but who would genuinely like to put into practice the wild theories which they have so long been germinating in the shadow of the Russian autocracy.[2]

The War Cabinet considered its general policy towards Russia in the light of Balfour's memorandum and concluded:

It was difficult to foretell how strong the Bolsheviks might become, or how long their power might endure; but if, as seemed likely, they maintained an ascendancy for the next few months only, these months were critical, and to antagonise them needlessly would be to throw them into the arms of Germany. There were at the moment signs that within a few days, when the elections for the Constituent Assembly had been completed, the Bolsheviks would be installed in power not only in a *de facto*, but also in a constitutional sense.[3]

The Constituent Assembly duly met, with the Social Revolutionary Party commanding a large majority. The Bolsheviks dissolved it by force within twenty-four hours of it meeting. This denied them any legitimacy, but they remained the *de facto* government of much of Russia. However, their hold on the more peripheral territories of the Russian Empire was either tenuous or non-existent.

Four days later, Lord Robert Cecil and Sir Edward Carson, the former First Lord of the Admiralty, who now coordinated government propaganda, made an astonishing suggestion: that Trotsky was a German agent. Leon Trotsky (the pseudonym of Lev Davidovich Bronstein) was, with Lenin, one of the most striking figures among the Bolshevik leaders. He was also a Jew, as were many of the leading Bolsheviks. The most vivid contemporary picture of Trotsky comes from the pen of Robert Bruce Lockhart, who had every opportunity to study him closely in the first half of 1918:

He struck me as perfectly honest and sincere in his bitterness against the Germans. He has a wonderfully quick mind and a rich, deep voice. With his broad chest, his huge forehead, surmounted by great masses of black, waving

31

hair, his strong, fierce eyes, and his heavy protruding lips, he is the very incarnation of the revolutionary of the bourgeois caricatures. He is neat about his dress. He wore a clean soft collar and his nails were carefully manicured. I agree with Robins. If the Bosche bought Trotsky, he bought a lemon. His dignity has suffered an affront. He is full of belligerent fury against the Germans for the humiliation, to which they have exposed him at Brest. He strikes me as a man who would willingly die fighting for Russia provided there was a big enough audience to see him do it.[4]

This suggestion was to have pernicious and long-lasting consequences. Neither man produced any evidence to support the claim. At the time it does not seem to have excited any discussion among the members of the War Cabinet, and perhaps it was what a group of frightened men wanted to believe. The Conservative *Morning Post*, perhaps prompted by Cecil, angrily observed that 'Russian Jews of German extraction', who were paid by Berlin had betrayed the Allies. It was a view that reflected at least some of the feeling in the Foreign Office. The allegation was made by the Assistant Foreign Secretary, the very man who had been instructed to carry out the War Cabinet's fateful decision of 3 December to support any responsible body in Russia that would actively oppose the 'Maximalist' movement.[5]

At a meeting of the War Cabinet on 21 December Cecil had argued that Britain must either support the Ukrainians, Cossacks, Georgians and Armenians, or the Bolsheviks; she could not do both. He claimed the forces in southern Russia had a fair fighting chance of success if the Allies supported them, while alternatively the government had to accept that the blockade of Germany would be at an end. He did not need to spell out the consequences of that. It was decided that a three-man special mission, consisting of Cecil, Macdonogh and Lord Milner, should proceed at once to Paris.[6]

Milner was an administrator, a bureaucrat. He had once stood in the Liberal interest for Parliament but had been defeated, and that was the limit of his contact with the democratic process. Lloyd George stated of him, 'He knew nothing of the populace that trod the streets outside the bureau. He did not despise them. He just left them out of his calculations. A study of the ways and thought of the crowd constituted no part of the preparation for entry into the civil service or for success afterwards.'[7] He was sixty-three in 1917, and still unmarried. He had been born in Germany, in Hesse-

Darmstadt in 1854, and been educated there before studying at King's College, London, and Balliol College, Oxford. He flourished at university where his academic record was distinguished and he obtained a first-class degree, later becoming a Fellow of New College, Oxford. A Freemason, his politics were broadly Conservative, but he did not share all Conservative views, favouring as he did higher taxes and extensions of social welfare.

Above all, he was an Imperialist. A colleague of Cecil Rhodes in Africa, he had been largely responsible for the Boer War through his intransigence in his negotiations with President Kruger. After that war he combined his existing posts of High Commissioner in South Africa and Governor of the Cape Colony with a new one as Britain's administrator of the newly annexed Orange Free State and Transvaal. While his administration may have been efficient in a bureaucratic sense, aspects of it – notably a plan to draft in Chinese labour to work the South African gold mines – led to anger and fierce criticism at home.

Like his mentor, Cecil Rhodes, he gathered round him a coterie of ambitious and able young men whom he used as his lieutenants. Among them were John Buchan, Waldorf Astor, Lord Henry Seymour, Geoffrey Dawson, Mark Sykes, Hugh Wyndham, Lionel Curtis, Leopold Amery and Philip Kerr. This group became known as 'Milner's kindergarten' and when Milner was invited into the War Cabinet, his kindergarten found themselves placed in influential posts.

Milner stated in his *Credo*, 'I am an Imperialist and not a Little Englander, because I am a British Race Patriot.' This was a view he shared with most of the British elite of the time, the greater number of whom genuinely believed the British 'race' to be supreme, a view founded on the existence of a worldwide empire, together with the nonsensical but influential idea of 'Social-Darwinism'. Professor Hewins reportedly noted in April 1917 that, 'Milner said the one thing he was anxious about was that we should get out of the War a really consolidated Empire.'[8]

Lord Robert Cecil was the third son of the third Marquess of Salisbury, Queen Victoria's last Prime Minister, and a member of that powerful family which had been involved in English government since the reign of Elizabeth. This made him a cousin of Balfour since his aunt, Lady Blanche Gascoigne-Cecil, had married Balfour's father, James Maitland Balfour. Devoted to the

Conservative Party and the Empire, Cecil was described by Lord Beaverbrook as 'a sombre figure and a stalwart supporter of the Church'.[9]

In 1917 he was both Minister of Blockade and Parliamentary Under-Secretary for Foreign Affairs, rising to be Assistant Foreign Secretary. He was described by the man selected to establish unofficial links with the Bolsheviks as '...supremely sceptical of the usefulness of establishing any kind of relations with the Bolsheviks...'.[10] He was an ardent interventionist. While Milner may have disliked and despised Bolshevism, Cecil hated it with passion. So impatient did he become with British policy that he was to resign from the Government over it on 7 June 1918. He wanted intervention of the strongest and most decisive kind, seeing that as the only way to counteract 'the progress of our enemies in Russia'.[11] His life was to take an unusual path after the war, when he became an untiring advocate of the League of Nations and disarmament. He gained fame through this and took part with President Wilson in drafting the Covenant of the League. He was ennobled in his own right as Viscount Cecil of Chelwood in 1923 and awarded the Nobel Prize for Peace in 1937.

The meeting in Paris took place on 23 December and Georges Clemenceau, the French Prime Minister, Monsieur Pichon, the French Foreign Minister, and Général Foch represented the French Republic. It revealed that the French Government was not only ready to accommodate the policy of the British War Cabinet, as expressed on 3 December, but had already taken active steps of its own.

The British delegation found complete accord with the idea of maintaining relations with the Bolsheviks through unofficial agents, hoping thereby to dissuade the Bolsheviks from placing any trust in the Germans, while persuading them to keep both their artillery and their wheat districts out of German hands. Simultaneously, both the British and French Governments agreed to give support to the other groups in Russia that held out the promises of continuing the war with Germany and denying her the resources of Russia. The British team also found the French to be especially keen to support the Ukrainians. The resulting agreement divided Russia into French and British spheres of influence, with the French taking responsibility for the Ukraine, the Poles and the Czechoslovaks, while the British were to handle the Armenians, Cossacks and the Caucasus.

Cecil presented this agreement to the War Cabinet on 26 December. It duly approved the policy with minimal discussion, merely adding a paragraph regarding the obligation of honour that Russia had towards Serbia.[12] The apparently perfunctory manner in which the War Cabinet passed this policy is frightening. It was a policy pregnant with civil war for Russia and one that threatened to burden the Allies with extensive new commitments. More than that, the attempts to support the new regional 'governments' were unquestionably interference in Russia's internal affairs. It was from these meetings and decisions in December 1917 that the deeds of this history flow.

Nevertheless, there were still voices that questioned the wisdom of pressing this dagger in up to the hilt. Thus, when Francis Lindley, Counsellor in the British Embassy in Petrograd, suggested that the British Government should enter into relations with all the *de facto* regional authorities in Russia the War Cabinet decided, 'It would be better for the present not to commit ourselves so far, and to continue our present policy of communicating with the Bolshevist government through Mr Lockhart, as decided by War Cabinet 316, Minute 16.'[13] Since steps had already been taken to form links with some regional authorities, even if they stopped short of formal relations, British policy was ambivalent rather than cohesive.

One of the voices opposed to open intervention in Russia was Arthur Balfour, the Foreign Secretary. He expected a rupture to come between Britain and the Bolshevik government and in his mind the question was, which of the two powers would occasion the rupture? Nor was Balfour alone in his doubts. The Prime Minister was also chary about rushing into commitments beyond the reach of Britain's resources, arguing 'that it was no concern of the British Government what socialist experiment or what form of government the Bolsheviks were trying to establish in Russia.' He urged his colleagues to regard the situation in much the same way that Balfour had:

> ...it was necessary to bear in mind that the Bolsheviks were a formidable menace to Austria and Germany, and that our information regarding the internal conditions in Austria was such as to encourage the view that the internal political condition of that empire was seriously embarrassed by the spread of Bolshevism.[14]

It was at this time, the beginning of 1918, that the British Government sent a new man to Petrograd to form unofficial links with the Bolsheviks. This was Robert Bruce Lockhart. 'Scottish by birth, romantic cosmopolitan by inclination, spendthrift by habit, he had studied at several European universities and sought his fortune in Malaya before entering the British foreign service.'[15] Engaging as is this summary, it does not disclose one aspect of Lockhart's character that led to him to leave Malaya and apply for a post in the British consular service.

When in Malaya he fell in love with the ward of the Sultan of Negri Sembalan and the two cohabited happily in Lockhart's bungalow. However, this resulted in a considerable scandal and one Lockhart should have been aware would happen. It just was not done for the daughter of a Malayan Sultan to live together with a white rubber planter. The episode might be considered unimportant, but for what it reveals about Lockhart's irresponsibility and instability. Lockhart's diaries show him to have been a man who enjoyed the high life, but who did not have the self-discipline to know when to stop. They also show that while he was intelligent and quick-witted, he was prone to working with furious intensity before lapsing into lengthy periods of lassitude.

He had been serving as a Vice-Consul in Moscow since 1913, but had been recalled in 1917, aged thirty, as a result of another extramarital affair. The official excuse was overwork. This meant he had missed the Bolshevik Revolution. The floundering British Government turned to him in their need for an informal ambassador to the new regime. Lockhart's acute observations of Russian politics and personalities from his original posting had clearly not been forgotten.

Or had they any relevance at all? Lockhart's role in Russia in 1918 has been depicted as that of a diplomatic official, whose advice often went unrecognized and unacknowledged and who was caught up in clandestine deeds at second-hand, almost as if by accident. I consider this a false portrait, designed to mislead. Among the people whom Lockhart met in London in the month before going back to Russia, two names stand out prominently: Sir Arthur Steel-Maitland, at the time Parliamentary Secretary to the Board of Trade, and Alfred Lord Milner.

Lockhart's initial task was to serve as an Agent of Influence, similar to that being performed by Sir William Wiseman in the United States. Agents of

Influence are charged with persuading, beguiling, or even bullying the leaders or governments to whom they are attached into shaping their policy according to the designs of the British Government. At the beginning of 1918, Lockhart's duty was to persuade, beguile or press the Bolshevik leadership into making war on Germany and keep Russia's resources of food and raw materials from the grasp of the Central Powers.

There was, however, little prospect of any bullying being done by him given the manpower crisis that threatened both Britain and France. Sir Auckland Geddes, Minister for National Service, showed the scale of the potential crisis in a paper he presented to the War Cabinet. He pointed out that without new and draconian legislation, 'it would be quite impossible to obtain for the army, anything like the number of men demanded for it.' There were serious obstacles to any new legislation – the prospect of serious disorder in Ireland and the pledges given by the former Prime Minister, Mr Asquith, and subsequently by Mr Arthur Henderson, regarding the protection to be given to skilled workers. He continued, 'To get even a proportion of the men required for the army it would be necessary to cut down shipbuilding, food-producing, or [the] munitions program or all three. It was not likely that any considerable further number of coal miners could be obtained without a serious strike...'[16]

The government had good reason to fear strikes. There was a threat from Bolshevik, later Communist, ideas and the Western Allies were very much alive to it. By the end of 1917 the realities of war for most of the population of Europe were empty bellies, deprivation of political rights, heavy losses and declining hope, a combination guaranteed to try the strongest of unities. The Bolshevik seizure of power marked the advent of a new instability, for the events in Russia fired the imaginations of many throughout the war-ravaged continent.

The new Soviet state towered over war-shattered and exhausted Europe like a colossus attired in the garb of freedom, offering to liberate poverty-stricken workers from the shackles of injustice, servitude, war and exploitation. It is, perhaps, difficult now to imagine the dramatic effect of the Bolshevik appeal on the war-torn and starving population of Europe, but in the last fifteen months of the war the new credo of internationalism was stronger than it has ever been since, and it sounded in the air like a tocsin. As we have seen, this situation was to have the most profound effect on the policy and strategy of the Allies.

There was no doubt that the British elite did regard the ideas of Bolshevism as a danger to their way of life – 'civilization' as they interpreted it. Those ideas terrified its members, threatening as they did the whole class system that gave them both prestige and material comfort. More immediately, they threatened the very conduct of the war. Sovnarkom's appeal to the subject races of Asia has already been noted, but the peril was not confined to the overseas Empire. As early as January 1918, Arthur Henderson, the Labour Party's representative in the War Cabinet, reported that Trotsky's name had been cheered on Clydeside.

Throughout the winter of 1917–18, the Director of Military Intelligence gave the War Cabinet a daily report on the number of German divisions that had moved from Russia to the Western front. A massive German offensive was to be expected. To face this, every available man would be needed on the Western front; there were going to be none to spare to bully the Bolsheviks. This was the other key factor that directed the Allied choice along the clandestine path.

George Macdonogh had little straw with which to build bricks. Sir George Buchanan, the British Ambassador in Petrograd, was on his way home having lost the trust of the Bolsheviks because, as he cabled to the Foreign Office on 29 November 1917, Trotsky knew he had been in touch with Kaledin and the Committee of Public Safety and had supplied the latter with funds.[17] The Committee was a bourgeois organization set up to try to win control of the situation in much the same way as the body of the same name had done in Paris in the French Revolution. In Russia, however, it proved entirely powerless and soon fell apart. A new way would soon be found to provide financial backing for the Cossacks without, it was hoped, the British Embassy being seen to dirty its hands. Buchanan was also considered to be too much a representative of the diplomacy of the old world to deal effectively with the Bolsheviks. His replacement, Lockhart, would need time to build effective links with both the Bolsheviks and the opposition groups. One organization already existed in Russia that might serve to sustain and enhance the opposition groups in Russia. This was the British Military Equipment Section, under Major-General Frederick Cuthbert Poole.

Poole, an artillery officer, had been recalled from retirement on the outbreak of war, and sent to Russia to try to organize and coordinate the demands for, and delivery of, British military supplies to the Russian forces. In the face of almost insuperable difficulties, largely occasioned by Russian inefficiency and duplication, he had accomplished much. Now, in February 1918, Lindley reported to London, 'Poole's organisation only working concern here at present with the necessary staff.'[18]

With the armistice and the beginning of peace negotiations on the Eastern front, the British Government decided to send no more military *matériel* to Russia. In the new circumstances, it was agreed that the Foreign Office would ask the War Office to place Poole at their disposal so that his organization could be converted into a body to prevent strategic material going from Russia to Germany.[19] This organization was known as the Committee on Russian Supplies, or Rusplycom, and it rapidly developed an Intelligence role.

Before the birth of Rusplycom, George Macdonogh had forged another instrument to act as a channel for his new responsibilities in Russia. On 30 January 1918 a section was created in the Department of the Chief of the Imperial General Staff for both Intelligence and Operations work and called 'Military Intelligence Operations', or MIO. It dealt with all matters concerning Russia, Romania, Siberia, Central Asia, the Caucasus, Persia and Afghanistan. It was formed from the personnel of the Military Intelligence section MI2(c) and the Military Operations section MO2.[20]

This section was placed under the leadership of Lieutenant-Colonel Richard Alexander Steel, of the 17th Cavalry of the Indian Army. He was the elder brother of Sir Arthur Steel-Maitland. Educated at Rugby and Sandhurst, he was married twice. In 1899 he had been appointed Aide-de-Camp to the Viceroy of India, Lord Curzon. In 1917 he had been head of MO2, one of the components of the new section. A closer study of its subsections shows that in reality it was responsible for the campaign in Mesopotamia, questions relating to the defence of India, military operations in Afghanistan, Baluchistan, Chitral, Persia and Aden as well as colonial campaigns and operations. This latter included the campaign in East Africa, where the German General von Lettow-Vorbeck was running a highly successful irregular campaign against the British.

39

His replacement as head of MO2 was an Intelligence officer with wide and successful experience in the field, including East Africa, where he had been head of Intelligence from 1914 to 1917. This was Lieutenant-Colonel Richard Meinertzhagen of the Royal Fusiliers. Tall and powerfully built, he was a sometimes awkward individual, opinionated, and, with full confidence in his own judgement, he did not fit readily into the War Office. He was an avid student of natural history specializing in ornithology, in which field he gained a sometimes controversial reputation that rivalled his distinction as a soldier.

His partner in MIO was the head of MI2(c), Major Frederick Kisch of the Royal Engineers whose deputy was Major L.R. Hill of the Royal Field Artillery. Kisch was another brilliant Intelligence officer, both Jewish and a Freemason, an unusual combination. After the war he was to turn his back on a potentially successful military career and go to Palestine to work for the Jewish settlers there.

Irregular warfare, where often untrained and indifferently equipped civilian militias fought regular armies according to their own rules of engagement, is as old as formal engagements between regular soldiers. It has always functioned best in rugged or close terrain where the training and weaponry of regular forces is at a discount. Equally important for its successful prosecution is a spacious theatre of operations, where the irregular forces can disperse, regroup and be difficult to locate.

There had been notable examples of successful irregular warfare in modern times, and which all the above-mentioned officers would have been familiar with: the American War of Independence, the Russian campaign of 1812 and, more recently, the Boer War. Both Steel and Meinertzhagen would have been familiar with the East Africa campaign, Steel as a staff officer while Meinertzhagen had first-hand experience. Moreover, Meinertzhagen also had the benefit of his experience of the Arab rising against the Turks when he had been head of Intelligence to Allenby in Palestine in 1917.

Such record as exists of the work of MIO shows that it was this form of warfare it planned to introduce into Russia while the Allies lacked the regular formations to send there. Links between MIO, Rusplycom, and Lockhart are clear from a number of official documents. Nearly all the documents from the officers of Rusplycom and from Lockhart were being sent to the Director of Military Intelligence and one or more branches of MIO. Of even greater importance is the revelation contained in a small collection of Foreign Office correspondence that Poole was taking his orders from Steel and running his communications through MIO.[21] This points to Lieutenant-Colonel Steel and MIO directing a major campaign of subversion against the Bolsheviks and to Rusplycom and Lockhart both being instruments of this strategy.

Sir George Buchanan had given the Bolsheviks an assurance, on instructions from the government, that Britain would not interfere in Russia's internal affairs. This was to be entirely contradicted by MIO and the men on the ground.

The Germans had not been idle in maintaining their influence with the Bolsheviks. As with the Allies, money was the tool that sustained it. In January 1918 N.M. Weinberg, a German-Jew who was the agent in Petrograd for Mendelsohn & Co., the Berlin bankers, had paid the Bolshevik leaders 12 million roubles from the account of the German Government. He was specific that the money had been paid directly to 'Lennin [sic Lenin], Trotski [sic Trotsky] and Derjenski [sic Dzerzhinsky]'. The payment had allegedly been made against receipts signed by the three Bolsheviks and they had been forwarded to Mendelsohn's Bank in Berlin.[22] The money enabled the Bolsheviks to consolidate their position.

There was to be a terrible reckoning for Weinberg. He was arrested in November 1918 and personally interrogated by Dzerzhinsky in the infamous Butirski Prison. Dzerzhinsky's objective was to recover the receipts, illustrating just how very sensitive the fact that they had received large sums of money from the Germans remained for the Bolsheviks. Since Weinberg could not surrender them, he was finally taken to the inspection room at the prison, where he was stripped and flogged, before being dragged out and shot.

The Germans had been using the nascent Ukrainian nationalism as a tool to fragment the Russian Empire and in July 1917 the Ukraine had claimed the right of self-determination, which the Provisional Government felt itself forced to concede. As Russia descended further into chaos, the Ukraine's newly founded sovereign assembly, the Rada, grew stronger, and at the end of the year declared independence. An ultimatum was sent to the Bolsheviks, who gave it short shrift and the Rada declared war on Soviet Russia. The British sent Harold Williams of the *Daily Chronicle* and Captain Edward Noel from Petrograd, with the concurrence of Sir George Buchanan, to see if they could exploit the possibilities among both the Ukrainians and the Cossacks and enlist their menfolk for the struggle against Germany.[23] In late December, Sir George Barclay, the British Ambassador to the Romanian Government at Jassy, sent another officer, Major J.K.L. Fitzwilliams, to the Ukraine bearing eight bills of £5,000 each and the authority to provide up to £10 million more. He was also to furnish another report on the Cossacks and Ukrainians.[24]

Then came the agreement of 23 December with the French, whereby the Ukraine became part of the French sphere of influence in Russia. The British were apparently happy to follow the French in all dealings there and at the beginning of 1918 it looked as if both Allied Powers were about to recognize the Rada as the government of an independent Ukraine. Then Général Taubouis, the French emissary to the Rada, dropped a bombshell:

> General Taubouis considers present political situation unsuitable for making any official notification to Rada and advises waiting to see if Ukraine intends making separate peace with Central Powers independently of Bolsheviks. Leaders of Rada strongly Austrophil.[25]

Taubouis had stopped the whole process in its tracks, not that it was ever a genuinely practical policy from the start. The Allied policy of bribing the Ukrainians to keep the front active was little more than selfish opportunism since it had no realistic chance of attaining its immediate military objective. The French wanted to form a union of Poland, the Ukraine, Romania and the Don Cossacks. The men of the French Military Mission scattered promises wholesale, but at no stage did they proffer the recognition that the Ukrainians demanded. The promises the French made were soon seen to be empty, as the French had no troops on the spot and it soon became clear that they could not even contemplate sending any.

The war with the Soviet regime that the Ukrainians had so rashly ventured into was proving disastrous. The minority Bolshevik party in the Ukraine had set up a parallel government to the Rada, and with the aid of Soviet bayonets had occupied Kiev. Early in February the Rada, having already sold itself to the French, now prostituted itself to the Germans as the only people who could help it.

The peace negotiations at Brest-Litovsk had by now broken down and war between Germany and Bolshevik Russia had resumed. Not only did Trotsky delay and complicate the negotiations, but the Bolsheviks had appealed to the German workers and soldiers to rise and slaughter the Kaiser and his Generals. It was a crass and irresponsible move that resolved any remaining dilemma the Germans might have felt about renewing the war in the East. They did have troops available and swept forward into the Ukraine. With their aid Kiev was reoccupied. French policy lay in tatters.

The question of what other avenues lay open to the Allies after the Ukrainian debacle can best be answered by turning to Transcaucasia and Transcaspia. There was already a small British Military Mission to the Caucasus, based at Tiflis, under the command of General Offley-Shore. On 14 December Macdonogh told the War Cabinet that,

> ... he had communicated the decision of the War Cabinet promising assistance to the Armenians, and had received from General Shore a telegram to the effect that the Armenian fraternity had collected a sum of between 5 and 10 million roubles, and giving figures for the cost of mobilising 20,000 men and maintaining 40,000 men for three months. The Director of Military Intelligence stated that the most valuable help in this part of the world might be expected from the Armenians, who had every reason to fight the bitter end.[26]

The reason for the Armenians fighting to the bitter end is found in their treatment by the Turks in 1915. Then, the Turks, believing that the Armenians had been helping the Russian Army fighting against them in the Caucasus, forcibly deported them, a process that resulted in the slaughter of millions of Armenians by starvation and mass murder.

The idea of forming what was virtually an autonomous Armenian Army had originated with Alexander Kerensky, but little had been done. Under the conditions now operating – the disintegration of the Russian Army, the armistice on the Eastern front, the opening of peace negotiations at Brest-Litovsk and the prospect of a German and Turkish advance across Central Asia towards India – the idea was resurrected from the files of the War Office. There were conditions that made it a matter of the utmost gravity that some sort of resistance was offered to the expected German and Turkish incursion into the Transcaucasian and Transcaspian regions.

It was one of Germany's avowed war aims that the British Empire would lose India as a price for going to war against Germany. With Britain's Grand Fleet controlling the seas, there was no prospect of a direct attack on British India. The only other options, both of which Germany adopted, were to employ Indian nationalists or to try to infiltrate German and Turkish teams into India and Afghanistan in order to incite an invasion of India by Afghanistan and simultaneously inspire the Indian masses to rise against the British.

The only overland routes by which they could achieve this were through Persia, or across Transcaucasia and Transcaspia. Whilst Russia remained in the war the latter route was completely blocked, although the Germans tried to instigate a revolution among the Georgians through the nationalist Prince Machabelli and others. With the cooperation of the Turks, the Germans persistently attempted to sneak clandestine parties across Persia to their goals, and strained to incite the Persian Government to go to war with Britain and Russia. To counteract these efforts both the British and Russians intervened in Persia, and successfully blocked these attempts though, on too many occasions for comfort, it was a near run thing.

The Russians had a more immediate interest in the region in that they were fighting the Turks in open, conventional warfare on the Caucasian front. Their Army of the Caucasus had performed magnificently, driving the Turks back into Asia Minor and capturing the major city of Erzerum. The Russian Army of the Caucasus, under the command of General Baratoff at the end of 1917, coordinated its actions with the British forces in Mesopotamia, first under General Maude and then, after his death, under General Marshall. The dissolution of the Russian Army caused by the Revolution reached the Caucasus in the winter of 1917–18 and this meant a huge hole was left in British strategy for the defence of India. It also left a dangerous gap on General Marshall's right flank, exposing it to a potentially devastating attack by any Turkish or German force that cared to exploit it.

To plug these holes, in the words of one of the Intelligence officers active in Russia, 'we started another adventurous policy – sending a minute force up from Mesopotamia to the Caucasus with instructions to endeavour to organise the Georgians and Armenians for resistance to the Turks and to secure the flank of the Mesopotamia Force.'[27] This was an attempt to open a new front using a native population as irregular forces, stiffened, trained and directed by small bodies of professional regular British officers and non-commissioned officers.

The British had been endeavouring to finance both the Armenians and Cossacks through their one centre of influence in the region, the British Consulate at Tiflis. Kaledin received some of the money he needed from funds drawn on the British Embassy and distributed by the British Military Mission in Transcaucasia. Otherwise, such small sums of roubles as the Consul, Mr P. Stevens, received, he held at the disposal of Colonel Pike, who was left in command of the British Military Mission pending the arrival of the commander of the 'minute force' from Mesopotamia. In the end, a stop-gap solution was engineered by purchasing 2,808,000 roubles from the Imperial Bank of Persia, a sum to be redeemed in London at a value of £48,264–14s. The rouble notes were taken to Tiflis by King's Messenger.[28]

The 'minute force' was called Dunsterforce after its commander, Major-General Lionel Dunsterville, who was sent to replace Offley-Shore as head of the British Military Mission in Tiflis. Dunsterforce was the child of MIO and originally consisted of forty-one officers and seventy non-commissioned officers, who assembled at Baghdad early in January 1918. Further officers and non-commissioned officers were ready to leave England to join the force later, and the CIGS reported to the War Cabinet that Russian officers were also leaving England for the Caucasus where General Baratoff hoped to raise a force to cooperate with General Marshall. Dunsterforce was well equipped with cars and lorries for the sake of speed.

A neutral, the weather, thwarted these expectations. On 4 February 1918 after setting out from Baghdad, Dunsterville and his convoy of forty-two vehicles arrived at the foot of the Hamadan Pass, in the Zagros Mountains of Kurdistan, en route to Tiflis, Georgia and the Caspian Sea. Unfortunately, the pass was blocked by snow. Major G.M. Goldsmith, who was to take up post as British Military Agent to the Army of the Caucasus, had preceded Dunsterville, so he could report on the condition of the roads and likely camping places for his force. On arriving at Hamadan on 31 January, he had observed a great deal of anti-British ferment brewing there, and separate attempts were made to assassinate both Goldsmith and his companion, Major Sir Walter Bartelott.

On 3 February, Brigadier-General Offley-Shore arrived from Tiflis, and 'In his opinion success depended on the rapidity of Major-General Dunsterville's arrival in Tiflis.'[29] With Dunsterforce trapped at the foot of the Hamadan Pass, Goldsmith now sent an urgent request to Dunsterville, urging him to ride over the pass with Colonel Duncan on Kurdish horses. In the meantime, he recruited Kurdish labour from Hamadan to clear the pass for the rest of the force.

Goldsmith was sent ahead again to reconnoitre the road as far as Enzeli, the embarkation point for crossing the Caspian Sea, which Dunsterforce needed to do to reach Tiflis. He successfully arranged for the safe passage of Dunsterforce to Enzeli through territory controlled by the Jungali tribe under their chief, Kuchikhan. Goldsmith then went ahead to Bolshevik-controlled Baku, but was informed that Dunsterforce was being held up at Enzeli by Bolshevik troops. Again, Goldsmith set to work negotiating and was once more successful, only to find that Dunsterville had returned to Hamadan.

Another of the tasks allotted to Dunsterforce was to gain control of the Caspian Fleet. It was intended to do this simply by purchasing it and to this end Goldsmith entered into secret discussions with the Armenian leaders and forwarded his reports on these discussions to Dunsterforce. He then proceeded to Tiflis, as suggested by Dunsterville, and came under the command of Colonel Pike, who had taken over the British Military Mission after Offley-Shore's departure. He relieved Goldsmith of two of his duties: the purchase of the Caspian Fleet, and the arrangement for a rapid communications network running from Tiflis via Baghdad to the War Office in London. These tasks he gave to Captain Noel, Goldsmith being informed that he was now at Pike's disposal and was to take his orders from him.[30]

MIO's first military venture into Russia had hardly been a resounding success, but this was by no means the end of British clandestine operations in the area, for Dunsterforce was to return to the scene later, in a different guise and with different purposes. So, too, would other British Intelligence officers who, while not attached to Dunsterforce, would be part of the overall scheme.

Siberia was recognized, like Transcaucasia and Transcaspia, as one of the keys to controlling Russia. It too was one of the breadbaskets of the Russian Empire, along with southern Russia and the Ukraine. On 11 February the War Cabinet learnt of a development that could open the door of Siberia:

> The Deputy Chief of the Naval Staff reported that he had received a message from HMS *Suffolk* at Vladivostok, which stated that the result of the Cossack Conference at Iman was highly satisfactory. A resolution, condemning Bolshevik policy and repudiating attempts to make a separate peace, was carried by 42 votes to 4. The message from HMS *Suffolk* also stated that financial and material assistance was urgently required from the Allies in order to enable the Cossacks to organise a force to establish order in Eastern Siberia, and that inquiries were being made by the Cossacks as to whether the Allies were prepared to give such assistance.[31]

The cruiser *Suffolk* had been stationed at Vladivostok in order to observe and report on the situation in the region and protect British lives and interests.

Certainly from the date of this report the British began surreptitiously supporting counter-revolutionary movements in Siberia. A telegram from Sir J. Jordan, the British Ambassador in Peking, contained in the files of the Political and Secret Department of the India Office, shows this clearly. Its subject is the difficulties involved in financing these different movements. Among those whom the British were financing was the Ataman Semenoff, a singularly unruly and unpleasant individual who, operating from the safety of China, made repeated incursions into Siberia. These were reputedly anti-Bolshevik, but by all accounts they bore more resemblance to unlicensed pillaging expeditions.

Jordan's figures show that Henry Sly, the British Consul at Harbin, was responsible for these payments and had received two original grants of £20,000 for this purpose, and these had realized 897,993 roubles. The money had been dispersed as follows:

1. Semenoff's forces, February 420,000 roubles. March 115,000.
2. Officers Corps, February 125,000, March 200,000, April (advance) 30,000.
3. Cost of despatch of Howitzers 7,993.[32]

Jordan's message gains additional significance from the fact that it is dated 22 June 1918. It goes on to state that the French Legation through its

Military Attaché had placed 4 million roubles at Semenoff's disposal. The Ambassador was naturally concerned that the French would have entire control and influence under these arrangements, and funds provided by the British might thus be used for furthering enterprises opposed to British policy. On 4 July the Foreign Office replied, informing Jordan that he could authorize Sly to pay Semenoff a further 500,000 roubles to cover the arrears for March.

The significance of the date lies in the fact that in April the British had instructed Semenoff that he was to cease his activities in eastern Siberia. Whenever Semenoff is discussed in standard histories of the intervention, this decision has been regarded as final and writers on the subject attribute his continuing activity to his seeking and receiving Japanese support. Jordan's telegram indicates that the situation was far more complex. No historian in the Anglo-Saxon world appears to have given the French a second thought, nor to have considered that British funding might have been continued.

British policy with regard to Semenoff was effectively hamstrung by what appears to be the common ailment of trying to have it both ways. Lord Robert Cecil spoke to the Japanese Ambassador, Baron Goto, and reported to the War Cabinet:

> Then there was the question of Semenoff. The Japanese were supporting this General, but we had told the Bolshevik Government that we were not doing so, and that he was advancing at his own risk. The Japanese wished to know what our attitude was in regard to the Semenoff movement. Lord Robert Cecil continued that he thought we should deal perfectly frankly with the Soviets. He himself was prepared to back Semenoff, provided that his activities were part and parcel of an Allied movement, otherwise we should have nothing to do with him.
>
> The opinion was expressed that we might leave Semenoff entirely to the Japanese, and say nothing to Trotzki [sic Trotsky], unless the matter were raised by him. It was suggested, however, that this would not be dealing frankly with Soviets, as, should intervention in Siberia ever materialise and Semenoff become part of the Allied movement, we should naturally support him. To recognise Semenoff now, on the other hand, was to recognise an avowed enemy of the Bolsheviks.[33]

Semenoff's activities were typical of the majority of Allied initiatives in this chaotic and complex period. They would seek to fund anyone who was prepared to state they would fight the Bolsheviks and so, at one remove, the Central Powers. This was entirely in keeping with the traditional British policy of subsidizing continental opposition to a sovereign or country that threatened to establish hegemony over the continent. It had been a tried and trusted weapon against Philip II, the Bourbon kings and Napoleon. In Russia shortage of suitable candidates sometimes meant backing unsavoury individuals such as Semenoff. Yet he was a mere sardine in the ocean in the broader context of what the Allies were trying to achieve in Siberia.

On his own, this sardine could never be a threat to Bolshevik rule much less to German domination of Russia. The problem, as General Poole wrote to Colonel Byrne, his liaison officer in London, was that Siberia consisted of 'A series of small republics with a strong tinge of Bolshevism and anarchism. No probability of a Central Govt. being framed in the near future.'[34] Without a central government to subvert, or alternatively one that was strong enough to carry the flag for the Allies, the strategy pursued by MIO and the French had no focus. That could come only from an outside force, and that effectively meant the Japanese, who alone could deploy an army in Siberia.

Lord Robert Cecil and the former Military Attaché in Russia, Colonel Knox, had been advocating Japanese intervention since December 1917. It was in January 1918 that the British War Cabinet started giving the prospect serious consideration. After debating the issue for nearly two weeks, a majority of the War Cabinet finally agreed to favour it on the 24th.

Although the Japanese Government favoured military intervention, they demanded the political support of the United States before taking any active step. Months of diplomatic wrangling ensued as the British, French and Italians attempted to pressure and persuade President Wilson to embark on this venture. The President would have none of it. Ultimately, the military interventions with American backing did take place once the British and French contrived to gain Wilson's support through the use of further clandestine manoeuvres, but this was to come later in the year.

The Kingdom of Poland had been partitioned three times in the eighteenth century by Austria, Prussia and Russia. However, national feeling and identity continued to flourish. Poles were conscripted into the armies of each of the occupying powers, but those powers soon recognized the necessity of appealing to their diverse populations, and for the Poles the only

49

meaningful inducement was the promise to restore their independence. There was an embryonic Polish Army in existence in 1914, led by Jozef Pilsudski, a highly disciplined and focused patriot. He founded a small Polish Legion, which he backed with a surreptitiously created underground army in Russian Poland. He believed that the only way to liberate his homeland would be to use his Legion to fight alongside the armies of the Central Powers. Meanwhile, another Polish patriot, Roman Dmowski, believed the Allies would win the war. He formed a Polish National Committee in Russian Poland, together with his own Polish Legion to fight beside the Russian Armies.

The defeats suffered by the Russians meant that most of Russian Poland was occupied by the Central Powers. The German General Staff anticipated raising a large contingent of Poles to fight at their side. To further this, on 5 November 1917, they announced that the Kaiser had decided to grant Poland independence and appointed a Regency Council as a government-in-waiting for the Poland they expected to establish under their aegis. They began to recruit a new Polish Army to serve the new puppet government. This foundered once it was discovered that the soldiers had to swear loyalty to the Kaiser rather than to Poland.

On Christmas Day 1916, the Tsar had decreed the formation of an independent Poland. This swelled the numbers of Dmowski's Legion, so that at the end of 1917 no less than three Polish Army Corps were serving with the Russians on the Eastern front. These were some 75,000 men strong, but in addition to them there were approximately another 675,000 Poles in Russia, including 20,000 orphans. The upkeep of this diaspora had been found by the Russian Government at a cost of 4 million roubles monthly. The Bolshevik Government was swift to cut off this funding, causing considerable distress to this Polish community.

At the end of November, the Polish situation was discussed in London by Balfour, Carson, Lord Milner and Macdonogh. They asked if the commander of the Polish forces, Lieutenant-General Dowbor Musnicki could get in touch with the Romanians, the Czechoslovak and Serbian Divisions and the Ataman Kaledin of the Cossacks. They were hoping to establish a bloc of non-Russian troops to recreate the Eastern front, and promised financial and material help for this.[35]

The Provisional Government had created a Polish Central Civil Committee to supervise the welfare of the Poles. Two of its members, Grabski and Wielovcieski, called on Sir George Buchanan at the British Embassy on 23 December 1917. In Buchanan's words:

> They suggest Allies either open credit for 10,000,000 roubles at an allied bank here to be put at disposal of Polish Central Civil Committee and later repaid by Russian Government, or else guarantee of loan for same amount to be raised by [the] Committee and later (? by), Russian Government. They state that Committee of Regency at Warsaw have offered their help and that acceptance would have deplorable effect on Polish opinion as it would practically mean accepting aid from Central Powers. I think we ought to meet them if possible. [36]

Buchanan also informed the Foreign Office that the Poles required 9 million roubles at once and a further 8 million each month. They also said they would 'much appreciate' the help of some British Army Service Corps officers to help with their supplies. The Military Attaché in Petrograd sent a telegram to the Director of Military Intelligence advocating that this policy should be followed, thus providing a strong degree of British control. Once again the prospect was enticing. Not only was there the prospect of a ready-made Army, but the promise of forestalling the Germans and the Council of Regency.

Now, however, the Anglo-French agreement of 23 December intervened, and matters Polish passed into French hands. The problems of forming a national army on foreign soil in the face of a hostile or indifferent government were soon to display themselves. Early in the New Year, the War Cabinet heard from the Chief of the Imperial General Staff, who 'reported that a French report from Russia indicated that difficulties were being encountered in the formation of the Polish Army'.[37] This was, if anything, an understatement.

In February 1918 the Prime Minister poured a much-deserved dose of cold water on the grandiose expectations of what could be expected of the Poles. Stressing that the Bolsheviks were the *de facto* Government and their internal policy was no concern of the British, he continued:

> In regard to the Polish movement, he gathered that the Polish armies in question were engaged not in fighting the Germans and Austrians, but in fighting the

51

Bolsheviks. This was no concern of ours, and they could only be regarded as friends if they directed their armies against the Germans or Austrians, or, as was suggested, to the assistance of our Roumanian Allies. [38]

Worse was to follow. The Poles were in an impossible position without either money or supplies, or the prospect of meaningful Allied help. With the Germans on one side of them and the Bolsheviks on the other, survival was the order of the day. Less than a month later, the CIGS 'reported the receipt of information that the Poles had crossed the frontier and had placed themselves under the orders of the Regency Council, which was tantamount to joining the enemy.' [39]

However, not all was lost. The Polish National Committee had fled Russia for Paris. What was more, part of Pilsudski's Polish Legion also managed to escape to France. There they served as a nucleus for the Polish Corps that the French began to form from prisoners-of-war and Polish émigrés. They soon had not a Corps, but an army 100,000 strong.

As early as 26 November 1917, the British Military Attaché in Romania had percipiently observed:

1. It is impossible count upon any assistance from the Poles, Armenians and Czechs who have no organisation or discipline.
2. The only possible assistance will therefore be from the Cossacks; Ukraine might also find up to half a million but she is most unlikely to find any at all. [40]

Three months later the accuracy of his words had been amply born out. The Allies had proved unable to help the Poles and Ukrainians by clandestine means. The Armenians were bogged down in chaotic conditions in Transcaucasia and Dunsterforce had been unable to reach them. This left the Cossacks.

IV

'...what must develop into a civil war'
Winter 1917–18 (II)

◄o►

The elements within Russia that the Allies tried to use to fight the Germans and the Bolsheviks all laboured under the same disadvantage. All were completely landlocked and the Allies could not send them any direct assistance. Money, not men, was all that could be offered. Isolated officers, such as Noel, Fitzwilliams and Goldsmith could cross hostile territory, but once they reached their destinations they were effectively on their own. Individually, or even when thinly spread over a larger area, as the officers of the French Military Mission had been in the Ukraine, there was little practical help or inducement they could offer to the peoples they were trying to win over to the Allied cause.

Sir George Buchanan had been left to make detailed arrangements for the establishment of Ukrainian, Cossack, Armenian and Polish banks in the directive of 3 December 1917. The only clue given in the instruction to the origin of the idea of founding these banks was a reference to Buchanan's telegram No. 1886 of the 28 November 1917. However, investigation establishes that the idea was originally a Russian one and had been put to Buchanan five days beforehand. On 23 November 1917, Buchanan had been approached by Prince Shahovskoi, whom he described as a 'Russian Banker', with a proposal to found a Cossack Bank.[1] The idea was to create a bank that could, with Allied backing, finance the Ataman Kaledin and the Cossacks.

The Cossacks had a degree of autonomy under the Tsars, and won even more under the Provisional Government. Under the Bolsheviks they saw this coming to an end together with their land ownership and prestige. These were matters of minimal concern to the British Government. They were interested in people who would fight the Central Powers. Buchanan forwarded the proposal to the Foreign Office, whose response, marked 'Urgent', suggests that it was greeted with near incredulity:

> Your private and secret telegram of November 23rd (Counter Revolution in Russia).
> In order to save the Roumanian Army it may be necessary to give financial assistance to the Cossacks with as little delay as possible.
> Scheme for a Cossack Bank seems at first somewhat fantastic. Does any other scheme suggest itself to you in which the desired end could be rapidly and safely attained?[2]

There was no better scheme and Buchanan was warming to the idea of the Cossacks achieving something. The words 'Counter Revolution in Russia' in the Foreign Office response above indicates that recreating the Eastern front was not the only goal they had in mind in financing the Cossacks, whose leadership rejected Bolshevik rule, but to effectively and deliberately finance counter-revolution and civil war.

In light of the promise given to the Soviet Government it was decided to try to use the British Embassy to Romania, now at Jassy with the Romanian Royal Family and Government, as the channel through which to finance the Cossacks. From there the Romanians still managed to play a marginal role in the war, for although their country had been largely occupied by the Central Powers, their army had been reorganized and retrained by the French Military Mission under Général Berthelot. However, their position was precarious since it had been dependent upon Russian support, which was now a thing of the past. This plan proved impractical and when the War Cabinet met on 21 January 1918:

> Lord Robert Cecil reported that considerable difficulties had been experienced in getting financial assistance to the Cossacks and other friendly persons in South-Eastern Russia. In this connection, he drew attention to two telegrams that had been received from Major Keyes, in which he suggested that if we could advance 5,000,000*l*. to an un-named capitalist it would be possible for us to get control of five banks that had branches in the friendly territory, which would enable us not only to finance the Cossacks, but also to obtain control of important industrial resources in Southern Russia.
>
> The Chancellor of the Exchequer felt some difficulty in making such an advance to an unknown person, even on Major Keyes' recommendation.

General Knox stated that the unknown capitalist was probably Mr Poliakoff [Vladimir Poliakoff, Commercial Director of the Siberian Bank], who was subsequently ascertained to be a Jewish banker of Rostov-on-Don, and who was known to General Poole.[3]

So who was Major Keyes and what was he doing advising the advance of £5 million to an unnamed capitalist? Terence Humphrey Keyes was the brother of Admiral Sir Roger Keyes, who rose to fame in the war through his command of British submarines in the North Sea, his work as Chief of Staff at the Dardanelles, and as the Commander of the Dover Patrol who initiated the dramatic raids on Zeebrugge and Ostend in 1918. He was a fire-eater, bold and always ready to take risks. Terence, although a good man in a tight spot, was a more subtle character. With his wiry physique, a narrow jaw, narrow eyes and the slightly cynical smile playing on his lips, his face spoke both of craftiness and strength. It was doubtless these facets of his character that had singled him out for the Political Service of the Government of India.

Rare qualities were required in its members, which was recruited two-thirds from the Indian Army, and one-third from the Indian Civil Service: subtlety, tact, confidence (but not overconfidence) and the ability to apply pressure without being seen to do so. Above all, they needed to be masters of intrigue with not only the ability to mount their own, but to smell a hostile one before it became dangerous. They were attached to the courts of the Indian princes in order to keep them, if not friendly to the British, then from doing any harm by fomenting nationalist trouble in India. Such a man was Terence Keyes.

In the summer of 1917 he was attached to the Russian Army on the Romanian front to conduct a propaganda campaign designed to persuade the Russian soldiers to fight and stand by the Romanians. It soon became clear that the Russians were too demoralized for Keyes to have any appreciable effect. He could not make water run uphill. More pressing needs arose for his abilities, and he was summoned to the British Embassy in Petrograd where he arrived shortly before the Bolshevik coup. The task he had been called to perform was, in his own words, 'nominally running military propaganda, I was really doing political intelligence for the Ambassador.'[4]

Général de la Panouse, the French Military Attaché in Russia, reported that 'Major A. Keyes who was in uniform at the station of Ungeni was pushed and robbed by the soldiers.'[5] This personal insult could only sharpen his nascent contempt for the Bolsheviks.

The 'political intelligence' was to raise money to finance the Don Cossacks and others. With their increasing independence and hostility to both the Provisional Government and then the new Bolshevik regime, they acted as a magnet for the disaffected of the political right and right of centre. Trotsky ordered the new Bolshevik Commander-in-Chief of the Army, N. V. Krylenko, to 'wipe off the face of the earth the counter-revolution of the Cossack Generals and the Cadet Bourgeoisie'.[6] The South Eastern Confederacy had been joined by several politicians from the previous regimes, among them such notables as Miliukov and Rodzianko. They now called themselves the Party of Collection, hoping as they did to collect the different elements of the disintegrating Russian Empire into a unified whole.

The situation was already confused and became more so with the creation of a new force, the Volunteer Army, a formation composed partly of officers and partly of former soldiers of the old Russian Army, who still retained fighting spirit and were both loyal to the Allies and entirely antagonistic to the Bolsheviks. It was under the twin command of Generals Kornilov, the former Commander-in-Chief under Kerensky, and Alexeyev, the last Chief of Staff to the Tsar. Composed of seasoned fighting men, its military value was high, but its numbers were small. It was also hopelessly isolated. Without powerful allies, it appeared inevitably doomed.

They pinned their hopes on the Cossacks, doughty warriors under a leader prepared to stand against the Bolsheviks. The Party of Collection saw the chance to build a bloc from the Cossacks and Volunteer Army that would be strong and committed enough to overthrow what they saw as the Bolshevik usurpers. They pressured both Kaledin and the leaders of the Volunteer Army to work together, threatening to withhold their support if they did not. That mattered because they controlled the money sent by the bourgeoisie of Moscow and Petrograd, without which both parties would find it impossible to survive. They also had the ear of the Allied representatives in Russia who, they said, were prepared to assist if and only if the parties united.

Thus, on 31 December 1917, the Volunteer Army, the Cossacks and the other anti-Bolshevik groups in south Russia became allies under duress. Such a potentially powerful union dominating the rich provinces of south-eastern Russia represented a glittering prize for the Allies, if they could grasp it. Its most urgent and immediate need was money, and it was in search of that vital commodity that Prince Shahovskoi had gone to see Sir George Buchanan. The task of arranging the details was given to Keyes.

Based in a flat at Morskaya Street, 52, Petrograd, Keyes began work. In his papers held at the British Library, he claims to have been the guiding light in this policy, drafting all the telegrams, and maintaining that the Party of Collection 'held the germ of the salvation of Russia, and was the one sound and constructive idea'. When news of the division of Russia into British and French spheres of influence became known to the Embassy in Petrograd, he was outraged:

> When I saw the telegram outlining this policy I went in to see the Ambassador and inveighed against the folly of putting the very delicate political business of assisting the Party of Collection under a General from Mesopotamia whose primary task was a military one [Brig.-Gen. Lionel Dunsterville]...Moreover what we were setting out to do in the Caucasus was the same capital mistake the French were making in the Ukraine – military opportunism in a delicate situation with immense future possibilities. The Ambassador told me to write him a note on the subject, and I dashed off a rather strongly worded note. The next day I was told that my note had gone off as a telegram to the Foreign Office with the addition of 'with reference to Mr. Balfour telegram number so and so Major Keyes makes the following remarks.'[7]

Keyes argued in favour of taking a longer view, and claimed that the Georgians and Armenians were entirely out of touch with the South Eastern Confederacy. Moreover, he said it was extremely unlikely that Dunsterforce could both form a Georgian-Armenian bloc and establish a barrier against Turkey's Pan-Turanian movement while protecting the flank of the army in Mesopotamia. He concluded that since the movements comprising the South Eastern Confederacy were influenced from Petrograd, the Embassy there needed to guide it by keeping in constant touch with the British representative on the Don, General de Candolle, a railway expert who had been detached from the Military Mission in Tiflis. Keyes summed up the different prospects on the Don and in Transcaucasia thus:

> Marked political difference between trans-Caucasus and South Eastern Confederacy must also be borne in mind. Former is at present predominantly Socialist and anti-Militarist while the latter is constitutional with tendency towards Monarchism and possesses strong military element. Constant danger of friction between the two makes it imperative they should be dealt with on different lines.[8]

The project almost collapsed through that old fault of British administration, the lack of coherence between government departments, when each pursued its own policy in isolation. On 21 December, Macdonogh ordered Keyes to Tiflis to assist in exploiting the situation in Transcaucasia. Buchanan's agitated response was prompt. On Christmas Day he telegraphed home that Keyes was engaged in 'work of the greatest importance' and begged to be allowed to keep him in Petrograd,[9] renewing his plea two days later, arguing 'that it is essential that Major Keyes (? at any rate) should stay for this and other important work.'[10] The 'begging' worked and Keyes remained in Petrograd. The scheme to finance the South Eastern Confederacy was put into motion on 28 December 1917.

Such was the secrecy that necessarily surrounded the project that money had already been advanced to Kaledin from the British Consulate in Tiflis, without Britain's Allies being told. However, the sums derived from this quarter were irregular and never enough. Keyes explained the predicament he found himself in:

> At this time the Bolsheviks had partially nationalized the banks, and, though the Embassy had several million roubles in various banks, it was unable to raise any for propaganda or secret service, and I was told off to raise a fighting fund. This job led me into relations with financiers of all grades and politicians mixed up in finance. The party of collection was in desperate straits for money. There was a great dearth of money tokens in the towns of the South....Something big was required to raise an army and finance what must develop into a civil war. Alexeyev appealed to us through certain statesmen of high reputation, and, as the Ambassador had assured the Bolsheviks that the Embassy was not engaged in any counter-revolutionary plot, I was told off to examine the question and interview Alexeyev's agents.[11]

With Britain teetering on the edge of bankruptcy after financing the Allied war effort for nearly three years, the burden of financing a civil war fell on the Americans. They were not shy of shouldering the burden, as Lord Robert Cecil explained:

> It has been intimated to us confidentially that President Wilson is in favour of the provision of Allied support for the above elements, and that while he has no power to lend money direct to such un-organized movements, he is willing to let France and England [sic Britain] have funds to transmit to them if they consider it desirable.[12]

Deepest secrecy was essential, less because of the assurance Buchanan had given the Bolsheviks that the Embassy was not engaged in any counter-revolutionary plots – that seems to have been entirely insincere – but because 'The Allies could not back it openly, as this would have been an act of war against the Bolsheviks, which they were then unable to undertake.'[13] Alexeyev had originally asked for £15 million but the Embassy was unable to supply this directly. The Bolsheviks had decreed that dealing in foreign exchange was a capital offence in order to prevent the export of capital that threatened their policy of confiscation. Attempts were made to raise the money by selling British Treasury Orders, but it was soon discovered that it was impossible to keep this secret. Keyes recorded that in the attempts to do this, four of his seven agents were caught and shot.[14]

It was not just the attraction of an army hostile to both the Bolsheviks and the Germans that drew the British into these proceedings but also, according to Keyes,[15] the fact that the Party of Collection had an organization behind them in Petrograd and Moscow. This was composed of former officers of the old army, civil servants and the professional classes, those who had most to lose in terms of status and income at the hands of the Bolsheviks. These people provided a fruitful recruiting ground for the Allied Intelligence Services in the coming months. In the meantime, they could provide potentially priceless information about conditions and feeling in central Russia, and about the plans and movements of the Red Army the Bolsheviks were creating.

It was the agents of the Confederacy in Moscow and Petrograd who broached the subject of finance with the British, reporting that there was a shortage of money tokens in southern and south-eastern Russia. In a report completed on 27 August 1918 the British Economic Mission to Russia, which had investigated the proceedings, related:

> The first overtures in Petrograd were made by M. Pokrovsky, ex-Foreign Minister, who had been appointed pleni-potentiary [sic plenipotentiary] by M. Rodzianko and General Alexeyev, leaders of the party of Collection. General Kaledin, Hetman of the Don, had endorsed this appointment personally, but was unable to do so on behalf of the whole South Eastern Confederacy without calling a meeting which would have given the matter too great publicity.[16]

While the economic problems of the Confederacy were real enough, the requests for finance can be seen to have originated with politicians and soldiers for political ends. All the British documents bear this out. The British Economic Mission's *Report* sums it up with the greatest clarity and simplicity:

> It appears to us important in the first place to bear in mind the objects with which these negotiations were originally entered upon. These objects were almost wholly political. We understand that the negotiations were initiated as a means of meeting the difficulty of providing Russian currency for political and military purposes, without which the South-Eastern Federation would have been practically helpless.[17]

Rodzianko figured in the next move, too. Due to tension with the Cossacks, who did not trust him, he chose to remain in the background and it was his cousin and agent V.M. Vonliarliarsky, who introduced the Party of Collection's financial agent, Karol Yaroshinsky [Jarosznsky in Polish]. Keyes, promoted to the temporary rank of Lieutenant-Colonel from 6 January to help in dealing with such august figures, was directed to examine the proposals the group had in mind. Yaroshinsky, aged thirty-nine in 1918, was a Russian Pole, the scion of a very old Polish family. He was the son of a large landowner and owner of sugar refineries in the Kiev Government of south Russia. His father died when Karol was young, which meant he was forced to accept heavy responsibilities at an age when most young men are not considered experienced enough to control a business. He also inherited the equivalent of £350,000. He was both energetic and resourceful and soon proved himself more than capable of running the business. A report by the British Secret Service produced in 1919 stated:

> As Kiev, however, did not present large enough scope for his activities and brain, Mr. Iaroshinski decided to come to Petrograd where he started on quite a new departure, namely finance. He felt that in order to become a great and conspicuous man it was necessary to dabble in large sums. He worked out a great financial plan based more upon speculation than love for the actual creation or development of industry.[18]

The service's informant, a Russian, also stated:

> Mr. Iaroshinski himself is a very educated man, very clever and a perfect gentleman in his manners and speech. These characteristics have all played in his favour and in Petrograd financial circles he is looked upon as A1, but one must bear firmly in mind the important fact that Russian financial men themselves, I mean bankers and Company promoters, are of such a standard and code of ethics that many a businessman of Western Europe would not like to accept.[19]

Yaroshinsky was essentially a speculator. He started by using his land and sugar refineries as security to borrow large sums of money that he then used to purchase considerable numbers of shares in Russian banks. He then used the shares as security against which to borrow more money that he used to buy more shares; in fact it was a pyramid operation. This built him a reputation as a credible man, for his contemporaries saw someone who could command great wealth and was trusted with large sums of money by others. However, he was more interested in influencing politics to maximize his financial returns than he was in building a business on sound lines. He was the sort of man who gained people's confidence and then used them, or their perception of him, to further his own ends.

The early death of his father may explain Yaroshinsky's desire to be 'a great and conspicuous man', both compensating for his own loss and perhaps also fuelling a desire to better his father. Whether this was so or not, Karol Yaroshinsky seems to have had a well-developed ego.

Perhaps it was his ego as well as self-preservation that led him to adopt an anti-German stance. Keyes noted:

During his meteoric career he had contracted enmities with certain bankers who happened to have come within the German orbit. The Germans were already in treaty with certain banks, and he was compelled, in order to keep his flag flying and realise his ambition, to stand out against the Germans.[20]

Keyes had many meetings with Yaroshinsky, Pokrovsky, and Vonliarliarsky to thresh out the details of the scheme, not without considerable risk in the conditions prevailing in both Petrograd and Moscow that winter. There was not only the danger of arrest by the newly formed Cheka, the Bolsheviks' Secret Service. As Keyes explained:

> It was impossible to meet anyone connected with financial matters except secretly by night. Flats with entrances to two different streets were generally selected, the interviews always took place after 11 o'clock at night, and it was generally stipulated that I should wear a different fur coat and cap every time. There was anything up to 100 robberies with violence every night – the victims [sic victim] being generally stripped to his vest and drawers in a temperature of frost. Snow was not generally cleared away, but was piled in great heaps at the sides of the streets, giving good covert to the armed gangs which infested the town. I was out for 22 nights out of the 28 in February, was attacked three times, twice with revolvers, and once with a bomb, saw three murders and several hold ups, and got involved in two general melees.[21]

These dire conditions were the fruit of the breakdown of law and order that followed on the heels of both Russian Revolutions in 1917. The police had vanished, the prisons broken open and their inmates released, bands of anarchists who had taken over some of the largest houses in both cities roamed the streets robbing at will, while former officers got together and lived by robbery. Above all was the uncertainty that seeped into the very fibre of society and sapped its cohesion. There was neither restraint nor any other motive than to survive by any means.

Even the Bolshevik leaders were not immune from the consequences of these conditions. John Wheeler Bennett recounts that Moisei Uritsky, who rose to be head of the Cheka in Petrograd, was robbed and stripped naked, though Edvard Radzinsky relates that Uritsky was robbed of only his fur coat; even the pockets of Lenin's coat were rifled and his automatic pistol stolen.[22]

While the territories more or less controlled by the Confederacy contained enormous natural wealth, it could not be realized without a bank that could issue currency in anticipation of it. The formation of such a 'State' bank was thus imperative, but it would be unable to carry a large issue of notes with a value comparable to that of the Kerensky rouble unless it was based on strong backing from the great financial institutions of London or Paris. That could not be done openly since it would have laid the British and French Governments open to the charge of fomenting civil war when the British Ambassador had expressly promised the Bolsheviks that the Embassy would do no such thing.

The arrangement Keyes and his fellow conspirators reached to achieve the same ends but by indirect means was to establish a Cossack Bank, backed by five, later seven, of the major Russian banks. This is where Yaroshinsky was to play the key role. He already owned enough shares to control three of these banks and was determined to group all of them under his wing. He needed money from the British and, ultimately, the Americans to achieve this.

The banks that were seen as the bedrock of the scheme were the Russian Commercial and Industrial Bank, the Russian Bank of Foreign Trade, the Kiev Private Bank, the Union Bank, the International Bank and the Volga Kama Bank. This last was later dropped from the scheme at the suggestion of Yaroshinsky, to be replaced by the Siberian Bank. Ownership of these banks would not only allow the foundation of a Cossack Bank, with Anglo-French backing, but this coalition would also have controlled almost the whole of Russia's economic life under normal circumstances and no Russian Government would have been able to function effectively without its support. Keyes explained the prospects in a memorandum:

> These banks own or control practically all the sugar concerns in the Ukraine valued at 400 million roubles, several railways, 1¼ million acres of easily accessible forest, 300,000 acres of irrigated cotton land in Central Asia, nearly all the insurance concerns of Russia, beside large oil, coal, cement and other concerns.

The addition of the Siberian Bank would bring with it

> …great influence over the most extensive, but only partially developed grain tracts of Russia, and over the butter business of Siberia, but has concessions in

Mongolia and for a Mongolian Bank which should give it almost a monopoly in that country. This Bank being more thoroughly under our control than any other should prove the most useful instrument of policy.

Keyes was certainly thinking on the grand scale, for he continued:

> We have the right to nominate our own directors to all these banks and to all the companies controlled by them, and Yaroshinski undertakes to place at least 100 young Englishmen in his banks and companies.
>
> These banks with their 300 odd branches and their interests in numerous commercial and industrial concerns offer us an unrivalled commercial intelligence system for investigating old and new undertakings. They offer us the means of setting on their feet such of our concerns as have suffered during the disorders, and of handing out loans and other financial interests.[23]

There was still another bonus. By controlling this conglomerate of banks, Britain, and to a lesser extent the Allies, would exclude the Germans and cripple their attempts to dominate Russia economically. This was a most desirable objective and it surfaced repeatedly as an object of policy.

It would be appropriate to describe the scheme that was evolving from all these discussions, without hyperbole, as momentous. It was using banking as an instrument of policy. It was Imperialism on a grand scale. If the mechanics of the scheme had worked, it would have reduced the Russian Empire to the status of a satellite of the British Empire. An understanding of the mechanics of the scheme is necessary, for they were the means by which this goal was to be achieved.

The original plan was to provide Yaroshinsky with £5 million – or 200 million roubles – at 3½ per cent interest. This sum was to be secured against shares in railways, oil, cement, sugar, timber, flax, cotton and coal owned by the banks, most of which were outside Bolshevik control. These shares were worth 350 million roubles. For his part, Yaroshinsky was not merely to buy the shares, but was to give the British half the seats on the Board of Control. This board was to consist of four members who would control and direct the policy of the banks in accordance with British interests. Yaroshinsky nominated himself and Pokrovsky to be the Russian members. An additional enticement was that seats on the boards of all the banks involved, and all the companies controlled by the banks, would also be given to the British.

Apart from financing the Confederacy and the Volunteer Army and preventing the Germans from gaining economic hegemony in Russia there were other far-reaching objectives. These included federating the component nationalities of the Russian Empire, thus preventing the breakup of Russia and maintaining it as a counter-balance to the German Empire, but also to provide the machinery for an economic blockade of the Central Powers as future circumstances might dictate. There was also the provision of unlimited opportunities for post-war trade with Russia and for handling Britain's enormous government and private financial interests.

Keyes summed up the prospects in a despatch to the Foreign Office on 21 January:

> 200,000,000 roubles at present is Five and a half million pounds: this could not be regarded as [a] large sum for blocking German schemes and securing such great advantages for British trade even if it were (? given). It is however loan on good security. Our man is willing to deposit with us shares of conservative valu-ation of 350,000,000 roubles in railways, oil, cement, timber, flax and cotton majority of concerns being in country outside Bolshevik control [.] [Control] over banks and their dependent concerns will be wielded by Board consisting of himself, one nominee of his and two of ours.[24]

Before the scheme could crystallize there occurred an incident of the sort that bedevils British officialdom and never more so than with regard to policy towards Russia in 1918–20. Buchanan left Petrograd for London at the beginning of January 1918, leaving affairs in the hands of the Embassy's Counsellor, now Chargé d'Affaires, Francis Lindley. It appears questionable how much of the scheme had been revealed to Lindley for, on the 11th, he telegraphed the Foreign Office 'recommending an exchange operation to assist Yaroshinski in obtaining control of the Bank of Foreign Trade'.[25]

Yaroshinsky had approached Lindley independently of Keyes: perhaps he was unsure about Keyes' financial acumen; perhaps, with so much at stake, he was simply hedging his bets. More probably, this initiative strengthened his hand in dealing with the British, in that it left both Keyes and Poole with little alternative but to agree to new proposals he was to make at a meeting on 6 February. Be that as it may, Lindley seized the bit between his teeth and, without consulting Keyes, sent his telegram. He considered that gaining control of this bank could be carried out without reference to the larger scheme, on the grounds that 'To have insight into its workings is alone worth exchange operation.'[26]

Confusion was the natural outcome and the *Report* of the British Economic Mission to Russia emphasized this when it observed that not only did the fact that the scheme was a political one present difficulties from a business viewpoint, but

> Closely connected with this difficulty is the fact that there does not seem to have been perfect co-operation between the two persons chiefly concerned in the working out of the scheme in Petrograd, viz. Mr. Lindley and Col. Keyes. Thus Col. Keyes in his Memorandum refers to a telegram having been sent without his being consulted on the matter. Hence there is a double thread to follow, viz. (a) Foreign Office and Mr. Lindley, and (b) Foreign Office and Col. Keyes.[27]

The reason for Lindley's apparently headstrong action was that four pro-German directors of the bank were anxious to flee Russia, but feared to do so unless they had substantial funds abroad. Yaroshinsky and his Russian colleagues could not afford to give the directors the foreign currency they were desperate for, and suggested that if the panicky directors deposited 6 million roubles in London, the sterling equivalent would be held ready for them.

Lindley feared that if the Embassy did not act, then the directors would turn to the Germans who would, and in the process win control of the bank. The Foreign Office consulted the Treasury and, perhaps over-anxious to forestall the Germans, on 16 January authorized Lindley to accept the offer, provided the 6 million roubles were rouble notes and not bank balances. Lindley replied that only 350,000 roubles could be sent in cash while the remainder would be in negotiable cheques, but as they were drawn on a bank balance in Petrograd that could not be touched, he had therefore declined the offer. However, two days later he reported that he had been assured that the money would be transferred direct to south Russia. The Foreign Office thereupon sanctioned the offer provided the money reached General De Candolle.

The Treasury now intervened, stipulating that the sterling equivalent would be paid only if they held a lien on an equivalent sterling sum, until they learnt that the roubles had actually reached De Candolle. This was telegraphed to Lindley and was made a condition of his accepting the offer. Lindley then made a strange move. In the words of the Treasury official who investigated the case, 'For some reason, which is still not clear, Mr Lindley is stated to have made arrangements for remittance to the South-East of only five out of the six million.'[28]

According to the same source, at or about this time Yaroshinsky 'seems to have informed' both Lindley and Keyes that he was able to remit to Kiev not merely 5 million roubles, but an additional 10 million roubles. A clerical error on the part of the Foreign Office now compounded an already complex situation. Telegram no. 88 to Lindley referred to telegram no. 104 instead of telegram no. 95. As a result of this error Lindley believed he had been fully authorized to accept Yaroshinsky's proposal without application of the safeguards laid down.

Yaroshinsky took what steps he could to carry out the agreement and messengers with bills drawn on Kiev were reputed to have left Petrograd. Yet February saw fighting between Soviet Russia and the Ukraine, together with the German advance into Russia after the peace negotiations at Brest-Litovsk had broken down. In the resulting chaos the fate of the messengers was still unknown to the British in April, although one was reported to have been murdered. In the meantime Yaroshinsky went into hiding.

Early in February Lindley asked that the sterling equivalent of 10 million roubles might be credited to Hugh Ansdell Leech, who was then running the 'Cosmos' Telegraph Agency on behalf of the British Government. He had been brought into the scheme as the intermediary between the two parties. Yaroshinsky placed 6 million roubles to his credit. However, in a witnessed statement made at Ziarat, Baluchistan, on 28 June 1922, Keyes claimed that he had expressly warned Yaroshinsky, 'that if any payments were made on his demand to Mr. Leech, the British Government would in no way be responsible, and obtained from him a document in which he admitted that he understood this.' The document would appear to have been one of those burnt when the British Embassy left Petrograd.

So far as the Treasury was aware, the roubles Yaroshinsky offered had not been received either at Petrograd or Kiev, or by De Candolle in south Russia. Another comedy of errors followed. Lindley's original telegram of 11 January had not been received and, when it was repeated on 18 February, it reached London in such a corrupt form that it was impossible to act on it.

Further demands for payment came from Leech. Yet there was still nothing to show that the roubles had been transferred to Kiev or the south-east. Nor was there any evidence to show what had become of the roubles or who held them. Since no British official had laid hands on the roubles, or even set eyes on them, the Treasury very correctly refused to make any payment against them.

As regards Leech's role, the Treasury observed that they 'have received certain indications casting doubt on his disinterestedness in his capacity as agent between the representatives of His Majesty's Government and the Russian parties to the transaction.'[29] Indeed, there was considerable scope for any individual who had an eye to lining his own pocket. As Robert Chalmers, the Treasury official who investigated the case observed, 'I am to remark at this point that the rate [of exchange] specified would have placed a considerable sum of money into the pockets of Monsieur Yaroshinski or Mr Leech.'[30] The Treasury was right to be on its guard.

The waters had been considerably muddied when General Poole and Keyes went into the final round of the negotiations with Yaroshinsky, whose hand had been significantly strengthened by his acquisition of the Bank of Foreign Trade.

Although working with the Embassy, Keyes was responsible to General Poole and his approval was necessary for the scheme to go ahead. Poole, Keyes, Yaroshinsky and Poliakoff met on 6 February by which date all knew that conditions in southern Russia were reaching crisis. With the arrangement with Lindley behind him, Yaroshinsky was now proceeding on different lines and needed £500,000 to immediately complete his control of the Union and International Banks and, in conjunction with them, take over the Siberian Bank. However, he needed a decision that day on whether the British would provide this amount as several directors of the bank were, he said, about to flee. Poole and Keyes felt they had to agree to the modification and it seems that their motive was to forestall the Germans, who were known to be interested in the Siberian Bank. The £500,000 was promised against the security of shares to the value of 35 million roubles, but with the interest increased to 5¼ per cent at Poliakoff's behest. Yaroshinsky undertook to form the Board of Control immediately.

The Germans were in hot pursuit of the Siberian Bank and Yaroshinsky found he had to pay more than he had expected for the shares he wanted. His purchase was achieved by a further £428,571–8s 7d from the British via Keyes. The Germans were forestalled by just a single day.

In his submission to the Foreign Office and Treasury after he had returned to London, Keyes still thought he had achieved a good deal:

> We have thus lent Yaroshinski £928,371:8:7 at 5¼% on the security of shares worth 35,000,000 roubles in commercial concerns and shares in the Siberian Bank for which he is paying 66,000,000 roubles.
>
> The shares in Companies stand in my name in the Commercial and Industrial Bank and the transfer of shares in the Siberian Bank are distributed as follows:
>
> (a) Transfer of shares deposited in Russian Banks in original with Poliakov, duplicates with me.
>
> (b) Transfer of shares in French and British Banks in original with me, duplicates with Poliakov.
>
> (c) 1018 shares deposited by me in Legation in Christiania.
>
> H.M. Government was willing to advance £5,000,000 at 3½% on securities worth 350,000,000 roubles to prevent certain banks falling under German influence and to obtain control of them for certain political and commercial aims. The formation of the Cossack Bank is in abeyance. The Volga Kama Bank has been dropped out, but the control of the other banks has been obtained for less than one million sterling at 5¼ instead of 3½% and with securities worth 101,000,000 roubles.[31]

Before Poole met Yaroshinsky and Poliakoff, the personnel for the Cossack Bank, including the engravers, had left for the Don. It was all too good to be true.

The British Government still had no idea of who the financier was; all they had to go on was the comment from Colonel Knox who had told them that it was 'probably' Poliakoff. Instead of asking Keyes or Lindley for his name and background, they hastily agreed to the scheme on 22 January:

Following for Keyes

The Government are so anxious to give immediate financial assistance to our friends that if the advance can be utilised immediately to assist them and on the understanding that the unnamed financier is Poliakoff of whom they have good accounts the Government will sanction proposal. They desire me to point out that they are prepared to take this course entirely on your advice.[32]

It was not until 7 February that Lindley enlightened the government as to the real identity of the mystery financier.[33] It must have come like a douche of cold water in London, especially when Lindley added the caveat that 'I do not consider matter should be finally settled until it has been thoroughly threshed out and Keyes will probably have to go to London to explain it.' The message created immediate distrust and that was to prove one element in the unravelling of the scheme.

A combination of other factors then completed the unravelling. Poliakoff had to go into hiding because the Cheka, who knew more about what was going on than the British realized, were searching for him. Not only that, he had not been informed of the political aims of the scheme, though when he was, he came in wholeheartedly behind them. Further delay was caused when the Bolsheviks imprisoned Pokrovsky.

To add to the confusion, the purchase of controlling shares in the Siberian Bank took on a life of its own and became, in effect, a separate proposition, recognized as such by the British Economic Mission, who termed it 'Proposition B' as opposed to the initial scheme, which was termed 'Proposition A'. This was because the major shareholder in the bank, M.N.K. Denisov, had arranged with Keyes and Yaroshinsky to be paid in instalments for the shares he was selling. These were valued at 65,044,500 roubles, of which 15 million roubles were to be paid on 1 March. The next instalment, worth 25,022,250 roubles, was due on 28 January 1919 and the final instalment, for the same amount, was due on 28 July 1919.

Keyes was responsible for the fulfilment of this contract by the due dates. Should he fail to make the payments then he was obliged to pay a sum equivalent to double the amount due as a fine for breach of contract. However, the various banks at which the shares were deposited had made loans to Denisov against their value, thus effectively mortgaging the shares. Denisov had agreed that these loans should be continued to Keyes, with the proviso that should the banks that granted the loans not be willing to continue the loans to Keyes, Denisov would arrange for other institutions to grant loans in their place. Charges on the loans were to be borne by Denisov until 1 March 1918, after which they became Keyes' responsibility.

By the terms of the contract Keyes was obliged to sell the shares to Yaroshinsky, who was to pay Keyes the 15 million roubles for the first instalment between 20 February and 1 March 1921, together with interest at 5¼ per cent, and then pay the other two instalments thirty days before the dates they were due. Keyes was to have voting control at the General Meeting of the Bank and was to then place two seats on the Board of Management at Yaroshinsky's disposal. As seats on the Council of the Bank became available on the retirement in rotation of its members, Yaroshinsky was to have the right to nominate half the directors to the vacancies.

There were a number of uncertainties implicit in this arrangement, but the main objection raised by the British Economic Mission applied to both strands of the scheme:

> It would appear that eventually all the shares and all the voting power in the Siberian Bank will be in M. Yaroshinsky's hands, and any control that we may wish to exercise over this bank will depend as in the case of the other five banks (proposition A) on M. Yaroshinsky's good faith and goodwill.[34]

Yaroshinsky's good faith and goodwill were not stable platforms on which to base a policy with such momentous aims.

Worse than that, the banks had been nationalized by the Bolsheviks, who had expropriated their assets and cancelled their shares. To try to circumvent this, the conspirators had pre-dated the contract that was signed in February 1918 to October 1917. As the British Economic Mission to Russia commented, 'Such a procedure, obviously taken to circumvent the Bolshevik order of nationalisation, was illegal, and makes the contract null and void should either party wish to take advantage of the fact.'[35] Not only were the banks nationalized, but also dealing in bank shares was prohibited and eventually the shares themselves were cancelled by a Bolshevik decree.

It is understandable that both the Treasury and Foreign Office in London began to have serious doubts about the project. This is reflected in a meeting of the Russia Committee on 15 February 1918. This Committee was one of several that had been created by the War Cabinet to advise it on the details of events and policy in several key areas that were crucial to Britain's conduct of the war. At its head was Lord Robert Cecil. The Director of Military Intelligence was a member and, if he was absent, Lieutenant-Colonel Steel took his place. Major Kisch was one of the Committee's secretaries. Lindley had cabled London over the confusion created by trying to operate two banking schemes, and raised doubts about Keyes' financial proposals. The Committee considered the draft of a reply and its minutes record:

> The draft was to the effect that no advance of funds should be made to Yaroshinsky until after Major Keyes had returned to England and explained the full bearing of his proposals.
>
> Lord Robert Cecil, while agreeing that no further obligations should be entered into, said we could not repudiate any action which had already been taken on the strength of the authority which had been given to Major Keyes, who, it appeared had pledged himself to the extent of half a million pounds. Mr. Ward agreed to refer the draft to the Treasury for further consideration, in view of the Chairman's observations which expressed the general feeling of the Committee.[36]

On 20 February the Foreign Office instructed Lindley and Keyes not to advance any further money to Yaroshinsky until Keyes' explanation had been received. Factors beyond the control of either the Treasury or the Foreign Office were also crowding round. With the breakdown of the peace negotiations between the Bolsheviks and the Central Powers, the armies of the latter advanced deep into Russia. The Bolsheviks had so undermined the Russian Army that little effective resistance was possible and German troops reached the outskirts of Petrograd. The British expected its imminent fall.

In the meantime the South Eastern Confederacy had collapsed. The Cossacks, the linchpin of the whole operation, were in a weak strategic position to begin with, surrounded as they were by Bolshevik forces that also controlled some of the main railway junctions that gave access to the rest of Russia. However, that was not the main problem. That lay in the fact that the Bolsheviks had established a Cossack Department under Lagutin and Nagaev, two Cossacks who had turned Bolshevik. The purpose of the

72

Department was to subvert the Cossacks from their traditional loyalties and agitators were sent into the Cossack territories. Moreover, younger Cossacks who had been serving at the front and were imbued with the spirit of Bolshevism were now flooding back into the homeland. They were not interested in fighting wars they saw as imperialist and they did not recognize the title of 'Ataman', which had been resurrected from history.

The Bolshevik forces began their long-feared concentric advance against the Cossacks in accordance with Trotsky's directive. Divided within, assailed by superior forces and still without money, Kaledin's regime crumpled. Faced with disaster and with his hopes shattered, Kaledin resigned and then shot himself. He was an honourable man who had been caught in an impossible situation. He deserved a better end. The Don territories were swiftly occupied by the Bolsheviks, who put General Nazarov, Kaledin's successor, in front of a firing squad.

This left the Volunteer Army isolated and unaided. Alexeyev wrote a despairing letter to Général Berthelot in Kiev. It was intercepted and published by the Bolsheviks. The continuation of the heroic struggle by the Volunteer Army in impossible conditions stands as one of the epics of military history. Yet it is not one that lies at the centre of this history.

When the Allied Embassies fled Petrograd, the staff of the British Embassy burnt many of the official documents, including all of Keyes' memoranda and documents on the Banking Scheme. Keyes recalled:

> By the time, [at] the beginning of March that the Allied Embassies had to leave Petrograd in a hurry, burning their archives (several important papers of mine were burnt), it had become clear that the Bolsheviks were getting hold of the financial system and that the banks over which we proposed to get control would possibly not be able to deliver the goods, we therefore managed to reduce our commitments to just under a million [pounds sterling]. To show for this we had a controlling majority of shares in certain banks. [37]

Keyes, having been recalled to explain the scheme, left with the staff of the Embassy, but his departure was jeopardized. Despite the secrecy with which his machinations had been surrounded, they had not escaped at least some notice from the Cheka – or so we may judge from what was to occur when his departure was arranged.

Like all members of the diplomatic community, Keyes was subject to the need to obtain a visa. It fell to Lockhart to obtain exit visas for Keyes and the other members of the diplomatic community. He was referred to one Lutsky at the Foreign Office, whom he described as 'an unpleasant Jewish lawyer'. Lutsky, apparently enjoying his position of power like many another petty official, refused all visas other than those for genuine diplomats. Keyes' passport was, therefore, not among those for which a visa was approved. Lockhart tried to argue the case and requested permission to telephone Trotsky, but proceedings were diverted by the arrival of the Marchese della Torretta, the Italian Chargé d'Affaires. Lutsky and the Marchese engaged in a ferocious row, of which Lockhart took advantage by slipping Keyes' passport into the pile of approved ones that Lutsky's secretary was stamping.[38] On the strength of this, Keyes was able to cross the Finnish frontier and return to London.

Keyes was to lament, 'The Treasury got cold feet when I had spent a million and called the show off.' It was broadly true. After his return to London, Keyes found himself the subject of detailed inquiries by two Departments of State: 'For two months I had a dreadful time with the F.O. and Treasury. The latter dishonoured my signature for £920,000, but eventually paid up.'[39]

Allied, and specifically British, policy in south Russia was left in tatters. The Banking Scheme had initially been described in the Foreign Office as 'somewhat fantastic' and, looked at in hindsight, it might well be deemed to have been so. However, within the limits imposed on Allied initiatives by the promise given by the British Ambassador and the fact that the Central Powers and the Bolsheviks barred direct access to southern Russia, it could equally be considered to have been a dynamic and courageous policy. That it was an imaginative one cannot be denied.

It might have fared better had the people involved spoken to each other. Lindley and Keyes were pulling in different directions at times, just as their respective Departments in London, the Foreign and War Offices, were. Nevertheless, Lindley's failure to inform Keyes about Yaroshinsky's approach in January seems unforgivable.

This reflected the position in London. It is a matter for wonder that the War Cabinet and Foreign Office both allowed themselves to assume that the financier handling the proposal was Poliakoff. Why did they not ask; why did they not make sure of their information before giving both Keyes and Lindley the authority to proceed? Equally, both Lindley and Keyes are subject to criticism for not informing, or at least enlightening, their political masters of the true identity of their financier. This is especially so after the Foreign Office telegram of 22 January that authorized Keyes to proceed on the express 'understanding that the unnamed financier is Poliakoff'.

It can be difficult to remember now that in 1918 the main means of international communication was the telegraph, depending on often defective wires running over hundreds if not thousands of miles and subject to interruption by weather, accident and, in time of war, enemy action. The telegraph line from Britain to Russia was particularly bad and was often prone to interruption. This could account for the muddle over the telegrams between Lindley and the Foreign Office, but neither excuses the clerical error made by the latter nor the failure to correct it immediately the error was discovered. Nor does it explain why the Foreign Office did not request clarification of the corrupted telegrams as a matter of urgency.

It was not as if the Foreign Office was alone in such slipshod methods. The War Cabinet remained at sixes and sevens, or so we may judge from the events of 25 February, when the Prime Minister was absent from the meeting. Colonel Maurice Hankey, the secretary to both the War Cabinet and Committee of Imperial Defence, recorded in his diary:

> They made 2 thoroughly stupid decisions: firstly to withdraw our Embassy from Petrograd owing to the Bolshevists having made peace; secondly to let the Japs loose into Siberia, which in my opinion will do no good, and may result in the starting of the 'Yellow Peril'.[40]

Hankey worked anxiously to get the decisions overturned, pointing out that it would mean the loss of all first-hand knowledge of events in Russia together with the loss of British cipher communication. The War Cabinet 'eventually' saw sense and agreed that someone with a proper cipher should remain there. According to Hankey, Lloyd George telephoned him later to express his dissatisfaction with the War Cabinet's decision.

Against this background it might be easily assumed that the Banking Scheme had little chance of success. Now the debacle seemed complete, but the banking scheme was not going to lie down and die. Like a ghost, it was to make three reappearances in the period covered by this history.

In January George Clerk, a permanent civil servant who was then head of the War Department in the Foreign Office and was later to be knighted, had minuted:

> The only forces we can use to meet the situation are
> 1 Money.
> 2 Armenians, and if we can get hold of them Poles, for these are the only peoples in Russia who have something definite to fight for and are prepared to fight.
> 3 An Allied occupation by Japanese, American and British troops of Vladivostock and possibly of Siberian railway.[41]

The first two options had now been attempted and had turned to dust and ashes. The third option, armed intervention, in the minds of several British policy-makers since the end of 1917, was yet to be tried. The case for this was to gather pace in the coming months. First there was the final denouement of Brest-Litovsk to be played out.

V

Where there is No Peace

January–March 1918

◄o►

The war dominated Allied thinking. After three years of monstrous bloodletting and severe social and economic dislocation, the political leaderships of the Allied Powers can be forgiven their fear of Russia signing a separate peace. The Associated Power, the United States, could alone afford to take a more distant view. With its deep reserves of manpower unimpaired, its industries thriving, its territory unoccupied and its economy booming, it was not dependent upon Russia to provide numerical superiority or divide the German forces.

The Bolsheviks' rise to power owed more to their promises of bread and peace than to the German gold they had undoubtedly received. Now they needed to deliver on their promises in order to establish their power. The winter of 1917–18 had been a fraught one with plot followed by attempted coup. The Cadets moved first, with an attempted rising in November 1917. A more serious if less immediate threat was posed by the general strike of state employees in December. The civil servants and employees of banks, and state or public enterprises stopped work in protest at the Bolshevik coup. The Social Revolutionaries then made their move. They tried to win the support of two Guards regiments of the old army, arm their supporters, and endeavoured to bring back soldiers from the front on the pretext of their attending a military university. They plotted to kidnap the whole Council of Commissars, which came to nothing, but they were implicated in an attempt to murder Lenin in the course of which Fritz Platten was wounded in the hand. In March the Cadet Party conspired with the advancing Germans to overthrow the Bolsheviks.

These continual threats provided sufficient reason for a step that was to have terrible consequences in the long term. This was the foundation of the

All-Russian Extraordinary Commission for Combating Counter-Revolution and Sabotage on 20 December 1917. Commonly called 'Vecheka' (VChK) or 'Cheka' (ChK), it was founded six weeks after the Bolsheviks seized power. Under its various guises – GPU, OGPU, NKVD and KGB – it was to become one of the most formidable political police forces in the world, as well as the most terrifying tool in the hands of its Soviet masters.

At its head was Felix Edmundovich Dzerzhinsky, who was memorably described with an artist's insight by the sculptress Clare Sheridan, Winston Churchill's cousin:

> He sat for an hour and a half, quite still and very silent. His eyes certainly looked as if they were bathed in tears of eternal sorrow, but his mouth smiled an indulgent kindness. His face is narrow, with high cheekbones and sunk in. Of all his features his nose seems to have the most character. It is very refined, and the delicate bloodless nostrils suggest the sensitiveness of over-breeding. He is a Pole by origin.
>
> As I worked and watched him during the hour and a half he made a curious impression on me. Finally, overwhelmed by his quietude, I exclaimed: 'You are an angel to sit so still.' Our medium was German, which made fluent conversation between us impossible, but he answered: 'One learns patience and calm in prison.'
>
> I asked how long he was in prison. 'A quarter of my life, eleven years,' he answered. It was the Revolution that liberated him.[1]

Dzerzhinsky, born in 1877 into a noble family, had turned towards revolution as a young man, joining first the Polish Radical Socialists and then the Bolsheviks, before being imprisoned for his pains. He was a man without pity and, as with all fanatics and zealots, he acted upon the conviction that he was working towards the establishment of the perfect state, whereby the end justifies any and every means. To men and women with this frame of mind 'The People' are everything; persons are of no account. He was described by Lockhart as 'a man of correct manners and quiet speech, but without a ray of humour in his character',[2] and it may have been his experiences in a Tsarist prison that scrubbed the basic humanity from him. In terms of the tasks facing the Cheka, he was the right man in the right place.

While the Bolsheviks proved able to defeat their internal enemies, a far greater danger loomed to Russia's west. Russia was still at war with the

Central Powers and Trotsky's delaying tactics at Brest-Litovsk kept alive Allied hopes that Russia might be persuaded to continue the struggle. Although they had no delegates present at the conference, the Allies, and certainly the British, were well informed of the course of the negotiations. Not only had the Bolsheviks insisted that the negotiations take place publicly, they broadcast the events to the world by wireless, a completely revolutionary means of conducting diplomacy.

The British were gaining precise information from one of the Russian delegates. The Royal Navy and the Imperial Russian Navy had established close links during the war and none more so than in the Intelligence sphere. This collaboration had paid handsome dividends as early as September 1914 when the Russians captured the codebook of the German cruiser *Magdeburg*. They had sent the codebook to the Admiralty in London, where it became one of the foundations for the justly famous code-breaking exploits of Room 40.

After the Bolshevik seizure of power many Russian naval officers maintained their contacts with the British when they could. One of those was Admiral Altvater, who was the Russian naval delegate at Brest-Litovsk. He kept the Royal Naval Attaché, Captain Francis Cromie, well informed of the course of negotiations. On 19 February Cromie wrote to Commodore Hall that, 'I had some gratifying news from Admiral Altfata [*sic* Altvater], one of the Russian peace delegates at Brest-Litovsk...'.[3] Yet even such inside knowledge of Trotsky's stand did not assuage the scepticism that many in London and Paris seemed determined to cling to.

Nevertheless, Lloyd George was being advised that Trotsky's attitude, even with the prospect of Russia having to leave the war, was actually beneficial to the Allies. In the previous month Colonel Maurice Hankey, the influential Secretary to the War Cabinet, wrote to the Prime Minister:

> The enemy's outlook is, fortunately, on the whole, even more menacing than our own. This, however, depends, to a considerable extent, upon what happens in Russia. It appears to me that Trotsky is really our best ally. He is completely disorganising Russia in every respect. Every Branch of the Government and Administration is being let down. The railways are rapidly deteriorating. The coal output is not likely to increase. The land has been taken from the big landowners, who cultivate it well, and handed over to the peasants who, I understand,

cultivate it badly. The greater the chaos Trotsky can produce in Russia, the smaller the prospect that the enemy will derive much benefit therefrom. Perhaps the greatest danger is that the Germans will invade Russia and restore order, but this will expose them to the contagious disease of Bolshevism – Trotsky's strongest weapon.[4]

While he engaged the delegates of the Central Powers in debate, Trotsky engaged the unofficial representatives of the Allied and Associated Powers in negotiations to discover what assistance Russia could expect from the Allies should the German demands prove intolerable and the Russians refuse to agree to them. Certainly by mid-February the negotiations at Brest-Litovsk had reached stalemate, with Trotsky finally declaring that Russia was unilaterally withdrawing from the war and demobilizing her armies. The very idea, summed up as 'No war, no peace', stunned the delegates of the Central Powers and drew the exclamation *'Unerhört!'* ('Unheard of!') from General Max Hoffmann, Germany's Chief of Staff on the Eastern front.

For all its drama, Trotsky's speech did not alter the hard military facts. After due deliberation, the Central Powers broke off the armistice and resumed the offensive in the East on 18 February. There was little practical resistance. Bolshevik propaganda had done its work well. The Russian Army was a wreck. Many of its men had deserted and the majority of those left in uniform had had enough of fighting. The Bolsheviks made a desperate appeal for a *levée en masse*, but to no avail. The armies of the Central Powers swept forward rapidly over vast tracts of land, including the rich wheat lands of the Ukraine.

The Bolsheviks had pinned their hopes on popular discontent with the renewal of the war culminating in revolution in Germany. The time was not ripe. The potential for revolution had been temporarily stifled when the January strikes, often called the dress rehearsal for the German Revolution, had been crushed. With the German revolutionary leaders such as Karl Liebknecht and Rosa Luxemburg in prison and many of their associates together with the men who struck conscripted into the army, this particular sword had been knocked from the Bolsheviks' grasp.

To avert nemesis the Bolsheviks now turned to the Allies for help. They approached the French, who abandoned their covert support for the

Volunteer Army, to which they had already paid the equivalent of 50 million roubles through its supporters in Petrograd and Moscow. On 21 February Trotsky asked the French Ambassador, Joseph Noulens, through an officer on Lavergne's staff, Captain Jacques Sadoul, and also Général Niessel, what support Russia could expect from France to resist the Germans. Noulens, who had been consistently anti-Bolshevik, now swung like a weather vane and assured Trotsky that he could rely on military and financial assistance from France.

In the meantime British and French officers in Russia were trying to help those Russians who would fight. These efforts could only have strictly limited success. The story of Colonel Joseph Whiteside Boyle and Captain George Hill shows what could be achieved, but also the limits imposed on the achievement by the circumstances.

Boyle was a larger-than-life character, a Canadian who would fit wonderfully into an adventure story for young boys. He was both a self-made man and a man of action. He had been by turns a fireman in Chicago, amateur boxing champion of the United States, manager of world heavyweight boxing champion Frank Slavin, a gold-miner in the Yukon and the founder of a gold-mining company that made him a millionaire. He had been considered too old for the Canadian forces in 1914, but nothing daunted, he set himself the task of raising a motor machine-gun company at his own expense. At the end of 1917 he was serving in Russia.

Such a character did not sit comfortably with the older regular officers of the British Army. Colonel Byrne, Poole's link in London, sent his chief several telegrams that shed light on this; they also show that Poole was broad-minded enough to employ Boyle despite the misgivings of more conventional officers:

> Boyle has cropped up again, and no one knows what to do with him. Being a Canadian, our WO [War Office] are not anxious to touch him, and I understand the Canadians are not able to, as he is a sort of freebooter. If nothing has been settled before you get this, and if he is still a burning factor, a wire with a definite suggestion as to his disposal would be welcome.[5]

A month later Byrne was still perplexed:

> I can't find anything out about <u>Boyle</u>, except that he is looked upon as an infernal nuisance. Your letter about him and De C. [De Candolle] is disquieting, as you make me think B. [Boyle] is the better man. No doubt he is an able man, but his ways are his own, and I see no place for him in any orderly organisation, even if he were top of it himself.[6]

In spite of such misgivings, Boyle was soon able to show how his unconventional abilities and drive could get things done. The most pressing need was to relieve Romania. That country was in a hopeless position, with most of its territory overrun, facing the armies of the Central Powers, completely isolated now Russia was leaving the war. As if this was not peril enough, the Bolsheviks had declared war on her. Boyle resolved to try and bring peace between the two, but knew that the Bolsheviks would not accept a direct approach.

Concealing his true intention he offered Nevski, the Commissar of Ways of Communication, his skills as a railway expert to clear the bottleneck in the Donets area, which was preventing the transport of badly needed food and coal to Moscow and Petrograd. Boyle went south to Kharkhov, accompanied by Captain George Hill of the Royal Flying Corps, and Lieutenants Nash and Crutchley. All these officers served Rusplycom.

Boyle swiftly won the confidence of Anotonov, the Commander of the Bolshevik Army fighting the Cossacks, and persuaded him to re-employ the railway experts, the superintendents and traffic managers who had been sacked on the grounds that they were bourgeois. In twelve days this measure had led to an increase of 47 per cent in supplies to the cities and Northern and Western fronts.

Boyle's party then travelled to Sevastopol where Nash and Crutchley left to proceed to the oil port of Batum in the Caucasus. In Sevastopol Boyle won the confidence of M. Spiro, Chairman of the Black Sea Congress, who was alarmed by the German advance further north and requested Boyle to go to Odessa and do what he could to stop the war with Romania. There, Boyle called a conference of Allied officers and officials and persuaded them to open negotiations with the Supreme Council, the Bolshevik body that ran affairs in southern Ukraine. After five days the Supreme Council, thoroughly discouraged by the unpopularity of the war with Romania and the consequent lack of recruits, sent a Note to the Romanian Government at Jassy that was carried by Boyle in an aeroplane. The Romanians accepted the Note and Boyle flew back to Odessa with their consent. He had almost single-handedly brought the war to an end, largely by the force of his personality. Boyle returned to help the beleaguered Romanians, while Hill remained in Odessa until the Germans approached. With two Secret Service officers he then went north to Nicolaievsk and Kherson.

At Kherson he joined Colonel Muraviev, a Left Social Revolutionary and commander of the Bolshevik forces in that region. Hill 'fostered his desire to offend Germany' and Muraviev's army did try to fight, but was hopelessly outnumbered in men and guns and retreated in disorder. Hill turned his attention to sabotage and recorded that 'a fair amount of destruction was indulged in' and one or two small bridges destroyed.

The British Consul at Kherson, Mr Blakey, his assistant Mr Gillespie and Mr Carouana the Vice-Consul, were all working hard to hinder the German advance and destroy as much material as possible. They introduced Hill to some of the French miners, who had been brought into the area in better days to modernize the Russian mines, with a view to destroying the mines and machinery. Hill next made contact with the District Mine Owners' Union and, through them, with a man described as 'Engineer X' of the Donets District Miners' Federation who arranged the destruction and sabotage of certain mines.

Finally, Hill arranged for the safe passage of the British and French Military Missions from Romania to Moscow, whence he returned in March.[7] These deeds have been outlined less as tales of derring-do than to illustrate the scope and scale of the activities conducted by Intelligence officers under trying circumstances. Bringing peace between Russia and Romania was a notable achievement in difficult circumstances, but otherwise the sabotage and similar operations would be little more than a hindrance to the Germans. If a few men could accomplish this much, what might not more do?

The Bolsheviks, riven between factions that wanted a Holy War with the Central Powers, those who wanted peace at any price and those who simply could not choose between Scylla and Charybdis, still had to find a coherent response before significant French or Allied aid would become available.

Trotsky favoured waging a partisan war from the depths of Russia. Lockhart duly reported this to London and the first mention there of it was on 26 February, when Macdonogh reported to the War Cabinet: 'In telegrams received at the end of the previous week it was stated that M. Trotsky had talked of the possibility of guerrilla warfare taking place.'[8]

The War Cabinet considered the policy more closely two days later:

> The Prime Minister drew the attention of his colleagues to the very conflicting information from Russia, which was probably due to divided counsels, as indicated in Mr. Ransome's dispatches to the *Daily News*. Some of the telegrams indicated mere surrender, while others suggested an intention to resist. In this latter category, he referred to the latest telegram from Mr Lockhart (No.595), in which M. Petroff was reported to contemplate a withdrawal to Nijni-Novgorod and the formation there of an army of 1,000,000 men, for which he desired Allied assistance. The Prime Minister asked whether the possibility of a formidable guerrilla warfare had not been underrated. History in Spain and elsewhere had shown that large numbers of troops could be occupied by these means, particularly in forest country.
>
> The Director of Military Operations pointed out that developments of modern warfare, such as aircraft, armoured cars, and machine guns, were all in favour of regular, and against guerrilla, troops. He admitted the possibility, however, that an active guerrilla warfare in Russia might still be very troublesome to the enemy.[9]

The military advice from the Director of Military Operations was sufficient to prevent this strategy receiving British support. Nevertheless, the episode does stress that Trotsky and some of his colleagues were prepared to fight to the bitter end, and that London was indisputably aware of the fact. The message should have been clear enough even to people like Cecil.

Faced with a military disaster that could spell the end of their regime, the Bolsheviks sought to remedy the situation at the front by creating a new Russian Army. This was to be the armed vanguard of the workers of the world and so was not termed the 'Russian Army', but the 'Red Army'. However, a rabble of armed men does not make an army. To do that the armed men need to be trained, disciplined and organized.

There was no doubt about the purpose of the new army. The Political Intelligence Department of the Foreign Office in London observed of the

Bolsheviks: '…the fact that they are now intending to use it against Germany is fully consistent with their general statement of policy both before and since their accession to power.' The Department went on to hope that this would be done when the Red Army was strong enough, and 'there are grounds for hoping that the Sovyet [sic Soviet] Government will welcome Allied assistance – British, French and Japanese.'[10]

Of potentially greater significance was the fact that the Allied representatives suggested to Trotsky that Allied officers should train the Red Army. A ready tool lay to hand. Général Berthelot's Mission, fresh from its unsuccessful intrigues in the Ukraine from whence it had been driven by the advancing Germans, had retired to Moscow. On 22 February the Central Committee of the Bolsheviks met to consider the offer. They were bitterly divided, with Bukharin and his supporters fiercely advocating a Holy War, though how they were to fight without an army he did not explain. Lenin was not present, but his was the deciding voice. He sent a slip of paper that put his decisive vote in favour of accepting Allied assistance with the words, 'That Comrade Trotsky be authorised to accept the assistance of the brigands of French imperialism against the German brigands.'[11]

There was not enough time for the Allies to transform the realities on the ground. The Bolsheviks were left with no choice but to sign a peace treaty on terms which the Central Powers, chiefly the Germans, laid down, and which were now even more severe than they had been when negotiations broke down. By them the former Russian Empire lost the Baltic provinces, the Ukraine, Russian Poland, Finland, and the Aaland Islands – 34 per cent of her population, 32 per cent of her agricultural land, 85 per cent of her sugar beet, 54 per cent of her industrial undertakings and 84 per cent of her coal. The peoples of the Caucasus were left ostensibly to determine their own destiny, but in reality Germany and Turkey left the region open to invasion and influence. It was shattering, but totally in keeping with the German Empire's long-term ambitions in Eastern Europe.

Nor did the treaty bind Germany to respect the territorial integrity of what survived of Russia. For the next two months it actually served as a basis for gradual encroachment and infiltration by them. They were seeking to forestall any Allied intervention from Siberia by moving eastwards to occupy strategic points. This mask suited both Germany and the Ottoman Empire in that both were drawn towards the east, the Germans because they were determined to threaten Britain's Indian Empire, and the Turks because they sought a great Pan-Turanian empire that embraced the Turkic peoples of the Caucasus.

There was one other consequence that appeared trivial at the time. Trotsky would not sign a 'shameful peace' and, to help expedite matters at Brest-Litovsk, he resigned as People's Commissar for Foreign Affairs. Lenin made him Commissar for War. His deputy, George Chicherin, took his place in charge of Foreign Affairs.

Although a treaty had been signed between the Germans and Bolsheviks, it still had to be ratified. Until it was the situation remained fluid and the Germans reached the outskirts of Petrograd, which the Allied Embassies fled on 28 February. Hard on their heels followed the Bolshevik leadership, who left the city early in March for what was to be the new capital of Russia, Moscow. Lockhart and his unofficial mission accompanied them, thanks to Trotsky. The British Embassy left for London, the other Allied embassies for Vologda, approximately 300 miles to the north-east of Moscow. The British left a skeleton staff in Petrograd, under Captain Francis Cromie, the Naval Attaché.

With the treaty still not ratified and the Bolsheviks bitterly divided, the Allied representatives in Moscow continued to hope that they could persuade the Bolsheviks to make common cause with them against the Germans. A committee of Allied officers was established to supervise the initiative and Trotsky formally requested military help from it and, on its behalf, Lavergne agreed to it. The French Military Mission to Romania, under Général Berthelot, which had reached Moscow thanks to George Hill's work, were detailed to provide the assistance. To all appearances the Allies were on the brink of securing their aims.

In serious anticipation of Allied military support, Lenin and Trotsky had sent Kamenev on a secret mission to London and Paris late in February. Initially all seemed set fair and the French Embassy stamped Kamenev's passport with a special diplomatic visa.

However, Lockhart related how disaster swept the promise away:

Two days later the whole scheme was wrecked. M. Noulens had intervened. General Lavergne was hauled over the coals for exceeding his powers, and

General Berthelot and his staff of officers were ordered to return immediately to France. The barometer of Trotsky's temperament suffered a severe depression, and the *Izvestia* came out with a leading article declaring that 'only America had known how to treat the Bolsheviks decently, and it was the allies themselves, who, by disregarding the wishes of the Russian people, were preventing the creation of a pro-Allied policy.'[12]

In fact the process was more complicated than Lockhart's portrayal indicates. Although suspicious, the Allied Ambassadors consulted their governments and reached an agreement on 3 April. They put forward a four-point plan whereby the French and British would help to organize the Red Army provided the Bolsheviks reintroduced military discipline; the Bolsheviks were to consent to the Japanese Army entering Russia with small Allied contingents to lend it a multinational flavour; the Allies were to occupy both Murmansk and Archangel; finally, the Allies were to refrain from interfering in the internal affairs of Russia.

This would have been a combination that any government would have found difficult to accept, especially the Bolsheviks with their distrust of the Japanese. The proposals left too many opportunities for the Allies to renege on their promise not to interfere in Russia's internal affairs.

Any grounds for optimism founded on Kamenev's Mission vanished as soon as he set foot on British soil at Aberdeen. Here he was searched, most of his possessions seized, including his diplomatic bag and a cheque for £5,000. His claim to be a diplomatic agent of an independent foreign state was wilfully ignored. The French Government forbade him to enter France, which led to the British Government insisting that he return to Russia. He reached the Finnish frontier where, at the instigation of the German military authorities, he was arrested and remained in prison until July when he was exchanged for several Finns who had been arrested in Petrograd. As the German saying goes, 'The friendship of the French is like their wine, exquisite but of short duration.'

Well might Trotsky react with obvious frustration and fury at these apparently clumsy manoeuvres. When Lockhart saw him on 11 March:

He cursed our ignorance bitterly and said we and France were the only people who did not realise what was happening. We were accusing him with false documents of

Germanophilism, while his best friends were running him down for having placed too false hopes on a pro-entente policy. He said our democratic government was pitiable, that our diplomacy throughout the war had been distinguished by a total lack of decision and that our F.O. [Foreign Office] was like a man playing roulette and scattering chips on every number.'[13]

Two observations need to be made here. The accusations that Trotsky and Lenin were Germanophile and German agents had recently gained new life from a set of forged documents that have become known as the Sisson Documents, after the individual representing Mr Creel, the head of American War Propaganda in Petrograd, who purchased them on behalf of the US Government. The forgeries, being pressed on the different Allied missions by anti-Bolshevik Russians, purported to come from the German General Staff and gave orders to Trotsky in the manner that they would give orders to a secret agent.

The British Secret Service had bought photographs of the original documents. They were acquired by Lieutenant MacLaren, Commander Boyce's deputy. He had obtained them from two officers who had worked in Russian Counter-Espionage under the Tsar, Ossendovsky and Seminoff. He was convinced they were bona fide,[14] but debate raged in London where the British reaction was more cautious. The opening pages of the file reveals a division about their veracity that neither the Director of Military Intelligence nor the Foreign Office could resolve. The general conclusion was that it was practically impossible to establish the truth and the Foreign Office should employ a man in Russia specifically to examine such documents.[15]

Perhaps significantly, the photographic copies were placed into the hands of Major W.W. Van Someren, DSO of MIOA, another officer of the Indian Army who was to be head of Field Intelligence for General Poole's force that was to be the spearhead of the intervention in north Russia.

Unfortunately, Sisson took them at face value and purchased them, no doubt in the belief that he had managed a singular coup. There was no one in Washington, DC, to sound a note of caution. The Bolshevik press published the documents on 12 March, soundly ridiculing them. Among them were some from the British counter-espionage section and later it was found that the Sisson Documents had been written on the same typewriter.

However, this is not the only case of forgery. Lockhart's diary reveals a different kind of forgery, or rather, attempts to mislead. In *Memoirs of a British Agent*, Lockhart corrupts the reference to the Foreign Office being like a man playing roulette into 'Your Lloyd George is like a man playing roulette...' He also changes other parts of the diary entry and alters the date to 23 February. It is far from being an isolated case, for Lockhart twists his contemporary diary entries on too many other occasions. His *Memoirs* cannot be regarded as a sound record unless corroborated from other sources.

In spite of Allied behaviour and Bolshevik suspicion and rhetoric, the latter were prepared to collaborate and give the Allies what they supposedly wanted more than anything else – the reopening of the war on the Eastern front, if the Allies were prepared to help. Different offers and even appeals to the Allies continued until late May 1918, yet all were rejected or answered with platitudes. The Allies took this stance because they had already decided upon military intervention in Russia. This was well before serious attention was being paid to the supposedly vast quantities of stores that were alleged to be piling up at Archangel and Vladivostock, allegedly in imminent danger of being seized by the Germans.

The initial tool for military intervention was to be the Japanese Empire. The Government of Japan had resolved as early as March 1917 to crush the Russian Revolution, but intervention against the Provisional Government would have been unacceptable. (In April the Bolsheviks published the secret telegrams found in the files of the Provisional Government's decoding service that revealed this intent.)

Throughout the war it had consistently been British policy to work with any and every Russian Government that would keep the Eastern front alive. When the great German Spring Offensive broke on the Western front on 21 March, this became a matter of extreme urgency for the British and French Governments. If the Bolsheviks were not prepared to fight the Germans, someone else must fight in their place. In Britain members of the War Cabinet had been anxiously pressing for Japanese intervention as early as 24 January.[16]

Japan had a very capable army of 250,000 men who were not engaged elsewhere. They were also only a short distance from Siberia. The thinking was that they could move into Siberia with ease and then move westwards to deny the Central Powers the resources of Siberia and reopen the Eastern front. There were just two obstacles to this dream. The first was the likelihood of a hostile reaction from not only the Bolsheviks but from many other Russians. The second was the guaranteed hostility of the United States.

It needs to be squarely recognized that many members of the British Government had been consistently in favour of intervention. The Prime Minister, Lloyd George, made matters clear in response to criticism voiced at the end of May by Lord Robert Cecil over the delay in intervening in Siberia. Lloyd George retorted:

> ...that Lord Robert Cecil's note implied that the whole delay, involving the loss of four months, had been due to the action of the British Government. He could not accept this criticism, nor admit that it was fair. He pointed out that the policy of the British Government had been steadily in favour of intervention. It had, however, been difficult to secure the necessary support of the United States' Government in the matter. At the same time, the Japanese had said that they would not act unless the Americans co-operated, and this the Americans had refused to do.[17]

Lloyd George's words summed up the negotiations that had been taking place over four months. Two related policies were being pressed on the diplomatic front; one was to persuade the Japanese to mount a full-scale military intervention and this they refused to do if the Americans declined to support it. The Allies had been consistently, even desperately, pressing President Wilson to agree to intervention. He had wavered once, in February, but had then returned to his staunch policy of non-intervention. The other policy was to try to pressure and persuade the Bolsheviks to agree to military intervention. This they would not do, since they did not want to be caught in the middle of what they regarded as an imperialist war. Allied capitalism was as hateful to them as German militarism. While the Germans presented the greatest and most immediate threat they were prepared to accept Allied support, but on their own terms. They were not prepared to allow large numbers of foreign troops onto their soil, especially when the ultimate purpose of those troops might well be the overthrow of the Bolshevik regime and its replacement by a capitalist government.

When Lockhart met Lenin on 2 March, this was made abundantly plain to him. He summed up Lenin's view on the subject: 'They were not to be made a cat's paw for the Allies.'[18] The point was emphasized a month later, when Chicherin (and not Lenin as Lockhart claims in his *Memoirs*) told Lockhart that 'sooner or later it appeared that Russia would become a field of battle for two opposing imperialistic groups and that Russia wished to put the decision off for as long as possible. This is Lenin's point of view.'[19]

Whatever either Lenin or Lockhart might have desired, the situation had already slipped beyond their influence. The British Government had invited the Japanese to intervene through Siberia on 4 March, the day after the Treaty of Brest-Litovsk had been signed. Lockhart's advice was dismissed on the following day:

> The War Cabinet had under consideration Telegram No. 1, dated 4th March, 1918, from Mr. Lockhart, in which he urged a suspension of the proposed intervention of Japan in Siberia, and Mr. Balfour's reply, No. 1, dated 4th March, 1918, in which he had fully explained the policy of the British Government. This latter telegram was approved, subject to the suggestion that it might have been added that if the Bolsheviks proposed to put up a fight against the Germans, they might enlist the Japanese as Allies.
>
> The Secretary of State for Foreign Affairs undertook to consider the desirability of sending a further telegram in this sense.
>
> The War Cabinet also approved Mr. Balfour's telegram No. 198 of 4th March, 1918, in which he initiated the invitation to the Japanese to take action.[20]

This policy, even though driven to a considerable extent by an understandable fear, remains cynical, especially in the sneering remark that the Bolsheviks might enlist the Japanese as allies.

Nor were the Bolsheviks ignorant of what was planned. They read foreign newspapers. According to Chicherin, 'the Japanese press was energetically preparing public opinion for intervention in Siberia' in March.[21] Moreover, Lockhart saw Trotsky on 13 March 'and told him about the dangers of Japanese intervention'.[22] At this time Colonel Knox, the former British Military Attaché to Russia and one of the most vociferous proponents of Japanese intervention was denouncing Lockhart in London, on the grounds that he 'acts as Trotsky's official spokesman'.[23] The interventionists were in the ascendant.

The Japanese landed at Vladivostock on 5 April, on the excuse that two – or three, depending on which sources are consulted – of their subjects had been murdered there. Royal Marines from HMS *Suffolk* then landed to support the Japanese. However, in the face of fierce American protests, the Japanese would go no further.

There had been another Allied landing, in north Russia, but this took place with the consent and cooperation of the Bolsheviks and illustrates what might have been achieved had the Allies chosen to pursue this course. The White Finns had defeated the Finnish Bolsheviks in the civil war that had broken out in Finland after she seized the opportunity to gain independence from Russia in the chaotic conditions of summer 1917. Now the Allies, especially the British, feared that the Germans and White Finns were about to seize the port of Murmansk, which was Russia's only ice-free port opening to the West, and that the Germans would create a U-boat base there. For their part the Bolsheviks also acted from fear, the fear that Russian territory was going to be seized by Germans and White Guards.

Lenin, Trotsky and Stalin all pressed Alexei Mikhailovich Yuriev, the Chairman of the Murmansk Soviet, to accept help from the Allies to repel the Finnish White Guards. He concluded a verbal agreement with the British and French representatives that authorized them to land troops to defend Murmansk, so a small force of Royal Marines came ashore on 31 March and drove off Finnish skirmishers. However, the Bolsheviks were anxious to keep the agreement secret, demanding that the Murmansk Soviet should publicly deny press reports that the Allied landings had been invited and approved. The verbal agreement meant that any collusion could be denied.[24] Later the Bolsheviks were to deny it and denounce claims that there had been an agreement as lying capitalist propaganda.

There was one more national group that remained for the Allies to approach and they fell into the French orbit under the terms of the Anglo-French agreement of 23 December 1917. These were the Czechoslovaks, former prisoners-of-war amounting to an army corps of two well-armed and disciplined divisions. These were in the Ukraine when officers of the French Military Mission began negotiating with them. Parallel negotiations were being conducted between officials of the French Embassy and the Czechoslovak National Council, first of all in Petrograd and later in Moscow. The Czechoslovaks were keen to fight for the liberation of their peoples from Austro-Hungarian rule, but they did not want to remain in Russia, which they could readily see was falling apart around their ears. Equally they wanted to fight the Germans, not the Bolsheviks.

Agreement was reached with the French at Kiev on 14 February, by which the Corps was to move eastwards, across European Russia and then through Siberia to Vladivostock where the men would embark to sail to France where they would fight on the Western front. They crossed the new Ukrainian-Russian border at Kursk where they voluntarily surrendered most of their heavy equipment, including all their artillery and several dismantled aeroplanes. The French and Czechoslovaks had agreed with Lenin that the Corps could leave for Vladivostock on 16 March after giving up its heavy equipment, and all parties had abided by the agreement. Accompanied by officers of the French Military Mission under Commandant Alphonse Guinet, the move eastwards began.

The Germans understandably took a dim view of such a strong reinforcement for their enemies in the west. They pressed the Bolsheviks to halt the movement of the Corps, which was gathering Czechoslovaks in Russia and various stragglers of other nationalities who chose life with the Czechoslovaks rather than face either the Germans or Bolshevik rule. On Trotsky's orders, the Corps was stopped at Penza on 20 March. However, on the 23rd progress was resumed after the Corps had agreed to give up most of its remaining arms.

March also saw an approach made to the British by one of the Russian cryptographic team's top members, Ernst Constantinovich Fetterlein. He had been one of the Tsar's leading code-breakers and now offered his services to the British, provided they would also accommodate his wife and family and provide him with employment. On 9 March the Naval Attaché at Helsingfors reported to the Admiralty:

FETTERLEIN cipher expert to Russian F.O. [Foreign Office] for 25 years who worked all war with Russian D. I. D. [Director Intelligence Division] offers his services and full information of German position square (*sic*) Austrian Military

93

and diplomatic codes. He is highly recommended by many well known to D. I. D. but will need financial aid for himself and wife to reach England.[25]

The British swiftly agreed to his terms and by June he and his wife Angelica were in London. They became naturalized British subjects in 1920. A.G. 'Alastair' Denniston, one of the original volunteers for Room 40, described Fetterlein as 'a highly experienced but elderly man who could not be made pensionable.' His arrival in Room 40 gave the British an inestimable advantage, Denniston said, since

> The Revolutionary Government in 1919 had no codes and did not risk using the Czarist codes which they must have inherited. They began with simple transposition of plain Russian and gradually developed systems of increasing difficulty. The presence of Fetterlein as a senior member of the staff and two very competent girls, refugees from Russia, with a perfect knowledge of the language, who subsequently became permanent members of the staff, enabled us to succeed in this work. We were also able to borrow certain British Consuls who could not return to Russia.[26]

Thus from the middle of 1918 the communications of the Soviet State were an open book to British Intelligence.

One final event of March needs to be recorded. On the 15th one Second Lieutenant Sydney George Reilly, of the Royal Flying Corps, whose real name was Sigmund Georgievich Rosenblum, reported to 'C's' office at 2 Whitehall Court, London. He was prepared to go to Russia for the Secret Service, but he appears to have had a hidden agenda of his own. Ten days later, he boarded the Danish *Queen Mary* and sailed for Russia. 'C' informed the head of the SIS station in the British Embassy at Vologda, Commander Ernest Boyce, RN:

> On March 25th Sydney George Reilli [*sic* Sydney George Reilly], Lieutenant, RFC leaves for Archangel from England. Jewish-Jap type brown eyes very protruding, deeply lined sallow face, may be bearded, height five foot nine inches. He will report to Vologda during April. Carries code message of ID to Vologda. On arrival he will go to Consul and ask for British Passport Officer. Ask him what his business is he will answer 'Diamond buying'. He has sixteen diamonds value £640.7.2 as most useful currency. Should you be short of funds

he has orders to divide with you. He will be at your disposal utilize him to join up your organisation if necessary as he should travel freely. Return him to Stockholm if possible end of June. More to follow.[27]

His orders were clear: he was to land at Archangel, from where he could reach Vologda and Moscow by rail. Instead he landed at Murmansk where he was arrested. Why he did this is not known for certain. His most recent biographer, Andrew Cook, suggests that it might have been to get a direct rail connection to Petrograd where he might have had family, business and/or possessions. This might be the case, but it remains conjecture.

Rear Admiral Kemp, the officer commanding the Royal Navy's White Sea Station, was unsure about Reilly's story and summoned Major Stephen Alley, the former head of MI1(c)'s Petrograd Station to see whether he could vouch for him. Reilly was prepared and took a microscopic coded message from under the cork of an aspirin bottle immediately Alley appeared. Alley recognized the Service's code and directly had Reilly released.

Instead of going to Moscow as 'C' required, Reilly went to Petrograd. He would spend the greater part of April there, but little is known about his activities while in the city.

VI

Fleets and Duplicity

April–mid May 1918

◄o►

The heart of the problem facing the Allies at the end of March was thrown into sharp relief at a meeting of the War Cabinet on 21 March 1918, the very day the great German Spring Offensive broke upon the British Fifth Army in Picardy. The War Cabinet was divided over policy but all agreed, 'that the real question was whether there was any prospect of the Bolsheviks really making good the intentions of renewing the contest.'

Nobody knew what the precise situation in Russia was. It was changing so rapidly that few in Moscow knew, much less in capitals such as Paris, London and Washington, DC, thousands of miles from the seat of events, hampered by seriously poor communications and hopelessly partial information. The War Cabinet considered the likely effect of the formation of the Red Army and a speech by Trotsky in which he had declared himself in favour of drastic discipline in the Army and the abolition of the election of officers.

The greeting afforded to these measures was less than enthusiastic:

> It was suggested that M. Trotsky's action was mainly aimed at trying to prevent Japanese intervention. The success of the Bolsheviks had lain throughout in the very fact that they were for peace at any price, and, although it was true that the anti-Bolshevik forces which we had previously attempted to organise for the defence of Russia against Germany had failed us, there was nothing to show that the Bolsheviks were either able or determined to renew the war with Germany.
>
> The Chief of the Imperial General Staff said it was fantastic to think that Trotsky or anyone else in Russia could put up a fight against the Germans.[1]

Predictably, the War Cabinet could not reach a conclusion and resolved to await the return of General Poole from Russia and hear his views.

Of paramount importance to the British was the fate of the Russian Navy. Its two major segments, the Baltic Sea Fleet at Kronstadt and the Black Sea Fleet at Sevastopol, lay in the path of the advancing Germans. The fear that the Germans would seize the ships and turn them against the Allies was very real, especially for a maritime power whose safety, strength, wealth and Empire was founded upon command of the seas.

As early as 23 November 1917 the War Cabinet had been thoroughly alarmed by the prospect, as Maurice Hankey's Diary shows:

> War Cabinet 11.30 the Admiralty having received information which leads them to believe that the Bolsheviks mean to hand the Russian fleet over to Germany, the following action by the Admiralty was approved: (1) British submarines to be destroyed and the crews brought home; (2) Russian officers faithful to the allies to be encouraged to man the Russian destroyers and make a dash for the entrance to the Baltic; (3) Russian officers to be induced to blow up the four Russian 'Dreadnoughts'. The v. [very] serious political consequences were not overlooked.'[2]

The desperation apparent in this diary entry speaks louder than any official document. Admiral Hall, the Director of Naval Intelligence, sent an urgent telegram the same day to his Russian counterpart, Admiral Egoriev, that seriously suggested he should consider the reckless second step the Admiralty had approved:

> I am perturbed as to safety of Russian officers in event of Revolutionary Committee surrendering ships to Germans. Suggest you consider proposition of officers bringing all latest type of destroyers to South end of Sound on given date and time. Arrangements could be made to have forces to distract the enemy and assist vessels through Sound to England – Please reply through same channel (stop) Your friend Indivisant.[3]

Just over a week later, Hall had another serious concern: 'In view of present situation, I earnestly beg you to burn all documents and papers connected with our mutual work. Should situation improve, I can replace everything & will keep you advised.'[4] Fortunately the Germans did not move to seize either the Baltic Fleet or the messages and codes, nor did the Bolsheviks surrender them. Nevertheless, the prospect that either might happen played on British minds.

To avert either eventuality there was a continual procession of British personnel to see Trotsky. On 22 April Lockhart took Engineer Commander George Wilfred Le Page, Captain Cromie's deputy, to see Trotsky to discuss both Russian Fleets. They saw him again three days later. On 11 May Cromie himself arrived in Moscow from Petrograd with Captain McAlpine, General Poole's deputy in Russia.

Lockhart's diary for 12 and 13 May has only very brief entries, while the 14th is left blank. Precisely what these men were discussing must be left to the imagination, but the whole background suggests that they were, at the very least, plotting the destruction of the Baltic Fleet by sabotage, besides much else. Lockhart finally took Cromie to see Trotsky about the Fleet on 15 May and found him 'in very good humour and conversation quite satisfactory'.[5]

Lockhart explained the satisfactory nature of the conversation to the Foreign Office:

> On May 15th I took Captain Cromie to see Trotsky with regard to destruction of Baltic Fleet. Trotsky stated this should be carried out in case of necessity, that special men had been chosen for this task, and a sum of money set aside for them and their families in the shape of special reward.
>
> He also confirmed news that Black Sea Fleet had escaped from Sebastopol and that in this case, too, he had given categorical orders to destroy fleet rather than let it fall into the hands of Germany.[6]

The Russian Navy appeared safe and, as we will see, proved to be so.

Simultaneously, Allied pressure for the Bolsheviks to accept their aid in reopening the war against Germany was continuing. Eventually, faced with continuing German encroachment and hostility, Trotsky invited the Allies to make a formal proposal of aid. This request was prompted as much by the internal pressures caused by rising discontent towards Germany's activities as it was by the more obvious, direct perils of the German encroachments.

Relations between the Allies and the Bolsheviks were growing warmer. The news had reached the War Cabinet on 19 April that,

> M. Trotsky wishes the Allied Governments to submit to him, at the earliest opportunity, a full and proper statement of help which they could furnish to

enable Russia to carry on the war against Germany, and of the guarantees the Allies are prepared to give in this direction. M. Trotsky had added that, if the conditions are friendly, he considers the conclusion of the agreement both necessary and desirable.[7]

It is possible that Trotsky might have been using the Allies in this way to put pressure on the Germans. If they knew of the offer, entailing the reactivation of the Eastern front that would have condemned them to certain defeat, then it might well persuade them to cease their aggression in Russia.

However, such a policy of deception would have been as great a risk for the Bolsheviks as it was for the Allies. The Bolsheviks were *in extremis* at this time and genuinely desperate for any help they could get. Lenin would not have given his approval lightly to such a policy; there was, after all, nothing that could seriously stop the Germans from seizing Petrograd before a single cartridge from the Western Allies could arrive. The Allies undoubtedly took Trotsky seriously, for they earnestly began formulating a common plan for aid to Russia.

The day before the information about Trotsky's proposal reached the War Cabinet, Hankey recorded their deliberations had been

...devoted mainly to the question of Japanese intervention in Siberia. After a long discussion, the P.M. [Prime Minister] on my initiative, pointed out that, while we had discussed different aspects [of] Russian policy in some detail e.g. Archangel, Siberia, trans-Caucasia etc., we have never presented either President Wilson or Trotsky with a comprehensive scheme of policy, and the Foreign Office were instructed to draft one.[8]

Less than a week later the divisions within the War Cabinet were sharper than ever, even to the point where the Foreign Secretary showed some reluctance in carrying out its decisions. Hankey recorded:

The P.M. has very stubbornly and adroitly resisted pressure from Foreign Office and War Office to rush the Japs in to 'down' the Bolshevists. He has always trusted Lockhart, our agent in Russia, whom F.O. and W.O. mistrust. Now Lockhart has actually received an invitation from Trotsky for the Allies to put up the scheme, and, as a first step, we are putting one up to President Wilson. Balfour was very 'sniffy' about it, and eventually sent it beginning 'I am asked by the War Cabinet to send the following' instead of treating it as though it were sent from the whole Government, including F.O.[9]

President Wilson's attitude, together with the shortage of British and French troops, especially in light of the great German offensive on the Western front, meant there could be no significant intervention from the Western Powers. We have consistently seen that military intervention was what a significant number of them desired. Since this goal was unattainable, they turned to the Japanese as surrogates.

They were also using their Intelligence Services in a new role, that of destabilizing Russia and overthrowing the Bolsheviks by fomenting and harnessing internal discontent. They were prepared to use the Bolsheviks' internal opponents as surrogates, even though these same internal opponents' priority was to use the Allies to overthrow the Bolsheviks on their behalf. Both parties were expecting more from the other than it could deliver.

Reports such as the following were commonplace:

> Various organisations throughout Russia have informed the Allied Ministers and Mr Francis that the Russian people most emphatically desire Allied intervention but whether such desire would take physical form is not stated. Lack of explanation is doubtless due to the severity with which the Bolsheviki treat every such movement, terming it Counter Revolutionary.[10]

However, the 'Russian people' referred to were either former officers or members of the bourgeoisie, the very people who would welcome intervention from either the Allies or the Germans, provided it restored their own position. It is, at best, questionable whether this was the general feeling among the population of Russia. The writer, who is not identified, almost certainly had little or no contact with either the peasantry or the industrial workers.

Lockhart was to put these claims into perspective the following month, when he advised London:

> I would also like to add that the Allies in general and French in particular are inclined to attach far too much importance to elements favourable to Allies in

Russia. I would beg you to have no illusions on this subject and not to expect any substantial assistance at the beginning of our intervention. If intervention is successful it will be supported strongly, but in the present state of demoralisation in Russia it would be foolish to hope for too much from Russians themselves.[11]

The Allies were faced with a new enemy in Moscow. On 26 April the new German Ambassador, Count Wilhelm von Mirbach, presented his credentials to Sverdlov in Moscow. Mirbach was forty-seven years old and the head of a wealthy family of Prussian Catholics. He was a career diplomat who had been Counsellor in the German Embassy in St Petersburg between 1908 and 1911. He was, however, a diplomat of the old school, which made him less than an ideal choice to deal with the Bolsheviks and the unstable situation in Russia.

Relations between the Germans and the Bolsheviks were under severe strain, as the Treaty of Brest-Litovsk had left borders undefined and German troops continually encroached upon the territories of rump Russia. The Soviet Government sent a Note to Berlin protesting about the violation of the Brest treaty by Germany. Mirbach replied on 30 April that the German advance would cease if the Allies evacuated Murmansk and Archangel. Lockhart informed the French Military Mission in Moscow of the fact.

Richard Pipes states that the German Foreign Office instructed Mirbach to support the Bolshevik Government and under no circumstances should he enter into communication with opposition parties. 'He was to inform himself of the true situation in Soviet Russia and of the activities there of Allied agents.'[12] This line tended to ignore the deeply unstable situation in Russia. Mirbach found the Allies were bidding for the support of a host of opposition groups and felt the continuation of Bolshevik rule was uncertain. If they fell, or were swept away, the Germans would be left high and dry without any effective ally in Russia.

Mirbach rapidly saw the dangers and advocated a more flexible policy towards Russia. He wasted little time in approaching the Cadets. The British Consul-General in Moscow, Oliver Wardrop, also had links with the Cadets who informed him that the

German Ambassador is making great efforts to obtain support of Cadet Party. A leading member of that party tells me that Mirbach made overtures soon after his arrival but these were immediately repulsed. He renewed his proposals on May 9th suggesting a constitutional (? Romanov) monarchy comprising greater part of old territory, a complete reversal of Brest policy and revision of Brest treaty, free access to Baltic by restoration of considerable part of occupied territory in that region and suppression of Bolsheviks.[13]

German fear of Allied intrigues in Russia was real and should not be underestimated. This is demonstrated by a telegram that Berckheim, the German Foreign Office's Liaison Officer at General Headquarters, sent to the Foreign Office:

> General Ludendorff would be grateful for information about Count Mirbach's reports on the internal political situation in Russia. The General thinks that it is not impossible that a government hostile to us might take over the helm and considers it advisable to prepare for this possibility by helping circles acceptable to us to take over the reins of government.[14]

Mirbach's response, on 10 May is important as it discloses both the Allied response to Trotsky's request for aid and the danger this presented to Germany:

> I have heard from a good but not yet fully proven source that the representatives of the Entente countries here, under the chairmanship of Francis, yesterday approved an ultimatum to the Soviet Government, which they delivered today and in which the Entente solemnly offered to continue even now to support Russia with food, arms, and raw materials for its fight against Germany and held out hopes of recognition of the Soviet Government by the Entente in the event of a general mobilization. Karachan and Radek did not tell me of this event, perhaps because the official reaction was not to be discussed until this evening.

Mirbach noted that the Bolsheviks had not informed him of the Allied initiative, and he seems to have been unaware that it had stemmed from a Bolshevik invitation. He continued:

> I heard, after the event, that the Entente had this evening made further urgent approaches to Sverdlov with important offers to organise the transport of food from Siberia, and that the non-Bolshevik Socialist parties, also this evening and in line with the steps taken by the Entente, had offered to let bygones be bygones

and to co-operate with the Bolsheviks for the salvation of Russia. I am continuing with my secret efforts to ensure the rejection of both offers. [15]

The central problem facing the Germans was that, while the Bolsheviks were not their natural Allies and had the worst intentions towards Imperial Germany, there was no other party in Russia that would suffer the Treaty of Brest-Litovsk. The Germans were alert to the fact that any bourgeois government that seized power in Moscow would inevitably turn to the Allies to overthrow the Treaty.

Mirbach's chief tool in his 'secret efforts' was money or, to put it bluntly, bribery. The money that Germany had originally used to help the Bolsheviks to power had terminated in January. German money was now suddenly made available again.

The Germans were right to be alarmed by the clandestine activities of the Allies. The record through April and the first half of May shows ample cause for concern. In eastern Siberia the Consuls of the Western Allies including, surprisingly, the United States, were acting with the Japanese.

On 15 March the Chinese Government, that had committed itself to the Allies largely in order to counterbalance Japanese expansionism at China's expense, had promised the Bolsheviks that Semenoff would not be allowed to cross its border with Russia or to interfere in Russian affairs. At Allied instigation they informed the Soviet Government on 6 April that they would no longer abide by their promise. Semenoff promptly renewed his activities.

On 16 April a new anti-Bolshevik Government was formed in Peking. This was known as the Far Eastern Government and was led by Prince Lvov, the first Prime Minister of the Provisional Government after the February Revolution, with General Horvath as Premier and Admiral Kolchak as Minister of War. On the following day the Bolsheviks arrested Japanese spies at Irkutsk, and documents found on them showed that the Japanese Consul was involved in espionage. These spies were not operating in a vacuum, but were engaged in preparing the ground for armed intervention – an invasion in all but name – by the Japanese Army.

The information provided under interrogation by the spies, together with that gleaned from their documents, led the Bolsheviks to the house of one Kolobov, a member of the Far Eastern Government. When Lockhart and Le

Page saw Trotsky on 25 April about the Russian Fleets, he faced them with the 'discovery of documents in Kolobov's house in Vladivostock [that] show he was member of the so-called Siberian Government and in touch with the other members of that Government who are at Pekin.'[16]

The documents left no room for doubt that the Allies were, if not directly behind the conspiracy, at least elbow deep in it and largely responsible for the formation of the Far Eastern Government. The Allied Consular Corps at Vladivostock had already, on 9 March, threatened to cut off food supplies from Siberia if the Bolsheviks interfered with the administration there.

It is indicative of how closely all these clandestine moves were orchestrated in that on 17 April the Allied Consuls at Vladivostock had sent a joint Note to the local Soviet and the press, proclaiming that the landing of Japanese and British troops was 'purely a police measure and not hostile to any section of the population'. They also promised that the landing parties would be withdrawn as soon as satisfactory measures for safeguarding Allied property existed.[17]

The Bolshevik Government demanded the recall of the Allied Consuls on 25 April, which was not surprising and which they were both fully entitled and justified in doing. They offered the Allies the courtesy of a golden bridge, an opportunity to withdraw with grace from what would normally have been considered a highly embarrassing position. Implying that the Consuls had been acting without the express authority of their governments, the Bolsheviks requested the Allied governments to investigate the activities of their Consuls, and also to define their attitude to the hostile actions of their representatives in Russia.

There were dangers nearer to the Kremlin than those in Vladivostock. On 6 May, Berckheim told the German Foreign Ministry:

> The Maximalist government was to be overthrown by the Minimalists, on the instigation and with the financial support of the French, the English, and the Americans. The appointed date, 1 May, had to be postponed because the organization was incomplete. The dictators of the Minimalist government were to be Chernov, General Schwarz, Kriwotshein [sic Krivoshein], and Gavenko [sic] and also, supposedly, Kerensky in Petrograd. After the victory of the counter-revolution, an army of 30,000 to 50,000 men was to attack the German troops in Finland or Estonia, in order to ease the burden on the French front. The

Maximalists were warned of the imminent counter-revolution by Monarchists and the Soviet government arranged for the arrest of the Minimalist dictators. A French firm is evacuating large quantities of metal, crude rubber, and motor tyres from Petrograd. German delegates were not able to seize this opportunity, as they had no authority to buy. Large and favourable offers were made to them.[18]

The 'Minimalists' were the Mensheviks. There is, unsurprisingly, no supporting evidence in French, British, or American files that suggests they were involved in this attempted coup. However, while this means the evidence must be treated with some circumspection, it should not be dismissed out of hand. A considerable amount of material has undoubtedly been withheld over the years by the governments concerned, while a significant proportion of British Intelligence files were destroyed when the Arnside Record Repository was bombed in September 1940.

What may be more noteworthy is the report's contention that Russian Monarchists betrayed the plot to the Bolsheviks. This underlines the fact that the former were divided into factions, though which faction was complicit remains unknown. Like most of those involved in these events, their action would have been the fruit of expediency, in the same way as the cooperation between Germany and the Bolsheviks had been. It is arguable that some Monarchists saw the Mensheviks as a greater danger to their ambitions than the Bolsheviks, especially as there is some evidence that at least some of the latter were contemplating a restoration at some stage.

The idea that Kerensky would be in Petrograd to play any part in this attempt is ridiculous. Even the German author of the document expresses his reservations about Kerensky's alleged role with the caveat 'supposedly'. What was certainly true was the detail about the Allies, in this case the French, removing material from Petrograd. At this stage the efforts to keep strategic materials out of German hands were in full swing and occupied much of the time of Allied Intelligence officers.

Lieutenant-Colonel Boyle, following his remarkable coup in arranging peace between Bolshevik Russia and Romania, now came under the orders of the British Military Attaché to Romania, Brigadier-General C. Ballard. He had been instructed by the Foreign Office to embarrass the enemy in any way he could, without limit of any kind. These were sweeping instructions.

In Ballard's own words, 'I discussed with him [Boyle] all his plans and told him that he must be the judge.'[19] Again, this gave Boyle the widest possible latitude and it is important to observe that, as far as can be ascertained, such wide-ranging arrangements were common for clandestine operations at this point. It meant that while the officers directly involved were free from restrictions, their activities might not always have been what the Government had in mind when issuing the instructions. Moreover, it meant his operations were technically deniable by the officials, and this carried the risk that the momentum of operations could easily run away with events. Ballard was criticized by the Foreign Office in 1919 for the high level of expenditure incurred by Boyle's operations.

Ballard gave Boyle 1 million Romanian lei to start work and some blank cheques of his own for use as required. Boyle's stock was so high with the Bolsheviks that they were prepared to trust him and accept his cheques. The majority of Boyle's agents were indeed Bolsheviks, though there were a few officers who gave him considerable assistance. He created an organization around this kernel, authorizing them to hire men for 'wider destructive work, especially on ammunition depots, and on railway lines and bridges'. Some idea of the scope and scale of their activities can be gauged from Boyle's eventual report:

> The Odessa group claim to have done damage to the extent of 80,000,000 roubles. I am satisfied that they worked the big explosion at the Odessa ammunition depot, another at Kharkhov, and smaller explosions elsewhere. These men went in danger of their lives all the time; at least 8 of them were killed. They claimed 8,000,000 roubles and I succeeded in settling with them for 2,000,000 roubles.
>
> The Kiev group worked a big explosion at Kiev and at least two others. I settled with them for £20,000. To pay these two sums I gave one cheque for £100,000.
>
> Of the original organisation there were about 350 men in Kiev working on the Railway and in Workshops. They organised the big strikes in June and October 1918. Consequently they were left without means of living. I kept up the organisation with a view to future necessities; but I reduced the organisation by 200 men, whom I paid off with instructions that they should join General Alexeyev's Army in Kuban. For this I gave one cheque of £10,000.[20]

This was a considerable organization that caused a great amount of damage, denying the Germans much of the blockade-breaking materials they anticipated gaining. Given the relatively short time in which it was operating, Boyle's organization compares very favourably with the French Resistance of the Second World War, which had the backing of both the Special Operations Executive and de Gaulle's Free French.

In financial terms it had cost the British taxpayer 1 million Romanian lei in cash and £1,110,000 paid in seven cheques. For what had been achieved, it was money well spent. Ballard summed up Boyle's contribution:

> First, it helped to detain a large force of the enemy in the Ukraine to deal with the unrest and guard the bridges and depots; up till the end of September there were no less than 20 German Divisions and 10 Austrian Divisions there. Second, it disabled the Black Sea Fleet to a large extent. Third, it prevented the enemy from collecting as much supplies as they might have done had the Railways been working well. In fact the results were far greater than those of the mission of Sir J. Norton Griffiths, were less expensive, and were carried out in circumstances of greater danger.[21]

Ballard is exaggerating when he claimed that Boyle had 'disabled the Black Sea Fleet to a large extent'; he undoubtedly contributed to this but others, including the Bolsheviks, contributed more. Sir John Norton Griffiths was the British explorer and adventurer who thoroughly sabotaged the Romanian oil wells as the armies of the Central Powers were occupying the country in the winter of 1916–17.

Boyle was not operating in isolation. A British official called Litch was as influential on a larger scale. He was responsible for most of the anti-German agitation in the territory of the Russian Empire. Over the spring and early summer of 1918 he spent 150 million roubles towards this end. His agents are known to have been active in the Ukraine and Estonia and for a short time he was able to boast that through his work Germany was forced to keep fifty divisions under arms in the Ukraine.[22]

One final point needs to be made about operations of this nature, one that explains why generally few records survive. Ballard explained:

> In order to preserve the secrecy I have kept no notes on this subject; there was a possibility that the Germans might raid our archives in Jassy. At present no one

has any idea of our connection except Colonel Boyle and myself. I have not informed even the British Minister of my action, so that he may be able to give an official disavowal of our action if necessary.[23]

Extensive sabotage, backed by British money, was one way of denying the Germans the resources they sought. In central Russia other tactics were needed. Whereas the Central Powers occupied the territory in which Boyle was operating, central Russia was under Bolshevik rule and Soviet Russia was legally neutral. The Bolsheviks had their own Evacuation Committees to prevent vital raw materials being seized by the Germans. The central Evacuation Committee was based in Moscow and there were regional branches throughout all Bolshevik-controlled territory. Sabotage by Allied personnel here would have been more of an act of war against the Bolsheviks than against the Central Powers. The Allies were not in a position to make a formal breach with the Bolsheviks – yet. Nothing could be moved without the consent of the Evacuation Committee, as the following telegram from Captain George Hill to General Poole of Rusplycom makes clear:

> Mac(?alp)ine [sic McAlpine] instructs me to report to you direct. I am in Moscow as liaison between Mission and Lockhart as control of military and vital stores largely depends on Bolshevist permit without which it is extremely difficult to move anything.[24]

We see here the shadowy umbrella that embraced the seemingly different British organizations. Hill, Poole and his deputy, McAlpine, were all representing Rusplycom that ostensibly dealt in the removal of the 'military and vital stores', though Hill later became an officer in the Secret Service. Lockhart was ostensibly an unofficial diplomatic agent. The distribution list reveals more. It includes the DMI and sections A and B of MIO.

Appended to the document is a handwritten question from Lieutenant-Colonel Steel, in charge of MIO, 'What is all this about? Anything which DMI or I should see?'. This indicates that although the different organizations were parts of the same machine, they did not necessarily run in an altogether synchronized fashion. While it is evident they were working towards a common goal and in conjunction with each other, liaison was not as perfect as it should have been.

The Russian Evacuation Committees were creating chaos, according to Hill:

> At that time the Bolsheviks were evacuating some of their towns and stations to the west of Moscow, without any order or judgement, but with such activity that they blocked the lines, not only to the West, but also to the East of Moscow, with the rubbish they were saving.[25]

In Hill's opinion, 'The chief difficulties in front of the Evacuation Committees were:

1. Lack of order and direction.
2. Lack of fuel and transport.
3. Lack of organisation between the evacuation committees and the railroad controllers.[26]

He states that to

> ...facilitate our effect on evacuation I got into very close touch with Trotsky and was appointed by him as 'Inspector of Aviation' and given extensive powers in that Department. This brought me into close touch with the Aviation personnel, and gave me an entrée into the Aviation Parks and Evacuation Committees.[27]

As an officer of the Royal Flying Corps, which since 1 April had become part of the new Royal Air Force, the Russian air arm was of special interest to Hill. His appointment as Inspector of Aviation was to have repercussions later on. The good connections that Lieutenant-Colonel Maund had made with the Russian aviators proved particularly valuable, though this bud did not really blossom until later in the year.

In order to solve the problems reigning on the Russian railways, Trotsky turned once more to Joseph Boyle. On 13 April Trotsky offered to make him head of the railways in Bolshevik Russia,[28] and Boyle accepted.

At the beginning of April progress was being made with the evacuation of strategic materials and the first truckloads were shipped eastwards. The role of the British here consisted largely in restoring order so the programme achieved its aims. This meant advising the Evacuation Committees on the priority with which materials should be evacuated, and pressing or persuading them to introduce stringent rules against the transport of less important or trivial items, such as furniture. It also meant smoothing over cases of friction between the Evacuation Committees and the Transport Controllers who, typically, viewed matters from entirely different perspectives. The Revolution had impressed many workers with the idea that as they now owned all materials of transport and production, they could work or not as and when they wanted to, so the British and French had to divert time and effort to keeping all hands up to scratch.

The achievement was considerable. According to Hill they took control of the material coming from Smolensk and further west as the existing arrangements were blocking the railway lines. All the material from Moscow was sent eastwards with Kotel'nich, Viatka, Nishni-Novgorod, Kazan, Sarapol and Penza selected as the main dumps. Contingency plans were prepared in case there was a sudden rush of traffic, such as might be caused by an extensive German advance. In that case the new line between Kazan and Sarapol was to be filled with rolling stock and the lines west of Kazan destroyed.[29]

In his new post as Inspector of Aviation, Hill was able to get the Russian air service to send a small party of men to Kharkhov. They prevented the aviation material held there from falling into German hands, destroying what they could not save before the Germans seized the city. Hill recorded that 'The month of May opened disastrously, as what with Socialist day, and the three days' holiday that followed it, Church holidays and a small strike, very little was got away until the middle of the month.'[30]

Progress was temporarily brought to a halt by the landing of the Japanese and British at Vladivostock. The Bolshevik reaction was to forbid any further evacuation to the east, presumably because they anticipated a push westward from the Allies. The forces landed were far too small for that and, as they made no move westwards, evacuation was resumed after the arrival of Mirbach in Moscow and the German occupation of Finland.

Hill continued to work on the identification of German units in Russia for Military Intelligence through April and May. However, in May this element of his work was no longer done directly on behalf of the DMI. At the end of April Lieutenant Ernest Boyce, the head of the Moscow Station of MI1(c) sent two of his officers, Lieutenants Urmston and Small, to make contact with the Intelligence section of the old Russian General Staff. The Bolsheviks had originally suppressed this but, faced with the German threat, they realized the importance of its work and re-established it. Initially the involvement of the Secret Service meant that there was overlap and duplication, until Boyce, Urmston and Hill agreed their efforts should be combined. They pooled their staff and continued to get sound information and 'from then on all cables went to DMI'.[31]

Hill also dabbled in propaganda. Despite limited resources, he considered that 'fair results were obtained',[32] though it is extremely difficult to measure such matters unless the results are dramatic, and that they were not. He also created a section to investigate Russian inventions with the twin aims of acquiring useful weaponry and dissuading the Russians from selling anything useful to the Germans. Most of the items studied were for anti-aircraft fire control and sighting systems. Aeroplanes, new machines, ideas, gadgets, automatic rifles and protector shields all fell within the ambit of the new section, but Hill concluded 'one felt that all exhibits had long been on the retired lists at home.'[33]

The tasks undertaken by Hill and his colleagues demonstrate how very wide was their field of operation. They were unquestionably influential in the mission that was their first priority, keeping raw materials and war matériel beyond German reach. Their conduct had been directed against the Germans at this stage, rather than against the Bolsheviks, but some of their work was laying the foundations for anti-Bolshevik action later. It is difficult to establish whether this was deliberately planned. There is no record of any instruction being given to the officers in the field in this respect, and it is most likely that at this stage they were 'hedging their bets'.

This is also suggested by the early activities of Sydney Reilly. His first report to 'C', from Petrograd, on 16 April, saw him argue that 'Every source of information leads to definite conclusions that today BOLSHEVIKS only real power in Russia', though opposition to them was constantly growing and if 'suitably supported' would lead to their overthrow. He advised pursuing two parallel policies – to work with the Bolsheviks for the attainment of immediate ends, such as safeguarding the stores and the Baltic Fleet from the Germans; simultaneously the British should be working with the domestic opposition to the Bolsheviks with a view to their eventual overthrow. Reilly proceeded to advise 'C' that if he was given £1 million he would try to achieve all these objectives! 'C' did not take the bait.[34]

The remarks from MI1(c)'s Stockholm station about Reilly's first report illustrate the relaxed attitude taken towards Secret Service officers, a fact doubtless due to the vagaries of their position when in an unstable or hostile environment: 'Received long wire from S.T.1 in Petrograd all politics <u>advising support of Bolsheviks</u>. He does not say why he went to Petrograd instead of Vologda as ordered.'

Below this someone had written, 'very odd' in blue ink.[35]

Audacious is barely an adequate term to describe Reilly's next move. He arrived on Moscow on 7 May and went straight to the Kremlin. He coolly informed the sentries that he had been sent by Lloyd George and demanded to see Lenin personally. Astonishingly he was admitted. He saw not Lenin, but, instead, his aide General Mikhail Bonch-Bruevich, the Military Director of the Supreme Military Council. According to Lockhart, Reilly told Bonch-Bruevich that the British Government was dissatisfied with the reports it had received from Lockhart and wanted a first-hand account of the aims and objectives of the Bolshevik Government. In fact, Reilly's account of the meeting shows that they discussed Bonch-Bruevich's position, a change of attitude towards the reorganization of the army among the Bolsheviks, and the abolition of the election of officers.[36] It is noteworthy that Reilly's report was distributed to the DMI and MIO.

The file containing Reilly's reports reveals that there were at least eight interviews between Reilly and Bonch-Bruevich between 9 May and 3 June. According to Reilly, he was told that, 'the moment is fast approaching when [the] Commissars are beginning to realize that [the] only safeguard for the Soviet Government is open war with Germany.'[37]

This is hardly the true position of the Bolshevik leadership at the time. They wanted neutrality, not involvement in what they saw as an imperialistic war. They played the Allies along, holding out the promise of joining them in the war against Germany. There was no prospect of that unless the Germans continued their encroachments into Soviet Russia and endangered the regime. Then, as a last resort, they might have accepted Allied aid and resumed the war, but only then. Like everybody else, they were trying to keep their options open and maintain their freedom of action.

Reilly now abandoned his direct approaches to the Bolsheviks. Did he recognize that they were not going to commit themselves? Did London order him to do so? There is no trace of any such order, but that does not necessarily mean there was none. Orders could have been given verbally, or the documents destroyed. Whatever the case, he now dropped the identity of a British officer and assumed a clandestine existence, disguising himself as a Greek businessman, Mr Constantine, while he was in Moscow. While he was in Petrograd he adopted the identity of Konstantin Markovich Massino, a Turkish merchant.

Now his penchant for seducing women served him well: in Moscow he inveigled his way into the good graces and accommodation of the actress Dagmara Karozus; while in Petrograd he moved in with an old friend, Elena Mikhailovna Boyuzhovskaya. It was while staying with the latter that he used one of his old acquaintances, the former judge Vladimir Orlov, to obtain identity papers for Sigmund Rellinsky, a member of the Cheka's criminal investigation department.

Contemporary Allied propaganda held that the later armed intervention in Russia was caused by the danger of the Allied stores at Archangel and Vladivostock falling into German hands, and historians in the West have frequently parroted this argument. However, it is clear that the stores were used as an excuse to justify the intervention that both the British and French Governments were seeking.

There certainly were considerable amounts of military stores and raw materials that had been poured into Russia over the previous year. However, there is little evidence that the Germans wanted to seize these stores at the ports and the available evidence shows that the Bolsheviks had no intention of letting the Germans take them.

A moment's thought will put the munitions question into perspective. Most of the artillery shells were for the Russian 3-inch field gun; others were for British 6-inch howitzers or 60-pounders that had been supplied in limited quantities to the Russians. The German artillery did not use these weapons; it had captured relatively few British guns and, though they had taken many more Russian 3-inch pieces, they never showed any inclination to adopt any considerable number of their enemies' weapons in the field. It would have meant retraining a considerable body of their artillery personnel and, as their own artillery was already extremely effective, they had no need to bother. As General Poole, the head of the British Military Equipment Section in Russia, explained at the end of 1917: 'I do not think that much importance may be attached to the supplies of filled shells at this port [Archangel] as these would not be of much practical value to the Germans.'[38]

Reports from officers of Rusplycom indicate how absurd were claims that the Germans would benefit from these stores. A letter from Denys Garstin in Petrograd demonstrates this:

> The silly perpetual attacks on the Bolsheviks in the English press – Lenin as a German agent, etc., etc. mislead people at home, & infuriate the Bolsheviks here. It's too childish. The French are worse, but the Yanks are playing more astutely. Anyhow we are giving the impression of capitulation to Germany which is terribly bad for our prestige, & our lack of any policy beyond a display of sulks is not adding to the dignity of our position.
>
> The Bolsheviks, being led by Jews mostly, are the only party with a definite plan & method. Trotsky is as much against German Imperialism as he is against ours, or what he imagines ours to be. He certainly represents the strongest anti-German party in Russia. In a land clamouring for peace, they have not yet made a dishonourable one. Being internationalists, they're not patriots, but then no one is, whatever they are.[39]

As late as March General Poole's man on the spot in Archangel could tell him:

> I assume that you have seen recent telegrams to and from the Consul with regard to the question of War stores here. The following considerations after a preliminary discussion (with him?) seem to be worth bearing in mind:
> (1) That only a small percentage of the goods here are of urgent need to Germany who should soon have the whole of Russia to draw on for war materials.
> (2) That only a relatively small proportion is of such importance to us as to justify use of tonnage to convey them to England. In the course of a week or so I shall send you alternative shipping programmes for the summer from here.
> (3) That however grand the plans for such despatch may have been despatch of war material from Archangel has been and is on a negligible scale. Further that there is no evidence that any of the goods already despatched will not

be absorbed and used in Russia. Most of the despatches have been sent to Moscow and I am asking PINDER who is there to trace what has happened to such goods so far as possible. The whole line at VOLOGDA is blocked by military goods which have been evacuated from [*sic:* to] the East from Petrograd. Some stores there had been even sent from FINLAND for the same reason.[40]

The unidentified Rusplycom officer proffered some advice about one of the British officers at Archangel, Captain Proctor: 'It is unwise at the instance of mad hatters of the Proctor type to adopt local policies.' The trouble was 'mad hatters of the Proctor type' had influential allies who could get them a hearing in Whitehall.

This is clear from a letter written by Knox on 25 April to Sir Eric Drummond, Balfour's private secretary:

I enclose some papers on the situation in Russia, which Captain Proctor has written in Scotland and has sent to me to put forward. I do not agree with all he writes but he has been three times longer in Russia than young Lockhart and his papers contain three times more sense than all Lockhart's telegrams.

The policy of the Japanese intervention has failed because it was never put up with proper insistence and determination; it has never been understood as one of the vital conditions for the winning of the war.

My advice has been brushed aside though I can prove that my prophecies have been correct. You will now see what help towards the winning of the War is to be had from Lenin and Trotsky and Lockhart.[41]

One of Proctor's papers is unarguably hysterical and reflects a disordered mind:

I can only emphasise that either Trotsky and Lenin are simple and incapable beyond words, which even Ambassador Francis and Messrs. Lockhart, Thompson and Robbins, do not assert, or else they and those who follow their beliefs are!! On the one hand, if they believe in Trotsky and Lenin's honesty and loyalty their credulity is indeed marvellous; on the other hand, if the proofs of logic, reason and circumstantial evidence do not convince them of Trotsky's and Lenin's guilt, the incredulity is amazing. A wonderful anomaly.

They must be particularly impressed with Colonel Thompson [*sic* Captain Thomson], who is reputed to have (mis)spent £100,000 of his own money in buying their company and goodwill!

It is worthy of note that people who know them unanimously assert that Lenin and Trotsky are most clever and accomplished men.

Germany's undoubted aim is not the annexation of the whole of Russia, but through Anarchy and extremism, secretly fostered and controlled by her agents, to reach reaction, German domination and a German controlled Monarchy.

Likewise, is it remarkable that the Imperial Family and the most reactionary of the Aristocracy are wonderfully immune from persecution and murder, while great Russian patriots, inveterate enemies of Germany, like Grand Duke Nicholas, Kaledin and others disappear or are 'removed' in characteristic German fashion.[42]

It might be wondered why this obvious nonsense was ever taken seriously. I do not consider that it was. It told some of its readers what they wanted to hear because they had already determined on pressing for armed intervention in Russia. It provided a justification for the position they had already adopted.

Proctor was responsible for the Allied munitions at Archangel. He had previously managed exports of flax for the Army Supply Department and the import of herring for the Restriction of Enemy Supplies Department. He boasted considerable commercial acumen and, rarely for a British officer or official, he spoke excellent Russian. Douglas Young, the British Consul at Archangel, described him thus:

> ...his general friendliness, his readiness to help anybody in any possible way had made him a universal favourite. Unfortunately, he succumbed early to the scare panic. He saw a German in Bolshevik disguise lurking behind every corner and went about putting people's nerves on edge with horrible stories of what was going to happen.[43]

He was instrumental in influencing the officer in command of the Royal Navy's White Sea Station, Rear Admiral Kemp, that Allied intervention was necessary to save Russia from Germany. Kemp did not need a lot of convincing. Having served in China during the Boxer Rising, Kemp tended to think of the Russian masses in terms of Chinese Boxers. In the words of Douglas Young, 'He had constant nightmares, not only of attacks upon Embassies and Consulates but also of the outraging and murder of women and children.'[44]

Proctor had originally gone to Petrograd where he had tried to alarm the British Embassy. The Embassy took a cooler and more realistic view of the situation than the rattled Proctor, who returned to Archangel. His fears seem to have swollen into an obsession, for he went to the Embassy a second time on the same mission. On this occasion he did not return to Archangel, but took ship to England instead. So it came about that he started to spread alarm and despondency about the Russian situation in Britain. It was, if not music to the ears of people like Knox and other interventionists, very handy ammunition for them to use to affright the government.

It was not so much the accumulation of material at Archangel that worried some people but rather its removal to Vologda. There is no doubt that Rusplycom knew the real reason for the evacuation of stores to Vologda, for Captain McAlpine made it clear:

> The Russian Government proposals for evacuation at Vladivostock closely resemble those already put into operation at Archangel. Their main aim [is] to convey raw materials for works into interior irrespective of the needs or demands of the Allies. There is no reason to suppose that this is due to any other desire than of keeping raw materials in the country which represent the development of capital, and of restoring the industries hereafter. Local reasons are obviously the cause for the demand for shell. Evacuation Commission will without hesitation try to rail away railway materials, foodstuffs and metals. There seems no point in forcing the issue on the point as shell etc. is clearly useless to Allies. From our experience at Archangel it is however quite clear that we must decide quickly what our attitude is to be as regards other stores, and I strongly urge you, act in concert with the Consul, to press strongly for a prompt decision on this point at home.[45]

So the evacuation of the stocks of raw materials by the Bolsheviks was to allow them to rebuild the shattered economy of Russia. McAlpine admits that the shells were useless to the Allies. The question of 'what our attitude is to be' was clearly a political question, hence the desire to press for a prompt decision at home. In its essentials the decision had already been taken.

London seemed determined to ignore information that did not accord with the picture the Foreign Office had chosen to paint for itself. On 18 April Lockhart received the following message from the Foreign Office:

We are informed stores are being moved from Archangel in increasing quantities to Vologda. We can do nothing to protect them there and they will be within striking distance of the Germans. Metals that could be moved eastwards and thus further from the Germans are being deliberately kept at Petrograd.[46]

Perhaps the gentlemen in the Foreign Office needed to consult their maps more closely. Vologda was roughly 700 miles from the German lines as the crow flies. With armies tied to the marching speeds of horses and men it is an absurdity to describe this distance as being 'within striking distance of the Germans', especially as the Germans would face opposition. As for the metals in Petrograd, the Evacuation Committees were straining to move everything of value away from the Germans; the only friction came from poor organization, lack of direction and shortage of fuel.

The second factor was that Lockhart had been no slouch where the stores were concerned. He had been negotiating with the Bolsheviks about their fate for some time. His negotiations were successful. His diary entry for 5 May reads: 'Arranged with T. [Trotsky] about Archangel stores – quite satisfactory agreement.'[47]

What did most to turn London towards intervention? The answer lies mainly in Poole's return there. He had prepared the ground in a paper dated 15 March 1918, where he claimed that only foreign forces could make the Russians fight the Germans. His proposals included a programme for policies in Russia that would justify armed intervention to the Russian people and he urged its energetic adoption lest the Germans steal a march on the Allies.[48] Eleven days later, Lord Curzon, the former Viceroy of India and now a member of the War Cabinet, presented a memorandum in response to Poole's that stated, in a nutshell, that the British Government ought to decide between 'abstention' in Russia as advocated by Lockhart, or intervention as espoused by Poole.[49]

It is not easy to see precisely what had changed Poole from favouring recognition of the Bolsheviks at the beginning of the year into an exponent of intervention less than three months later. Regrettably his personal papers on his service in Russia at this time have disappeared. His papers in the Liddell Hart Centre for Military Archives only cover reports he made when in south Russia in late 1918 and early 1919.

Perhaps the frustrations he faced in Russia had made him bitter, but this remains speculation. He thought the Red Army was a feeble force that a vigorous Allied thrust would readily overcome:

> Judging by what we have seen of the occupation of the Western Provinces of European Russia by the Germans, it would only be necessary to employ a small force to carry out such a policy. The Bolshevik troops are thoroughly undisciplined and disorganised and are quite unfitted to oppose any small body of Regular troops.[50]

No doubt an enterprising British commander, quite probably himself in view of his experience in Russia, could reproduce the startling advances made by the Germans in February. Then he could sweep to Moscow, inspiring the 'loyal' Russians, overthrow the Bolshevik rabble and drive the Germans out at the head of an irresistible tidal wave. Such dreams can fire the ego of any man.

Whatever the case, his appearance in London was to swing policy heavily in favour of armed intervention. The trail of Poole's deliberations and change of mind are found in the paper already alluded to, and another received on 9 May. In the latter, his assessment of the choices facing Britain and the Allies reduced them to four options: they could incite immediate armed resistance; they could organize armed forces to fight for several months but which could then have the support of Allied intervention; they could adopt a definite and energetic Allied policy designed to restrict the Germans to a commercial and economic invasion; or, in conjunction with the latter, launch a military occupation of Murmansk, Archangel and Vladivostock 'on the pretext of alleviating tonnage and transport difficulties'.[51] Poole dismissed the first two out of hand as impractical. He had sympathy for the third option, but threw his weight solidly behind the final proposal.

The use of the word 'pretext' by Poole in his outline of policy options needs to be heeded. The removal of strategic materials would only answer one of the questions posed by Russian neutrality; it was not going to lead to the massive transfer of German divisions from the Western front to Russia that the Allied leaders wanted as a matter of urgency. It also cannot be denied that there was never going to be anything so valuable as an Allied-friendly government in Moscow that would resume the war against Germany. Thus it was that the Allies continued to conspire with anti-Bolshevik factions in Russia. This is certain from the activities of Allied officials and agents with at least two of these factions.

Between March and May 1918 Joseph Ferdinand Grenard, the French Consul-General in Moscow, had paid the sum of 9 million roubles to two members of the Czechoslovak National Council. Oliver Wardrop, the British Consul-General in Moscow, followed suit by paying a further £85,000 to the same people. The documents establishing the proof of this were not discovered until July 1918 when the Cheka raided the offices of the National Council. In addition to this, of the 150 million roubles disbursed by Litch, 40 million were paid to the Czechoslovaks.[52]

It is crucial to note this. The Czechoslovaks were to use some of this money to subsidize several White organizations, so enabling them to take up the struggle against the Bolsheviks in the summer. This could not have been done without Allied knowledge or collaboration. The affair contradicts Richard Pipes' assertion that there was nothing that indicated the French were the instigators of the Czechoslovak uprising.[53] Without the generous financial support of the Allies, neither the Czechoslovaks nor the Whites would have been able to rise against the Bolsheviks in the summer of 1918.

April also saw the first serious moves made in London to retain the Czechoslovaks in Russia, as opposed to the official desire of the French Government to transport them to France. On 17 April, Balfour proposed that it might be possible to persuade Trotsky to agree to the Czechoslovak troops then at Kursk being redeployed to the Archangel or Murmansk districts, the ostensible aim of this being to prevent penetration of those areas by forces from Finland or by the Central Powers. A telegram was duly sent to Lockhart directing him to urge Trotsky to adopt this policy.[54]

On 27 April, the Military Representatives of the Allies' Supreme War Council met at Abbeville and backed this idea. They also resolved on Allied intervention through the north Russian ports. The military and naval forces were to be placed under the command of a British officer, and the British Government nominated General Poole. A small expeditionary force was to be sent to north Russia. Once there it was to train and equip the Czechoslovaks, together with a force of approximately 30,000 Russians who were expected to rally to the Allied standards. There would seem to be if not a hidden agenda then at least a double one. In a memorandum for President Wilson, Balfour had stated, 'it is of vital importance to us to retain Murmansk, if we desire any possibility at all of entering Russia.'[55] When Wilson read the memorandum, he does not appear to have attached any significance to those last ten words. The ultimate end of all these machinations can be seen poking its nose through the mask.

At this stage it was proposed that only the II Corps of the growing Czechoslovak Legion, which was forming around Omsk, should be sent to north Russia. The I Corps would continue on its way to Vladivostock and then embark for France. The French fell in with this plan and despatched a Colonel Donop from their Military Mission at Moscow to Archangel to superintend the arrival there of not only the Czechoslovaks, but a detachment of Serbians.

Joseph Noulens, the French Ambassador, safely ensconced at Vologda, but with his finger on the pulse of events – particularly schemes aimed at overthrowing the Bolsheviks – stated in April to the press that the Allied governments could not recognize a government that was not either in fact or in law representative of the true Russia.

Yet what was the 'true' Russia? Everything depended on which side of the divide one stood. Russia was fragmented. The Bolsheviks held central Russia and none of their opponents had the strength to overthrow them. All of them would have to rely on outside force. That meant either the Allies or the Germans. The Social Revolutionaries had won by far the majority of the seats in the ill-fated Constituent Assembly. They were the strongest threat to the Bolsheviks in terms of popular support. Could they claim to represent Russia? Did they have the strength to establish that claim? The Allies seem to have thought they had a chance and they chose to back it.

The Social Revolutionary Party had been founded in 1901 and its prime aim was a massive redistribution of the land in favour of the peasantry. On 6 November 1917 the party had split. The smaller portion of the split became known as the Left Social Revolutionaries, who cooperated with the Bolsheviks. The majority became known as the Right Social Revolutionaries, not because their policies were either conservative or reactionary, but simply as a mark of differentiation from their former colleagues. It was this majority party that the Allies were courting.

The most succinct summary of the early attempts to use the Social Revolutionaries is provided by Mirbach:

> According to a reliable source, situation in Petrograd once again precarious. The Entente is supposed to be spending enormous sums in order to put right-wing Social Revolutionaries into power and reopen war. The sailors on board the ships *Res Publica* and *Zarya Rossii*, and on the cruiser *Oleg*, which has sailed to Ino, are said to have been bribed with large sums; likewise the former Preobrazhenski Regiment. Stores of arms in Sestroretck armament works in the hands of Social Revolutionaries. Bolsheviks cannot find central office of this apparently well-conducted organisation. The movement is supposed to have opened relations with Dutov and the Siberian movement. Here, too, agitation has increased. I am still trying to counter efforts of the Entente and support the Bolsheviks. However, I would be grateful for instructions as to whether overall situation justifies use of larger sums in our interest if necessary, and as to what trend to support in event of Bolsheviks being incapable of holding out. If Bolsheviks fall, successors [*one word garbled*] to Entente have best prospects at the moment.[56]

These prospects were understandably unpalatable to the Germans. Kuhlmann, the Under Secretary of State, replied:

> In reply to telegram No. 122.
>
> Please use larger sums, as it is greatly in our interests that Bolsheviks should survive. Riezler's funds at your disposal. If further money required, please telegraph how much. It is very difficult to say from here which trend to support if Bolsheviks fall. If really hard-pressed, left-wing Social Revolutionaries would fall with Bolsheviks. These parties seem to be the only ones who base their position on peace treaty of Brest-Litovsk. As a party, Kadets are anti-German; Monarchists would also work for revision of Brest peace treaty. We have no interest in supporting Monarchists' ideas, which would reunite Russia. On the contrary, we must try to prevent Russian consolidation as far as possible and, from this point of view, we must therefore support the parties furthest to the left.[57]

Mirbach spent all the money at his disposal and managed to avert danger in the short term, but on 3 June he requested 3 million marks a month to combat the Allies, warning that a higher sum would be needed if the German Government wished to support other contenders for supremacy in Russia. The German Treasury agreed for 40 million marks to be placed at the disposal of the Foreign Ministry on 11 June.[58] By the time any of this money reached Moscow little of it could or needed to be used.

VII

'…up to the last moment'
Mid-May–Beginning of June

◄○►

G erman fears, inspired by the combination of Allied intrigues and the offer of Allied aid to the Bolsheviks, threw their purely selfish concern for the survival of the Bolshevik regime into sharp relief. Mirbach, showing he agreed with Kuhlmann's diagnosis, outlined the contours of their position in his message of 13 May:

> As far as can be judged from the opinions, the attitudes and the strengths of the various political strata and from the overall situation, it appears to me, as I see it from here, that our interests still demand the continuation in power of the Bolshevik government. [*One word garbled*] the efforts at insinuation and the professions of friendship of all the other parties, there is, in most cases, only the wish to be rid of the Bolsheviks. If they do fall, then all their successors will with the aid of the Entente, work for reunification with the ceded territories, especially with the Ukraine, and for the revision of the Brest peace treaty. Any further advance on our part might drive the Bolsheviks into the arms of the Entente or, in the event of their fall, bring successors favourable to the Entente into power.[1]

At a meeting held at General Headquarters, Spa, on the same day, the issues facing German foreign policy were discussed. The subjects included the difficulties faced in the Ukraine, where resistance to the Germans and their puppet government under Skoropadsky meant that little of the badly needed foodstuffs were reaching the Central Powers; the Caucasus, where there was friction with the Turks; the perennial problem of Alsace-Lorraine; the movement for Flemish independence in occupied Belgium; the fate of the Crimea. Finally, attention turned to Russia.

The Germans recognized their current policy of annexation by encroachment was playing into Allied hands and had become a liability:

State secretary von Kuhlmann explained that the Entente had apparently recently approached the Bolsheviks with promises, if the latter would reopen the war against Germany. He did not consider this alarming from a military point of view. The Bolsheviks were in any case under a severe threat from the left, i.e. from a party which paid homage to even more radical views than the Bolsheviks, who seemed to be trying gradually to orientate themselves towards the right. It would, at all events, be very much in our interests if it could be announced, once and for all, that our operations in Russia were definitely finished.

General Ludendorff replied that this was now the case and that it had presumably already been announced.

At the General's request, Colonel von Winterfeldt stated that he had told Under State Secretary von den Bussche that the demarcation-line was being drawn and that the advance had thus reached its conclusion.[2]

Improvement in Soviet-German relations did not take place overnight. The fact that German troops were no longer advancing by degrees led to an initial thaw in the frosty relations, but an exchange of notes between the two governments at the end of May and the beginning of June settled the unstable situation. It led to the creation of political and economic commissions to fix relations. The work of these two bodies was to culminate in the Supplementary Treaties to Brest-Litovsk in the summer.

Since the Bolsheviks were no longer in immediate danger from the Germans, the Allied offer of aid could be safely declined. It also meant that the main Allied pretext for military intervention in Russia vanished.

Lockhart grasped the point rapidly and tried to press it home in his reports to the Foreign Office. In one file alone, FO371/3286, between 23 and 29 May there were no less than seven reports in this vein.[3] Some of these repeat the message more than once, and one of them reiterates it four times. Just one example will suffice to show how the realization that the Allies had been thwarted dawned:

Situation here has undergone marked change during the past ten days. This is chiefly due to sudden alteration which Germans have made in their policy. For reasons which are partly unknown to us but which I shall try to explain later, they have announced to Bolshevists that their military operations in Russia are completed, that they have no intention of occupying Petrograd or Moscow, and that they are anxious to co-operate economically with present Russian

Government. They have therefore begun to play again with Bolshevists and are putting up to them various economic proposals.[4]

Lockhart had opposed intervention up to this point (and was regarded as far too close to the Bolsheviks) but he was now pressing, with increasing impatience, for it:

> The only other policy is policy of Allied intervention on a large scale preferably with the consent of the Russian Government but if not without it. I have never denied its difficulties and have always underlined the importance of preparing it in the most careful manner possible. As Bolsheviks consent will only be given in the event of further aggression on Germany's part, it seems to me that the only course is to prepare our intervention as speedily as possible and as secretly as possible, to continue to play with the Bolsheviks up to the last moment in the hope that some movement on Germany's part will gain us their consent, and, as soon as we are fully prepared, to seize the first favourable moment in political situation here to issue a well worded declaration to Russian people demanding their consent to intervention and to follow this up within twenty-four hours by a simultaneous landing at Murman, Archangel, and Far East.[5]

The idea that the British should 'continue to play with the Bolsheviks up to the last moment' are Lockhart's own words, notwithstanding the fact that the British and French Governments were more than ready to do just that. It raises important questions about the trust that can be placed in not only his words, but of those of many others in official positions.

Colonel Keyes, who we have seen working alongside Lockhart, was under no illusions about him. Keyes was to write, 'He was a very shameless opportunist. I don't think he had any convictions.' He went on to describe Lockhart's playing with the Bolsheviks: 'His performances, dirty as they were, had done us well, for they strengthened the Bolsheviks' intentions against the Bosche, and lulled their suspicions while we were preparing the ground.'[6]

For Lockhart any genuine attempt to reach an understanding with the Bolsheviks was now an irrelevance:

> From the Bolshevist point of view Lenin has again proved right, and unless the Germans attempt to attack the Bolshevists there is no use in our wasting time in

trying to secure their loyalty; what then remains to be done? There is only one answer, intervention and as soon as possible.[7]

Despite his friendly meetings with Trotsky and, increasingly, Chicherin, Lockhart was now firmly in the interventionists' camp. His conversion met with smug approval from the interventionists in London. On 22 May Lord Robert Cecil met the Japanese Ambassador:

> I told him that Mr. Lockhart believed that joint action in Moscow with the Soviet Government would be successful, but that he had now arrived at the conclusion that intervention was so urgent that we ought to act whether we obtained the invitation of the Bolshevist Government or not.[8]

A distinct line of cause and effect can be traced leading from Allied clandestine activity together with an offer of aid to the Bolsheviks, to the German announcement of the cessation of military action, through to the Bolshevik decision to reject the Allied offer. The intrigues in Siberia had temporarily stalled, but were now picking up their tempo. Whereas they had previously been directed mainly at resisting the Germans with the overthrow of the Bolsheviks as a welcome addition, the focus had now shifted to destroying the Bolsheviks. No formal decision seems to have been made. War's own momentum, together with the proclivities of influential individuals, carried matters forward.

The staff of Lockhart's mission was reduced at this time and his frustration is made clear in the message he sent on 1 June:

> I have had extremely difficult task keeping in touch with Bolsheviks and at the same time retaining confidence of other parties. I have naturally been forced to be extremely discreet regarding your policy and I am well aware that as a result of my silence I have been severely criticized by individual members of General Poole's Mission in Petrograd for being blindly pro-Bolshevik. In this connection I would point out that since March I have done my best to achieve complete concord regarding intervention amongst all Allied representatives in Russia and I am quite sure that latter would be the first to bear witness to this.[9]

It is worth noting that criticism was coming from members of Poole's Mission. Poole was still in London where he had successfully argued in favour of intervention. His organization, Rusplycom, had originally been responsible for preventing Allied stores and Russian supplies and raw materials from reaching the enemy, but now, in the words of the Foreign Office, 'the scope of his work had been enlarged'.[10] Indeed it had. Poole was now fully engaged on work of a military nature – the armed intervention in Russia, which was to be preceded by large-scale subversive operations to engage the support of the parties opposed to the Bolsheviks.

Lockhart ably sketched the way Allied thinking was developing:

> Events here are moving very rapidly and if once Bolsheviks persuade themselves that we are bent on an anti-Bolshevik intervention they are capable of accepting secret help from Germany and of causing us serious trouble in Siberia.
>
> On the other hand, if we can conceal our intention almost to the end, we can still disarm their suspicions and render any opposition they might offer ineffectual.
>
> There is no doubt their power is gradually diminishing and that Allied intervention will produce a counter-revolution which may easily be successful. In this respect we have much to gain by forcing Germans to back Bolsheviks.
>
> On the other hand, we should clearly understand that without Allies' intervention a pro-ally counter-revolution has no chance of success. If it were attempted and if it failed, our position here would be irretrievably damaged.[11]

He continued with recommending a nine-point programme for a successful intervention, which looks quite reasonable – on paper. He emphasized the need for speed above all else, urging that intervention must take place at the earliest opportunity, certainly not later than 20 June. In this he was to be disappointed. He seemed to imagine that the Allies could conjure up a large force of good troops and swoop on Russia in less than a month. With the campaign on the Western front still hanging in the balance there was no realistic possibility of this happening.

The Allies were surreptitiously bidding for the support of the Right Social Revolutionaries and this intrigue now bore fruit. Lockhart reported:

> On 23rd instant the Congress of Russian Social Revolutionaries of the Right passed a long resolution condemning ruinous foreign policy of Bolsheviks and inviting Allied intervention as sole means of saving Russia. Resolution naturally insists that Allies should respect integrity of Russian territory and also her sovereign rights as a nation. It also points out that intervention should be

genuinely inter-Allied and not the task of only one of the Allies, that is Japan, whose action might be interpreted as purely selfish and imperialist. As a result of this resolution the Bolsheviks are beginning a fierce campaign against Social Revolutionaries.[12]

The Cadets also threw their weight behind the Allies at a meeting on 26 May. Expectations were rising since 'everyone is eagerly expecting Allied intervention.'[13]

The Monarchists also approached the Allies. Lockhart was approached by what he describes as 'a very prominent member of the old regime' on 28 May, who informed him that the two most important monarchist organizations had been divided, one pro-German, the other pro-Ally. Lockhart's visitor said he had been approached two days previously by a member of the pro-German faction, who had told him his organization was now hesitating in its attitude in view of the recently improved relations between the Germans and the Bolsheviks. He suggested that if the Allies would only act quickly, they would get the support of both factions.[14]

Unsurprisingly the Germans did not see the action of the Right Social Revolutionaries in this light. Trautmann, the Counsellor in the German Foreign Ministry, submitted a paper to Kuhlmann for the benefit of Count Rödern, the State Secretary of the Treasury, in support of the Foreign Ministry's appeal for more money for the Embassy in Moscow:

> The Bolsheviks have, for the moment, been successfully restrained from steering into the waters of the Entente, but every day may bring new surprises. The Social Revolutionaries have completely sold themselves to the Entente which, with the help of the Czechoslovak battalions, is trying to undermine the supremacy of the Bolsheviks. It appears that the Bolsheviks have, for the moment, succeeded in overcoming the attack of the Czechoslovak troops. Nevertheless, the next few months will be taken up with internal political strife. This may possibly even lead to the fall of the Bolsheviks, especially as one or two of their leaders have already reached a certain degree of resignation as to their own fate.[15]

The fact that Trautmann refers to the Czechoslovaks in the same context as the Right Social Revolutionaries raises important questions. Was there a link between the two? There is evidence of cooperation between them. It was certainly under the protection afforded by the Czechoslovak Legion that the

129

Right Social Revolutionaries were able to establish two democratic governments in Omsk and Samara. These enjoyed only a brief life, but that was hardly the fault of the Czechoslovaks. The Samara Government was faced with overwhelming military odds and it proved quite incapable of forming an effective army. The government at Omsk was a coalition government, involving Populist Socialists, Cadets and Mensheviks. It was riven by internal dissension and eventually foundered, being supplanted by the more conservative Siberian Provisional Government.

The Czechoslovaks were quite unquestionably the tools of the Allies. Without them there could have been no dangerous risings against the Bolsheviks, much less a full-scale civil war. The usual story that has been handed down is that the rising of the Czechoslovaks stemmed from a clash between them and returning Hungarian prisoners-of-war at Cheliabinsk in western Siberia. The story relates that a trainload of Czechoslovaks and a trainload of Hungarians were stationary and adjacent to each other, when one Hungarian threw a lump of metal, perhaps from a stove, at the Czechoslovaks, killing one of them. The Czechoslovaks immediately surged from their train in a fit of rage to mete out justice and, when the local Red Guards tried to quell the disturbance, the Czechoslovaks turned on them, thus beginning the conflict.

The story is nonsense. The Czechoslovak rising took place over approximately seven thousand kilometres of the Trans-Siberian Railway. It would have had to have been coordinated over that vast distance and what amounts to a minor incident at one station would not have inspired a rising on that scale. Who was coordinating the rising on this scale? The French were most closely involved with the Czechoslovaks and, with the British, were funding them. Lockhart admits that he had been 'in close touch' with the Czechoslovak National Council,[16] but undoubtedly he deliberately left no public record of the discussions. An officer of the French Military Mission, Commandant Guinet, was responsible for the Czechoslovaks in their anabasis to Vladivostock. It has also been claimed that one French officer travelled with them in the guise of a Red Cross nurse and, in Samara, another joined them disguised as a nun.[17]

Moreover, the Czechoslovak National Council had decided at Cheliabinsk that the Legion would, if need be, fight the Bolsheviks in Russia instead of travelling to the Western front to fight the Germans. This was in accord with British planning. The Bolsheviks were desirous of avoiding trouble with the Czechoslovaks and were actually anxious for them to leave Russia. This is emphasized by the reaction in Moscow to the outbreak of fighting with the Czechoslovaks. The news broke in Moscow on 25 May. Six days later Chicherin asked Lockhart to use his influence in settling the incident.[18]

In his *Memoirs*, Lockhart gives a misleading account of his meetings with the Allied Ambassadors at Vologda, chief among whom was Noulens. Lockhart relates how the two men discussed the question of the Legion from 'all its angles' on 29 May, and decided that the Czechoslovaks should be evacuated as rapidly as possible. Lockhart continued, 'After the meeting I said goodbye to M. Noulens. He was all smiles and affability.' It was only when he returned to Moscow that he heard of the clash between the Legion and the Bolsheviks.[19] The implication is that Noulens knew what was about to happen and kept the information from Lockhart, yet the information Lockhart had sent to the British Government from 23 May onwards showed that he was acting in collusion with Noulens.

Lockhart was almost certainly acting on instructions from London, for a special Committee of the War Cabinet had been formed to review the situation in Russia and recommend future policy. Its members were General Jan Christian Smuts, the South African, after whom the Committee was named, Lord Milner, together with the First Sea Lord, Sir Rosslyn Wemyss, and the Chief of Imperial General Staff, General Sir Henry Wilson. They met on 11 May and the official record of their discussions leaves no room for doubt about the course of their thinking in relation to the Czechoslovaks. The consequences were considered only insofar as they impinged on the war:

> It seemed also anomalous that, while great efforts were being made to secure the intervention of Japan in Russia, the Czecho-Slovak troops should be removed from that country to the Western front. The Shipping Controller reported that any transport of Czecho-Slovak troops would simply divert tonnage from equivalent numbers of American troops, and it appeared inadvisable to ask for Japanese tonnage for the purpose at the very time when we were pressing Japan to undertake intervention in Russia, which would absorb all her tonnage. We therefore came to the conclusion that the Czecho-Slovak troops now at Vladivostock or on their way to it should be taken charge of there and be

organised into efficient units by the French Government, to whom the above difficulties in the way of their transport to France should be pointed out, and who should be asked that, pending their eventual transport to France, they might be used to stiffen the Japanese as part of an Allied force of intervention in Russia.[20]

The Secretary of State for War undertook to send a telegram in the above sense to Clemenceau, the French premier. General Poole was to go to Russia as soon as possible as the British Military Representative to take charge of military affairs 'and to advise the War Office as to all steps to be taken in regard to our intervention in Russia.' Rusplycom's London Office would collect the necessary officers and NCOs 'more or less along the lines of the Dunsterville mission, to assist him in organising the Czecho-Slovaks and other forces of intervention from Archangel and Murmansk'.

The First Sea Lord undertook to send 200 marines for the defence of Archangel, and the War Office was to send such munitions and supplies as Poole might consider necessary. Poole 'was to consider, while holding and safeguarding the positions at Murmansk and Archangel, how far he could work up from Archangel towards Vologda with the forces at his disposal.'[21] The 'fact' that so many military stores were supposed to be ready and waiting at Archangel seems to have been left out of the account.

On 17 May Lloyd George suggested to the War Cabinet that Britain might intervene in Russia without the Americans and Japanese if they continued to withhold their consent. He argued, with justice, that German troops from the Russian front were attacking on the Western front, and the British Army was bearing the brunt without any material American contribution. He considered that the Czechoslovaks could be used in Siberia with minimal Allied assistance.[22] Balfour thought such action would force the hands of both the Americans and Japanese and lead them into joining the intervention.

Lord Robert Cecil thought that the rest of the Allies would soon conform if the British took active steps to intervene in Siberia. He added, 'The French Government had always been pressing for intervention in Siberia, and he thought that if they realised we meant business they would consent to the Czecho-Slovaks being used for the purpose.'[23] Milner pointed out that as the

Czechoslovak force was 'entirely the creation of the French,' it was imperative that Britain should obtain their co-operation before deploying them in this manner. The War Cabinet decided that the General Staff should ascertain whether anything could be done in Siberia using the Czechoslovaks as a nucleus, without the cooperation of the Americans and the Japanese. Lord Robert Cecil was directed to approach Mr Benes and discover whether the Czechoslovaks were willing to be used in this way, if it was explained to them that the objective was to fight Germans. Finally, if it was decided to mount the operation, the Foreign Office was to take 'such diplomatic action as might be expedient with the United States of America, Japan, and France'.[24]

The War Cabinet also adopted the Smuts Committee's suggestion that the French should be told that there was not enough tonnage to transport the Czechoslovaks from Vladivostock to France, so overcoming any reluctance on the part of Clemenceau. Evidently the prospect of a successful intervention in Siberia without reducing the tonnage available to bring badly needed American troops to France in numbers was persuasive enough to lead him to agree; either that, or the French had already adopted a very similar plan. Milner was able to inform the War Cabinet as soon as 23 May that, 'he had received information from M. Clemenceau that the latter agreed to the use of Czecho-Slovak troops at Murmansk and Archangel, except such as had already arrived at Vladivostock.'[25]

The plan the British were manufacturing was clear. They were going to use the Czechoslovaks as a nucleus, supported by whatever Allied detachments were available, to rally the domestic opposition to the Bolsheviks and so mount an intervention by proxy. The small force being sent for General Poole was to act in the manner of Dunsterforce, the offspring of MIO. The plan bears all the hallmarks of MIO, and Poole was ultimately responsible to them.

Equally apparent is the plan that Poole should press south from Archangel to Vologda. There the railway line from Archangel to Moscow joined the Trans-Siberian Railway, and that was the point where he was to link with the Czechoslovaks and the Russian forces that rallied to them. After that options remained open. Once in possession of Vologda, food supplies from Siberia could be denied to the inhabitants of Bolshevik Russia, leading to starvation, discontent and a rising that would sweep the Bolsheviks away. Alternatively, the combined forces could march on Moscow and, in conjunction with an Allied-inspired rising within the city, destroy the Bolsheviks in their own territory.

This process was in operation at the outset of the Czechoslovak rising. Chicherin, writing in 1919, stated: 'Almost concurrently there occurred a number of counter-revolutionary insurrections – among others in Saratov –- all of which were the work of the secret agents of the Entente, at that time mainly of French agents.'[26] The Allies began to reveal their hand a little over a week after the Czechoslovak rising had started and only four days after Chicherin had requested Lockhart to use his influence to settle the matter. The British, French and Italian representatives went to the offices of the People's Commissariat for Foreign Affairs on the afternoon of 4 June and declared that their Governments considered the Czechoslovak forces to be Allied troops who were under their protection, and that any attempt to disarm or interfere with them in any way would be considered as a German-inspired act and unfriendly to the Allies. Lockhart describes the scene:

> The Bolsheviks listened to our protests in silence. They were scrupulously polite. Although they had a case, they made no attempt to argue it. Chicherin, looking more like a drowned rat than ever, stared at us with mournful eyes. Karachan seemed stupidly bewildered. There was a painful silence. Everyone was a little nervous and none more than myself, whose conscience was not quite clear. Then Chicherin coughed. 'Gentlemen,' he said, 'I have taken note of what you said.' We shook hands awkwardly and then filed out of the room.[27]

The day before this meeting, Lockhart had received a visitor from Murmansk, Captain W.M.A. McGrath, who had been commissioned in the Royal Engineers in October 1916. Since 14 October 1917 he had been listed as a 'Captain, with Local, Temporary, Acting and Honorary Rank Whilst Specially Employed.'[28] In fact he was now an officer in the Secret Service and was to be one of the main intriguers in what was rapidly becoming a very dirty game. According to Lockhart's diary, the information McGrath gave him did not amount to anything sinister. The pertinent part of the entry in question reads: 'From what McGrath says things are not very far advanced and there is no policy in England at all. Nothing apparently will be done until Poole reports home!'[29]

We know this to be untrue. The policy had been decided and was already in action. Was Lockhart being kept in the dark deliberately, so he could neither protest nor, perhaps, betray anything by careless words? Or is his diary entry deliberately misleading? Maybe it was a mixture of both. There was the real risk that the Cheka might seize his diaries if they were suspicious enough to raid his premises. In that case he had very good reason to exercise the greatest discretion about what he committed to paper. He recorded nothing about his conversation with Cromie, who accompanied McGrath, no doubt for precisely the same reason. Also, neither Poole nor his staff knew when they would engage in their part of the plan. Archangel was still frozen by a belated winter and the composition of Poole's force had not yet been finalized. Perhaps McGrath was being legitimately circumspect.

The genuine reason for the Czechoslovaks being turned against the Bolsheviks at this time is made clear in July, when the Prime Minister sent a telegram to Lockhart explaining:

> The Czecho-Slovak successes give us an opportunity of restoring an Eastern front and revitalising Russia which may never return. Unless we take fullest advantage of this opportunity of reconstitution of an Eastern front I frankly do not see how we are to bring the war to a satisfactory end in 1919.[30]

This echoes Chicherin's view that 'French diplomacy had persistently conceived the re-establishment of the eastern front as an outcome of intervention, stepping across the corpse of Soviet Russia crushed by the Entente powers.'[31] By the summer of 1918 both the British and French were working together in pursuit of this policy.

The Allies showered money on the Czechoslovaks who were far from being mere mercenaries fighting simply because they were paid. Their real objective was political. In December 1917 the French had signed an agreement with the Czechoslovak National Council over the use of Czechoslovak troops. The Italians did the same in April 1918. Although these agreements were aimed at achieving the use of Czechoslovak troops on the Western front and at disintegrating the Austro-Hungarian Army in Italy, they were, in effect, recognition of Czechoslovakia as an independent state. Only London remained laggardly.

The Czechoslovak Legion in Russia was a very considerable bait to bring all of the Allies on board. Its deployment in Russia was a price the Czechoslovak leadership were prepared to pay in return for independence. Benes, in charge of the National Council in Paris, said the Legion was what 'I used for our political recognition in France and England.'[32]

Apologists for the intervention have made much of the argument over the years that the Czechoslovak troops did not 'want' to fight in Russia. They probably did not. Their views carried as much weight as did those of the rest of the populations of the belligerent powers – it was negligible. It was politicians who made the decisions, not the people or the rank and file of the army. All the governments of every state proclaimed their respective countries were either under attack or threatened with attack to rally their peoples to war. The Czechoslovaks were rallied with the claim that they were going to fight the Germans, who controlled the Bolsheviks.

It is easy now with nearly ninety years' hindsight to recognize the magnitude of the error made. Yet in June 1918 there was nothing to suggest to the Allied Governments or General Staffs that the German offensives had spent themselves. There was still less evidence that an Allied victory was less than six months away. So much was ultimately to depend on the indefinable state of morale, influenced by a multitude of factors, that the prospects could not be forecast with any hope of accuracy. The Allied Governments saw 1919 as the year of potential victory, and the idea of the dramatic German collapse of the summer and autumn of 1918 would have been dismissed as wishful thinking.

Reference has been made to the plan for Poole's force and the Czechoslovaks, acting in conjunction with an Allied-inspired uprising in the Soviet heartland. This plan was well under way and its chief tool was to be Boris Viktorovich Savinkov. Like Lenin, he was a son of the Russian nobility, variously described as 'the Hamlet of the Revolution', a terrorist, a renegade, and a patriot. He was essentially an intriguer against authoritarian regimes that held power in Russia, both Tsarist and Bolshevik. The underground organizations he led had scored two notable triumphs in the assassinations of Plehve, the Tsar's Minister of the Interior, and the Grand Duke Serge. His latest Western biographer, Richard B. Spence, sums him up thus:

His complex character was riddled with flaws; vanity, mendacity, and faith-lessness were not the least charges that were made against him, nor being an outright sociopath the worst. Yet he was also a man of immense charm, wit, intelligence, and occasionally, real vision. He was capable of inspiring deep loyalty and affection, but in the end Savinkov left almost no admirers to preserve and polish his memory. During his career he burned every bridge behind him and bit every hand that fed him. What he did leave was a legion of disillusioned followers and bitter enemies, who are inclined either to minimise his influence or erase his memory entirely.[33]

In 1918 he was undoubtedly scheming with both the British and French. On 17 May Lockhart informed the Foreign Office that two days previously he had a long conversation with an agent sent by Savinkov, who claimed that Savinkov's organization was probably the only counter-revolutionary organization with a pro-Ally policy. The agent told Lockhart that Savinkov did not feel strong enough to act at that moment, but urged that his counter-revolution should coincide with Allied intervention. Lockhart proposed to maintain informal connections with Savinkov through third parties. The minutes accompanying Lockhart's message reveal that there was no objection to Lockhart maintaining discreet relations with Savinkov. Writing on 25 May, the day Lockhart's message was received at the Foreign Office, George Clerk commented:

> I believe that the Bolsheviks know pretty well everything that goes on, I am not quite sure of our ciphers and I am confident that unless Mr. Lockhart gets direct instructions to the contrary he will continue to keep in touch with Savinkov. I should therefore leave this unanswered for the present.[34]

Lockhart did indeed continue to keep in touch with Savinkov, as his more detailed report of 26 May shows:

> I had today a long conversation with one of Savinkov's agents. This man whom I have known for years and who can be trusted states that Savinkov's plans for counter-revolution are based entirely on Allied intervention. The French mission has been supporting them and has assured them that intervention is already decided. Savinkov proposes to murder all Bolshevik leaders on night of allies landing and to form a Government which will be in reality a military dictatorship.

Following names are mentioned as likely to take some share in New Government – Alexeyev, Kolchak, Sazonov, (?Kis)hkin, Avkentsiev, Savinkov.

Savinkov is afraid French are trying to force him to make his attempt before Allies intervention. He wishes to impress upon Allies absolute necessity for immediate action as he is quite prepared to act with every day's delay the risk of discovery is greater.

He bases his hopes for success mainly on discontent of population with famine conditions. He proposes to win peasants sympathies by declaring free trade between all Governments and removing unpopular bread monopoly. His agrarian policy is to leave land to peasants and compensate land-owners.[35]

While the British trod cautiously, it is clear that Savinkov was operating far more closely with the French. He had made contact with them through René Marchand, the Russian correspondent for *Le Figaro* and *Le Petit Parisien*. Marchand was impressed by Savinkov's determination, energy and lack of scruples and put him in touch with a secretary at the French Embassy, who in turn arranged a meeting with Général Lavergne, Consul-General Grenard and, according to Spence, Martial-Marie-Henri de Verthamon, identified by Gordon Brook-Shepherd as a French naval officer sent to Russia to conduct sabotage operations.

Savinkov's organization was called the Union [it can also be translated as 'Alliance'] for the Defence of the Fatherland and Freedom. It had no political alignment and included anyone who opposed the Bolsheviks apart from the out-and-out monarchists. Its fighting men were mainly former officers, many of them from the Grenadier and Guards Regiments of the old Russian Army. Organized on military lines, with its membership divided into battalions, companies and platoons, it had started in a small way due to the shortage of funds. Spence states that it had only sixty to seventy active members at the end of March.[36] The Czechoslovaks remedied the shortage of money, using their Allied funds. Savinkov was later to claim that the Czechoslovaks gave him 200,000 Kerensky roubles. Tomas Masaryk, the leader of the Czechoslovak struggle for independence, later cast doubt on this, but he had a reputation to defend when he wrote his memoirs and was anxious to avoid antagonizing the Soviet Union.

Masaryk is known to have met Savinkov on 2 and 5 March. One of Savinkov's right hand men and co-conspirators, Flegont Klepikov, recalled one meeting between them at which Masaryk would not agree to Savinkov's request to instigate a rising against the Bolsheviks by the Czechoslovak Legion that could then be joined by the anti-Bolshevik Russians. He did offer to promise Czechoslovak assistance short of fighting if Savinkov succeeded in starting a rising. Savinkov asked Masaryk for money to support the planned rising and Masaryk agreed to supply some. He insisted on using intermediaries since he wanted no direct links to Savinkov. The money was made available and Lieutenant Georg Kletsando handled the transfer for the Czechoslovaks and Klepikov on behalf of Savinkov.

Several instalments totalling 200,000 roubles were paid by early April.[37] The money saved the Union in the short term until the French stepped in. According to Spence, the first French subsidies were modest, but when Savinkov agreed to undertake a full-scale rising, funds began to flow more freely, with another 2 million roubles being put at his disposal. Savinkov was to estimate that the French provided him with 2.5 million roubles altogether, while Colonel A.P. Perkhurov, one of the Union's small staff, estimated that the Union received 100,000 roubles, mainly from the Czechoslovaks during March, another 500,000 from the French during April, and at least 1 million more during May.[38]

All the usual suspects are present in the Savinkov plot: the French, the British, their Czechoslovak tools, together with Alexeyev and other White leaders. It was all too good to last. To create an underground army in the heartland of the enemy is to ask for trouble. Too many people are in the know and somebody is bound to say something. It appears that a young officer cadet, Nikolai Ivanov, fell in love with a nurse at Moscow's Iberian Hospital. His feelings overcame his discretion and he advised her to leave the city because of the imminence of the rising. The most reliable Western sources give two different accounts of what happened next. Spence claims that the nurse 'dutifully reported this information to the commander of one of the Latvian regiments, who in turn passed it on to the Cheka'.[39] The Latvians were the Bolsheviks' most reliable troops and have been described as the praetorian guard of the revolution. Brook-Shepherd says the nurse 'foolishly gossiped about this alarming news' and the Cheka picked up on the gossip and swooped on the hospital.[40]

Both Spence and Brook-Shepherd use apparently reliable sources. Spence relies on Mel'gunov's *Soius*, supported by Taybov and Christiakov, while

Brook-Shepherd uses the unpublished *The March of Time: Reminiscences by Alexander Orlov*. Orlov was a General in the KGB, successors to the Cheka, and the highest-ranking Soviet Intelligence officer ever to defect to the West. Although he had not personally taken part in the events, he had been posted to the Moscow headquarters of the GPU during 1924–6 and had investigated the struggles of the Cheka against the Allies and the Bolsheviks' domestic opponents. He had the singular advantage of being able to speak to the men who were involved.

Whichever is more accurate, the Cheka had discovered the Union's activities and raided the Iberian Hospital. There they found a number of Union officers and through them were able to pounce on Dr N. Grigoriev's clinic on 29 May, where four small rooms served as the Union's meeting place and its *de facto* headquarters. Grigoriev managed to remain at large, but the entire cadre of officers there was arrested.

Lockhart recorded in his diary that on 31 May Moscow was in a state of siege due to 'another' counter-revolutionary plot having been discovered. He gives no clue as to the identity of the plotters despite the fact that he knew about Savinkov, but states that five hundred arrests had been made.[41] Shortly after this, on 4 June, Lockhart reported:

> Your telegram not numbered of May 30th
> I had already some days ago destroyed all my papers and documents. I would only add that if you do not intervene within the next few weeks or days if possible we shall lose a (? golden) opportunity.[42]

Apart from the naïve view that a major military operation could be mounted in the space of a few weeks or even days, this suggests that Lockhart was ordered by the Foreign Office to destroy his papers and documents. This can only have been to ensure the destruction of compromising material. It is probably safe to conclude that more material on British relations with Savinkov and the Czechoslovaks was contained in those papers and documents.

The raid on Grigoriev's clinic was a major blow to Savinkov, one that was to irretrievably shatter the Moscow branch of the Union, and Savinkov now led a fraught existence there, hiding in basements and the homes of friends. The Cheka also discovered the names of the leaders of the Kazan cell, together with passwords and the addresses of safe houses. The Union had been organized so that cells were distributed in Moscow, Kazan, Rybinsk, Yaroslavl, Murom and Kaluga. The Cheka swooped on Kazan, effectively neutralizing the cell.

While Savinkov's organization was thrown into disarray, Allied agents were preparing the ground for the forces of intervention, the Czechoslovak Legion and the Whites who were expected to rally to them. George Hill received a request from General Poole for hydroplanes (fast, flat-bottomed motor boats) and personnel to be sent to north Russia. The official pretext for this was to protect the northern ports from German submarines. However, the prospect of the Germans being able to establish U-boats at Murmansk or Archangel had diminished to the point where it could no longer be regarded as realistic. When one considers the waterlogged terrain in the summer in north Russia, there is a much more plausible reason for this request.

With the rivers being the main means of transport and much of the land being waterlogged, the need for hydroplanes is at once apparent. They would be a sound means of moving troops and supplies. However, Hill was unable to secure any – the Bolsheviks had evacuated both the hydroplanes and flying schools to the Volga district. Instead, Hill sought to use his contacts with the Russian Air Force to initiate the movement northwards of Russian personnel who were 'experienced enough to acquaint themselves quickly with the British machines'.[43] It was in June that Hill began recruiting Russians to act beside the forces of intervention. He had established a special section to supervise this operation, under Lieutenant-Colonel Kazakov, who had been awarded the St George Cross under the Tsar. Kazakov founded the recruiting service in Moscow, while Captain Barkovski handled the organization of Flying Units. According to Hill, he did much to recruit Air Force personnel and worked constantly for the Allies.

Hill also briefly states that he contacted the Czechoslovaks and sent a message to them.[44] Other than dating the message 'June', he does not reveal when the message was sent, from whom it came, or what the message was. What it does reveal is the continuation of the circle.

A courier service was also organized to carry information from Moscow to Poole in north Russia. This was established under Captain Vezenkov of the

11th Hussars. Not only did he organize the service, but tested it by travelling in person over the selected routes. Hill described his efforts as 'brilliant work'.[45]

Hill was building for the future. In the meantime every effort was being made to prevent the Baltic Fleet falling into German hands. The importance attached to this is demonstrated by the telegram sent to Consul Woodhouse in Petrograd:

> Please hold at immediate disposal of Captain Cromie 1,500,000 roubles from embassy or other available accounts. Lockhart has been asked to facilitate in any way possible your operating on these accounts. You should take any steps open to you to make the money available to Cromie when he wants it. He will advise you as to rate at which he will require the money. He may be able to help you in overcoming obstacles on part of bank officials. If you have any difficulty in satisfying Cromie's needs in full, advise us immediately.[46]

Lockhart was instructed to do anything in his power to assist Woodhouse in this, and was specifically told that it was much more important than the transfer of funds to Moscow.[47] Lockhart proceeded to issue promissory notes to wealthy Russians in exchange for ready money. Promises redeemable in Britain were worth more than roubles at this time of great uncertainty.

When Cromie and Lockhart met Trotsky to discuss the issue of the Russian Fleets on 15 May, they were assured that arrangements had been made and men detailed for the destruction of the ships should there be any threat from the Germans. Cromie was not convinced:

> Just returned from a flying visit to Moscow *re* official schemes of destruction and transfer of transports. The former is very fine on paper, but has little or no prospect of developing unless crews are compensated, and is even then doubtful, owing to present large number of parties in the Fleet.[48]

However, in the event Cromie's misgivings proved unfounded. Indeed, Trotsky had also confirmed that the Black Sea Fleet had escaped from Sevastopol to Novorossisk, except for a few vessels that had been scuttled. Trotsky had given categorical orders to destroy the fleet there rather than let it fall into German hands, and this is precisely what happened when the Germans approached Novorossisk later in June.

As for the Baltic Fleet, it became less a question of keeping it out of German hands, than of destroying it to assist Allied intervention. Lockhart made this clear in a telegram to the Foreign Office:

> It is becoming increasingly clear that with the change in (?Germany's) policy towards the Bolsheviks (group undecypherable) the (groups undecypherable) intervention will be extremely problematical. The most we shall be able to achieve will be that their opposition to it will not be serious. In view of these considerations the question of destruction of Baltic fleet with aid of Bolsheviks becomes equally improbable. If however, we are to intervene without Bolsheviks as now seems probable, it will be absolutely necessary for us to destroy Baltic fleet. I have had several conversations with Captain Cromie on this subject. As you are aware, he has made arrangements of his own towards this object. He does not think, however, they will hold good very long. It is therefore extremely important that intervention itself should be hurried on as quickly as possible and that destruction of fleet should take place almost simultaneously with our intervention.[49]

The clandestine measures taken by the Allies in Russia had exerted a significant effect on German policy, pressuring the Germans into being more accommodating towards the Bolsheviks. This in turn made the chances of the Bolsheviks renewing hostilities against the Germans more unlikely, so the pressure for direct Allied military intervention grew. The focus of Allied clandestine activities now turned decisively. Broadly speaking their previous endeavours had ultimately been directed against the Germans; any consequences for the Bolsheviks and Russia as a whole were not regarded as central to them. Now they assumed a new direction. The Bolsheviks were to be regarded as enemies as much as the Germans, and their consent to Allied military intervention was seen as, at best, irrelevant. It was what many in the political elites of Paris and London had always desired.

VIII

The Horns of a Dilemma

June 1918

━◖◗━

The beginning of June saw a major development in the management of the Intelligence intervention in Russia, with the dissolution of MIO. The official history of the Directorate of Military Intelligence states that this was because, 'The experiment of combining intelligence and operations work in one section was not a complete success.' There is truth in this, for MIO's activities had not realized the goals that had been set for it. However, it is not the whole truth: now military intervention had been decided upon MIO was effectively surplus to requirements, since Intelligence was to adopt a more conventional role, that of supporting the military intervention. The operations side of its work was transferred back to the Director of Military Operations and a new section, MO5, was formed under Lieutenant-Colonel Steel to handle it. The Intelligence work returned to MI2 and another new section, MI 2(d) under Major Kisch was created to deal with that.

The sheer scale of the work in the coming months meant that MI2 was soon overwhelmed. Its small staff was struggling with Intelligence concerning twenty countries spread over four continents. As a result a further reorganization was carried out and another section called MIR was formed under Kisch, who was promoted to temporary Lieutenant-Colonel to match his new responsibilities. MIR was responsible for Russia, the Caucasus, Central Asia, Persia, the Far East and for liaison with the General Staff of the Indian Army.

A section of the Directorate of Military Operations, MO3 under Lieutenant-Colonel the Duke of Northumberland, was charged with the consideration of special operation questions in conjunction with the Director of Military Intelligence.

There was one other weapon the Allies were using in their clandestine war in Russia, which has not attracted significant attention, probably because of the shortage of reliable sources. Throughout the war the British Admiralty's Room 40 had scored a series of notable triumphs in breaking German codes, enabling them to read German naval and diplomatic traffic. The most spectacular example was the decoding of the telegram from State Secretary Arthur Zimmermann to the German Ambassador in Mexico, proposing an alliance between Germany, Mexico and Japan against the United States whereby Mexico was to regain much of the territory it had lost to the United States during the nineteenth century. The telegram was instrumental in persuading the reluctant President Wilson to go to war against Germany.

These skills were now to be turned against the Bolsheviks, or so we may judge from the message sent to Smith Cumming at the beginning of June:

> Following for 'C' from MacLaren.
> There is a possibility of obtaining copies of direct wires from Petrograd to Berlin as sent you before. Have you any use for these, if not please instruct Petrograd. Meanwhile have told Petrograd to carry on.[1]

There is no trace of any reply to MacLaren's question. However, there can be no doubt at all that the British were reading Bolshevik coded messages. Whether this was because the skilled operators of Room 40 had already broken the codes, or whether it was the result of the work of Cromie and MacLaren it is impossible to say. The evidence would appear to have been destroyed.

The Bolsheviks' codes were simple compared to those used by the Great Powers, since they hesitated to use the advanced ones that had been developed under the Tsar. Their problems were also compounded by the defection of some of Russia's leading cryptographers, and it took until 1920 for the Soviet Government to realize their weakness in this respect. On 21 August 1920, Chicherin wrote to Lenin, explaining that he had always regarded Soviet codes with scepticism. As an alternative he recommended using special couriers to carry the most secret reports. Lenin, replying the same day, proposed altering the key to the cipher daily and changing the system or its details frequently.[2] The Soviet Government changed its codes after this, though the British soon broke the new ones.

MacLaren was a Lieutenant in the Royal Navy and the deputy to Moscow's MI1(c) head of station, Commander Ernest Boyce. By the end of June his activities had become so obvious that they had attracted the attention of the Cheka. Wanted by the Bolsheviks, it was useless for him to remain in Moscow or Petrograd, so 'C' advised Colonel Thornhill, General Poole's head of Intelligence, that he should remain in Archangel or Murmansk and organize Secret Service there.[3] That was what happened.

The hollowness of the accusations levelled against the Bolsheviks that they were German agents was underlined by the proposals made for the scuttling of the Russian Black Sea Fleet on 8 June. Trotsky suggested to Lockhart and Cromie that Royal Navy officers could take control of the Fleet and, if necessary, sink it. How enough officers were to get to Novorossisk that quickly was never considered; it proved to be quite impossible. The Bolsheviks duly ordered the Fleet to return to Sevastopol, but Trotsky had secretly arranged for its vessels to be scuttled and the Russian crews duly performed this task.

The Allies were not acting alone in what was now an attempt to subvert the Bolshevik regime. Soon after the Bolshevik Revolution, the British Government confiscated the funds of the Russian Embassy in London and withdrew the privilege of its corresponding in cipher with other Russian institutions abroad.[4] It was represented by the Chargé d'Affaires, Constantine Nabokoff, who had served both the Tsar and the Provisional Government in that capacity. On his return from Russia, Lockhart met Nabokoff and recorded this rather patronizing impression, though it is important to remember that by this time Nabokoff was a justifiably bitter and frustrated man:

> Nabokoff was not very impressive. He is not very clever and complains bitterly of the way we have treated him. Poor little man! He looks so pathetic and so like the part of the man who is made to be badly treated. Said he had rendered the Allies one service by persuading Lloyd George to abandon idea of Stockholm Conference![5]

A lot depended on Nabokoff. According to his own memoirs, he maintained close relations with the British Government, chiefly through George Clerk, and he also cooperated with the Admiralty, War Office and the Foreign

Office. The British were, however, soon providing the funding for the Russian Embassy. They were to do so until 31 May 1919. According to Nabokoff, the sum lent by the British to the Embassy amounted to 'about £190,000'.[6] Despite these links the available papers reveal only a small portion of the tip of the iceberg.

The British Government had formed the Russia Committee to study the Russian problem in greater detail than could the War Cabinet. Lord Robert Cecil chaired the Committee. Later in the year it was to discuss Nabokoff's position:

> Mr Gregory raised the question of M. Nabakoff's position at the Russian Embassy, pointing out that M. Nabokoff had been doing very useful work in co-ordinating the efforts of the various Russian 'Governments' with whom touch had been established. Mr Gregory suggested the desirability of increasing M. Nabokoff's facilities for the dispatch of information to such 'Governments', and of allowing him the use of a cypher for this purpose.
>
> Mr Dudley Ward pointed out that the proposal would involve increasing the funds placed at M. Nabokoff's disposal, but recognised the advantages to be derived from such course.
>
> The D.M.I. mentioned that the War Office had found M. Nabokoff sympathetic and helpful on such occasions as he had been approached in connection with military questions.[7]

The Committee decided that Nabokoff should be allowed to communicate in cipher with his colleagues abroad, and that Gregory was to consult him and prepare a scheme for increasing his staff, while the Treasury was to be consulted about improving the financial position of the Russian Embassy. Nabokoff used the facility as the Russia Committee and Naval Intelligence desired. The Russian Ambassadors in Paris, Peking and Tokyo were the main focus of his activities.

William Dudley Ward was a Conservative MP who was listed in the *Navy List* as a Lieutenant-Commander in the Naval Intelligence Division (HMS *President*) from 31 May 1917.

The British Intelligence services were using Nabokoff and the Embassy staff in London to coordinate the actions of the different White organizations and governments and this is manifest in the message that Admiral

Hall, the Director of Naval Intelligence, sent to Rear Admiral Kemp at Murmansk:

Following for Wassilieff.

O.K. Embassy is in open direct communication with Vladivostok, and with Horwatt [sic Horvath] through Pekin.

Both claim to represent whole Siberia.

In accordance with Allied policy Nabokoff has informed Vladivostok and Horwatt [sic Horvath] that co-ordination between local Siberian Governments is essential for progress [and] Allied assistance.

Vladivostok Government unreliable.

Allies will not recognise any one Government to the exclusion of others.

It is important to establish direct communication with Alexeyev in order to definitely ascertain his whereabouts and to enable Embassy to remain in touch with him Alexeyev's activities being most valuable in view of information contained in your last message.[8]

This mutual support went far deeper than the political plane. The telegram addressed to Wassilieff and prefixed O.K. reveals clandestine collaboration that went back to the end of 1917. 'Boris Wassilieff', who was really Commander Bezkrowny of the Russian Navy, was the main agent of a spy ring that was the child of the Russian Naval Attaché in London and run by one of his officers, Commander Okerlund. It was from the latter's name that the identification 'OK' was taken for the system. Okerlund was a Finn serving in the Russian Navy. He had been a member of the Russian Naval Mission to the British Admiralty, where he became well known to Admiral Hall. He was, apparently, 'a faithful friend' of the British Naval Attaché, Captain Francis Cromie.[9] The circumstantial evidence makes it highly probable that Cromie and Okerlund were working together.

Using the diaries of 'C', Alan Judd points out that on 8 December 1917 Smith-Cumming went 'to Hall's office to meet Admiral Volkov and Lieutenant Okerhand [probable] of the Russian service.'[10] Volkov, the Russian Naval Attaché, and Commander Okerlund – presumably 'C's handwriting wrong-footed Judd – offered the British their ring which, they claimed, was worth the £15,000 a month that it cost. The advantages of a

Secret Intelligence Service in Russia that was staffed by Russians, run by Russians, and immediately responsible to Russians is obvious.

The outcome of the negotiations is clear. The official Secret Service did not get this plum, but Admiral Hall and Naval Intelligence did. The available evidence suggests that it provided sterling service from June 1918 into early 1919. Volkov was responsible to Nabokoff, and the latter's direct involvement is made transparent by the following 'Personal' telegram from Admiral Hall:

> Following for Wassilieff from Nabokoff:
> O.K. Begins. Please convey to General Poole my sincere appreciation of his letter delivered by Kassianoff. Inform him that in my endeavours to collect Russian officers I encounter many difficulties. I am doing my very best and I know that hundreds of officers would be available on the continent were it not for technical obstacles which may still be overcome when Allied Governments realise more clearly that it is imperative to establish cooperation with Russians in authority in Allied countries on a proper basis. I am in direct touch with the War Office on the question of recruiting officers, and hope to achieve much if the British military chiefs will lend me a helping hand.[11]

Nabokoff twice mentioned Russian officers. The recruitment of Russian officers worked in two main respects. The first was their use in Intelligence. Admiral Hall sent a message to his Liaison Officer in Paris, Commodore Heaton-Ellis, asking him 'Please convey following message to Lieutenant Hesse c/o Russian Naval (begins) 'Following from ABAZA, your presence here urgently required for a few days keep your journey secret and come direct to Russian Embassy before seeing anyone.'[12]

Alexander Alexeyevich Abaza was one of Volkov's staff. He was the son of Vice Admiral Alexei Mikhailovich Abaza. In recent years he has gained notoriety as the officer who handed the White investigator Nikolai Sokolov the deciphered version of the infamous telegram allegedly written by Beloborodov that purported to show that the imprisoned Imperial family had been murdered. Abaza did not decipher the telegram, but acted as the link between the White Russians and British Intelligence. Sokolov described the man to whom he gave the coded telegram as, 'a Russian whom I had known long since to be particularly competent. Before the revolution he had worked in the government code department for many years.' This description could only apply to Fetterlein, the Russian code expert who had defected to the British in March 1918. Sokolov's reticence about who really decoded the telegram was an attempt to conceal the close links between the British and the White Russians, so avoiding embarrassing questions about why the British sought to disguise their involvement, one that would raise serious questions about the authenticity of the telegram had it been known.

The extent of the collaboration between the British and the Russian Embassy in Intelligence is further emphasized by another telegram from Admiral Hall to Rear Admiral Kemp at Murmansk: 'Lieutenant White RNVR on his way to report to you. He is a Russian Naval Officer, gallant fellow and prepared for any job you may give him. You can trust him.'[13] 'Lieutenant White' was in reality Lieutenant Commander Dmitri Nikolaevich Fedotov of the Russian Navy. He had joined the Royal Naval Volunteer Reserve in the winter of 1917/18. The precise purpose of his mission to north Russia remains unknown, but since he was operating with Admiral Hall, it is reasonable to conclude that it was not unconnected with Intelligence.

The other respect in which Russian officers were used was in an attempt to form a unit of Russian volunteers to serve as an embryo for the anti-Bolshevik Russian army that the Allies hoped to raise in north Russia. That much is clear from a telegram sent by Wassilieff to Hall early in June, two days after he had reached Murmansk on 6 June:

> Wassilieff wishes following transmitted to Weyman, Christiania [Oslo]. Begins – Russian Volunteers are required here for special units being formed for purpose of fighting Germans and Finnish White Guard now invading Russian Territory. These units would be attached to British E force operating in vicinity Pechenga. Conditions of enlistment are following. Officers N.C.O.s and men will be taken if of good health not over 40 years of age and ready to fight. They will all first join as troopers and be submitted to Military Law as per British Army Regulations 482 they must understand discipline is strict and that no politics will be tolerated. Arms, clothing, rations, and payment will be on British Army lines.[14]

All the officers who would accept the above terms were to report to the British Consul at Kirkenes, a Norwegian town on the Russo-Norwegian border to the immediate west of Murmansk. He had been instructed to give all necessary assistance to them. It was left to Rear Admiral Kemp to organize recruiting on similar lines in neutral Sweden and Denmark, with the caution that it was necessary that nothing about the movement should become public and all concerned were enjoined to work with the utmost secrecy.

It looked, as did so many of these ideas at the time, to be a perfectly sound project in theory. However, the difficulties of getting a sufficient number of officers to north Russia on the one hand, together with the general lack of fighting spirit among Russians by that time, crippled the plan from the outset. What all this does show is that the British, and particularly their Intelligence services, were actively preparing for armed intervention from May 1918, even though American support for the venture remained lacking.

The British Government and the whole interventionist policy were nearly thrown into disarray at the beginning of June by the resignation of Lord Robert Cecil over what he saw as the lack of progress towards intervention.

Lloyd George, in his reply, put his finger on the key problem: 'President Wilson in spite of continuous pressure from all the Allies, had refused to assent to the proposal, and that consequently nothing had been done up to the present.'[15] This lay at the heart of the reasoning behind the clandestine intrigues the British and French adopted. With the war in its fourth year, both countries lacked the manpower to embark on a military intervention. While the United States stood aloof, these intrigues were really the only answer they had to the problem of the disappearing Eastern front.

The Allies had won over most of the parties in Russia that opposed the Bolsheviks. One group still lay outside their grasp and that was the Monarchists. The more extreme Monarchists were the only party in Russia that favoured German intervention — that way they saw the Russian autocracy restored together with the positions and prestige they held under the Tsar. However, they were a minority who could not hope for power without the help of foreign bayonets.

Germany's long-running flirtation with the Monarchists owed much to both the original concept of their plan for a *Mitteleuropa*, a huge Central European constitutional-monarchic bloc under German leadership, and the nature and proclivities of the ruling elite: the Kings, Grand Dukes and Princes of the German Empire, backed by one of the staunchest upholders of the principle of monarchy – the Kaiser.[16] Thus it was that plans were laid for the Duke of Urach to be consecrated King of Lithuania, and Prince Friedrich Karl of Hesse to become King of Finland, while the Archduke Karl Stephan of Austria-Hungary was a serious contender for the throne of the intended puppet kingdom of Poland.[17]

Most of the more extreme Monarchists had rallied in Kiev, capital of the German puppet state of the Ukraine, where the Germans had installed a former Tsarist General, Skoropadsky who had, perhaps fittingly, been elected as the state's titular head in a circus ring. This clique intrigued for a restoration of the monarchy, sometimes with the backing of the Germans, and sometimes without. In this respect everything depended on how strong relations between the Bolsheviks and the Germans were, which in turn depended on German perceptions of how long the Bolsheviks were likely to survive.

These intrigues went on through the spring and into the summer of 1918. The numerical and military weakness of the Monarchists proved to be their undoing. In August Admiral Hintze, the new German State Secretary for Foreign Affairs who was not opposed to the Monarchists in principle, recognized that their weakness was such that they would require large-scale German military support: 'People have talked to me of the Monarchists as possible vehicles of a counter-revolution; they are officers without an Army, the Kadets do not go out into the street...'[18]

There is no doubt that the British were aware of these intrigues, if not their ultimate outcome. Captain Cromie's deputy, Engineer Commander George Wilfred Le Page, sent home a report on them that received wide circulation. It is worth quoting in full:

> Following information received from Staff of Ludendorff. German General Staff consider in a month their attack on Western Front will render Allied Armies incapable of taking the offensive for some considerable time. They then propose

152

to turn to Russia break Brest peace and declare a Monarchy. This has not yet been finally agreed to by Reichstag Party. Conditions will be more favourable than Brest Peace Conference, return of all territory to Russia even Ukraine, Estonia, ?Finland, Courland to be autonomous under either German or Russian Suzerainity [sic suzerainty], ?but German culture of Baltic States to have full sway. Finland to be independent under Russian ?protection. Economic conditions will be onerous but less so than at present.

Candidate for Throne is Grand Duke Michael and a high German Agent has already been sent to Perm to open negotiations but Grand Duke has temporarily disappeared.

My informant a high Russian Officer whose name must remain secret a personal friend and in whom I have complete confidence has lately travelled much and has been much in contact with peasants, says until further famine is threatened, the crisis will be in July and it is then ?Germans will declare Monarchy, in August new harvest will be available and all this will be put down to new Monarchy regime.

He considers Monarchy only means of saving situation and in view of German purpose it would seem such is the case and that it would be to Allies advantage to forestall Germans.

A Dictatorship is not possible, there are three candidates Generals Alexeyev and Boldereff and Admiral Kolchak neither of whom would be a success in my opinion in that position. He gives Allies one month to arrive at decision and that it is most urgent to start operations in East (so often put forward by Allies Representatives now in Russia) and form a ?front on ?Volga ?taking advantage of present Czechs ?Slav movement, if possible get ex Emperor and ? principal other members of Imperial Family into our hands not ?allow them to be exploited by any political party.

Central Russia would then rally round our standard but anything other than a Monarchy would drive all capital and landowners over to German side and these would be followed by intelligent classes who at present, in feeling, are anti German, also it would split up Right Centre drive one section to extreme Right and other to extreme Left.

I venture to suggest this proposition in view of new German plan to be taken into very serious consideration.

In Ukraine there are 200,000 Officers of whom 150,000 will at once join up only in support of Monarchy, he himself is not a monarchist but he views the situation such that a Monarchy is the only way out especially as regards difficulties of position.

Grand Duke M. is most popular candidate but it is also certain no member [of the] Romanoff Family ?could accept throne unless requested by representatives of majority.

Present German activities are merely side play of main objective.[19]

'Grand Duke M' was Michael Alexandrovich, the younger brother of Nicholas II who had been made the heir to the Russian throne in the latter's Instrument of Abdication. He had held the throne for one day, before abdicating in the face of the hostility of the Muscovites and the absence of any guarantees for his personal safety. He had lived under house arrest at Perm and disappeared from his hotel room there on the night of 12/13 June 1918. The official version of his fate – that the Bolsheviks murdered him – rests on the wholly unreliable account given by Nikolai Sokolov, the man chosen by the White Russians to investigate the fate of the Romanovs. However, there is a powerful body of evidence from German, British and Swedish sources that indicates he was rescued from Perm.[20]

The stakes had been raised when Noulens, the French Ambassador, promised the Monarchists French support. The Germans were suitably alarmed:

We have to acquire contacts with the right-wing monarchist groups and influence them so that the monarchist movement would be governed by our wishes as soon as it gained influence. The Entente has also recognised the importance of this movement. According to reliable information the Entente has already promised its support to the Monarchists through Minister Noulens at a meeting of conservative elements, and proposed the introduction of a constitutional monarchy. The proposal was acknowledged politely but so far has not been answered.[21]

The implications of the promised support for the Monarchists from the French Ambassador are thrown into sharp relief when we read a telegram from Armin von Reyher, one of the staff at the German Consulate-General in Petrograd. It was sent to Prince Henry of Prussia, the Kaiser's brother, who had been given personal responsibility for the Romanov case. It stated:

I have learnt that His Imperial Highness was in Perm almost one month ago and held under close arrest at first and then with the permission he held he moved into an hotel with his secretary, where His Imperial Highness proved to have much sympathy on the part of the people... I have learnt from a trustworthy source that the Grand Duke has been brought by ship to Rybinsk (a town on the Upper Volga), which was certainly a result of the struggle with the English and French subsidised Czechoslovakians, that stands under the supreme command of the French Major Comte de Lubersac.[22]

Major Comte de Lubersac was the heir of the Marquis de Lubersac who was to be made responsible for the restoration of the devastated lands of the Western front after the war. The Major had been a member of the French Military Mission on the Eastern front and was now serving with Commandant Guinet and the Czechoslovaks in Siberia. Thus far the picture makes perfect sense. If the French wanted to gain the support of the Monarchists, they had to be able to offer them something in return. The rescue of the Grand Duke would have been a powerful inducement. It also caused increased concern among the Germans, who had toyed with the idea of backing Monarchist plans to place the Grand Duke on the Russian throne.

The British were equally obliged to offer the Monarchists something in return for their alliance, and it is clear that there were plans to rescue the Imperial family from Ekaterinburg. Cromie sent a message from Petrograd that establishes the intention beyond reasonable doubt:

> Following received via Christiania from Naval Attaché Petrograd for S.N.O. [Senior Naval Officer] Murmansk begins:
> I have received from Mr. Browd on behalf of the Murmansk Scientific Industrial Coy. the offer of the building to be erected on the Dived Companys land near the British Consulate Murmansk formerly intended for the late Czar and now offered for occupation by General Poole or Admiral Kemp. Buildings complete with heating Light utensils etc. and now in charge of Kambulin Engineer erecting them.[23]

The house was purpose-built by the Hudson's Bay Company to shelter the Tsar and his family. The prime mover within the company appears to have been Henry Armitstead, a descendant of a former Mayor of Riga. The message carries the unavoidable implication that there had been a plan to rescue the family and bring them to north Russia where they would be under British influence. However, that particular plan came to naught, or so we may deduce both from the reference to 'the late Czar' and the non-appearance of the family to take up their intended abode. On 28 August the

155

Admiralty informed Sir Mansfeldt Findlay, the British Minister at Christiania, that the offer of the house could be accepted.

Contrary to the beliefs of many aficionados of the Romanov case, the motive behind these manoeuvres can be seen to be a cynical political ploy to win over the Monarchists rather than any fellow feeling George V might have felt for his relative.

Whatever the realities on the ground, both the Allies and the Germans were frightening themselves with their respective Intelligence reports. Mirbach, having agreed with Kuhlmann that it was necessary to support the Bolsheviks in May, advised him on 25 June that the time had come to look elsewhere to fulfil Germany's ambitions:

> After two months' careful observation, I can now no longer give Bolshevism a favourable diagnosis. We are unquestionably standing by the bedside of a danger-ously ill man, who might show apparent improvement from time to time, but who is lost in the long run.
>
> Quite apart from the fact that Bolshevism would definitely soon, of its own accord, fall a victim to the process of internal disintegration which is devouring it, there are all too many elements working tirelessly to hurry its end as much as possible and to settle the succession favourably to their own designs.
>
> One day we might therefore be faced with what for us would be the most undesirable state of affairs possible, i.e. Social Revolutionaries, financed by the Entente and equipped with Czechoslovak arms, quite openly leading a new Russia back into the ranks of our enemies. Of course this is not so terrible from a military point of view, but politically and economically it could not possibly be less desirable.[24]

He stated that the Monarchists were too 'confused and too lazy' to be worth recommending. Yet the Intelligence reports of the enemy's activities fed fears in both the Allied and German headquarters. This lent the Monarchists a far greater weight than their actual strength entitled them to. Whether they were serious contenders for power or not, the British, French and Germans embarked on a struggle to woo them, their suits fuelled by their mutual fears.

It is worth emphasizing this point, as the contest for influence in Russia between the Allies and the Germans was central to the dynamic of the unfolding events. Fear of a German coup early in June was real. Lockhart bears witness to this:

There is no doubt that they [the Germans, under Mirbach] are also carrying on active propaganda among various officer organisations here and are spending money with great freedom. Further, refusal of Allies to take any decisive action or to spend any money for counter-revolutionary purposes is causing number of our supporters to decrease from day-to-day.

From various sources and also (gr. undec.) (? of) German attempts to buy over Lettish regiments which are main strength of Bolsheviks. It is said that these efforts have met with some success.

Two points seem to me especially clear. Power of Bolsheviks is decreasing rapidly and, two, danger of pro-German counter-revolution is now imminent.

In the circumstances it is obvious whether we like it or not we shall be forced to intervene sooner or later. Surely America must realise that if we intervene after a pro-German counter-revolution we shall find ourselves at a serious disadvantage and that from every point of view we have far better reason or excuse for intervening now when the country is in a state of anarchy and when majority of Russian people is crying for intervention of any kind.[25]

Lockhart need not have worried, for General Poole returned to Russia in June to lead the intervention. He was accompanied by two Secret Service officers, Major John Scale and Captain W.M.A. McGrath, and had been welcomed by those who rested their hopes in the Allies. His visa was granted by Maxim Litvinov, the Bolsheviks' representative in London (who had been denied official recognition by the British Government), on the pretext that he was going to Russia to work for the Red Cross. Colonel Keyes had also returned to north Russia. So had a new British diplomatic representative. This was Francis Lindley, the former Counsellor with the British Embassy at Petrograd. Lockhart greeted Lindley's return without enthusiasm, recording in his diary, 'Hear Lindley is coming out again. Wonders will never cease. I cannot possibly imagine any worse appointment than this.'[26] Lindley had been appointed High Commissioner and his real duties were to coordinate and handle the diplomatic side of the military intervention.

The Allies had been alarmed when Miliukov, the former Foreign Minister of the Provisional Government, had joined the German camp at Kiev. Among other as yet uncommitted groups was the Right Centre, also known as the Moscow Centre, a temporary combination of Monarchists, Cadets and disparate conservative fragments. Among its leaders was Alexander

Krivoshein, the head of one of the more powerful Monarchist factions. He leaned towards the Germans and was known to have used intermediaries to approach Kurt Riezler, Counsellor at the German Embassy. He claimed his faction had the means and will to overthrow the Bolsheviks, but still needed German support. His price for doing this was a substantial revision of the Treaty of Brest-Litovsk. There was a real fear that the faction led by Krivoshein would follow the path trodden by Miliukov. It seems that the British diplomats were panicked by the prospect and Lindley sent Keyes to try and dissuade him from turning to the Germans.

In Keyes' own words:

> Anyhow, though it was the end of June the ice had not yet broken up, so he sent me on from Murman to try to get through to Petrograd and Moscow by Lake Onega, and, if possible to interview certain people in connection with the financial scheme and try to get the Monarchist party onto the right lines again. I had the most adventurous journey…Krivoshein, when I convinced him that the Allies were really going to do something, undertook to sit on the fence a little longer, and come down on our side if we really played up.[27]

Krivoshein had been one of the backers of the original Banking Scheme. Keyes was now to try to resurrect it in the hope that it could be used to finance the broader White movement and particularly the Volunteer Army in the south. Many of the officers who had been sent south to join the Volunteer Army were Monarchists or had been directed southwards by monarchist organizations.

While the Germans recognized that the extreme Monarchists were the only faction even remotely favourable to them, the Allies sought to unite all shades of Russian opinion against both the Germans and the Bolsheviks. German fear of losing their only alternative to the Bolsheviks and Allied fear that Russians other than the Bolsheviks might collaborate with the Germans threw fuel on what was in reality a very small fire.

The Germans were caught on the horns of a dilemma. Unless they were to abrogate the dictated peace of Brest-Litovsk, they were forced to rely on the Bolsheviks as the only party that would, however unwillingly, accept it. For this they sacrificed the potential for friendship with all other parties, except the extreme Monarchists, in Russia. The Allies faced a different kind of problem. They had decided upon intervention, but they sought to unite all the opposition parties in Russia into an anti-German and anti-Bolshevik crusade. The latter became increasingly necessary since the Bolsheviks were the real targets of the wrath of the opposition parties rather than the Germans.

There was another potentially formidable foe waiting in the wings that had not yet declared itself: the Russian Orthodox Church. The Bolsheviks could not legitimately complain about any antagonism they received from that quarter, for in their revolutionary enthusiasm they had occupied the Alexander Nevski Monastery early in February. The response from the Church was one that the Bolsheviks probably felt they could safely ignore at the time: the Metropolitan proceeded to excommunicate the whole party.

In June Sydney Reilly was negotiating with the Church with a view to using its still considerable influence on the Allies' behalf. He considered:

> That the Church must play the greatest part in a regeneration of Russia is self-evident. She is the one fundamental moral factor in Russian life which can be temporarily obscured, but which neither Bolshevism nor the Germans can destroy. To range this factor on our side would be an act of the most farseeing statesmanship and, in the long run, would be infinitely more worth to us than many Russian Army Corps.
>
> The purely practical difficulties in rendering the asked for assistance to the Church could, I am sure, be overcome. This matter should be transacted with the utmost secrecy, in Russia it would be known only to the Patriarch and to two or three of his most trusted advisers.
>
> The matter is urgent and it is desirable that it should be brought as soon as possible, to the attention of the Government.[28]

He spoke to N.O. Kuznetsov, the legal adviser and right-hand man of the Patriarch who was responsible for acting as the official intermediary between the Patriarch and the Bolsheviks. Reilly's report demonstrates the way the Allies hoped to wield this influence:

> He confirms the views which one hears on every (? side) that there is a considerable revival of religious feeling all over the country; that a 'renaissance' of the

Church is at hand, and that the Church will play the major and political [role in the] salvation of Russia.

He says that the Bolsheviks, notwithstanding all their bluster, fear the Church and its influence, and are now ready to revise favourably many propositions in their decrees regarding it.

They have had lately to drop an attempted accusation against the Patriarch for spreading in his address counter-revolutionary (? doctrines) on being told that 100,000 people will want to accompany him to the tribunal and that half a million will be there to follow him to prison, if he is convicted.

Kuznetsov dropped a hint that if the Church had money now, it could send 10,000 religious agitators into the country, and flood it with religious literature.

Kuznetsov is affecting [sic] to decide in favour of armed intervention on the part of the Allies. He thinks that only an (Allied) force could become the rallying point for the formation of a Russian Army.[29]

As Macdonogh saw it, the Church was the only element in Russian society that retained any real national feeling. He accordingly advocated that every effort should be made to ensure that its alleged renaissance should be identified with the Allied cause. Given the mass support that the Church was considered to command, its support for any Allied intervention had the potential to be highly influential and perhaps decisive.

With so many enemies gathering about them having been given life by Allied or German support, the Bolsheviks foresaw their doom. Numerous telegrams from both Lockhart and Mirbach informed their respective governments that the Bolshevik grip on power was failing. Both the Allies and the Germans were making ready to step in and promote their protégés when the expected fall came. The Bolsheviks realized this, for Lockhart reported: 'I am informed by two high officials in Bolshevik Government, whose names I do not mention for reasons of safety, that the Bolsheviks understand that their reign is coming to an end.'[30] From his conversations with these officials, Lockhart understood that the Bolsheviks realized that both German and Allied intervention was inevitable. The Germans were already concentrating troops at Smolensk and Orsha and a German-backed counter-revolution was 'quite close at hand'. The Bolsheviks had begun planning for a secret organization in case of a German occupation.

If the Bolsheviks needed any reminder of their precarious position, it came in the form of the assassination of their Commissar for Press, Agitation and Propaganda, Volodarsky, in Petrograd on 20 June. His murderer was Serge'ev, a Right Social Revolutionary, and Uritsky, the head of the Petrograd Cheka, made a bitter speech in which he accused the British of being behind the murder.

Meanwhile in Petrograd, the Consul General, Mr Arthur Woodhouse, reported the landing of General Poole at Murmansk. He went on to advocate intervention from both Siberia and north Russia. He added more fuel to the fire of fear when he continued, 'In present circumstances and if made quickly and participated in by European Allies, such move should have great chance of success. If we delay and Germans are to restore order and proclaim monarchy we shall once more be too late.'[31]

The momentum was clearly building up, but there was one British official in Russia who kept a clear head and saw matters in perspective. This was Douglas Young, the British Consul at Archangel, the port that was to be the centre of the military intervention in the north. On 7 June he sent a telegram marked 'Urgent' to London. It read:

Rumours of active Allied intervention at Archangel in the near future are current here and such a policy seems to be in high favour with newly arrived French Consul and Military mission.

In view of formal assurance given by Allied representatives at Murmansk and repeated here by me with your sanction and as such indications of your policy as have reached me all point to the contrary, I have hitherto discredited these rumours.

I have now received from General Poole at Murmansk request to find accommodation at Archangel for 600 officers and other British ratings, and impression that active measures are contemplated is otherwise confirmed.

Being completely in the dark as to nature and extent of operations contemplated and of advantages which His Majesty's Government hope to derive from them I cannot express a fair opinion even as to their probable local effect. In absence of such data I would however like to record my conviction that any premature military operations carried out without consent of the de facto local authorities will be attended with grave risks and without bringing any great permanent advantage will even if successful locally commit His Majesty's Government to ever increasing obligations from which they will be unable to free themselves without discredit and loss of prestige.

THE HORNS OF A DILEMMA

The most which I have ever contemplated or advocated is presence of Allied cruisers as passive force in the first instance in order to give local influence favourable to us an opportunity of declaring themselves. [32]

Apart from the prescience of Young's view, four significant facts are disclosed here. The first is that rumours abounded that the Allies were going to intervene in north Russia, which effectively meant that any chance of surprise had been lost. The second is that intervention had already been decided upon before Poole arrived in Murmansk, and that the seizure of Archangel was going to be the first step. Thirdly, in the best traditions of the British Government, the men on the spot seem to have been the only ones who were kept in ignorance about what was planned. Finally, it is abundantly clear that a solemn official promise had been given to the local Soviet that the Allies had no designs on the territory of north Russia. This raises serious questions about the veracity of official communications.

The men on the spot, who might have given sound advice, were not being consulted and this had left a vacuum that was filled by interventionists such as Cecil, Knox and Proctor. Their efforts were complemented by the advice received from the Chief of the Imperial General Staff and the Director of Military Intelligence, who were both dependent on the information they received from their Intelligence agencies. Among the latter must be numbered MIO, whose brief inevitably coloured its reports.

Young was not alone in being kept in the dark. Lockhart had been ordered to work towards Allied intervention, but was apparently kept in ignorance of its location, timing and strength. London seemed to prefer to rely on officers from the Secret Service and MIO to establish the links and lay the plans for combined action. This, as we have seen, meant that the intention to intervene could honestly be denied by British officials. Lockhart found himself left in mid-air, lamenting:

Our position here is now extremely disagreeable and humiliating. The other parties are demanding help and above all for instructions and advice regarding a common plan of action. We are not allowed to give them money and we are not in a position to give them any information beyond the vaguest assurances. Any day now may see the crisis arrive and if we are not to make a sorry mess of the whole affair we must be prepared to act immediately. [33]

Young's telegram was too late to change the events that were now afoot, even had there been any will to do so. On 23 June, the first of General Poole's forces landed at Murmansk. This was 'Syren' Force, which had originally been called 'Develop'. In common with Dunsterforce, on which it was modelled, it was composed of senior officers and experienced non-commissioned officers, whose task it was to train the masses of men from the anti-Bolshevik parties that the Allies expected to flock to Murmansk.

The expedition had been shrouded in the deepest secrecy; nobody below the rank of colonel had any idea of their destination before their ship sailed. There may well have been a hidden agenda behind the expedition, an agenda that has not been discussed in any of the British files so far released. We have noted, too, how General Poole's private papers covering this part of his service have disappeared. It has the appearance of a calculated attempt to stifle the real motive for intervention in Russia. There is one clue that more might have lain behind the expedition. It comes from the testimony of one of the few junior officers in the expedition. Lieutenant E.J. Furlong was one of the Flying Officers in 'Syren' who were to fly the DH4 aeroplanes that were the aerial component of the expedition. When asked to what extent the veil of secrecy was lifted once they were at sea, Furlong replied:

> Well of course then it was open; we were told then once we had got away from the quay – where presumably we could not divulge the information – we were told that we were going to Archangel – no Archangel wasn't mentioned – we were going to Murmansk, North Russia, where we were going to 'take over' whatever that meant and we were told that we were going to train Russians who were not in the Bolshevik outfit who were assembling round about Murmansk, and they were going to make up an expeditionary force largely of Russian personnel which we would train.[34]

While this is not sufficient by itself to support the view that the British Government and military were intending to 'take over' when they intervened in Russia, the context of the whole plan suggests there might be truth in it. There were factors in play that demonstrate that the restoration of the Eastern front was a declining influence, while the Allied stores at the ports were a mere pretext.

Shortly after 'Syren' Force's landing at Murmansk, Admiral Hall received one of the first reports that can be traced to Wassilieff of the Okerlund system. He, in turn, had received the information from people outside the organization. It was news of another attempted coup in Petrograd:

Situation Petrograd end of June was as follows: – Party who were secretly preparing a counter-revolution were discovered by Bolsheviks. Head of organisation General Shouiffo took refuge in German Embassy. Bolsheviks only arrested a few people. The above party was composed of elements of both pro-German and pro-ally but a large majority of latter. On being discovered party (? dispersed), and split when news was received of Grand Duke Michels [sic Michael's] proclamation in Siberia and also when allies move at Murmansk became known. Both these events have had a most salutary effect and allies are rapidly gaining ground. All news from districts around Petrograd Pskoff, and generally North Russia seem to indicate that although Soviets are anti-ally, intelligent classes of peasants and social revolutionaries are realising there is a Russian Country and that they must unite to oust Soviets and Germans.[35]

This attempted coup has all the appearance of being timed to coincide with the Allied intervention. In the event the conspiracy was discovered before its participants could strike.

The clandestine operations of the Allies increasingly were becoming clearly aimed at overthrowing the Bolsheviks. They were courting the widest possible range of political elements in Russia to create, it was hoped, a national force that would be powerful enough to crush the Bolsheviks with the aid of limited Allied forces. Their intrigues embraced every anti-Bolshevik party from the Right Social Revolutionaries to the Monarchists and, with these last, they were in direct competition with the Germans. The range of these intrigues bore out the truth of Trotsky's jibe to Lockhart that the British Foreign Office was like a man playing roulette and scattering chips on every number.

On 9 June the small Allied force at Murmansk, 'Syren' Force, began advancing south. There was scant opposition, but fearful of an attack on its flank from Finland, progress was slow. This push was to considerably disturb the Bolsheviks.

By the end of June the British and French Governments might have considered that their plans were destined for a favourable outcome. Most of the significant opposition groups in Russia had been enticed into their corral, while the Monarchists had at least been persuaded to remain neutral. The one flaw, a flaw that was to exert an increasingly malevolent influence as time went on, was that the differing aims of the various parties created such tensions between them that their unity was superficial and rarely lasted very long.

The Allies viewed developments in Russia through a telescope marked 'War' and their efforts were bent towards forming a united anti-German front in Russia. As the Bolsheviks would not go to war against Germany and their overthrow was at the heart of the programmes of the opposition parties, they became just as much the target as the Germans.

There was another difficulty in that Anglo-French policy contained the inevitable implication of using Russians as cannon fodder, whether against the Germans or the Bolsheviks. Apart from a relatively small number of people, the Russians wanted an end to the war. This had been the main motive behind popular support for the Bolsheviks in 1917. The fact was ignored in the Western capitals as was the fact that the opposition parties did not speak for the mass of the Russian people.

IX

Vicissitudes of Assassination
July 1918 (I)

—◀○▶—

The Germans had more immediate difficulties than the apparent imminent collapse of the Bolsheviks and the decline of their position in Russia. Their Embassy received anonymous letters warning that members of the Embassy staff would be killed. Strangers were seen photographing the Embassy building. Men posing as electricians visited the Embassy and inspected the rooms. There was also an informer who claimed that an assassination attempt was being prepared against members of the Embassy staff. This was to be accompanied by a coup against the Soviet regime. The Embassy approached Dzerzhinsky about these new perils and the latter interviewed the informer, Vladimir Ginch, in the presence of an official from the German Embassy. Dzerzhinsky decided, 'the allegations were undoubtedly false and designed to blackmail the Germans and lead the Cheka astray.'[1]

Some act against the Germans might reasonably have been anticipated. Mirbach was advocating Germany turning away from the Bolsheviks and founding her policy in Russia on new allies. The extreme Monarchists were chief contenders for this role. The High Command of the German Army had lost patience with the Bolsheviks and was pressing for their overthrow at German bayonet point. Matters went so far as Ludendorff presenting the Chancellor, Hertling, with a lengthy memorandum on 9 June that advocated precisely that.[2] The Chief of Staff in the East, Max Hoffmann, went so far as to contact representatives of the Tsar's former Government and the Provisional Government.

The Bolsheviks knew more about these activities than the Germans liked – and the Germans knew that the Bolsheviks had some knowledge, or so we may judge from the telegram sent by Riezler to the Foreign Ministry on

20 July: 'Bolshevik distrust of German-backed counter-revolution has further increased due to revealing communications with General Krasnov.'[3]

General P.N. Krasnov was the new Ataman of the Don Cossacks. He had been elected to the post by the Krug, but only on condition that they gave him virtually dictatorial powers. He recognized that the Don Cossacks could not survive without German goodwill and one of his first acts was to write to the Kaiser. Krasnov and the Cossacks needed arms and ammunition; the Germans were the only power that could provide them in the quantities needed. He received at least eleven thousand rifles, forty-six field guns, and eighty-eight machine guns from them.[4]

Yet Krasnov retained his links with the otherwise isolated Volunteer Army. They, and the Allies, might have disapproved of his links with the Germans, but they chose to look the other way since Krasnov passed approximately half of the arms and ammunition he received from the Germans to them. As Krasnov eloquently summed up the position: 'The Volunteer Army is pure and undefiled. And I, Ataman of the Don, accept with my dirty hands German shells and ammunition, wash them in the waters of the quiet Don, and hand them over clean to the Volunteer Army.'[5]

All of this focused hatred on the representative of Imperial Germany in Russia, Count von Mirbach. The opposition within the Bolshevik Party to the ratification of the Treaty of Brest-Litovsk had been fierce. Some leading Bolsheviks, among them Joffe, Radek and Bukharin, wanted to wage a revolutionary war against Imperial Germany. The Left Social Revolutionaries, who had generally cooperated with the Bolsheviks but fell out with them over the restitution of the death penalty, not only agreed with them but were prepared to act.

The Fifth All-Russian Congress of Soviets opened in Moscow on 4 July, with the representatives of the Great Powers observing from boxes at the Bolshoi Theatre. Among them was Mirbach. The representative of the Ukrainian peasants rose and denounced the German occupation of the Ukraine and the Bolsheviks' share in allowing it, finishing with the words, 'The dictatorship of the proletariat has become the dictatorship of Count Mirbach!' Pandemonium broke out and the assembled delegates, led by the Left Social Revolutionaries, howled for his blood. They got it two days later.

At 3.30 p.m. on 6 July gunshots and an explosion echoed in the German Embassy. Two men, Andreev and Blumkin, raced out and leaped the Embassy fence and dived into a waiting car. Inside the Embassy, Count von Mirbach lay dead. The two men seen fleeing the Embassy were both members of the Left Social Revolutionary Party. Lockhart informed the Foreign Office about the murder on the basis of an account he received from Radek:

> Two well dressed men arrived German embassy in a motor car & presented document signed by President of Commission [Dzerzhinsky] for combating counter-revolution. They stated they had come to inform Mirbach of a plot to assassinate him. As soon as he entered the room they both fired at him with revolvers. German Counsellor who was also present dashed out of the room for help. Profiting by his absence murderers jumped out of window & in order to make doubly sure threw a hand bomb into the room. Mirbach died almost immediately.[6]

The assassination was the signal for the Left Social Revolutionaries to rise in Moscow. They seized the telegraph and telephone exchange, also the headquarters of the Cheka together with its leaders, Felix Dzerzhinsky and M. Latsis.

The only reliable troops the Bolsheviks held at their disposal were men of the Latvian Rifle Division. Riezler described them as the praetorian guard of the communists [Bolsheviks became the Communist Party in Feb. 1918]. Like other provincial units of the Russian Empire, they had been raised for war service, but the combination of radical local traditions, German occupation of their homeland and insulation from the old army by their language led them to maintain their discipline and cohesion.

Their commander, Colonel Vatsetis, was summoned to an empty and gloomy Kremlin on the night of 6/7 July. Matters were at such a pass that Lenin faced him with a simple, direct question: 'Comrade, can we hold out until morning?'[7] Vatsetis moved quickly and decisively, regrouping his forces in the Moscow area and surprising the Left Social Revolutionaries with a speedy and effective counter-attack.

Lockhart recorded in his diary:

> Radek came to see me. Mirbach's murderer Blumkin lived in our hotel in room 221. He was a member of the Extraordinary Commission. The Left Social

Major Terence Keyes with pony and dog, Turbar-i-hind, India.

General Alexei
Maximovich Kaledin.
Kaledin and his
Cossacks were the
main targets of the
Banking Scheme.

Felix Edmundovich Dzerzhinsky, Head of the Cheka.

Lord Robert Cecil, Minister of Blockade and Assistant Foreign Secretary. He was one of the strongest advocates of intervention.

Count Ernst von Brockdorff-Rantzau, German Ambassador to Copenhagen, who recognized the importance of Parvus.

Left to right: General Pustovoytenko, Nicholas II and General Alexeyev. Alexeyev led the Volunteer Army, which the Allies tried to use.

Seated far left to right: Générals Lavergne and Niessel and Ambassador Noulens.

Count Wilhem von Mirbach,
German Ambassador to
Russia, 1918.

Boris Viktorovich Savinkov.

"Morning, J.O.!"

Caricature of Admiral
Sir William Hall,
Director of Naval
Intelligence. G.P.
Mackeson, one of the
staff of Room 40,
probably drew the
caricature.

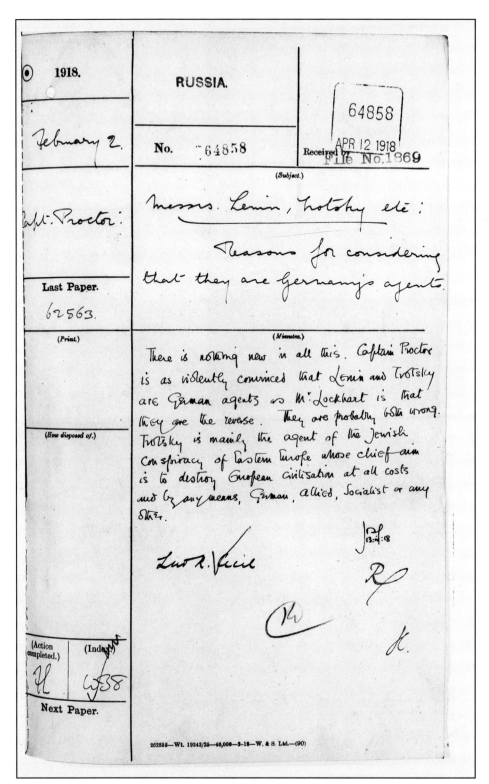

1918.

RUSSIA.

64858

APR 12 1918
File No.1869

February 2.

No. 64858

Received by

Capt. Proctor:

(Subject.)

Messrs. Lenin, Trotsky etc :

Reasons for considering
that they are Germany's agents.

Last Paper.

62563.

(Print.)

(How disposed of.)

(Minutes.)

There is nothing new in all this. Captain Proctor
is as violently convinced that Lenin and Trotsky
are German agents as Mr Lockhart is that
they are the reverse. They are probably both wrong.
Trotsky is mainly the agent of the Jewish
Conspiracy of Eastern Europe whose chief aim
is to destroy European civilisation at all costs
and by any means, German, Allied, Socialist or any
other.

Lord R. Cecil

13.iv.18

(Action completed.) *(Index.)*

Next Paper.

262855—Wt. 19343/25—40,000—2-18—W. & S. Ltd.—(90)

The horns of a dilemma – Captain Proctor's alarmist submission with reference
to Lockhart's more restrained assessment in the minute.

Captain Francis Cromie, D.S.O,
RN. The British Naval Attaché,
Petrograd.

Consul Douglas Young
and Mrs Young,
Archangel.

Revolutionaries during their short revolt arrested Dzherzhinsky...Their resistance was very weak, but for a time they held the telegraph. This was afterwards retaken by Hungarian war prisoners internationalists. Many of the Social-Revolutionaries have been arrested including Alexandrovich, Vice-President of the Extraordinary Commission. He is to be shot immediately. All papers suppressed. No trains to Petrograd or anywhere, no telegrams to abroad.[8]

Several more leading Left Social Revolutionaries were to share the fate of Alexandrovich in the coming days. Their figurehead, the veteran revolutionary Maria Spiridonova was seized and Dzerzhinsky released. Blaming himself for his failure to act on the warnings he had received about the assassination and the attempted coup, together with the fact that some of the leading conspirators had been members of the Cheka, Dzerzhinsky requested to be suspended as its Chairman. This was done with effect from 8 July and was to last until 22 August 1918. Although the Cheka now formally passed into the hands of I. K. Peters, Dzerzhinsky apparently continued to direct it from behind the scenes.

Riezler, who was a sick man, temporarily took over the German Embassy.

There has been some dispute about whether the assassination had in reality been contrived by the Bolsheviks. It is true that Mirbach's murder dislocated German ideas of overthrowing the Bolsheviks, and it is equally true that Blumkin, who initially fled to the Ukraine, was to eventually return to Russia and serve the Bolsheviks. The majority of the Left Social Revolutionaries who were arrested received extremely lenient sentences given the magnitude of their offences. Moreover, there are doubts whether the attempted 'coup' was a genuine attempt to seize power, however precarious Bolshevik rule then was. The rising in Moscow was limited and, once having seized a few key points, the rebels sat tight and took no further action to secure power. The apparently all too ready dismissal of the threats brought to Dzerzhinsky's notice is equally suspicious, giving rise to the idea that he knew more about it than has been publicly admitted and was either happy to let matters take their course, or was even quietly encouraging them.

Against this must be weighed the fact that the conspirators genuinely sought war with Germany and their assassination campaign did not cease with the death of Mirbach. On the 30 July Field-Marshal von Eichorn, the

German commander in the Ukraine, was blown up and killed by a young man called Boris Donskoi and a woman, Irina Kakhovskaya, both Left Social Revolutionaries. The leniency shown to the Left Social Revolutionaries after the July 'coup' could be explained by the fact that the Bolsheviks recognized them as fellow travellers who might be won over to the Bolshevik cause, as several of them were. There is also the fact that the Left Social Revolutionaries were rooted out of the Cheka in the aftermath of the 'coup'.

Nevertheless, this is hardly conclusive. We noted that Blumkin fled to the Ukraine, where the Left Social Revolutionaries were waging a fierce guerrilla struggle against the occupying Germans, one that hopelessly disrupted German efforts to secure wheat and cereals from the country. However, they did not act alone. The Bolsheviks were surreptitiously providing them with funds and weapons for this. Moreover, Lockhart was to state that Chicherin and Karachan received the news of Eichorn's death with unconcealed joy.[9]

Yet it is an error to study these events, in a time of great confusion and peril, solely through the spectacles of party. Behind the different party labels lay many personal disagreements and characters. Different people act and react in ways dictated by their different personalities. Many of these human attributes are on display in the Moscow of July 1918 and the only individual who stood above the very human cauldron was the remorselessly logical and calculating Lenin, who seems to have been lacking the emotional and spiritual attributes that normally define human beings.

Although it may not be possible to trace any formal alliance between the Bolsheviks and Left Social Revolutionaries over this issue, there is enough material that suggests there was some degree of collusion. In the tangled web that represented politics in revolutionary Russia, it paid everybody to make alliances of convenience and expediency and to hide their traces. The consequences of failing to do so were often fatal. Any such alliance between the Bolsheviks and Left Social Revolutionaries was probably not a formal one, but made between cliques and even individuals at a lower level than the formal party leaderships.

Of more immediate concern to the Bolsheviks was the reaction that might be expected from Germany. It was of paramount importance because Germany was the only one of the warring powers that appeared to be in a position to intervene in Russia with enough military strength to make or break governments. Fear of German invasion was the immediate priority for the Bolsheviks. As Lenin reportedly said to Sverdlov, 'There is ample occasion for it. Now at any price we must influence the character of the German report to Berlin.'

The Germans expected nothing less. Radek promised the Germans that the Bolsheviks would do 'everything'. They would send someone to Berlin immediately and send their apologies and condolences to Mirbach's family by wireless. Alfons Pacquet, the journalist, novelist and poet who was in the German Embassy in Moscow observed, 'The least which Germany can require now, is that an end is made of the organisations and agents of the Entente on Russian soil.'[10]

A veritable procession of Bolshevik leaders visited the German Embassy to offer their condolences. Radek, Chicherin, Karachan and Dzerzhinsky all came, followed by Lenin and Sverdlov. One of the first demands the Bolsheviks faced from the Germans was the right to station a battalion of German troops at the Embassy as a guard. Of course, given the German approaches to the parties of the right, such a force could readily be used as a spearhead in an attempt to overthrow the Bolsheviks. Officially, the Bolsheviks stood their ground and refused to allow this. In Sverdlov's words: '… after the murder of Mirbach, the Germans demanded that they be allowed to send a battalion to Moscow. We categorically refused and were within a hair's breadth of war.'

As usual, the situation was much more complex than this. Wheeler-Bennett states that the Bolsheviks agreed to an increase in the staff of the Embassy to 300, with additional and undefined 'forces' being allowed to come to Moscow in groups of thirty, but without arms or German uniforms. In addition, the Bolsheviks promised to provide an adequate guard for the Embassy.[11] It was suggested that this guard might be found from the German settlers from the Volga Basin. This offer from the Bolsheviks does not appear to have been accepted, yet when the German Embassy pulled out of Moscow and went to Petrograd, British travellers in Russia reported: 'German Embassy at Moscow arrived at Petrograd on August 9th accompanied by 800 German soldiers in Russian uniform who guarded German Mission after assassination of Mirbach.'[12] Much necessarily depends on the reliability of the witnesses, but as there was more than one the information was probably reasonably reliable.

It is fair to ask where these 800 German soldiers had come from, why were they in Russian uniforms and when had they arrived in Russia? They certainly were not German settlers from the Volga. The fact that they were reported as wearing Russian uniforms complies with the conditions given by Wheeler-Bennett. It suggests that the Germans, in an arrangement with the Bolsheviks, had agreed to disguise their men. Then the Bolsheviks would not be embarrassed in the eyes of everybody by appearing to be either German tools or subservient to the Germans, a charge to which they remained extremely sensitive.

French sources support the view that the Bolsheviks did submit to German demands. Général Lavergne informed the Minister of War in Paris:

> From a reliable source: 1st German conditions were: execution of 25 sentries who were guarding the German Consulate and German Ambassador.
> Government had responded: first conditions accepted and it admitted the presence of a battalion at Moscow.
> 2nd [condition] Government had discussed declaration of war against the Allies, but had renounced it because they knew that neither public opinion nor the army would be persuaded.[13]

Armed German troops were undeniably in the Embassy. According to Pacquet, by 28 July:

> It is likely that all these threatening rumours are exaggerated, but remind us to be careful, that the house is guarded by 72 rifle-armed soldiers in the cellars, 5 machine guns, everybody in the house have pistols in front of them and nobody goes out without a Browning.[14]

He further informs us that 'Captain von Zychlinski, who has come from Berlin, is now the palace commandant. This man goes through the streets with a monocle.' The footnote to this tells us that von Zychlinski was 'Commandant of the 300 men of the Embassy guard arrived from Berlin.'[15] There is little room for reasonable doubt that before the end of July the Bolsheviks had agreed to a German guard at the Embassy. At that stage the guard did not amount to a battalion, but approximately half a battalion. It may have been strengthened later as the Embassy evacuated Moscow. Sverdlov's words were contained in a message to the Ural Soviet, so it is probable that he was telling its recipients what he wanted them to know, perhaps to lull suspicion or to quell a rising panic, perhaps to restore confidence in an all too obviously shaky government. Any suggestion of either cooperation with the Germans or subservience to them was anathema to the Bolshevik leadership and steps would be taken to disguise the truth of the matter.

The new German Ambassador in Moscow was Helfferich, formerly Chief Secretary to the Treasury and the man who had been responsible for approving the money the Germans spent on supporting the Bolsheviks. He arrived on 28 July 1918. He did not remain there long – in fact barely a week.

On the surface, Helfferich sought to pursue a more conciliatory policy towards Bolshevik Russia but his brief taste of Muscovite life under the Bolsheviks saw him hasten back to Berlin, perhaps speeded on his way by the threat of assassination. As Oliver Wardrop, the British Consul-General in Moscow reported:

> From another source I learn that Helfferich has been told that he is condemned to assassination and that two unsuccessful attempts against him have already been made. In one case at least machine gun fire was directed against an aeroplane flying low over the German diplomatic Agency.[16]

On his return to Berlin, Helfferich was to strongly advocate that the Germans should overthrow the Bolsheviks and replace them with the Monarchists. The seed fell on stony ground. The Germans finally recognized that the only way of preserving their influence in Russia was by clinging to the Bolsheviks, however unpalatable that may have been.

The wheels were rapidly falling off the German wagon in the aftermath of the assassination of Mirbach. Panic was beginning to spread. There were suspicions that the Left Social Revolutionaries were acting in concert with the Allies. Both the Allies and the Left Social Revolutionaries sought the same end – war by Russia against Germany. Richard Spence states that the French Consul-General, Grenard, was supplying funds to the Left Social Revolutionaries, among others. He cites Savinkov's later suspicion that the French, '...knowing that the Left SRs planned a revolt in Moscow, deliberately shifted our forces to the upper Volga, in order to coordinate our operation with the Left SR uprising.'[17]

The suspicion is strengthened by the fact that the Bolsheviks faced still another blow from the left. The commander of the army facing the Czechoslovaks, Muraviev, was a Left Social Revolutionary. On 10 July he tried to turn his army against the Bolsheviks. Chicherin claimed that, 'Bribed by the Entente, commander-in-chief Muraviev betrayed us and opened the front to the Czecho-Slovaks.'[18]

To date there has been no formal evidence to support Chicherin's allegation that the Allies bribed Muraviev, so the claim must be treated with caution. However, Muraviev was hardly acting in isolation – the very timing of his action coincides too closely with the rising of the Left Social Revolutionaries for that. It also fits the Allied plan rather too closely to be dismissed out of hand, especially when it is recognized that his action was calculated to open the door to those tools of the Allies, the Czechoslovak Legion. When we remember that the Allies were trying to make common cause with every shape and form of opposition to the Bolsheviks, the excuses deployed to distance the Allies from these events look ever less convincing.

For all the immediate danger Muraviev might have represented, his venture came to grief when he fell into a Red Army ambush. It has been claimed both that he was killed in the ambush and that he committed suicide. Whichever was the case, the immediate threat from this quarter was over and the front against the Czechoslovaks held.

General Groener, Chief of Staff of the German forces in the Ukraine, had no doubt about who was ultimately behind these upheavals. He wrote bitterly in his diary on 10 July:

> That the Entente was behind the murder of Count Mirbach can hardly be subjected to any more doubt. The authors were the Social Revolutionaries, who were minded to be Entente-friendly. The English and French agents work with much money and aptitude, while in such things we neither have one nor the other.[19]

The hostility Keyes encountered on his journey south to see Krivoshein was experienced in the aftermath of Mirbach's murder, and it was occasioned by the belief that the Allies were behind the assassination.

Other Germans actually saw a glimmer of opportunity in the circumstances, with Pacquet rejoicing at the prospect of a serious breach between the Bolsheviks and the Allies and the further prospect of a formal alliance between Germany and the Bolshevik Government.[20] One step that seemed to point in this direction was the anticipated German demand for the expulsion of the various Military Missions which the Allies still maintained in Russia, the most active of which was the French. After discussions with the Germans, Radek, according to Pacquet, stated: 'We go to Lenin at the Kremlin now. Yet that should happen tonight: dissolution of the Military Missions, banning the operations of the Entente organisations and agents.'[21] Not only were the missions and agents of the Entente to be suppressed, but Russian newspapers friendly to the Allies were to suffer the same fate. Lockhart reported:

> Official Govt. announcements of murder state that it was carried out by agents of Anglo-French imperialists. Radek considers Germans will either advance immediately or demand enormous compensation from Bolsheviks. He considers in latter event they will demand departure of allied missions from Russia but that Lenin will not consent to this. The Bolsheviks are very alarmed by what has happened and are carrying on fierce propaganda against all other parties who they state are trying to draw Russia back into war by foulest provocation. One result of murder will be complete & final break down of all relations between Bolshevik & Left Social Revolutionaries.[22]

The Bolsheviks had every reason to be 'very alarmed'. They were perfectly accurate in their accusations that the other parties were trying to draw Russia back into the war. That was the greater part of the reason for the Allied association with those parties.

On 12 July a telegram was received from Lockhart via Paris. Among other matters, it reported that, the 'Minister for Foreign Affairs [Chicherin] considers it likely that Germans may demand expulsion of Allied Missions from Russia. He states Government will not agree to this, unless our action at Murmansk forces them to take this step.'[23] There were also fears that reprisals would be taken against Allied diplomats and officers in Russia.[24]

A report from British Military Intelligence referring to events in July throws further interesting light on the movements of German troops in disguise, and much else besides:

The following *résumé* of the situation is given in a military report, dated 23rd July, from a Russian who (? group omitted) General Staff at Moscow. The death of Count Mirbach has been a signal for a renewal of activity of the Germans. Orders have been issued by the Staff at Pskoff to be in fighting readiness for an advance towards Gatschina. The Staff of the 10th Army has arrived in Minsk, the Staff of the 48th stationed at Minsk has moved to Orsha. One of our agents who was exceptionally well informed but who unfortunately was murdered on evening of 18th July, reported on the 12th and 13th July that von Lusius was in Petrograd and that 120 officers under the disguise of sanitary officers passed through the Finnish Station there. That was just at the time when the German Government demanded the introduction of a German battalion into Moscow. According to the informant (one group undecipherable) there seems to be in the circumstances of Mirbach's death much doubt and mystery. It is a remarkable coincidence that two weeks before his death the rooms of the Embassy were all photographed, and that six days before his death Major Sisholz, of the Prussian Army, who is the chief of the White Guards organisation in Minsk, asserted in a conversation that it was daily expected that an attempt would be made upon the life of one of Germany's diplomatic representatives. It was thought then that the blow would fall upon Biermann. The same agent intercepted and deciphered a wireless message at station Alexandrovskaya, from which it appears that Mirbach had received the order of recall two days before his death. It was impossible to obtain further information on the above in view of the murder of the agent referred to, and the information is, however, worth noting, though it may appear disconnected. German policy towards Russia has been deeply affected by the events on the French and Czech fronts.[25]

Apart from the faintly amusing information about German officers disguised as sanitary officers passing through Petrograd, this part of the message throws light on other matters. An attempt on the life of one of the German diplomats was expected, as well it might be after the threats that the Germans had consulted Dzerzhinsky about. The movement of German forces towards Minsk put them in a position to march on Moscow, a threat that might well have persuaded the Bolsheviks to compromise on their opposition to a German battalion at the Embassy. Mirbach's recall fits the context of the time, since Berlin was by then considering him to be 'Bolshevized' and, as the Germans were seeking other partners to the Bolsheviks, they would require an ambassador who would implement that policy with more commitment.

The twin strands of German policy are revealed here in the reference to Major Sisholz. The Germans were switching their weight between the Bolsheviks and extreme Monarchists in order to keep Russia divided and to enable them to apply pressure to either party should one or the other not meet German demands. By playing them off against each other, they could reasonably expect to wield considerable influence over whichever party held power in Russia. The German-backed White movement was so numerically small as to be derisory, but the threat of increased German support may well have lent it a potency beyond that merited by its numbers.

Clearly the British had a very well informed agent in Central Russia, one who had access to at least some of the wireless traffic through the Alexandrovsk Wireless Station. That would imply that the agent also had access to the codes used. The identity of the agent is not revealed here and cannot be stated with certainty. Perhaps he was the victim of the anticipated reprisals against Allied officials mentioned in Lockhart's report above.

Finally, the reference to the influence of the French and Czechoslovak front is to the fact that the great German offensive on the Western front had failed. Indeed, it was on 18 July that the Allied counter-offensive under Général Mangin opened at Villers-Cotterets, an attack that heralded the turn of the tide in the Western theatre. In Siberia the Czechoslovak Legion was continuing to make headway. Germany's position was becoming increasingly critical.

The Bolsheviks were not only assailed from the left of the political spectrum, but the right. Savinkov's Union launched risings at Rybinsk, Murom and Yaroslavl on 6 July, all on the upper Volga. Success would have isolated Moscow from the north and east. Possession of Yaroslavl would have cut the Trans-Siberian Railway and presented an ideal position to link up with the Czechoslovaks from Siberia and also the Allies, who were expected to sweep down from the north.

The attempts to take Rybinsk and Murom were defeated. Yaroslavl was seized but held for only seventeen days by a force commanded by one of Savinkov's most trusted lieutenants, Colonel A.P. Perkhurov. His detachment of the Union was joined by Right Social Revolutionaries, Mensheviks, workers, peasants and even some German prisoners-of-war. The seizure of the town was followed by the execution of the local Bolshevik leaders while others were imprisoned on a 'death barge' on the Volga. Equally ferocious were the reprisals the Bolsheviks took against the participants in the rising whom they captured when they regained control of the town. Perkhurov and some of his key officers managed to escape, but the Union's strength had been shattered.

Savinkov was to argue that the French had been responsible for what came to be regarded as the premature launch of his rising. Grenard and Noulens both denied any involvement with his attempt. Lockhart considered that they had been behind it. Where does the truth lie? Was Savinkov trying to lay the blame at the door of others for the waste of life?

On the night of 12 July, in the aftermath of the assassination of Mirbach, the rising of the Left Social Revolutionaries and Savinkov's stroke, Radek called on Lockhart and stayed with him for about three hours. According to Lockhart, 'He inveighed at great length against the French who were [?]ired up in every anti-Bolshevik movement including Yaroslavl.'[26] The Bolsheviks knew more about Allied support for the anti-Bolshevik movements than the Allies would have liked. It is possible that Radek was seeking to give Lockhart a veiled warning about entangling himself in anti-Bolshevik conspiracies. If Lockhart had heeded the warning, then a division would have opened between British and French covert operations, one that would have meant Allied intervention would have been seriously enough cumbered to at least delay it.

There are other factors linked with the abortive attempt that provide some necessary context. The first was that there was another secret organization in Russia beside the Union: the National Centre, often known simply as the Centre. Its leaders were Professor Peter Struve, Mikhail Feodorov, Avinov, Shippov and Astrov. It was a union of anti-Bolsheviks, comprising Cadets, members of the disintegrating Right Centre, and some members of the dissolving Left Centre – Right Social Revolutionaries, Popular Socialists and members of Plekhanov's Socialist group. Most of the latter represented themselves rather than their party. The Allies began forming links with it at the end of June. Its political programme was based on a deceit, as Lockhart was to report: 'It favours a monarchy, but does not consider immediate proclamation of monarchy desirable. Its plans of operation are based entirely on (?friendship of) Allies. They have already begun active measures with Czechs.'[27]

Since the restoration of a monarchy was to remain hidden for the present, its immediate goal was the establishment of a military dictatorship that would probably be entrusted to General Alexeyev of the Volunteer Army. He was to be supported by a civilian administration, the only purposes of which were to be conducting war and restoring law and order. It was to leave all internal questions, including decisions on the future form of government in Russia, until the end of the war. It was hoped that the administration would, as far as possible, be both national and contain as many parties as possible. This latter hope was almost certainly vain.

The link to the Czechoslovaks follows the familiar pattern, but the picture becomes more fully rounded with Boris Savinkov's encouragement of the formation of the National Centre. That also explains much about its composition, for the creation of a non-party organization to fight both the Bolsheviks and Germans, that embraced all shades of political opinion except the most extreme, was Savinkov's constant dream. Nevertheless, Savinkov's character would not allow him to place himself or the Union for the Defence of Fatherland and Freedom under its control. He wanted, above all, to take centre stage himself.

He was later to claim that the Centre had sanctioned his rising, yet when it was crushed the Centre denied ever having done so, making Savinkov a political scapegoat for the failure.[28] Lockhart demolished the Centre's argument when he informed the Foreign Office that, 'Centre has come to complete agreement with Savinkov's League.'[29] Lockhart was told that the Centre preferred that Russia should be a second Belgium, heroically resisting the German invader, rather than a second Bulgaria that was seen as a helpless German satellite. Lockhart concluded his message, 'We should help it. I can (? raise) money here. Please reply by wireless from Paris.'

As early as 7 July Lockhart had been advocating financial support for the Centre:

I would also beg you to give me power immediately to spend up to ten million roubles in supporting those organisations which may be useful to us in the event of intervention. This is of supreme importance as without money it is difficult to do anything. So important do I consider this question that in event of our having to leave before I receive any reply from you I am seriously considering advisability

179

of giving such sums as I can collect on my own responsibility to Centre here which now contain [*sic* contains] all parties who are favourable towards allied intervention.[30]

There is no doubt that the Allies were supporting the Centre. While urging the British Government to support them, Lockhart used the fact that the French had already given them money, the sum of 'two and a half million roubles', to persuade London to open its purse. The Centre still needed more. Lockhart continued, '... in the event of our having to leave Russia I venture once more to ask you to authorize me to finance group as the one solid organisation likely to assist us in event of intervention.'[31]

The Centre was expecting military intervention from the Allies, since 'In view of all that has been said by Allies regarding intervention, everybody in Russia now believes intervention is about to take place.'[32] Although Lockhart might not have been specifically alluding to the Bolsheviks, 'everybody' was bound to include them. The plans for intervention must rank as one of the worst-kept secrets in history. Lockhart continued: 'French have told Centre that intervention has already been decided on. Centre has therefore committed itself inevitably and is sending down its leaders to South to Alexeiev [*sic*] & to Czechs and Samara.'[33] The same promise seems to have been made to the Centre as Savinkov claims was made to him.

Lockhart's dealings with the Centre were concealed for many years. He refers to them only twice in his *Memoirs*, which reflect a tone of injured innocence and the role of hapless dupe. He states there that 'Until the decision [to intervene] was brought to my notice I gave no support to the Whites either in cash or in promises.'[34]

This myth was originally dented by Richard K. Debo in 1971.[35] Gordon Brook-Shepherd drew attention to the fact that Lockhart submitted one paper to the Foreign Office that served as a fig-leaf for his true activities and could be used to deceive the public and Parliament.[36] Another, secret, Memorandum, dated 5 November 1918, to which the public was not granted access for a further fifty years, contained a stronger element of truth. That document opened with the words: 'Up to the 27th July my anti-bolshevik [*sic* Bolshevik] activities in Russia had been limited entirely to negotiations with the "Centre" in Moscow.'[37] This establishes Lockhart's complicity in the plot with the Centre, but it carefully omits other clandestine activities in which he was engaged.

So what were Lockhart's real relations with Secret Intelligence? There are two immediate pointers that strongly suggest these were closer than the usual story that is printed, namely that Lockhart was a diplomatic agent and not a Secret Service agent. The opening paragraph of his Memorandum states that interviews with the Centre's leaders were kept to a minimum except when strictly necessary, otherwise 'I maintained relations with this organisation through Lieutenant Webster, the Passport Control Officer at Moscow.'[38]

Webster was an officer in the Royal Naval Volunteer Reserve, attached to MI1(c). Britain's Secret Service had a small regular staff; most of its officers in the field were attached or loaned to it from the various branches of the armed services. One of the most frequent guises used by Smith Cumming's men was that of Lieutenants in the Royal Naval Volunteer Reserve. Passport Control Officer was a position often used as cover for Secret Service officers. The official guise conferred a degree of legal immunity in the host countries, a fact of considerable value to any Intelligence officer. Until it was officially exposed – the capture of the Passport Control Officer in the Netherlands, Captain Stevens, by the Nazis at Venlo in 1940 effectively made it public, so destroying its value – it was priceless in that few would expect such a relatively innocuous official of being connected with espionage unless they were either especially security-conscious or utterly paranoid.

Terence Keyes' association with Lockhart has already been noted. Keyes was involved in other anti-Bolshevik activities as well as the Banking Scheme. His services were called upon by Lockhart to supply the urgently needed funds to the Centre. The first intimation of this occurred on 25 July, when Lockhart told the Foreign Office:

> Having received no reply from you and being absolutely (? convinced) of supreme necessity of doing something (? that might support) centre and to prevent further repetition of incidents such as Miliukov decided today after consultation with Colonel Keyes to give immediately half (? a) million roubles (? to the centre) at the same time I would point out that far more (group undecipherable; possibly: financial) aid than this will be required and I (? await) your answer on this question with impatience.[39]

Three days later the matter became more pressing. Lockhart argued this was because Alexeyev was now without funds and the Allies had an obligation to support him. He told the Foreign Office that the Allied military representatives in Russia entirely agreed with the Centre and a sum of 10 million roubles was required. At this juncture it is clear that the French joined with Lockhart, since

> They begged us to give them immediately 2,000,000 (? roubles) (four groups undecipherable). On receipt of instructions from Vologda or from London, I agreed, after consultation with Colonel Keyes to give one million while French Consul General gave (? the other). I regret that I was forced to take this decision without your sanction. I would point out that the (? actual) (? responsibility) would have been far greater if I had refused altogether. I trust that my action will meet (four groups omitted) for Alexeiev [sic] 10 million roubles. For Centre itself 81 million roubles. For Shuwgin [sic Shulgin] at Kiev 500,000 roubles. French will certainly bear at least half of this expenditure. I am also conferring with Americans (? on) the same (? subject).[40]

This was an extremely serious effort, with the sums initially involved totalling 2.5 million roubles, of which the British supplied 1.5 million roubles. The projected expenditure amounted to an additional 91.5 million roubles. The money was raised locally by issuing promissory notes redeemable in London to wealthy Russians who realized their wealth was wholly insecure in the Russia of 1918. The British Government had been committed in much the same way as it had been over the £500,000 loaned by Keyes to Yaroshinsky in the Banking Scheme, and by the same officer.

Of just as much significance is that Lockhart is shown to be acting in the closest fashion with a man he knew to be an Intelligence officer. He was prepared to take this step without London's official approval. Were he and Keyes secure in the knowledge that their initiative would receive the backing they needed from 'C'?

Lockhart's telegrams did not reach London until 25 and 28 July respectively. This was due to the hazards of communication we have already recognized. The Foreign Office responded promptly, informing Lockhart on 30 July that his action had been approved and could be continued.[41]

This is not the only case where Lockhart misleads readers of his *Memoirs*. He claims in them that on the evening of 17 July he received official news from Karachan that the former Tsar and his family had been murdered at Ekaterinburg and that he was the first person to 'convey' the news to the world.[42] His diaries make no reference to any meeting with Karachan that evening, or to the receipt of any such news from the Bolsheviks, that evening or ever. Now that the pertinent British files have long been open, it is a certainty that he bore no such news to the British Government, let alone the world. Study of his diaries shows that he did not hear of the alleged murder of the whole family until he was safely back in Britain and read an article in *The Times* by Robert Wilton, a thoroughly discredited source who, in 1917–18, was taking his orders from Poole's deputy Captain McAlpine. Lockhart's diary entry for 9 February 1919 reads: 'It now appears that both the Tsar and Tsarina and all children have been murdered, also the Grand Duchess Elizabeth and probably the Grand Duke Michael.'[43] The claim in his *Memoirs* is perfectly fictitious.

The British were by then intercepting Bolshevik communications on a large scale. In the National Archives there exists a file containing Bolshevik telegrams between Moscow, Petrograd and Ekaterinburg that were intercepted by the British in July 1918.[44] They were channelled to British Intelligence officers at Archangel via Murmansk, where General Poole had established himself with his forces. The intercepts originated in Petrograd and are all marked: 'COPY.JL.' They shed revealing light on the desperate position of the Red Army defending Ekaterinburg against the Czechoslovaks. There is no doubt that this vital information was put into the hands of the Czechoslovak command as soon as possible. Lavergne certainly provided the Czechoslovaks with the Red Army's Order of Battle, particularly around Ekaterinburg, on 28 July.[45] The intercepts show that as early as 16 July the Bolsheviks recognized that Ekaterinburg was going to fall. On 22 July the commander of the Red Army troops resisting the Czechoslovaks, Reinhold Berzin, fled to Moscow.

What is important so far as Lockhart's claims are concerned is that the notorious telegram allegedly sent from Ekaterinburg by Commissar Beloborodov, the Chairman of the District Soviet, on the evening of 17 July stating that the family had 'suffered the same fate as head' [i.e. Nicholas, the former Tsar] does not appear in the intercepts. Had the telegram existed there can now be no reasonable doubt that it would have been intercepted

183

and Lockhart's words therefore might still be credible. Neither Karachan nor anybody else among the Bolshevik leadership could have known on 17 July that all of the Imperial family had been killed in Ekaterinburg, which in turn emphasizes the fact that Lockhart was peddling not so much fiction as a deliberate untruth.

Serious questions have been raised hitherto about the authenticity of that telegram. Those questions gain added weight from its absence from the intercepts. Indeed, had the telegram existed the British Government could have used it later to discredit the famous Anastasia claimant.

The question is, who, or what, motivated this deception? We have seen that Lockhart had much closer links to the Intelligence Services than is presented by the official storyline. In his introduction to his father's *Memoirs*, Lockhart's son states that his father was offered the post of head of the Secret Intelligence Service, which in the period covered by this book was known as the Secret Service. Lockhart turned the offer down. If this is true, there can be no doubt that he did enjoy the closest ties with that Service. Such posts are not offered to rank outsiders.

If senior British officials wish to publish memoirs of their service, it is a standing rule that they have to be cleared by the authorities who can insist that sensitive material is omitted or, in a form of 'collaboration', arrange for the writer to include the message they want the public and foreign readers to hear. Bearing in mind the intimate links between the British Intelligence Services and the Russian Embassy in London, the prospect of Lockhart having penned this nonsense on his own initiative seems implausible.

Savinkov's intentions after successfully mounting his coup provide important context in relation to the backing he received from the Allies. Savinkov intended to assassinate – or murder – Lenin. According to Spence several plans were considered, including an attempt to plant a large mine under a railway line to blow him up together with his Government.[46] The removal of Lenin would certainly have been the most effective way to shatter the Bolsheviks. The French were the most closely associated with Savinkov and it is unlikely that they remained in ignorance of Savinkov's intent. Indeed, they would appear to have been more than willing to turn a blind eye to the crime. There is, however, no direct evidence to link the Allies definitely to any plot to kill Lenin.

The words of Douglas Young encapsulate the Allied view perfectly: 'The root of the whole evil lies in the assumption, long proved false, that the Russian "Whites" would speedily cut the throats of the Bolsheviks while the Allies looked the other way, and that the story of the pre-intervention proceedings would be buried with the corpse.'[47] The assumption that the Whites would do the Allies' dirty work for them has been repeatedly seen to be the case. If their Russian allies were prepared to murder Lenin and his colleagues, then it would vastly simplify the situation for them.

There was one final element that requires relation now. Late in July 'Syren' Force began pushing southwards from Murmansk. The only practicable route they could take led to Petrograd. Naturally the move caused consternation among the Bolsheviks. Lockhart informed the Foreign Office:

> I have received today (? further) note (? from) Minister for Foreign Affairs relative to our advance from Murmansk. What Russian Government really wishes to know is (? whether our) action is anti-German or anti-Soviet.[48]

In the same message that gave Lockhart approval to continue funding the Centre, the Foreign Office told him, 'Murmansk activity prompted entirely by first, and in no way by second, motive mentioned by you.' This was transparently incorrect. It has been shown that the Allies were forming a coalition from every anti-Bolshevik party or group in Russia.

The initial and perhaps ultimate momentum for this stemmed from the perceived need to restore the Eastern front, but that policy was necessarily anti-Bolshevik since inextricably bound in with it was the need to overthrow the Bolsheviks. There is no mystery why that should be so: the Bolsheviks would not go to war against Germany if they could possibly help it. Any alliance with the Whites was necessarily anti-Bolshevik as the primary aim of the Whites was the overthrow and destruction of the Bolsheviks. The Allies were thus implicitly bound into attempting to destroy them.

There was a community of interest between the Allies and the Whites, with both hoping to achieve their wider aims through using the other. In this respect the relationship differed little from that between the Bolsheviks and the Germans in 1917. That did not make the Bolsheviks German agents. Equally, the Whites were not Allied agents, though in one of those human ironies the Bolsheviks depicted them as such.

X

Not So Secret

July 1918 (II)

◄○►

The French had never abandoned the idea of forming armies from friendly diasporas within Russia, despite repeated setbacks. They now sought to organize a Polish Army in Russia at Murmansk in July. Although it was to be under the immediate command of General Poole, its direction was to lie in the hands of the Polish Military Commission in Paris, under the presidency of General Haller. However, in the middle of the month the Bolsheviks inconsiderately cut the telegraph for ten days, hopelessly disrupting the attempt to concentrate the Poles in north Russia. As one of the French officers observed, 'But the military concentration of the Poles in Russia is impossible before the occupation by the Allies of Archangel and Vologda.'[1]

It was clear the Bolsheviks were not taking any chances. On 22 July they interrupted the transport of the Poles to Murmansk. This threw French plans into further disarray. Unlike the Czechoslovaks, the Poles were not concentrated into a cohesive force and had to reach Murmansk from scattered locations. The above circumstances prevented Polish officers from reaching Murmansk. Worse still, under pressure from arrests, including that of 400 Poles at one swoop in Nijni Novgorod, pursuit and seizures, the Polish Military Commission in Moscow was unable to work regularly. Nevertheless, small Polish contingents did manage to reach Murmansk, as did a small number of Serbs. The French were also hoping to form the latter into a contingent and, although their numbers remained small, they were to prove influential in the unfolding of events.

The British, for their part, concentrated on native Russians. One of them was Captain Grigori Chaplin of the Russian Navy. He was reputedly a handsome man, who spoke perfect English, a colleague of Captain Cromie's from their joint service with submarines in the Baltic Sea. They renewed their professional acquaintance, as conspirators, in the spring of 1918. He was now serving Captain McGrath, who sent him to recruit men for the White armies. In May 1918, at McGrath's behest, Chaplin was disguised as 'Commander Thomson' of the Royal Navy and issued with a false British passport by Arthur Woodhouse, the Consul at Petrograd. While he and Cromie were sending recruits north to join the Russian army that the British were forming around Murmansk, the main focus of his activities was arranging a coup at Archangel to support the planned Allied landing. It was hoped to launch a corresponding coup in Petrograd at the same time.

The planned coups were part of a considerably larger scheme, as Cromie made clear:

> I have refused an offer of destroyers on Lake Ladoga, as we cannot give them any base unless we invade Finnish territory and would have great difficulty to supply them. If a small base can be formed at Perchguba or Brukoba both close to station Medvieja I can organise a small naval force on Lake Onega. At present I am in touch with bullet-proof motor boats 12 knots with sufficient kerosene for 80 hours which should leave this week ending 28th July towed by tug to complete repair. They will keep in touch with Gillespie at Vologda and are prepared to go anywhere. There are also four petrol boats 25 knots but sufficient petrol is not obtainable. Both classes carry 1 75 millimeter [*sic* millimetre] gun and 1 maxim. Am trying to raise armed tugs for same purpose. Many contact and electric mines are now being sent to P[etrozavodsk] and Archangel. If Naval cooperation on river & lake desired please inform me giving proposed bases and detailed plans ends.[2]

The question arises as to the identity of 'Gillespie' at Vologda. R. Bainton argues that the name was another of Reilly's suspected aliases,[3] but lacks any supporting evidence. Whoever Gillespie was, and it is more probable he was the assistant to Mr Blakey, the former Consul at Khakhov, the context firmly indicates that the different branches of British Intelligence were working together, not to save Allied stores, but to overthrow the Bolshevik Government.

The surviving documentary evidence places Reilly in Petrograd and Moscow rather than Vologda, continuing his work with the Orthodox Church. Rather than for any Intelligence plot in the conventional sense, the effort expended on the Orthodox Church was designed to win influence.

The Church was desperately short of money and had difficulty in maintaining itself. The money given by the British needs to be seen as a *douceur* that won goodwill through enabling the Church to continue its normal activities.

Reilly and Hill, travelling incognito, called on Patriarch Tikhon with two large suitcases stuffed with 5 million roubles, with an approximate contemporary value of £143,000. In return the Patriarch promised that, once the Bolsheviks were overthrown in the aftermath of the Allied intervention, solemn divine services would be held in Moscow to celebrate Russia's escape from the Bolshevik grasp.

A letter from Reilly informed Lindley that he was leaving that night for Moscow, where he was going to put the matter before Oliver Wardrop, the Consul-General, in accordance with Lindley's suggestions. This indicates that the British Embassy and Consulate-General were both parties to the intrigues of the time. There is an extract from Smith Cumming's diary, in Alan Judd's biography, which shows Lindley advising 'C' about the officers employed to keep in touch with Cromie and the head of station, Boyce. This makes clear Lindley was familiar with these men and their duties, and that he supplied them with funds:

> This came about following a call from a Mr Lindley, who 'stated that in reply to my question: 1) That he considered Boyce the best man to put in charge of our organisation. 2) That he ought to base on Moscow. 3) That he would provide my people with money if required. He showed a very high appreciation of their value, especially MacLaren and Boyce.'[4]

This is supported by a telegram he sent to Smith Cumming, via Mr Balfour:

> Confidential
> Following for 'C'.
> I have had long conversations with Boyce and MacLaren who have been doing excellent work.
> I hope you will leave Boyce as head of organisation he knows so well. He is better fitted for that job than MacLaren, who is first-rate in other ways.[5]

The British had started recruiting personnel for their Russian army in the north in June. The process became systematic in July, with George Hill being particularly successful as a result of the close links he had formed with the Russian Air Force as Inspector of Aviation, and the good connections that had been made by Colonel Maund. Several officers, from all services, were selected and given advances to enable them to reach north Russia. Hill was to write:

> When the recruits were wanted, about 45 were sent to North; the first party, under Colonel Kazakoff, consisted of six or seven officers. It was also through the Aviation that close relations were maintained with the Cadets and their organisations.[6]

Some of the men of the Russian Air Force who defected to the Allies did not go north, but were directed towards the Czechoslovaks. Hill reported: 'As most of the unit commanders were of our orientation, and in league with myself, this was very much encouraged, as we hoped to get whole squadrons deserting to the Tczecho-Slovaks [*sic* Czechoslovaks].'[7]

This stresses the fact that the Czechoslovak Legion was a tool of the Allies, whatever the men in it might like to think and whatever excuses might be made later on. Both the dimensions and purpose of the Allied web can be ascertained by the fact that Hill also reported that unit identifications continued and linked up with the south, where the Volunteer Army was fighting, and the Czechoslovak front in Siberia. As both these forces were fighting the Red Army rather than the Germans, there can be little room for doubt that the Allied machinations were now directed in the first place against the Bolsheviks.

As with the French, the British plan to form a friendly army in north Russia came to grief. Besides the Bolshevik countermeasures, which were as effective against Russians travelling to the north as they were against the Poles, some degree of incompetence was also responsible for the failure. R.H. Clive, on the staff of the British Embassy at Stockholm, reported:

EMPLOYMENT OF RUSSIAN OFFICERS:
This would appear to be a matter which solely concerned the Military Authorities, but I consider it my duty to report that I received a visit yesterday from General Maraschevsky, Chief of the Russian General Staff during the Kerensky regime, and General Prince Serge Beloselshi, who begged me to draw

your attention to the political aspect of the question. According to what they told [me], the present method of trying to recruit Russian officers for the Murmansk and Archangel Expeditions was a failure. There seemed no serious wish to engage these officers; the conditions of service were not made clear to them; no provision was made for their families; in fact the whole thing seemed to be haphazard, and consequently very few officers were coming forward.[8]

A combination of Soviet countermeasures, British incompetence, together with the understandable reluctance of many Russians to commit themselves until they could see that the Allies were in earnest, resulted in the British-inspired counter-revolutionary army in north Russia being a runt instead of a strapping lad.

Lindley mentioned that Boyce and MacLaren were doing excellent work. Few direct traces of this now remain. However, some flavour of the activities can be gleaned from Lockhart's Secret and Confidential Memorandum, where he wrote:

> During my stay in Russia I had little connexion with the British representatives in Petrograd, having no control over them. I was, however, on very friendly terms with Captain Cromie. At the same time I had no definite knowledge of the counter-revolutionary activities of the Allies in Petrograd, although I knew vaguely from both Captain Cromie and Mr. [sic Lieutenant] Boyce that they were interested in several organisations there, and that considerable sums of money were being spent.[9]

The Memorandum, though deliberately vague on detail, contains two further references to the clandestine British activities in Petrograd. One of them is of particular significance at this stage:

> From the evidence of Captain Schwabe whom we picked up in Finland it is also clear that in Petrograd the Allied representatives were in close touch with various counter-revolutionary organisations. Our whole position, indeed, was extremely difficult. Orders were constantly been received from General Poole, or his staff to send up counter-revolutionaries to the North or to finance various people. We had also to maintain relations with the anti-bolshevik [sic Bolshevik] forces on the other side of the Volga, and whether we had supported the anti-bolshevik [sic Bolshevik] organisations or not we should still have been regarded, after intervention, as the centre of the counter-revolutionary movement.[10]

Lieutenant Urmston sent a more revealing report to General Poole. It reveals how the clandestine activities all dovetailed:

> Following received from Lieut. Urmston:-
> (a) In Pskov and Petrograd districts many battalions have been formed by Germans. These battalions wish to put themselves at disposal of Allied forces and at given signal attack Germans and overthrow the Bolshevik power in PETROGRAD. The C-in-C of these battalions wishes to have an interview with you at any place you name.
> (b) Captain CROMIE has offer of three destroyers and five motorboats who wish to join us. CROMIE request that you advise him of our plans and if we are to advance down MURMAN line which port they can be sent.
> Please communicate for further details with Lieutenant Commander OKERLUND through MILKONT, Petrograd, if this is impossible we can do so via SOROKA, by courier.[11]

The lure of enemy forces turning their coats was to exercise a considerable influence on Allied clandestine activities. What is more immediately important is the revelation of the link between Cromie and Okerlund that was touched on earlier.

Although Russia's capital had now been moved to Moscow, the city of Petrograd still held enormous symbolic value. Not only was it the former capital city, it was the focus of revolution in 1905 and it was the city where the Bolsheviks had mounted their coup in November 1917, thus it would amount to a major triumph for the Allies if they could seize the city. There was also the perception that the city presented an easier target for counter-revolution than did Moscow. This impression influenced Lockhart, for in his diary he noted:

> Rang up Cromie... Feeling in Petrograd quite different from Moscow. Altogether quieter and further removed from the struggle. Anti-Bolshevism very strong and hardly concealed. At the cabaret jokes were made at Bolshevik expense which would not be tolerated in Moscow.
> Famine pretty severe and grave discontent among the workmen and sailors. Counter-revolution here possible any day.[12]

Cromie wrote to Admiral Hall:

> Our main scheme is in pretty good order, thanks to our more active policy in the north. The current expenses are heavy, but I am more confident of the results than I have ever been, after receiving some independent reports of the general feeling.
>
> Our small propaganda work has been fostering the growing discontent of the Esthonian [*sic* Estonian] and Lettish elements in Kronstadt against the Germans by spreading letters and reports (all true) received from Reval and district. I have been approached indirectly for opinion on official schemes for destruction of ships at Kronstadt.[13]

Cromie was hard at work preparing the way for the intervention force. His letter continued:

> We have put Merpert in touch with our needs and agents. One brigade that I have backed against local military (?) advice is likely to turn out well, and reports of an English officer sent off to meet an old friend of mine on the northern front [likely to be Chaplin] is very cheering. The recruiting started much too late, but we progressed slowly in spite of the difficulties of the route. I have nine river gun-boats at my disposal, but as usual cannot get a reply out of the north and dare not give them definite orders until I am sure of a base, but they could take Petrozavodsk any day. There is some danger in having so many irons in the fire, but I think I have enough friends to get me out even if it comes to flying. Evacuation has come to a standstill as far as we are concerned, but we will push the official lot as much as possible. We continue to delay trains of mines and guns for the north at very small expense.[14]

Cromie had to handle all these plots under the most trying circumstances, since the Germans had put a price of 100,000 roubles on his head and from May much of his covert work had had to be conducted by night. He was not the only one to feel the pressure. July also saw the downfall of Litch. According to Armin von Reyher of the German Consulate-General in Petrograd, the German Intelligence Services managed to so compromise him that he was recalled by the British. His expenditure had risen to 150 million roubles and he had run out of money. However, the relief for the Germans was short lived as Litch was swiftly replaced.[15]

The Bolsheviks were also feeling the pressure. Assailed from both left and right, leading Bolsheviks were preparing to flee. Riezler reported in June:

> For the moment their terror seems to have gained a little wind, but, in spite of this, Karachan has put the original of the Treaty of Brest ready in his desk. He intends to take the document with him to America and to sell it, with the Emperor's signature on it, to the highest bidder.[16]

The situation had worsened since then. The crisis caused by Mirbach's murder remained unresolved for most of the month. German invasion was seen as a desperately real threat, while the landing and advance of Allied forces was anticipated with dread. The Czechoslovaks looked unstoppable, while the internal opposition was showing its teeth. The Bolsheviks knew these latter were working with the Allies. They were like a man, threatened from two sides, finding the ground beneath his feet giving way.

The secret web the Allies had spun to ensure the success of their intervention without committing many troops was extensive. The key player for the military intervention in the north was to be Captain McGrath, who had been sent out by London for that precise purpose. After his arrival at Murmansk, he went to Petrograd and then on to Archangel. He operated in civilian clothes and thus was open to being shot as a spy had he been caught. In the words of the British Consul at Archangel:

> His mission was none other than to organise in Archangel a rising of the Anti-Bolshevik elements with the active assistance of Russian officers of the old regime, to overthrow the Soviet authority and then to invite the Allied forces at Murmansk to come in and help them. During his stay in Petrograd Captain McGrath had arranged the Petrograd end of the business with the late Captain Cromie R.N. . . . A Russian naval officer who had served with Captain Cromie in the Baltic shortly followed Captain McGrath. This officer, who may be known as Captain X [Chaplin], was to take direct control of the military side of the rising. To assist him in his plans he was given a British passport, issued by the British Consul in Petrograd [Arthur Woodhouse], under an assumed British name.[17]

As early as 4 March 1917 Smith Cumming had discussed with Samuel Hoare what was needed to continue Secret Service work in Russia. Hoare advised him that an official position and some ostensible duties were essential.[18] This was possibly the origin of the Passport Control Officer façade. However, as Lieutenant Webster already filled that position in Moscow, another cover would be needed for McGrath. His cover was his appointment as a Vice-Consul in the Siberian town of Krasnoyarsk.

He would henceforth be attached to the Foreign Office, ostensibly on leave from the Army. No documents on his appointment survive in the Foreign Office files in the National Archives; they were destroyed. However, traces of the appointment can be found in the Foreign Office card index where, under his name, can be found the references '52680/18 Acting Vice Consul at Krasnoyarsk – on leave,' and '93907/38900/18 Re: of giving him a post in Russia'.

The situation is likewise in the case of temporary Sub-Lieutenant Andrew Cunningham of the Royal Naval Volunteer Reserve, another of 'C's men. He was appointed as Vice-Consul at Samara, where delegates to the former Constituent Assembly were forming a new government, known as the Komuch, after the seizure of the town by the Czechoslovaks.

At this time the appointment of Vice-Consuls were also considered for the towns of Nicolaievsk, Habarovsk [sic Khabarovsk], Tchita [sic Chita], Irkutsk, Tomsk, Krasnoyarsk, Semipalatinsk, Samara, Kazan, Orenburg, Penza, Ufa and Nijni Novgorod. Most of these places had never merited a British consular official before and while certainly not all of the men appointed were Intelligence officers, it can definitely be stated that two were. The reason for this focus on the Siberian towns is obvious – the British Government sought to influence events there and provide support to its allies – the Czechoslovaks and Whites.

The Bolsheviks were alert to this chicanery. A report from Lockhart's mission at the beginning of August allows light to fall on some of their knowledge:

Please send urgently following telegram numbered 349 from Lockhart to M.I.1.C. Telegrams of following character are being received here from Archangel by Commissar Butenko who obtains information from Russian who was recruited in Russia and now apparently holds British Commission of Second Lieutenant. A. Giving terms of services with Allied forces. B. States Colonel Thornhill has arranged with two (? lately) arrived boats rendez-vous at (two groups undecipherable) for mapping of Archangel and Vologda district each received 50,000. Also giving names of telegraphist and railway officials in Allied pay. In all cases receipts were taken. C. States that General Denikin is going up north and that a supported motor relay service was being arranged for his transport. D. That in Archangel there are two men acting as recruiting agents for Allies – L.A. ginger-headed (? Jew) aged about twenty-three, other apparently Britisher, dressed in grey Norfolk, aged about thirty. E. Allied secret service was very efficient and worked chiefly from Consulates. A regular radio service is in operation.[19]

Scrawled across the face of the document is the legend: 'Copies sent to: C.S.S. [Chief of Secret Service] D.M.I.' This shows how seriously the news was taken – as well it might be.

Much about Allied secret intrigues and operations was revealed here. The Consulates were now hopelessly compromised and the Bolsheviks would be fully justified in taking steps to prevent any further abuse of consular position and privilege. The idea of Denikin travelling to north Russia by motor relay sounds improbable. Perhaps the informant was misinformed or simply mistaken; perhaps it was actually planned, but abandoned once it was realised the Bolsheviks knew about it. It is unknown what happened to the telegraphist(s) and railway officials in Allied pay. Presumably they were given short shrift.

The episode illustrates one of the key problems of the secret war in Russia, one that affected every party to the struggle. That was the reliability or otherwise of individuals employed, especially when attempts were made to employ people en masse as the Allies were persistently trying to do. There was not even a remote possibility that every individual was committed and loyal. The Bolsheviks had identical problems with the numbers of specialists they had to employ at staff and technical levels. As has been shown, people of this level were only too ready to pass information to the Allied Intelligence agencies, or to parties who were in touch with them.

This also raises questions about the reliability of the raw information Allied Intelligence Services received from these sources. In the great majority of cases this would be framed to persuade the Allies to act in a manner that would meet the desires of the informants. This happened in the case of the Sisson Documents. Evaluation of this material from such sources therefore called for a very high order of skill. This was not as common as would be the case in an ideal situation.

Attempts were made to coordinate operations in the north with those in Siberia and the Volunteer Army in the south. At least one British officer,

Captain Charles Kenelm Digby Jones, was sent from Archangel to liaise with the Czechoslovaks in Siberia. McGrath had in fact told Digby Jones to leave on 19 June, but it looks like he was delayed for some unknown reason, as he did not start until 8 July.[20] A civilian, Mr Reed, whose business remains unknown, accompanied him, as did a White officer, Lieutenant Meinov. He arrived in Ekaterinburg on 16/17 July, the night the Tsar and his family were alleged to have been murdered. He succeeded in making contact with the Czechoslovaks, and presumably passed on General Poole's orders to them. He was to die of illness – influenza leading to meningitis – in Cheliabinsk in the autumn.

In the wake of the Czechoslovak successes in Siberia, White 'governments' sprang up like mushrooms. Two of the most important ones were the Provisional Siberian Government at Omsk and a Right Social Revolutionary government, the Komuch, at Samara. Other, more localized governments with grand ambitions formed at Tomsk and Krasnoyarsk. There was also Horvath's Far Eastern Government and others. The Allies and their adherents were faced with a tremendous problem in either forcing or persuading them to work together.

Second only to the hatred these governments felt for the Bolsheviks was their hatred, jealousy and suspicion of each other. The Komuch, comprising members of the former Constituent Assembly, claimed to speak for the whole of Russia and would brook no compromise with any other element. Those with regional interests were reluctant to make common cause with those that had larger ambitions, for fear their own interests would be trampled underfoot. Those dominated by the military or Cadets were bent on smashing the Bolsheviks and drew little distinction between them and other parties on the Left. Each was jealous of its own little 'kingdom'.

The Czechoslovaks allowed these governments to form, but took little interest in them thereafter. Their focus was on more immediate problems. Those at Vladivostock turned westwards to link with their comrades in western Siberia. The latter were striving to get to the north, but were held for a time at Ekaterinburg. The fact that the movement of the Czechoslovaks from Vladivostock westwards complied with Allied strategy rather than the stated purpose of evacuation to France, indicates they were marching to a prearranged plan and that plan was an Allied one for destroying the Bolsheviks.

Communication between the different echelons of Czechoslovak troops was vital. Along the Trans-Siberian Railway from Penza via Cheliabinsk to Nijni-Udinsk, the railway stationmasters sympathized with the Czechoslovaks and assisted them when possible. Many of the telegraphists also sympathized with them; those who did not were replaced.

Commandant Guinet, who was organizing and coordinating the pro-Allied forces that were springing up under the aegis of these different governments in Siberia, congratulated the Czechoslovaks on their actions against the Bolshevik Government. 'Until recently,' he wrote, 'the represen-tatives of France tried to maintain normal relations with the Soviet author-ities, but now these authorities, in the opinion of the Allies and of all the civilised world, no longer deserve it.'[21] Apart from refusing to play the Allied game and go to war against Germany, it is difficult to see precisely what the Moscow government had done to cause such grave offence. The response in Moscow was naturally acerbic. Lockhart noted: 'French also blackguarded in the Press for a proclamation said to have been issued to Czechs in Siberia by French colonel attached to Czech mission.'[22]

To coordinate the actions of the Czechoslovaks at Vladivostock with those of their comrades in western Siberia, a British liaison officer, Captain Leo Steveni, was appointed to the staff of General Mikhail Dietrichs, who was commanding the Czechoslovaks in eastern Siberia. He was told to make every effort to ensure cooperation between the Czechoslovaks and White Russian military elements, and to smooth over any friction between the Czechoslovaks and General Horvath's Far Eastern Government. He was also responsible for liaising with Semenoff at Harbin and trying to keep General Dietrichs, Semenoff and General Horvath harnessed to the Allied wagon without squabbling. Dietrichs, he reported, was disdainful of the quality of Horvath's troops with the exception of the Cossacks under Kalmikov. In a bid to achieve the desired cooperation, he persuaded Dietrichs, Horvath and Kalmikov to meet on 1 August at Grodecovo. A degree of cooperation was achieved, with Kalmikov being detailed to cooperate with the Czechoslovaks under Dietrich's command on the Ussuri front.

Yet Dietrichs was not independent. He was in the pay of the British. Steveni forwarded a message from him to the DMI:

> I have permitted my assistant to leave me as Metcalf, who was instructed to pay my assistant and myself 35*l*. to 65*l*. per month respectively, has now left the party, and I have received no payment since June, and arrived here with no definite instructions from you. At your suggestion I agreed to undertake this journey and warned you through Metcalf that only if subsidised by you could I go.[23]

There would appear to have been those in Britain who saw a far-reaching role for Dietrichs. Immediately following his transmission of Dietrich's message, Steveni continued:

> ...consider his apparent disappointment due entirely to Metcalf, who, on journey, certainly gave General to understand that with British support when intervention came he would become (two groups undecipherable) in restoration of Russia.

With the commander, a Russian, of the Czechoslovaks advancing westwards from Vladivostock in British pay, pleas of Allied innocence in the rising of the Czechoslovaks in Russia can have no foundation. The Czechoslovaks had an importance far beyond being the military spearhead of the intervention, beyond even the hope they could cut off the food supplies to Moscow and Petrograd. They were a lever to bring the United States into the club of interventionist powers.

David Lloyd George saw the opportunity to use the Czechoslovaks in this manner at the beginning of July. It was then he sent a telegram to Lord Reading, the British Ambassador in Washington, DC, that urged just such a course:

> Secret. Following from Prime Minister.
> I hope you will do all you can secure complete American co-operation for policy of intervention in Siberia recommended to them by Supreme War Council to-day. President's arguments against it, especially his fears as to effect on Russian opinion of intervention by forces mainly Japanese have weighed strongly with me in the past. To-day however conditions have greatly changed and I am now convinced that if we do not act at once Russia and Western Siberia will be in

German hands before the winter. The Czecho Slovak successes give us an opportunity of restoring an Eastern front and revitalising Russia which may never return. Unless we take fullest advantage of this opportunity of reconstitution of an Eastern front I frankly do not see how we are to bring the war to a satisfactory end in 1919. I feel sure that President will accept recommendation of Supreme War Council, but I rely upon you to see, as you did so successfully in the case of American troops for Europe, that matter is pressed to practical conclusions without delay, as unless action is taken at once Czechs may be overwhelmed and chance of establishing ourselves in Siberia and Northern Russia before winter sets in may disappear.[24]

The argument that the Czechoslovak Legion might be overwhelmed without Allied support dangled a tempting moral carrot in front of President Wilson. He was being offered the chance to play the knight in shining armour riding to the rescue of a damsel in distress, or the US cavalry galloping to the rescue of a beleaguered wagon train.

One wonders just how much influence the Supreme War Council had on Lloyd George's change of heart, for there was a competitor for that honour. On 16 June, Sir William Wiseman, MI1(c)'s station chief in the United States, had sent a message deploring the fact that all the arguments in favour of intervention were 'virtually exhausted'. He added:

There remains only the Czechoslovak complication to use as a lever. Possibly an appeal to the President to extricate these unhappy people from their present grave position would be useful. The sympathy for them in the United States must be considerable and moreover, until they are disorganised by Bolshevist attacks or disintegrated by Bolshevist propaganda, they are of great military value along the Siberian railway. If they are to be saved at all intact as a force, or the military situation which they have created utilised at all, intervention if it is to be must be undertaken at once. At all events it seems worthy of consideration whether we should not make the most of this in dealing with the President.[25]

It cannot be stated with certainty whether Lloyd George ever read this telegram. If he did, then the insight of a Secret Service officer may have been the major influence.

With his commitment to self-determination, as announced in his famous Fourteen Points, Wilson was open to the idea of assisting the

Czechoslovaks. Through the influence of his friend Tomas Masaryk, Wilson held them in particularly high esteem. Theirs was a moral argument he would find difficult to resist. At a conference in the White House with his military advisers on 6 July, Wilson decided that small American and, remarkably, Japanese forces were to intervene in Siberia. The emphasis was on 'small'.

When the President presented his aide-memoire to the Allies on 17 July, it stated American military intervention in Siberia was allowed in order to 'help the Czecho-Slovaks consolidate their forces and get into successful cooperation with their Slavic kinsmen'. The military intervention was to be limited in scope and numbers, but the commitment had been made. The door was now open to the long-desired Japanese intervention.

This introduced a new player onto the Intelligence field. The difficulty was that the United States had no formal Secret Service at the time. This meant one had to be built up from scratch. The United States' Consular Service, led by the Consul-General in Moscow, De Witt C. Poole, provided the bedrock. According to Brook-Shepherd, Poole and his vice-consul led seven consular officers spread throughout the Russian Empire, a hardly generous allocation.

Beyond them were eight 'Especially Appointed Vice-Consuls', most of whom were former members of the Young Men's Christian Association. Finally, there were twenty-seven rapidly recruited 'Observers and Special Agents', nineteen of whom were serving under Xenophon B. Kalamatiano. Some of these were Russians. The rest, like Kalamatiano, were American citizens.[26]

The United States' Consul-General was swiftly involved in the clandestine war. Every day the Allied representatives in Moscow met at the American Consulate to plan their activities, the safest location since the Bolsheviks directed their wrath against the British and French, perhaps hoping to split America from the Allies by turning a blind eye to their part in the covert war.

On 13 July, Lockhart recorded that he 'Saw Keyes again and had a long talk with him.' The next day he went with Keyes to see an individual identified as 'P.B.' and had another long talk. On the 15th there was a conference between Grenard and Keyes. The long talks were not about the weather, for on 16 July Keyes left and McAlpine arrived from Petrograd. According to Lockhart, 'He gave us distressing news of Poole's plans.'[27]

Lockhart felt strongly that the forces the Allies were going to commit to military intervention were too small. He had consistently urged that if intervention was to be made, it needed to be made in strength. As late as August a message was received from him, informing the British Government:

> If therefore intervention does not take place and Czechs and Centre are left to their fate our positions in Russia will be irretrievably damaged. Two [sic The?] Centre warn us that if our intervention is to be successful it must be made in force and that the support we will receive from Russia will be in proportion to number of troops we send. This seems to me such an elementary truth that I must once more point out the serious danger we run in imagining that [I] we have only to send out officers to form and command troops composed of those Russians were willing to join us.[28]

The Allies, and particularly the British, made just this mistake. They sent out a small force along the lines favoured by MIO, consisting largely of officers with a small number of troops to serve as a nucleus around which 'loyal' Russians and foreign detachments could form.

The Allied plan of operations was simple. It was so simple as to be obvious to the Bolsheviks. They planned to sail from Murmansk, descend on Archangel, capture the port and from there march south to join hands with the Czechoslovak Legion and such White forces as had reached Kotlas, where the railway from Archangel to Moscow joined the Trans-Siberian Railway. The Allies, moreover, knew the Bolsheviks were aware of their obvious plan, for they were told in the report from the officer of the Soviet General Staff in Moscow who alerted the Allies to the 'doubt and mystery' of Mirbach's death:

> So far as we know, the Bolsheviks understand the intention of the Allies to join up with the Czechs through Kotlas. It is also appreciated that the Allies cannot move on Petrozavodsk whilst the Finns threaten their flank. The only feasible movement is considered to be in the direction of Obozerskaya and further to Kotlas, whither the Czechs are moving.[29]

There was thus no possibility of surprise, an all too common factor in Allied military operations during the First World War. Perhaps their perseverance was the fruit of overconfidence. The same informant also told Poole that the Bolsheviks were preparing four operation schemes and they had given at least one of these to a German officer. He continued, 'We are making every effort to obtain the operation scheme against the Czech front and we hope to succeed.'[30]

In anticipation of the military intervention the Allied Intelligence Services redoubled their efforts to undermine the Bolsheviks. The interception of Bolshevik communications had reached an advanced stage, if the charming story Lockhart recorded in his *Memoirs* is to be believed. In mid-July the Bolsheviks sought to persuade the Allies' Embassies to return from Vologda to Moscow. They sent Radek as their emissary. The Ambassadors and their staffs thought it probable that the Bolsheviks wanted them in Moscow so they could be used as hostages as and when the intervention came, so they refused.

Radek reported the failure of his mission by telegraph. The Allies intercepted his message and the United States' Ambassador, David Francis, had the pleasure of reading out Radek's account to the assembled Ambassadors. It included the observation that, 'Ambassador Francis is a stuffed shirt-front', while the British High Commissioner, Francis Lindley, was (presumably) embarrassed to hear that 'He practically admits that he considers Noulens's behaviour childish in the extreme.'[31]

Fearing for their safety, the Ambassadors fled Vologda for Archangel on 24 July. With supreme irony, their train met that of the Bolshevik commander at Archangel, Commissar Kedrov. He was returning to Moscow to report on the position at Archangel. It was a single-line railway and both trains had to halt. Kedrov and the Ambassadors talked while one of the trains moved to a siding.

With Allied military intervention now a certainty, British Intelligence officers made plans to stay behind when their diplomats and military missions left Russia. Hill enjoyed increasingly close relations with Sydney Reilly, whom he came to greatly admire, and who would appear to have had some influence in persuading Hill to remain in Russia. Hill's report to Poole on this aspect of his operations reads:

Experience had shown that Russian organisations (benefiting from our funds) had entailed great wastage with small results, therefore preparations were

202

commenced to enable one or two British officers to stay behind 'after hostilities had commenced' in order to organise the recruiting.

The idea of course was to combine identifications with destruction and recruiting. I found M.I.1.C. were also making preparations to leave an officer behind, (S.T.). However, at a conference with Lt. [Lieutenant] Boyce R.N.V.R. (M.I.1.C.) and S.T., they pointed out how likely it was the recruiting and organisations would be traced soon after it commenced to function and that this should, despite past experience be handled by a Russian organisation, but they suggested that the courier service already organised by myself, should be developed, and that I should remain behind. Recruiting went on, but it was intended to drop it as soon as we went underground.[32]

Hill makes far-reaching claims for the success of his courier service in his book on his activities in Russia, *Go Spy the Land*. However, his official report shows that it was beset by difficulties. The courier service was activated when the Bolsheviks forbade Allied officers from leaving the towns where they were based and from wearing their uniforms. On 12 July they also prohibited the transmission of coded telegrams by both officers and consuls.

Hill had estimated that 20 to 25 couriers would suffice to maintain constant communications between the Intelligence officers in central Russia and the intervention force in the north. This proved an underestimation and more would be required. The first couriers left on 8 July, one by each route. Hill related:

> Courier 1 returned after 12 days; he reported a difficult passage North, was twice arrested and searched. He returned by trickery direct from Archangel by train and so cut the journey in half. He said the nervous strain was very great and a good rest would be needed after every journey.
> Courier 2 went out on the Petrozavodsk route; he was away 20 days, and had similar experiences to No 1. His journey was however more expensive, as he had had to use horses in certain places.[33]

These experiences led Hill to increase the number of couriers on 1 August. He also made other preparations. In order to observe the expected increase in Red Army troop movements in response to the intervention, Hill also organized a number of agents to observe these movements in the Moscow railway knot. He also organized a small destruction gang, together with another small section for obtaining false passports, passes and documents. Sabotage was one of the tools common to all the Allies, and the French were planning destruction on a major scale. A telegram from Général Lavergne to the Deuxième Bureau reported:

> Intelligence Service Laurent has arrived to give great development to services and the manufactur [of] instruments: he requires however, that for Port Murmansk you make and send regular phials of sulphuric electronic detonators and ordinary ones that he cannot make.
>
> He would also like poison for livestock and rot for cereals and potatoes. Everything should be in sufficiently reduced packets by preference boxes of conserves.
>
> Altogether, the service requires 200,000 francs, of which 100,000 have already been allocated. Pray grant this supplement from the 1st August. In case of leaving Moscow I have the intention of according Laurent one million roubles. I ask that you let me know your decision by telegram.[34]

This highlights that favoured French ploy of starving the people of central Russia into revolting against the Bolsheviks.

The German and Bolshevik antagonism towards the Allied missions, together with the order banning Allied officers from travelling were marked by Reilly, during his interrogation by the OGPU in 1925, as the occasion when he turned from courting the Orthodox Church to actively opposing the Bolsheviks. He explained:

> From this very moment, I started my fight against Soviet power, which manifests itself mostly in military and political intelligence and in identification of the active elements that could be used in the fight against the Soviet government. For this purpose, I went underground and obtained documents from various persons; for some period of time, for example, I was a commissar in charge of transporting spare vehicle parts during the evacuation from Petrograd, which provided me with a good opportunity to travel between Moscow and Petrograd without any restrictions, even in the commissars coach. At this time, I resided mostly in Moscow, changing flats nearly every day.[35]

This is broadly accurate, but Reilly was only telling his interrogators what he wanted them to know and what he knew they already knew, so it needs to be treated with circumspection. What is left unclear is whether he was acting on his own initiative, or operating in accordance with the plans and orders of the British Secret Service.

The Bolsheviks increasingly turned against the Allies as a matter of sheer survival. They knew Germany was weakening, but they were not yet strong enough to resist further German aggression. Now they were confronted with the threat of Allied intervention. Chicherin summed up their position thus:

> In the meantime our break with the Entente had considerably strengthened Germany's diplomatic position against us. At the same time, the 'Bolshevist menace' threatening Germany had become palpable and not merely theoretical. The German press cast off the restraint which had characterised its attitude toward us in the first months after the Brest treaty. Our internal difficulties, the unrest among the peasants, and the counter-revolutionary insurrections gave the German Government an impression of our apparent weakness. Thus the decline of German power, which was already noticeable, was neutralised by the impairment of our position in relation to the German Government. [36]

Indeed, in the report from the officer spying for the British within the Soviet General Staff it was stated:

> All the defences against the Germans are in a still worse condition. Characteristic is the conversation of one of our agents with General Parski's Chief of Staff, in which the latter mentions that it had been decided not to defend any of the fortified positions against the Germans. At the first advance of the Germans, the Staff will retire to Tikhvin, and the troops will be moved east, the general hope being that they will be received by the Allies. [37]

On the other hand, they were certain they could crush all internal opposition unless strong foreign forces supported it and, since Allied military plans for intervention were so obvious, and the climate and terrain in north Russia so difficult, they felt they had a sporting chance of parrying this thrust. The chance would be even better if they could buy off the Germans and win an element of German support. There seemed every prospect of this. At the end of June, Lockhart had informed London that this was being discussed:

205

General Lavergne informed me this afternoon Wednesday, that Trotsky had stated to an officer of French Staff that at last night's (Tuesday) meeting of small Soviet the Commissars had admitted in principle that the only way of averting German intervention and consequent occupation of Moscow and Petrograd by Germans was for Bolsheviks [to] declare war on the Allies and conduct vigorous attack against their intervention in the North and Far East.

In this manner Bolsheviks think they will gain a few weeks more and if they declare war on us vigorously it will prevent Germans from forcing their aid on them.

Trotsky states Germans have already offered their aid in this connection but that Bolsheviks had refused it. This modification has not (?been) raised in connection with landing of 15,000 British troops at Murmansk on the 23rd June.

Matter will be discussed again tomorrow Thursday and a decision in this sense may be expected at any moment, and do not know how far may be bluff on Trotsky's part, but from Bolsheviks point of view there is nothing illogical in this policy which is on a par with the usual policy of blind opportunism.[38]

In light of the shaky position of the Bolsheviks, such a development might have been expected. Nevertheless, at that stage the Bolsheviks were still extremely wary of accepting help from the Germans. The cynicism of the Allied officials was also displayed in this document, for Lockhart went on to suggest it might be to the Allies' advantage if the Bolsheviks did declare war on them, since then the United States could scarcely refuse to take action in Russia. On those grounds, Lockhart argued, it could be in Anglo-French interests to provoke a declaration of war by the Bolsheviks.

What the Allies were actually doing was driving the Bolsheviks into Germany's arms. Their generally clumsy conspiracies, and the obvious threat of military invasion had reversed the situation in June when Germany's position in Russia was being destroyed. Survival was uppermost in Bolshevik minds, and they sought to ensure this by buying off the Germans while resisting the Allies.

All the military reports sent in by Allied agents over the previous two months had consistently emphasized the weakness of the Red Army. It was variously described as 'disorganised' and 'a rabble'. We have recognized that Poole thought it could offer no serious resistance, and the Intelligence reports reinforced this view.

Now the danger of collusion with the Germans, already suspected, stoked up the fires even more. Allied Secret Intelligence agents appeared to be the first targets. A report from Petrograd, titled 'Various Agents', stated:

It is intended shortly to take measures for the complete liquidation of the Allied activities in PETROGRAD. Especially experienced Secret Service men are expected to arrive from Germany. The allied agents are to be arrested by the Soviet, under the directions of the Germans. According to rumours, the organisations have documents, definitely establishing the connection of the Allied Missions with the right wing of the Socialists.[39]

This report turned out to be true, but the impact of these measures was not to be felt for nearly a month. The danger was clear to all parties in the clandestine struggle for, as the value of the prizes to be won grew, so the dangers swelled in proportion.

This is well illustrated by the events surrounding the Economic Mission the British sent to Russia in July. The Mission ostensibly had economic goals. Its members were Sir William Clark, Mr Peters of the Commercial Diplomatic Service, Leslie Urquhart, a Siberian manganese magnate who hated the Bolsheviks, and Henry Armitstead. Others have commented on the peculiarity of sending such a mission at this juncture, but have appeared broadly content to accept it at face value. Insofar as one can peep below the covers, a different story emerges.

One of the duties of the Mission was to examine the banking scheme that had been operated by Terence Keyes, and parts of the criticisms contained in its reports have already been seen. One of the Mission's members, Henry Armitstead, had been involved in creating the safe house for the former Tsar and his family at Murmansk. When in Moscow he had seen not only Lockhart, but also the head of the Secret Service's Moscow station, Ernest Boyce. The three men had lunch together on 23 July.[40] Lockhart, the only source for this, does not disclose anything about the discussions that might have taken place but, since Boyce and Lockhart were both engaged in subversive activity, one would have to be naïve to imagine that the subject never came up.

When the Economic Mission fled Russia on the eve of the Allied landing at Archangel they almost missed the ship and had to scramble aboard in undignified haste. Armitstead told one of Douglas Young's vice-consuls that he had left certain letters in the care of the Russian attendant of their railway carriage, requesting him to deliver them as soon as possible. Young explains what happened:

> My vice-consul, immediately scenting danger, doubled back as fast as he could to the train and recovered the letters. One of them proved to be from Captain Cromie, and the contents were such, if they had fallen into the hands of the Soviet authorities, as to give the whole show away and hang the lot of us.[41]

The flight of the members of the Economic Mission was the prelude to the Allied intervention. 'Syren' Force was already pushing south from Murmansk, but the real blow was to be struck by an additional force, called 'Elope'. This was also under Poole's command. When 'Syren' Force seized the small town of Kem, they captured three members of its Soviet. These were handed over to the Serbs to guard and were confined in a railway carriage. The Serbs, protégés of the French, were encouraged by them to promote the idea that the Bolsheviks should try to escape. As they did they were shot down. The excuse offered to the world was that they were resisting arrest and attempting to escape. This wanton act was to have potentially grave consequences in the next month.

There is an obvious discrepancy between the launch of the 'Syren' offensive and the landing of 'Elope'. Poole, like every commanding officer before and since, wanted more troops. While it was larger than 'Syren' at Murmansk, 'Elope' remained a small force that was unlikely to be able to master a strong and determined defence. Poole pressed the War Office for more men. They sent him a signal stating:

> I concur in your general conclusions, that is to say, that your arrival at Archangel should be deferred until the French detachment has joined you. The question of a British battalion to reinforce you is being taken up by us but in any case this cannot reach you before the middle of August.[42]

However, Poole was prepared to go ahead without the reinforcements. The real reasons for the delay were, first, the weather and second, the postponement of the expected coup. The port of Archangel is ice-bound between

September and May. In 1918 the thaw was seriously delayed. The frozen conditions continued into July, frustrating any idea of landing at Archangel. The second, the coup McGrath was arranging in Archangel, aided and abetted by Chaplin, was repeatedly postponed. The plotters planned to seize Archangel, murder the members of the local Soviet and then invite the waiting Allies at Murmansk into Archangel. The Allies at Murmansk were led to expect that the pre-arranged signal from the conspirators at Archangel was imminent. In the event it never came, because the plotters were reluctant to move on their own since the forces of the Red Army at Archangel, although small, were quite sufficient to crush any local rising.

Instead the alarm was sounded from an entirely different direction. After their conversation with Commissar Kedrov, the Allied Ambassadors resumed their journey towards Archangel. According to Douglas Young:

> Arrived at Kandalashka, Mr. Lindley, H.M. Representative, telephoned to the British Military Command at Murmansk that a 'rising' at Archangel might occur at any moment and that the British must consequently hurry in there immediately. The information was not exact; for no rising did, or could occur. But this action precipitated the despatch of the Allied Naval expedition from Murmansk.[43]

Poole had been expecting Chaplin's coup to take place on 5 August. The original plan had been to sail on that date, but on 22 July it was altered to 2 August.[44] So, at the end of July, he was being pressured by his immediate political superior to act with all despatch. This he proceeded to do on 30 July.

The delay to the Allied incursion at Archangel had an impact on Savinkov's rising of 6 July, along with that of the Left Social Revolutionaries. He has often been blamed for launching his rising prematurely, when there was no prospect of Allied support which, it cannot be doubted, had been promised. The Centre had also received an identical promise. The main site of Savinkov's rising was Yaroslavl, on the direct route from Archangel, Kotlas and Vologda to Moscow, so well placed to receive Allied support from north Russia – if any came.

As it was, Savinkov's men were left out on a limb. They could not be helped. To blame Savinkov for timing his rising badly under these circumstances neatly shifts the responsibility entirely on to his shoulders and quietly relieves the Allies of any accountability. It also distracts attention not only from the Allies' part in the plan, but disguises the fact there was a plan.

XI

The Grand Unravelling

August 1918

—◄o►—

When 'Elope' Force landed at Archangel on 2 August, it consisted of just two battalions, the French 21st Colonial Battalion and a British second-line Territorial Battalion, the 2/10th Royal Scots, together with some British Royal Marines and, significantly, sixty-four American soldiers from the 339th Infantry Regiment. They succeeded in taking the town, helped by one of Chaplin's men, Nikolai Startsev, a lawyer who had been distributing British weapons to Chaplin's followers in the area. They created a diversion at Shenkursk, south of Archangel, that drew away several hundred men from the meagre 800-man garrison that the Red Army had to defend Archangel. It was the only part of the planned coup that was successful.

The Americans had stipulated that their troops were to be employed only in guarding the ports and stores in north Russia. The Allies had agreed. In fact, when the rest of the Regiment arrived they were to be used as the spearhead for the push south from Archangel towards Kotlas and Vologda.

General Poole's optimistic view that the Red Army was an undisciplined rabble that could be brushed aside as he romped down the railway line towards the Czechoslovaks and Moscow betrayed both him and 'Elope'. The Allied advance after landing was slow and it was soon bogged down against stiff opposition.

More important than the armed troops put ashore by the Allies is the composition of the British staff for Elope. It was a disproportionately large staff for such a minuscule force, and it contained a large number of Intelligence officers for such a small force.

At the head of the Intelligence organization was Lieutenant-Colonel C.J.M. Thornhill, whom Lockhart described as 'a rabid interventionist'.[1]

His deputy was Major W.W. van Someren of the Indian Army, formerly on the staff of MIO under Lieutenant-Colonel Steel. There were also no less than five specially appointed Intelligence officers: Captains Garstin, A.F. Hill, J.J. Pitts, and Lieutenants L.P. Hodson and G.R. Tamplin. These five were to join the force once it was in Russia, and it is of some significance that Garstin, Hill and Tamplin were all members of Lockhart's Mission.[2]

Of the six cipher officers, two – Lieutenant A.E. Sturdy and Lieutenant-Colonel A.G. Burn – had been on the staff of Rusplycom in London. Captain Digby Jones was disguised as a Royal Engineers officer. His Personal Service Record shows that he was actually working for MI1(c). Among the interpreters were Alexander Proctor and William Gerhardi. The RAF contingent was headed by Lieutenant-Colonel A.C. Maund, while George Hill was to join in Russia, as was Second Lieutenant C.G. Tomling. Hidden among the infantry officers was a pilot, Captain John Sanderson Poole. This headquarters staff had an Imperial complexion, with a smattering of officers from all the Dominions, except New Zealand.

The Nominal Roll of officers for 'Elope' bears witness to the hand that pulled the strings. The document is stamped MO2(a) and handwritten on the top is the legend 'MI2(d) 2 copies'. MO2(a) had been part of Lieutenant-Colonel Steel's MIO, while MI2(d) was the successor organization for Military Intelligence in the region. The stamp also reveals the date 15 June 1918, confirming that the British War Office had every intention of invading north Russia however much the Foreign Office might prevaricate.

The purpose of 'Elope' is transparently clear. It was to form a small nucleus around which an army of White Russians could be formed. It was typical of the plans engineered by MIO, an organization that followed a long-standing British Imperial tradition. However, the problems faced in creating such a force in north Russia meant that the 'Russian army' the British hoped to form there never reached the anticipated strength.

The news of the Allied landing at Archangel reached Moscow on 4 August. Rumour and expectation had inflated the landing force to a size many times greater than it actually was. The figure of 100,000 men rapidly became current. Seven Japanese divisions were supposed to be advancing through Siberia to join them in a march on Moscow. Reaction from the Bolsheviks was swift. On 5 August French and British citizens were arrested and interned by the Cheka. At 4.30 a.m. both the French and British Consulate-Generals and the French Mission were raided at pistol point. Oliver Wardrop kept a cool head. He had already destroyed 'a great many confidential documents', as he put it, in anticipation of such an eventuality. He had also made preparations to destroy the remainder. The story is best told in his own words:

> The programme we had prepared was carried out to the letter and I would particularly mention the valuable assistance given by Vice-Consuls Lowdon and Wishaw, who, with coolness and skill, kept the invaders in parley till I had personally, in my bedroom, carried out the work of destruction to such a point, before the threat of violence had actually become effective, that I was at last able to appear in my sitting-room, half-dressed, knowing that there was little probability of any fragments of the burning paper being legible. I still, however, continued to engage the guards in conversation till I felt certain the holocaust was perfected. Meanwhile, clouds of heavy, acrid, poisonous smoke were pouring from the window and through the door. The men on watch outside at last succeeded in attracting the attention of those who were in my company. The latter demanded the immediate opening of the door and exhibited their revolvers to enforce the demand. The door was, however, locked and the key had been passed to one of the staff who was not immediately found. When at last the door was opened the fumes were so thick that my bed-room could only be entered, even with the protection of wet cloths over the nose and mouth, at the risk of asphyxiation and my Bolshevist visitors preferred to leave the apartment incompletely examined and obtained no view of the capacious fire-place. When they finally left, I broke the charred fragments very thoroughly and to the best of my belief, there is not now in this building a single scrap of paper of a strictly confidential kind. [3]

The conversation so skilfully deployed to delay and distract the Cheka revolved around the validity of their warrant, which ordered the immediate arrest of all 'well-to-do' British and French citizens, and in disputing whether it extended to Consular officers. The Cheka officers were unsure of their ground in these respects, so it made a valuable delaying tactic. Wardrop leaves us with no impression of his feelings when, 'one of the guards before leaving, told me privately that it was a pity I had burned my correspondence, as he and his comrades had no authority to make a perquisition or to seize papers or property of any kind.' [4]

Whatever his private feelings upon hearing this, Wardrop must have been relieved that he had taken this action when the Consulate-General was again raided by the Cheka at 4 p.m. This time Lockhart and Captain Hicks were with him and the official part of the building and its contents were sealed up. The next day, 6 August, the staff of the Consulate-General were arrested, although, curiously, Lockhart, Wardrop and Hicks were allowed to remain at liberty. The French Consulate was surrounded and Consul-General Grenard was arrested, as were Général Lavergne and the French Military Mission. All the Allied representatives who were seized were swiftly released, but then confined under a rather loose house arrest.

Lockhart had also destroyed his confidential documents and ciphers on 5 August, but under less trying circumstances. Why was there a need to destroy all this material? It was because Wardrop was in touch with the Cadets and Czechoslovaks, while Lockhart was dealing with the National Centre and also intriguing with others.

The Bolsheviks were still treading carefully, caught as they were between two fires. In his last letter to Admiral Hall, Cromie summed up their predicament thus:

> It is evident that the Bolshi wishes to avoid an open rupture with us and so be forced to definitely declare on which side they are, as it suits their purpose to sit on the fence at present. To declare war on us would put the people against them, whilst not to move against us will bring the Germans down on them, in fact it has been touch-and-go with them for the last week.[5]

The crisis the Bolsheviks faced after the murder of Mirbach was more prolonged than the accepted view in the West indicates. They did not want war with the Germans or the Allies; their long-term hopes were founded upon using propaganda to subvert the social structures of the belligerent powers, with Germany as their major target. For the moment they were under the most severe pressure from the Germans who held the Allies responsible for Mirbach's murder and the continuing instability within Russia. At the same time Allied policy was pushing the Bolsheviks increasingly towards cooperation with the Germans as their only means of survival.

That summer it had looked to most of the Bolshevik leadership that their prospects were slim. We have seen that Karachan was preparing to flee to the

United States with the original of the Treaty of Brest-Litovsk and there sell it for as much as he could get. Cromie reported that 'Lenin and Trotsky have been up here [in Petrograd] a great deal lately, and they seem prepared to flit – it is said to Switzerland.'[6] He also reported that 'Lenin is at Peterhof and a yacht under Swedish flag ready to take himself away.'[7] Hill, who was in Moscow at the time, reported that the fall of Kazan to the Whites, the Allied pressure in the north, and the fact that Trotsky had temporarily disappeared, 'caused much unrest in official circles. Many of the Commissars of the various departments were procuring passports and money and making general personal arrangements for safe departure.'[8]

Wardrop sent a contemporary report from Moscow:

> The Bolshevik leaders are well aware that their position is critical and in private the majority of them admit that they cannot last more than a few days. Lenin seems to favour the temporary disappearance of the party from public life; Trotzky [sic Trotsky] apparently wishes to go on as long as possible with the help of German troops.[9]

The help of German troops was not a figment of Wardrop's imagination. The Bolsheviks invited the Germans through Helfferich, the new German Ambassador, to march an army to north Russia along a route they would prepare for them. This was to run from the Finnish border to the north, avoiding Petrograd and Petrozavodsk. Such an advance would inevitably threaten any advance the Allies made from Murmansk and Archangel. In return, the Bolsheviks wanted the German army in the Ukraine to combat any attempt by the Volunteer Army to march north. Apparently Helfferich did not transmit the proposal to Berlin in its original form.[10] Instead he recommended that German troops should replace the Bolsheviks with a puppet government along the lines of the Skoropadsky regime in the Ukraine.

The Allied landings and intrigues combined to frighten both the Germans and Bolsheviks into near panic, which threw them together. As Cromie observed: 'Position of Soviet powerful in Petrograd is becoming rapidly untenable they are giving orders for evacuation of various units (group unde-cipherable). It is evident they are in touch with Germans.'[11] Being 'in touch with [the] Germans' was a mixed benefit. It is likely that the Bolsheviks and

Germans fed and fuelled each other's desperation, for Cromie reported that the Germans were equally panicky:

> So many people have been trying to get up North to join us, and so many detachments turning over to us that they got really frightened; this, coupled with further attempts on the German Embassy and the steady advance of the Tcheks [*sic* Czechs], spread a sort of panic amongst the Hun as well. The Hun has been very busy evacuating both from Moscow and Petrograd into Finland.[12]

The German Embassy abandoned Moscow on 7 August, getting held up en route by fighting between Red Guards and peasants around Orsha. On his return to Berlin, Helfferich pressed for the overthrow of the Bolsheviks, whom he detested, but the new situation created by the Allied intervention led to the Germans throwing their weight behind them. There was little alternative. The clandestine Allied moves had cornered the market in meaningful alternatives to the Bolsheviks.

The most immediate impact was felt on those clandestine activities. It has already been seen that German Secret Servicemen were being brought in to liquidate the underground manoeuvres of the Allies. They carried out sweeping arrests of 'class enemies' who might be expected to support the Allies, together with such Allied agents as they could catch. Cromie informed Admiral Hall of these events:

> The Hun got so nervy that they organised the wholesale arrest of officers and leading bourgeoisie as both they and the Bolshi no longer felt safe. Small parties were actually led by Hun officers who could hardly speak a word of Russian. In all some seven thousand arrests were made, mostly officers, who were sent to Kronstadt and packed sixty and seventy in a room with not enough room to lie down in, and without food for three days. Curiously enough the sailors, who are getting tired of the Bolshi, came to the rescue with food, &c. However, I am afraid very many met a bad end. The arrest was quite indiscriminate, ranging from mere lads up to veterans of seventy, and including men with one arm and one leg.[13]

We know Cromie was a wanted man and he did not escape the attentions of this sweep: 'My flat was visited and two nights later the house I had moved to, but I was away over the roofs before they got upstairs.'[14] Other officers had equally narrow escapes. From Stockholm came news that, 'It is reported by a Jew who arrived from Petrograd that McAlpine and Lessing have been condemned to death and are in Petrograd in hiding.'[15] Both officers were from Rusplycom, so increasingly involved in the covert operations in Russia. After his nocturnal adventure, Cromie opted to sleep in the Embassy building. Like Wardrop, he issued instructions for the destruction of compromising documents in case of need. He continued to work on the various plots he had in hand.

The mass arrests created a serious problem for the Allies' Secret Services. The people arrested were precisely those the Allies were conspiring with and counting on to rise in their favour as they advanced on Moscow and Petrograd. The arrests emasculated this strategy, leaving the small intervention forces effectively isolated from meaningful support in central Russia. In July George Hill had begun sending his information directly to MI1(c), and in August he was added to its strength. He tells us how the arrests were managed and what effect they had:

> In the middle of the week an order published by the Bolsheviks instructed all former officers, whether employed in any government branch, private business, or those out of work to report for examination and to receive new documents from the Soviet authorities. About 8,000 of the officers stationed in Moscow complied with this order, which broke up any hope of the White Guard organisations being effectively used against the Bolsheviks, as most of the officers examined were promptly arrested, put into barracks outside the town and disarmed. A similar movement had taken place in Petrograd, with the result that a great number of officers found themselves in Kronstadt and the White organisations were broken up by the Bolsheviks with equal success.[16]

The Bolshevik move also dislocated another French attempt to create counter-revolutionary forces in the cities of central Russia.

Wardrop informed London that Radek had told Mr Widerstrom, the Swedish Consul-General in Moscow, that the Bolsheviks, as a result of the murder of the members of the Kem Soviet by the Serbs, 'proposed to hold the Allied officials as hostages and shoot them successively by lot, as reprisals for the deaths of any Soviet authorities at the hands of the Allied troops.'[17] The measure had its desired effect, or so Cromie and Woodhouse reported from Petrograd:

French consul and his protector the Danish Minister have agreed to sign formal undertaking on behalf of French Government that French soldiers will not in event of occupation of Petrograd, carry out reprisals against Russians belonging to any party on account of political acts committed by order of the Soviet, on condition that no further arrests of French subjects be made. We have refused to sign similar document without instructions from Home Government.[18]

Prior to these setbacks MI1(c)'s Moscow station had been finalizing their preparations. Of 4 August, Hill wrote:

We had our last conferences for arranging affairs and Lt. Riley R.A.F. [*sic* Lieutenant Reilly] and myself gave Lt. Boyce M.I.1C. our plans, the proposed work of organisations and our estimate, approximately, of the amount of money we should require to carry on: Our proposals were accepted and authorised by Lt. Boyce M.I.1C.[19]

Hill then proceeded to list nine safe houses or, as he called them, Centres, in and around Moscow that were to serve as headquarters for a wide variety of different operations, including stores, a courier station, recruiting and meetings, sabotage, station control and passes, agents and money, indirect couriers, odds and ends, and a retreat and refuge.[20]

Reilly and Hill had previously arranged that their go-betweens would be women as they would be less likely to attract suspicion. It was an astute move. As an additional security measure, it was agreed that any meetings with the couriers would normally take place in public gardens where it would be difficult for agents of the Cheka to scrutinize them unobserved. They sent agent H.1 to Lieutenant Webster with a request to send all the money stored by MI1(c) to them as both Reilly and Hill felt it was no longer safe with the station. The transfer was agreed, but in fact to the United States' Consulate, from whence the British Secret Service officers could draw on it at need.

Of Hill's sabotage gangs, the one in Saratov seems to have been the most effective. They sent a courier to Hill in the second week of August informing him of their current plans. The destruction of naphtha and oils was temporarily suspended, but Hill suggested sabotage and propaganda directed against the proposed despatch of the Red Army's Saratov division to the Northern front, where it would face the Allies. Should this move prove imminent, Hill recommended the destruction of the railway lines. When the crisis was imminent at the end of the month, Hill reported that on 29 August the man in charge of the Saratov organizations saw him in Moscow:

> His report for the month was extremely satisfactory, and sabotage and deliberate frustration of the Bolshevik military plans had gone very well. Stores, ammunition and equipment trains were derailed, without doing any serious damage to the line, but causing three or four days blockage (Removing one line etc.).[21]

After the mass arrests of officers, Hill found himself faced with what he described as 'the shattered remnants' of the White organizations who turned to him requesting that their members might be sent to Archangel. Men going to join the Allies in the north had habitually been given a financial advance. Hill now told them that it was impossible to help them, because of 'the shortage of funds, and the small likelihood of any real attempt being made by these officers to get through to the North.'[22] This sounds cold and too sweeping. Undoubtedly some officers would have ventured northwards and some form of screening would have been more appropriate.

The Bolsheviks cut telegraphic communications in July and they continued to do so at will. They cut them again on 6 August, seriously disrupting Allied traffic. On 12 August Cromie was reduced to using a Norwegian called Jensen to carry telegrams by hand from Petrograd to the British Legation in Christiania.[23] The Bolsheviks clearly recognized that communications were a vital and vulnerable link in the Intelligence war. Even those between Allied organizations within Russia suffered. As Lavergne reported to Paris, the British diplomatic courier had been stopped and it was possible that the Allies' means of communicating privately through emissaries was no longer guaranteed.[24]

George Hill was forced to reorganize his courier service as results were 'so poor' and a large advance of money had to be granted to each courier, without any guarantee of reliability. Hill responded by trying to organize a large chain service, which inevitably demanded more personnel and more money. He considered the delivery of messages would be more certain, while the couriers could also make observations on their route north and report what they had seen to the Allied commanders.

It took time to arrange all this, but Hill sounds proud of the men and what he had achieved. In fact the service was never activated because it was over-taken by events and there is a barely concealed disappointment about the results:

> It was extremely difficult to find suitable men to volunteer for this work, but by the 22nd August an extremely fine batch of men were got together under expe-rienced and very keen leaders. All these men had suffered and lost everything they possessed owing to the Bolsheviks. They proved themselves from the very start, and had we continued the work, it would have been entirely satisfactory. The parties left Moscow on the 22nd August and the whole chain was expected to be in operation by the first days of September.
>
> On the departure of these groups we immediately set about procuring a further 20 men to replace the casualties that were bound to occur. (Note. Nine of the original number were executed by the 'Extraordinary Commissions' in Vologda District).[25]

In each village, town and city the Bolsheviks had formed 'Committees of the Poor' from the poorest peasants and menial workers. They were made responsible for checking the identity of all strangers in their areas, for knowing what their business was and for knowing who was living at each address. Every new arrival at a settlement was given a registration form that once completed, did not allow him to move from one village to another. It became virtually impossible to enter or leave a village or district undetected. This was a cheap and extremely effective method of extending the reach of the Cheka and it seriously hampered the covert activities of the Allies in central Russia.

On 17 August the British Consul at Archangel, Douglas Young, went home. He was the first of the Allied representatives to return from Russia. His work, under the most trying circumstances, had left him unwell, suffering from recurrent boils, generally run down and in poor condition, with dyspepsia and nervous exhaustion.[26] His doctor recommended at least two months' leave for Young; that the Foreign Office granted. Prior to his medical examination, Young had reported to the Foreign Office where he saw Sir George Clerk. What happened there can best be recounted in Young's words:

My suggestion that a mistake had been made in Russia appeared unwelcome to him (he was at the time Head of the Northern Department, with Mr. Gregory as his chief assistant). When, at my second interview, I stated to him my intention of sending in the usual routine report on events that led up to intervention (which report, I suggested, might help H.M.G. to get a clearer view of the real situation), Sir George Clerk anxiously and energetically deprecated the making of any such report, although I prepared it for use if required; for it would in any case have had to pass through Sir George's hands.[27]

The Government clearly did not want a critical record that would expose its underhand activities on file, nor did it want to take the opportunity Young was offering to withdraw from its position with grace.

It was now that most of the Allied clandestine activity unravelled in what has become known as the Lockhart Plot, though sometimes called the Lettish Plot or the Reilly Plot and even the Dzerzhinsky Plot.

George Hill, who was intimately involved in it, explained the reasoning behind this plot:

> The Allies, the Tchecko-Slovak [sic Czechoslovak] and White Guard troops were straining their utmost to join up with each other and to form a united front. The staged Yaroslavl affair had worn itself into a disastrous failure; the confidence of the White Guard organisation [sic organisations] were shaken in the Allies and it was impossible to rely on any mob of theirs for support of the Allied troops; especially was it the case after the arrest of the Moscow [and] Petrograd officers by the Bolsheviks, as already mentioned.
>
> The only sound scheme left was to back the Letts. This has been conceded as sound by most people who knew the conditions in Russia, but a few have had doubts as to the rights of staging a revolution internally in Moscow and Petrograd.[28]

This demonstrates that the Allied plan was much larger than is normally painted. It was a grand plan organized by the Allied representatives in Russia with the approval of their governments. It was based on 'expediency', that bogus chimera that so often proves decisive and compelling in human affairs.

In June, two men, Jan Bredis and Jan Schmidken, approached the British Embassy in Petrograd. They were in fact agents provacateurs who were working for the Cheka. They explained that they were Letts who were disillusioned with the Bolsheviks and wished to desert to the Allies, along with many of their fellow Lettish soldiers. Eventually they were introduced to Cromie. Their intentions appealed strongly to Cromie who we know was working on similar schemes. He put the men in touch with Sydney Reilly who agreed with Cromie that they should see Lockhart. They travelled to Moscow, armed with a letter of introduction from Cromie.

Cromie and Reilly had swallowed the bait whole. Lockhart was more cautious and tried to check on the men's backgrounds. Apparently Reilly reassured him that they were genuine. However, Lockhart still remained cautious and wanted to meet one of the commanders of the Lettish regiments who had the same feelings as Bredis and Schmidken. The two men reported this request to the Cheka, which chose Lieutenant-Colonel Eduard Berzin, the commander of the Special Light Artillery that guarded the Kremlin.

Meanwhile, seemingly would-be Lettish turncoats were further entangling Cromie. An Englishman, Hugh Trevenen Hall, provided a report on the new development to the Director of Naval Intelligence through the Naval Attaché in Stockholm. Hall's report is in a file called *Reports from Agents*, and it has the tell-tale Secret Service 'C.X.' prefix. This indicates that Hall was one of Smith Cumming's men and the plotting that was being done had the backing and participation of the whole British Intelligence organization. The report is curious in that Hall never uses the first person singular to identify himself, but always uses his surname and writes as if he was a third party.[29]

According to Hall, Cromie negotiated with two men called Sabir and Steckelmann. A man called Dick, the context of whose appearance in the report suggests his name was familiar to British Intelligence, had introduced Sabir to him. Sabir claimed to have been a lieutenant on the staff of Admiral Chastni, presumably Admiral Shastny, the former Commander-in-Chief of the Baltic Fleet whom Trotsky had had executed in July. Cromie seems to have been initially reluctant to trust him, but when Steckelmann produced a letter of introduction from Lockhart, he won Cromie's trust. Steckelmann then proceeded to 'white wash' Sabir.[30] They are said to have claimed to be White Guards and asked Cromie what they could do. Cromie allegedly proposed that their men should blow up the Ochta railway bridge that linked the Nicholas Station with the Finland Station in Petrograd, in case the Germans advanced from Finland.

Cromie was following the British policy of trying to unite all the anti-Bolshevik parties in Russia under a common banner. His visitors greeted the idea with good countenance. A wiser or more experienced man than Cromie might have been more cautious before going any further; it all seems too easy in hindsight. The use of *agents provocateurs* by the Russians had a long history of which Cromie seems to have been unaware.

Steckelmann baited the hook by telling Cromie he had 60,000 followers in his pay in Finland, and that the telegraph, telephone and railway officials were also in his pay and that on his signal they could disrupt the whole transport system and open the door to Poole's forces. It sounds a wholly improbable story yet Cromie apparently never queried how Steckelmann is supposed to have found the money to pay such a legion. Steckelmann also assured him that he had 25,000 Letts available to him. These, as Cromie well knew, were the backbone of the Red Army and responsible for the security of the Bolshevik leadership. Sabir was then to assert that he had Petrograd in his grasp, with the night guard in his pay and a battalion of officers ready to seize all the armoured cars in the city.

It was – surely? – all too good to be true. Yet Cromie, like a greedy duckling, gobbled it all up. Admittedly, there was pressure on time and the situation was extremely uncertain, but it would appear that Cromie's eagerness and naivety caused him to cast caution and common sense to the winds.

Even more incautious was a meeting Cromie organized at the Hotel de France in Petrograd of the chief conspirators, including General Yudenich, to meet Steckelmann and Sabir. Luckily the men Cromie had summoned did not keep the appointment, since this would have revealed the key figures of the Allied plot to them. Sabir and Steckelmann stated they would have to go and inspect their posts; there can be little doubt that they were discussing the next move with the Cheka and getting their instructions. When they returned, they telephoned the Embassy and said they had 'very important news'. Hall states that he was sent to them 'about mid-day' and Steckelmann told him the 'time for action was ripe and could not be delayed'. Hall managed to wring a two-day postponement out of him. They proposed meeting again at the Hotel de France, but Hall suggested the Embassy.[31]

Betrayal clung to the whole intrigue like a pungent and unsavoury scent. Two weeks previously, an officer named Kovalenski, of the Finnish Dragoons, was organizing a courier service to link Petrozavodsk with the Allies at Murmansk. Hall related:

> He had with him cipher messages, which he proposed to hide in the collar of his fox terrier. Two hours before he left, he was arrested at his home, and the first question asked was 'Where is the collar of the fox terrier?' Sabir was the only man besides Hall who knew of this.[32]

Hall does not enlighten us regarding the identity of the originator of the messages, though the implication is that it was either Cromie or Hall, or how he knew what had happened to the unfortunate Kovalenski. The episode demonstrates that the plot was well known to the Cheka, and there is little doubt that its informants were Steckelmann and Sabir.

The compromising of Lockhart was arranged through an equally simple trap. Lockhart met Schmidken and Berzin on 15 August. Reilly and Fernand Grenard were also present. Berzin succeeded in convincing the Allied representatives that the Letts could be recruited to their cause, but the operation would cost 4 million roubles. Lockhart, Grenard and Reilly promised to consider this. The prize was great. The defection of the Letts promised to open the door to 'Elope' Force and enable it to link with the Czechoslovaks advancing from Siberia. Lockhart took the step that the Cheka desired by compromising himself in writing out passes for Berzin that would permit deserting Letts to cross the Allied lines. They read: 'Please admit bearer, who has an important communication for General Poole, through the English lines.'

Lockhart entrusted the management of the operation to Reilly; that way he thought he could deny knowledge of it. Furthermore, if the Bolsheviks seized him, then he could not compromise the operation and they would find no documents. The first of a series of meetings between Reilly and Berzin took place on 17 August. Reilly was able to tell Berzin that the funding he said he needed had been approved and gave him 700,000 roubles in cash, though Brook-Shepherd cites Orlov as stating it was 900,000 roubles. Lockhart and Keyes had provided the money.[33] It has been claimed both that Reilly suggested to Berzin that the Letts should rebel against the Bolsheviks, and that Berzin suggested it to Reilly.

Gordon Brook-Shepherd relies on General Orlov, who stated that Grenard 'brought up the question of overthrowing the Soviet government and tied it in with the fate of Latvia'.[34] None of the available sources is contemporary or necessarily reliable; indeed, some were written to deceive. However, Orlov had no axe to grind, nor did he need to protect anybody, nor were his memoirs written for publication. When this is coupled with the fact that the overthrow of the Bolsheviks was an undoubted aim of the Allies, particularly the French, then in this instance it would seem to be the most historically reliable account, though it is not entirely faultless.

Lockhart met Grenard and Lavergne to discuss the proposition. Andrew Cook points out that in his *Memoirs* Lockhart told Reilly to have nothing to do with 'so dangerous and doubtful move', while in his Memorandum to the Foreign Secretary he states he told Reilly 'there was nothing to be gained by such action.'[35] The discrepancy is clear enough. Since Lockhart proves to be such a consistently unreliable witness, it is probably wise to doubt both versions. What makes either statement from Lockhart even more open to doubt is the fact that both Reilly and George Hill continued to meet Berzin and paid him a further 500,000 roubles in two instalments. Again, Lockhart and Keyes provided the money. Lockhart and the French representatives did more than this. Hill's report reveals that,

> The scheme which the Allied Diplomatic representatives worked for was: a definite relief on our Northern and Tcheko-Slovak [*sic* Czechoslovak] fronts, which was to be brought about by certain Lettish units turning over to our side and thereby weakening the main force against our troops.[36]

The conspirators resolved that the coup would take place on 6 September. Cook considers that Reilly favoured humiliating Lenin and Trotsky by marching them through the streets of Moscow without their trousers.[37] However, we are free to doubt this as Orlov wrote:

> The British agent [Reilly] outlined to Berzin the plan for overthrowing the Soviet government which, he said, had been suggested by a French general. According to the plan, two Lettish regiments would have to be transferred to the city of Vologda, where they would go over to the side of the Allies and open the front for the Anglo-French troops advancing from Archangel. The Lettish troops

remaining in Moscow would then assassinate Lenin and the members of his government.[38]

The French general was almost certainly Lavergne. The intention to murder the Bolshevik leaders gains further weight from eyewitness testimony that the Bolsheviks obtained about a conference of American, British and French diplomats and officers that took place at the American Consulate-General on 25 August:

> Reilly told the small audience that, in three days, on 28 August, a session of the All-Russian Congress of Soviets was to take place at the Bolshoi Theatre, with the whole of the Russian leadership in attendance. At this conference, he and his band of daring conspirators, armed with pistols and hand grenades, would be concealed in the theatre behind the curtains. Then, at a signal given by Reilly, the Lettish soldiers would close all exits and cover the audience with their rifles, while Reilly, at the head of his band, would leap on to the stage and seize Lenin, Trotsky and the other leaders. All of them would be shot on the spot.[39]

Against this must be weighed the claim from Reilly himself that it was his intention to humiliate Lenin and Trotsky. Reilly is not a reliable witness. Furthermore, the context of the Allied covert operations through the summer of 1918 lends further credence to the idea that it was the intention to eliminate Lenin and Trotsky by murder. Douglas Young's observation has been recorded, and it was undoubtedly Savinkov's plan to murder the Bolshevik leaders. The Allies had not protested or threatened to withdraw their support from him. At the very least, the Allies were more than willing to look the other way while either Russians or their own secret agents did the job for them. It strains credibility that such a puerile and petty move as depriving Lenin and Trotsky of their trousers would have been considered.

So how did the Cheka know what had passed at the conference of 25 August, and how did they know what Reilly had said? The answer lies in the French journalist René Marchand. Grenard had taken him into his confidence in the belief that he was an agent of the French President, Raymond Poincaré. He had taken him to the conference. Marchand was becoming increasingly disillusioned by the duplicity of Allied policy in Russia, so disillusioned that he decided to turn his coat and inform the Cheka of the details of the conference. The Consul-Generals of the United States and France, De Witt Clinton Poole and Joseph Ferdinand Grenard, together with their head Secret Service agents, Xenophon Kalamatiano and Henri de Verthamon, were there. Reilly was the only Briton present. This fact emphasizes that British diplomats contrived to operate at arm's length from espionage, though they were often responsible for initiating it and solving the political problems that it might arouse. This effectively made British Secret Service officers their country's effective representatives.

It has been suggested that Reilly was following his own inclinations in Russia in the high summer of 1918. He was unquestionably capable of this, but that should not be taken as meaning that he did so on every occasion. At first glance an explanation offered by Colonel C.N. French, the liaison officer between the War Office and the Secret Service, to the Foreign Office would appear to bear this out:

> Reference Secret demi-official W.165188 of the 7th October, to the D.M.I.
> REILLY is an officer who was sent to Russia as a military agent last March. In June it became apparent that his utility as a military agent was being impaired by the fact that he was in touch with Mr Lockhart, who was using him for some political purpose. Reilly had been warned most specifically that he was not to get into any official position, or to get mixed up with politics; therefore when it became apparent that he was doing so, a wire was sent ordering him to proceed to Siberia to report on German Prisoners of War Camps – this with the idea of getting him away from the Political atmosphere in which he was being involved.
> He apparently never went there; perhaps he was ordered not to do so be [sic by] Mr Lockhart. He certainly had no business to be doing propaganda, which he was apparently instructed to do by Mr Lockhart.[40]

This evades, probably deliberately, any reference to the plot of the summer of 1918. It tries to blame Lockhart for getting Reilly 'mixed up with politics'. While Lockhart had some influence in this respect, Reilly was operating with him – at arm's length – rather than blindly obeying his orders. Commander Boyce, the station chief, approved the plans that he and Hill had prepared. Reilly was only one cog in a much bigger operation. His ventures cannot be divorced from the context provided by those of Boyce, Cromie, Hill, Keyes, Litch, McGrath, the Americans or the French.

Moreover, none of these officers, including Reilly, faced any sort of disciplinary hearing when they returned to Britain. There is not a scintilla of evidence in his SIS file that he was ever criticized or censured in any manner for his conduct in the summer of 1918. Had he exceeded his orders in the manner suggested, he would assuredly have been subject to censure, as would all the other officers involved.

There is no record of the orders that might have been given to Reilly at the time in question, possibly because they were too embarrassing for the British authorities to allow becoming public knowledge. French's letter was written after the crisis of the summer of 1918 had passed and can be interpreted as a smokescreen designed to avoid awkward questions.

This is reflected in the influence that Reilly wielded. According to George Hill, he was 'receiving very excellent information from all possible sources,' including an agent inside the Kremlin who was identified by Hill as agent 'C', but more importantly,

> I considered that Lt. Riley [*sic* Reilly] knew the situation better than any other British officer in Russia, and as he also had the more delicate threads in his hands, I therefore agreed to co-operate with him, and leave the political control and our policy in his hands.[41]

The officers of the British Secret Service were far more than 'spies' in the accepted sense. The acquisition of information that might direct and guide policy and strategy was only one aspect of their task and it was not the most important one. They were heavily involved in politics. These were not the politics of formal diplomacy, but making arrangements behind the scenes and playing 'the more delicate threads' with people the British Government did not wish it known they were negotiating with. These were the men who were negotiating with the opposition parties in Russia and committing Britain to policies that were not necessarily approved in detail by the government. The French Intelligence officers were doing likewise, but with greater direct complicity from their government.

It has been seen how the British Ambassador in Jassy was officially kept in the dark about the operations of Colonel Boyle. An officer from MI1(c) conducted the clandestine political negotiations with the Bulgarian opposition while the diplomats remained in the background. Sir George Buchanan initiated the Banking Scheme and then left the arrangements to Keyes. Keyes' description of Lockhart's activities revealed the relationship between diplomacy and clandestine activity. In August 1918 Lockhart was standing at arm's length, but he had broad knowledge of what was taking place and he was paymaster for it.

The Americans had sprung into the clandestine world with a vengeance. The presence of Kalamatiano at the conference on 25 August along with De Witt C. Poole is important. In a remarkably short space of time he had created a formidable network. His origins are obscure. From 1908 onwards he was working in Russia for the agricultural machinery firm of J. I. Case. He seems to have been recruited for Intelligence work in 1915 by Professor Samuel Harper, whom he knew from his days at the University of Chicago.[42] His two principal agents were both soldiers, Colonel Friede and Major-General Zagriasky, the former on the staff of the Moscow military head-quarters and the latter a serving officer in the Red Army. They were able to provide Kalamatiano with high-grade information from within the Bolshevik high command.

With the French journalist, René Marchand's information in his hands, Felix Dzerzhinsky was faced with a dilemma. What his ultimate goal was is open to discussion, but it may have been to lure 'Elope' Force into a trap by using the Letts to open the front and, when it advanced, envelope it with overwhelming force. Whether this was so or not, the news of the Allied plot meant there was now no time for whatever plan he had to prosper. He must act swiftly and at the same time protect Marchand's identity. It was resolved, at Lenin's suggestion, to have Marchand write a letter to the French President, outlining the plot and then the Cheka would raid his flat and 'find' the letter. Once the plot was exposed the Cheka would be more than justified in seizing the Allied diplomats, their agents and their Russian allies.

The events of 30 August intervened and upset these calculations. That day a young Russian military cadet called Leonid Kannegieser shot and killed Uritsky, the head of the Petrograd Cheka. He made his escape by bicycle to the building that had until recently been the English Club, for British businessmen living and working in the area, and he was quickly cornered. In the evening of the same day, Lenin himself fell victim to an assassin. Dora

Kaplan, a Right Social Revolutionary, shot him twice with a revolver as he left a workers' meeting at the Michelson Factory in Moscow. He was critically wounded and there was genuine fear for his life.

Knowledge of the Allied plotting, together with the facts that Kannegieser had fled to the English Club, and that the Allies were in league with the Right Social Revolutionaries, led to an entirely justified outcry against the Allies by the Bolshevik press. Lenin had personally taken charge after he heard the news of Uritsky's assassination and before his own shooting. 'He ordered Dzerzhinsky to Petrograd and instructed him to swoop down on British and French embassies and consulates simultaneously in Moscow and Petrograd.'[43] The Cheka swung into action on 31 August. Lockhart was arrested at pistol point while still in bed. Consul Woodhouse and Engineer Commander Le Page were arrested shortly after midnight as they walked towards the British Embassy.

In the most striking incident, they attacked the British Embassy in Petrograd between 4 and 5 p.m. They knew that Cromie was in conference there with Boyce, Sabir, Steckelmann and Hall. The latter's presence at such a gathering of conspirators tends to confirm the view that he was in the Secret Service. Also in the building was Prince Shahovskoi, the Tsar's one-time Minister of Trade and Industry and councillor of the state bank [perhaps the man identified by Buchanan as Prince Shahovskoi (see p. 53)]. The party was awaiting the arrival of one more conspirator, General Yudenich.

Sabir had left the meeting for a short while, allegedly to check that his men were prepared, but it is almost certain that he was working for the Cheka and had gone to alert them, for within minutes of his return the Embassy was stormed. It is unclear precisely what happened, but there were reports that some within the Embassy, perhaps undisciplined sailors, had fired on the Cheka, who returned fire. Three of their own men were hit. Popular mythology painted Cromie maintaining a single-handed defence of the Embassy and perishing in the attempt. From the eyewitness accounts we have the events were less dramatic. The Cheka were extremely nervous when they broke into the Embassy and Cromie was shot twice in the back of the head as he ran down the main staircase towards the front doors.[44]

The Cheka searched the building, seizing all the documents they could find. These laid bare much of the Allies' intrigues and in a minute on the covering page of the report on the seizure of the documents, it was noted: 'Presumably the cyphers have been taken with the rest. I am afraid they will have got a good deal of compromising material.'[45] Admiralty cipher 01 was considered to be in doubt and M/1917 suspect. It was reported that Radek had stated that the Bolsheviks now had enough evidence against Lockhart to shoot him.

Should anyone doubt Lockhart's complicity in the plot, they need to remember that Reilly had gone to Petrograd to meet Cromie and his fellow conspirators on the eve of the assassination attempts on Lenin and Uritsky. The Embassy had been stormed and Cromie killed before they could meet. He returned to Moscow where he saw Hill, whose report discloses, 'He [Reilly] had already sent to Mr Lockhart his official report, and what he considered had happened.'[46] The question needs to be asked: why was Reilly reporting to Lockhart? The answer can only be because Lockhart knew a great deal more about the plot than either his *Memoirs* or his Memorandum reveal. It is clear from this that Reilly was operating under Lockhart's juris-diction and with his knowledge and consent. Reilly's report has never been made public. It is not in any file in the National Archives, nor is it in Reilly's SIS record. Perhaps it never got out of Russia under the conditions of September 1918, though then one is left to wonder why a further report was not written by him after he returned to Britain.

There is one final aspect of the Allied plot that requires comment. In his final letter to Admiral Hall, Cromie wrote:

> **The Hand that feeds this people will be the Master of Russia, in spite of any military force that may be sent against it,** and everyone agrees with my opinion that if the Allies can hold Vologda (and the troops are only waiting for us to come to turn over to us) we can call on the people of Russia to hold the railways for us and assist us to distribute Siberian corn to the big towns. They will do anything in return for food, and are at last convinced that the Germans cannot help in this matter, and that their present Government will not.[47]

The prospect of the people of central Russia rising against the Bolsheviks because of starvation has been a consistent thread running through this history. Starvation is a gambit as old as war itself. It was a threat implicit in the naval blockade of Germany. It was the prospect of food supplied by the

British that persuaded the Murmansk Soviet to make common cause with the British.

In spite of Reilly's later denial that the Allies planned to interdict the food supplies to the cities under Bolshevik dominion,[48] it is perfectly clear that this was part of the Allies' plan. It needs to be born in mind that Reilly was arguing for his life when he made that statement and was still trying to mislead his captors.

The Marchand letter, the only first-hand account in existence, would appear to establish the case:

> After that, two sabotage agents made a report about the steps they had taken to cut off Petrograd from food supplies. One of them said that everything was made ready to blow up the bridge which spanned the River Volkhov near Avanka. The other reported that he was only waiting for a specific order to blow up the Cherepovetz Bridge, which connected Petrograd with the Eastern provinces from where the city's food supply came. According to the plot, the blowing up of the bridges was supposed to be timed with the mutiny of two Lettish regiments in Vologda, in order to prevent troops of the Petrograd garrison from reaching the attacking mutineers.

One of the 'sabotage agents' was probably de Verthamon. When the Cheka raided the premises of the Allied officers and agents on 31 August, they found eighteen pounds of explosives in his flat at the French lycée where he had been using a teaching post as a cover, together with a code and 28,000 roubles. De Verthamon escaped.

The plan to sever the stronghold of Bolshevism from its sustenance by sabotage was the special sphere of the French. Yet sabotage was not the only tool. The main supplies of grain reached central Russia from the Ukraine, the Kuban and Siberia. The Ukraine was in German hands and was in chaos. The Kuban Cossacks had joined the Volunteer Army. Under the protective umbrella of the Czechoslovak Legion, the Whites controlled much of Siberia and there was the prospect of the junction of the Czechoslovaks and the Allies from the north. These factors opened the prospect of cutting off Siberian foodstuffs on a strategic scale. The plan was thus to work on two levels: an immediate threat created by sabotage; a strategic one founded upon domination of the grain-producing areas and their communications with central Russia. The effects on the citizens of central Russia may be readily imagined.

What, in the meantime had the Allies been up to in Siberia? The French had been particularly active there. They had supplied Semenoff with a credit for 4 million roubles between 14 May and 13 June inclusive. Four million roubles were provided between the 24 and 30 May. A further 2,936,000 roubles were transferred to the Russian Asiatic Bank at Harbin on 1 June to the account of Captain Pelliot, who was the officer charged with supporting Semenoff. Pelliot was left with 1 million roubles in his account to provide 'necessary payment' until 13 August, and he estimated that he would need a further 2.5 million roubles for the remainder of August.[49]

The pity of it is that Semenoff proved to be little more than a bandit and a frustrating point of friction in the ensuing campaign in Siberia. It is possible to understand the French championing him in the first five or six months of 1918 when there were few other contenders for the role of an anti-Bolshevik spearhead in Siberia, but the suspicion remains that the French had their own agenda and saw him as the means to carry French influence across Siberia.

Nor had the British been idle in Siberia. They decided to send Major James Mackintosh Bell from MI1(c) to Vladivostock in the guise of Vice-Consul (Acting). He was 'to be given every facility' by the British Consul there and would report directly to 'C' in London. Sir Charles Eliot, an expert in sea slugs recruited from the University of Hong Kong, was the newly appointed British High Commissioner for Siberia, and had recommended on 5 July that Bell should be attached to the Czechoslovak commander, General Mikhail Dietrichs, no doubt to keep him in tune with British policy and strategy. The British Consul at Vladivostock, R.M. Hodgson, followed this up by reminding the War Office: 'Please inform me whether my suggestion of Major Bell being attached to Czech General Officer Commanding is approved. Appointment would be well received.'[50] The Foreign Office replied, via Sir Conygham Greene, the British Ambassador in Tokyo, regretting that the proposal could not be accepted. Had the appointment been approved it would have clashed with the duties of Captain Steveni.

It would appear that this fact led London to turn down Hodgson's recommendation, since in August Bell was instead attached to the 25th Battalion the Middlesex Regiment as an interpreter.[51] That unit was another battalion of B-class troops that had been sent to establish a British presence in Siberia and thus stiffen the morale of the Czechoslovaks and White Russians. They had reached Vladivostock on 3 August. A French regiment had also been sent, but more important were 7,000 Americans under General Graves and a force of Japanese that rapidly swelled in number to 70,000 men. Bell's efforts in Siberia did not have a happy outcome. The new Director of Military Intelligence, Major-General Sir William Thwaites, who had taken over from Macdonogh at the beginning of September, sent a telegram to Major-General Knox, the British Military Attaché attached to Eliot, explaining the position:

> Bell went out originally under C. He was recalled for non-adherence to his duties and then was sent out once more. Again it was found that he totally failed to grasp his duties as an s.s. [Secret Service] officer and is quite unable to efface himself. I do not think he should have a third trial and consider Shaw would be better man for you to work with. I suggest that you arrange with Sir Charles Eliot that both Military and Political information should be obtained through one Secret Service organisation to avoid needless expense and overlapping.[52]

The events of August had been significant in a number of respects. They disclose the relationship between formal diplomacy, upon which most histories are based, and Secret Service. The latter was used to handle the hidden diplomacy that 'dare not speak its name'. They also re-emphasize the key importance of money. Without foreign finance most of the anti-Bolshevik organizations would have been powerless.

They also re-emphasize the problem of loyalty, which was identical for all parties to the struggle. All of them suffered from the ambiguity of loyalty, which is more frequently conditional than unconditional by nature.

Many of the British and French officers involved in the August plot are open to justified criticism for falling for what, in hindsight, were remarkably simple penetrations of their operations. The Cheka conducted these operations with skill, but given the gullibility of the Allies' representatives, their success was hardly remarkable. The Allies could be criticized for naively believing what they wanted to believe, but equally they were under great pressure.

It was not all bad news. The Bolshevik leadership was panicking and most thought their days in power were numbered. The scale of the enmity within the territories of the Russian Empire had been displayed with terrifying clarity. The Germans had been thrown on to the defensive and their hopes were dwindling. The flight of the German Embassy from Moscow was a considerable achievement. Against that must be set a new bond, the bond of mutual fear, which joined the Bolsheviks and Germans into a new alliance of expediency.

At the end of the month, the covert operations of the Allies in Russia were largely in ruins, which meant that the small military intervention forces had severely diminished prospects of achieving anything. Yet they were essentially all the Allies had left. It is to how the Allied Intelligence Services tried to deal with this situation that we must now turn, but bearing in mind that they were no longer the Allies' spearhead.

XII

Terror and Instability

September 1918

—◄O►—

Lockhart was asked a few questions and released, according to his own account, at 9 a.m. the morning after his arrest. He did not remain at liberty for long. On 4 September he was arrested again. He was luckier than most of his colleagues and the French. They were incarcerated in the notorious Butirski Prison, whilst Lockhart was to 'enjoy' the relative luxury of solitary confinement in the Kremlin.

The British Government was rightly concerned about Lockhart's fate. With neither credibility nor any diplomatic representative in Moscow, the openings for retaliation or effective protest were few. One bargaining counter to hand was the Soviet representative in London, Maxim Litvinov, who had no formal diplomatic status and who had been busily spreading pacifist propaganda. Complaints against his activities were voiced in the War Cabinet. The police seized copies of *The Call*, a leaflet calling for an immediate end to the war, if necessary by revolution. The War Cabinet considered that deporting Litvinov 'would be tantamount to a declaration of war against the Bolsheviks', so they decided to tread carefully. The danger lay in the fact that members of the War Cabinet believed that the combination of Litvinov and the propaganda of the British Socialistic Party, backed in this case by the Independent Labour Party, 'was tending to undermine the *moral* of the people.'[1]

Fears were exacerbated in February when Litvinov penned an article for *The Woolwich Pioneer* that the War Cabinet considered incited the munitions workers at Woolwich to revolution. He was also considered to have sought to 'tamper with the discipline' of British troops, notably Russian-Canadians. As we have witnessed on several occasions the driving force was fear, fear founded on dark anticipations.

He was placed under what the British called 'preventive arrest' and steps were taken to legalize the position under Regulation 14B of the Defence of the Realm Act.[2] Telegram followed telegram as the British sought to put pressure on Chicherin. Eventually an arrangement was reached whereby Litvinov and his companions were to be released in exchange for Lockhart, Wardrop and the other British officials held by the Bolsheviks: a straightforward exchange of hostages in fact.

The ship chosen to carry Litvinov and his party was HMS *Jupiter II*,[3] a paddle minesweeper hired from her civilian trade by the Admiralty in 1915 and commanded by Lieutenant James Fitzpatrick of the Royal Naval Reserve.[4] She operated from Dover and worked in her new role in the Straits of Dover. Her logbooks, recording a generally uneventful service, are available in the National Archives – or nearly all of them.[5]

The log for the period 18 September–14 December 1918 is missing. There is no obvious reason for this and requests for information from the Ministry of Defence are met with the response that the log has not survived the passage of time. This seems strange when all the other logbooks have. Further investigation suggests a possible reason for this discrepancy.

It was arranged for Litvinov and his party to embark from Aberdeen on 26 September, but planning had already started on 12 September. On that day Admiral Hall saw Lord Hardinge, the Permanent Under-Secretary for Foreign Affairs. The outcome of the meeting was explained to the Deputy Chief of Naval Staff the same day, when Hall wrote, '…Lord Hardinge is very anxious that until we get definite news that Mr. Lockhart and his party have arrived in Finland, Litvinoff should not get outside the jurisdiction of Great Britain.'[6] Hall then proposed the means by which this could be done, suggesting that it would be 'quite feasible' to embark Litvinov and his party at Aberdeen, 'giving the Captain instructions that he should have a machinery breakdown, which necessitated his putting into Lerwick. Once there we can detain Mr. Litvinoff until we know whether Lockhart and his people are safe or not.'[7]

If the Deputy Chief of Naval Staff agreed with the proposal, Admiral Hall suggested that a secret letter should be written to the Senior Naval Officer at Aberdeen, giving him full instructions as to what was to be done in order that the captain of the *Jupiter* would thoroughly understand what was required of him. The scheme was swiftly accepted, or so we should judge from the facts that Major Fenner was detailed to be ready to leave for Aberdeen with instructions the same night, while the C-in-C of the Grand Fleet at Scapa Flow and the Senior Naval Officer, Aberdeen, were informed by telegram.[8]

In the event none of this chicanery was put into practice. The Bolshevik response to the notes of protest entered by the British and French Governments was that they would release Lockhart and his party when Litvinov and his companions were freed, or at least once the Bolsheviks had heard that Litvinov had reached Bergen safely.

Lockhart and his staff were expelled from Russia, though held up at the Russo-Finnish frontier while the Bolsheviks waited to hear that Litvinov and his party had reached Bergen. Litvinov and his companions were embarked on the *Jupiter* on 26 September, and the ship sailed on the evening tide of the 27th, after the receipt of a signal from the Admiralty that the call at Lerwick would not be necessary.

A practical and convincing reason for the disappearance of this particular logbook of HMS *Jupiter II* is either it has been deliberately withheld or destroyed in an attempt to hide the duplicity that forms the background to this voyage.

Those of the Allied Missions who had escaped arrest took refuge in the United States' Consulate. It was now under the care of the Norwegians, who had agreed to look after American interests after the breakdown of relations. The Bolsheviks chose not to storm it, perhaps mindful of the tragic consequences of their action at the British Embassy in Petrograd. Instead they isolated it and cut off supplies of food and water in a bid to force the occupants to surrender. Unfortunately for them, the cellars of the Consulate contained the stocks of the American Red Cross, while the Bolsheviks had failed to turn off one source of water, which meant the occupants lived more abundantly than the inhabitants of Moscow.

There was one American who had not managed to reach the Consulate in time. That was Xenophon Kalamatiano. The Cheka had already searched his flat without success, but that told Kalamatiano that they were looking for him. He would have to be careful. He was wise enough to discreetly observe the situation outside the Consulate by daylight before making his move. He decided his best means of approach ran through the grounds of the British Church alongside the Consulate and it would be advisable to use the cover of night to make the attempt.

The one he chose was wet, which reduced visibility and persuaded the Bolsheviks surrounding the premises to take shelter. He would need to scale the fence that separated the church from the Consulate and, unfortunately for him, the fence was high. He reached the fence, apparently undetected, but carrying his stick in one hand he found it impossible to haul himself over the fence with the other hand alone. He had also omitted to take the watchman by the gate into his calculations. Disturbed by the noise, he seized Kalamatiano's waist and called for help. There was no escape. The prisoner was interrogated but maintained his silence. However, the fact that he would not release his stick aroused suspicion. When his captors examined it, they found it to be hollow and stuffed with compromising material – receipts from his agents, money and messages.[9] He joined the Allied operatives in the Butirski Prison. The seizure of the receipts and messages enabled the Cheka to mop up many in his network.

Still further damage had been done to the Allies' clandestine networks by a letter Reilly had sent to one of his mistresses, whose flat was being used as a centre for Reilly's couriers. Reilly would appear to have been remarkably lax or remarkably unfortunate in this, for he had arranged to meet Berzin there. He was late. While waiting for Reilly, Berzin

> noticed a sealed envelope which, the maid told him, had just arrived and was lying on the table. Berzin recognised from the handwriting that the letter was from Reilly. As it was not marked for him, the colonel did not open it. But what looked extremely useful was the return address which Reilly had put on the envelope.[10]

Berzin wrote the address down and gave it to the Cheka. It belonged to Elizaveta Otten, codenamed E.E., Reilly's chief courier and mistress, who was seized when the Cheka pounced on the Allies' networks after the assassination of Uritsky and the attempt on Lenin. According to Orlov's account, as related by Brook-Shepherd, Otten confessed all. She had relayed messages between Reilly and his agents and the conspirators had used her flat for meetings. The Cheka lay in wait in the flat and arrested all who called, among them Marie Friede, the sister of Colonel Friede. George Hill, whose information is contemporary, reported that on Sunday 1 September:

About midday Lt. Reilly's chief girl E.E. was arrested. Her house was thoroughly searched, and she was repeatedly asked whether she had not got some friend who was likely to give her away. She posed as innocent though showing much nervousness. Through two friends in the house the money she had in her possession was saved. She carried no documents. Just as the search party was about to leave the house with E.E., whom they assured would be allowed her liberty within a few hours, as nothing had been found against her, a girl by the name of Marie Friede, of the American S.S. [Secret Service] appeared. This woman was carrying messages, and on seeing the armed guards seemed to lose her head and gave away that she was carrying documents for E.E. This girl was likewise arrested, as a few hours later were her brothers, who also belonged to the American service.[11]

Orlov's version may have been exaggerated by hearsay over the lapse of several years. This view is based on the petition Otten made to the Red Cross Committee for the Aid of Political Prisoners.[12] While this must be treated with caution, in that Otten was concealing everything she could in the hope of saving her life and perhaps regaining her liberty, it seems clear from it that she had not confessed to anything, despite Orlov's claim. She portrayed herself as the dupe of Reilly and pleaded ignorance of what he was doing. However, Marie Friede and the purposes for which her flat had been used had hopelessly compromised her.

Meanwhile Lenin lay critically ill. What became known as the 'Red Terror' engulfed the territory held by the Bolsheviks. The slaughter was horrific, though there is some justification in the fact that it was a direct response to the Allied plots and fuelled by fear. It was both ruthless and ferocious.

On 5 September the assembled diplomatic corps in Petrograd, nearly all of them the representatives of neutral powers, under the leadership of the German Consul-General in Petrograd, Bretter, protested against the terror. Zinoviev heard them. The protest made little visible impact, but what did alleviate the position to some extent was the steady recovery of Lenin, a fact that calmed the Bolshevik leadership.

Relations between the Germans and the Bolsheviks underwent another revolution at this stage. The Supplementary Treaties to the Treaty of Brest-Litovsk had been signed on 27 August, regularizing the political and economic relations between Germany and Soviet Russia and confirming the stability of the western frontier of Russia. German troops began evacuating White Russia. However, a steep price had to be paid for this. The Germans imposed a severe indemnity on the Bolsheviks, disguised as 'compensation', and it had to be paid in gold. Nevertheless, friction remained. While the German press gloated over what was a considerable reverse for the Allies, on 2 September Hauschild presented the Soviet Government with a note protesting against the 'inflammatory articles' that appeared in the Russian press against Germany.

On 13 September he presented an even more caustic note about the Bolsheviks spreading revolutionary propaganda in Germany,[13] but the government in Moscow could and did deny it, on the technical grounds that it was the action of independent socialists, rather than the Soviet Government. This conveniently ignored the fact that the 'independent socialists' were effectively the tools of the Soviet Government, despite pretences of independence. The propaganda, together with that spread by the Allies, was undermining the will and purpose of both the German Army and people. Oppressed by near starvation, heavy losses and with the army forced into retreat on the Western front, Imperial Germany's foundations were rocking.

Could the Allies salvage anything from the wreck of their efforts in Russia? Hill thought so. On the afternoon of 3 September he sent a message to Lockhart, one that further implicates him in the subversive activity, telling him:

> I had been over the network of our organisation and found everything intact, but that there was undoubtedly a fair amount of nervousness among some of the agents. That I had got all Lt. Reilly's affairs under my own control, and provided I could get money it would be possible to carry on. That we had the greatest difficulty in getting up our messages to the North, and unless the new chain organisation produced a better result than the single messenger service had done it would be useless to carry on. However, I thought a lot might be done in destruction.[14]

The report was sent by messenger, who luckily reached Lockhart's flat shortly after he had been re-arrested. While the report had not reached Lockhart, neither had it fallen into the hands of the Cheka.

In London a minute on a report from Lindley about the discovery of the plot read: 'We have had the substance of this already by wireless, and it looks rather ominous for the safety of our missions. Unfortunately, there is no doubt a considerable foundation for the accusations.'[15] It is of perhaps more than passing interest to note that the official who penned this minute was E.H. Carr, who later wrote what was to be regarded as one of the standard English diplomatic histories of the Russian Revolution, one that suppressed or ignored the Intelligence element. It is comment enough on the way history is distorted for political purposes.

Nothing had been heard from Reilly. The British who were left at liberty in Moscow supposed he had been arrested in the debacle in Petrograd. Reilly had in fact travelled back from Petrograd in a first-class sleeper, reaching Moscow on 3 September, unaware of the events there. He was soon enlightened. Hill arranged for him to adopt his own alias as Georg Bergmann and it was in this guise that Reilly managed to escape to Riga and thence to Britain via Finland. However, his agent 'C' at the Kremlin was arrested. He was not the only casualty. Hill recorded that '12 of our couriers had been shot, as had also one or two of my independent agents.'[16]

Whatever the fate of the other Allied networks in central Russia, the Okerlund ring, run from the Russian Embassy in London, continued to function. Its head agent, Wassilieff, sent the news that after the expulsion of the Bolsheviks from Archangel, Rear Admiral Leonid Ivanoff had taken command of Russia's small Northern Fleet. As there were few naval officers at Archangel, he appealed for all those available to be sent to Ivanoff's head-quarters at Archangel.[17] A reasonably optimistic reply came from Nabokoff, the Russian Chargé d'Affaires, demonstrating once again the close ties between the White Russians and British Intelligence.

The Okerlund network was trying to expand and the ring it was trying to establish was at the forefront of contemporary technology, wanting to set up a wireless network linking Archangel with Petrograd, Moscow, Rybinsk and the Don. Wassilieff appealed to London for the 200,000 roubles a month he said were needed for this service.[18]

London showed no great enthusiasm, so Wassilieff continued to press the matter:

OK. Following for D.N.I. from WASSILIEFF:-
Reference my 16 over 8 an immediate outlay of 200,000 roubles is required in order to put into motion the wireless connection and secret service. Further

expenses will depend from the general position 18 over 10 (ends) (Begins):-
End of July URA and SEV arrived in PENZA. O.K. sent a courier to Crimea to
Alesha and has his man in Kiev. He requests to organise direct communication
through Weymarn. I am forwarding O.K. 300 pounds by the courier he sent and
OK requests you to remit him 500 pounds which I consider is possible through
neutrals because after Cromie's murder communication between Archangel and
the Petrograd British representative interrupted 19 over 11.[19]

'Ura', sometimes rendered 'Jura' and 'Iura', was an agent of the OK ring. Of
particular interest is the fact that the British still had someone in Petrograd
who was trying to fill Cromie's shoes and he was having difficulty communicating with General Poole. What is even clearer is Wassilieff's abiding
interest in a wireless network. Although wireless had been in use by all of the
belligerent powers since the outbreak of war, the technology was still novel
and while great strides had been made in its performance over the years of
war, its use for spying on the scale suggested here had still to be successfully
proved. The 'round generators' were generators designed by Captain
Round, the wireless expert in British Intelligence, who had been working
since at least 1915 on a wireless system suitable for Secret Intelligence
purposes.

The OK ring was being used to try and re-establish an Intelligence
presence in Petrograd to replace the services recently destroyed. Whether
this initiative came from Admiral Hall or was offered by the Russians is not
clear, but the British were not prepared to finance the wireless backup, for a
disappointing reply came from Admiral Hall:

Please forward following to Wassilieff:-
O.K. Begins. It is impossible to get money for organisation wireless without
having details. We already telegraphed you about this matter in our No. 43/10.
It is impossible at present to remit money through neutrals.[20]

In September it would appear that the British, and probably the other Allies
too, were transferring their weight away from the bourgeois parties in
Russia, feeling these parties could not command enough widespread
support in the country to enable them to crush the Bolsheviks. This indication appears in a telegram from Kassianoff, who doubled as a courier and

White Russian representative with the British, that was to be passed to Wassilieff:

> I have seen everybody. My impressions are as follows. The intention of England to destroy German influence in Russia is evident. Aim – the regeneration of Russia, as Allied Empire. Russian bourgoisie [*sic:* bourgeoisie] completely discredited with British who count upon support of the masses. Consequence – slight movement to the left in official circles. In case of disillusionment in the organising capabilities of social revolutionaries, a turn to the right may be expected. Russian influence exists here not sufficiently strong. General Alexeyev's name carries most weight. His strength lies in absence of political programme and desire for practical work. Many people are making undue use of Alexeyev's name.[21]

The attack led by the Intelligence Services had come to grief and Allied hopes now rested ever more strongly on conventional military means. The intervention forces, the Czechoslovaks, the Whites in Siberia, the Volunteer Army and the Cossacks were now the true spearheads of the Allies. Counting 'upon the support of the masses' was a vague statement that reflected an ideal rather than practical policy. Their different desires, prejudices, religions, trade and political affiliations, personal antagonisms and much else divide the mass of people in most societies. It is only occasionally that one single issue succeeds in uniting most of them into an irresistible force.

The 'masses' in Russia had no leader, other than the Bolsheviks who simply nominated themselves as the champions of the masses. If the Allies were to gain the support they desired, they would have to present a political, social and religious programme that would not merely be confined to a collection of fine-sounding platitudes, but be compelling enough to capture imaginations and so galvanize 'the masses' into being prepared to give their lives for it. This was less about the structure of society, or the forms of its institutions, than the spirit that animated them. It sounds simple but, as Clausewitz observed, 'Everything in war is very simple, but the simplest thing is difficult.'[22] If the attempt to rally the masses was successful, then leaders *might* arise among the masses. As it was, and in the absence of anything other than platitudes such as 'liberty', that meant next to nothing to most Russian peasants, the Allies were left with no alternative but to negotiate with the existing leaders and political parties unless and until they could impose leaders of their own.

This the British attempted to do at Archangel, where General Poole mounted a coup that was carried out by Britain's favoured conspirator, Chaplin. The coup took place on 6 September and the puppet government the Allies had installed there a few weeks earlier was arrested. It was an ill-considered move that brought down the wrath of the United States on Poole's head. In Washington, DC, the British Ambassador, Lord Reading, was summoned to see Robert Lansing, the Secretary of State for Foreign Affairs, who told him:

> That the attitude adopted by General Poole at Archangel was causing [the] United States Government considerable concern. United States Ambassador to Russia had reported General Poole had appointed a French colonel as Military Governor of Archangel: that latter had issued an order prescribing arrest of any one guilty of Bolshevik propaganda.

The threat came at the end of the message:

> Mr. Lansing asked me to inform you that he had taken the matter up with the President who took a serious view of it and that unless there was a change in high-handed attitude adopted by General Poole in appointment of a military governor United States Government would seriously have to consider with-drawal of United States contingent from General Poole's command.[23]

For the United States to have withdrawn its troops would have been a disaster for the interventionists, for it was American soldiers who formed the only worthwhile fighting troops among the forces under Poole's command. Urgent representations were made to Poole, who replied on 15 September. His reply tells us the new regime was only to be a fig leaf for military rule and American concerns were to be 'soothed' rather than dealt with:

> The matter has been discussed by me fully with LINDLEY and we have decided on a policy which we hope will outwardly give the Civil Authority control while at the same time Military interests will be fully guarded. On the grounds that the amount of territory which we have occupied does not justify their existence and

that the administration can be carried out by a Governor assisted by local Councils, who will be under the directions of the SAMARA Government, the Government whose policy was absolutely impossible from a Military point of view have decided to retire. Colonel Dourov is nominated as Governor. There will be no necessity to have a Military Governor if he proves willing to cooperate with us for ensuring Military security and all requisite military precautions for safety of the Port can then be carried out by purely Russian administration backed by us. This will I hope soothe the American susceptibilities.[24]

It is interesting to note that, in Poole's eyes, the North Russian Government had 'decided to retire'. Presumably it was of no concern that the decision was made at pistol point. The whole foolish ploy did nothing to 'soothe the American susceptibilities'; on the contrary, he fuelled American exasperation. The military administration was dissolved and the former government restored. Poole's position was rendered untenable by this act and he was recalled to London and command was handed over to Major-General Edmund Ironside.

In the same month the French Général Janin was appointed to supersede General Dietrichs as commander of the Czechoslovaks. This had been agreed in advance, but it meant that a Frenchman had supplanted an officer in British pay. Both the Allies had their own objectives in Siberia and this move looked likely to have repercussions later.

XIII

'...a double interest for us'

◄o►

If there was one fear that consistently haunted the rulers of the British Empire in the last four decades of the nineteenth century and the first decade of the twentieth, it was the threat to their Empire in India. In 1914 the Indian Mutiny of 1857, with its horrors and atrocities perpetrated by both sides, was still within living memory. No British statesman could afford to ignore the possibility that it might occur again. The beginning of the twentieth century saw a resurgence of Indian nationalism, and the Nationalists were quite prepared to employ terrorist methods.

Barely separable from this fear was the perceived threat to India from Russia. A full-scale military invasion was deemed possible, and for some seventy years British and Russian officers and Secret Service agents battled for control and influence in the borderlands beyond the North-West Frontier. It has become known as the Great Game. This covert struggle was not brought to an end until 1907, when both Powers signed an Entente delineating their spheres of influence and agreeing not to contest them. This had been prompted by their common fear of Germany's aggressive policies.

In 1918 the fear for British India had sharpened dramatically, and with good reason. The collapse of the Eastern front had created a new threat to India, as that champion of intervention, Colonel Knox, expressed it: 'The Government of India has worried for 80 years over the spectre of a Russian invasion; it will in future have something more real to fear, for German brains and energy are more effective than Russian.'[1] The threat to India was one that the War Cabinet could not afford to ignore. Its links with intervention in Russia were succinctly expressed by the Chief of the Imperial General Staff on the very day that the great German offensive in the West broke:

If the Germans once secured control of Siberia, their influence would extend south into Turkestan, and our whole position in India would be imperilled. The problem was, in fact, part of the same problem as that raised by the danger to Persia. It was a question of pulling Siberia out of the wreck, in order to save India.[2]

In one of the memoranda Keyes wrote to explain his activities in south Russia, he made the point abundantly clear:

By the end of 1917 this area [south Russia] began to have an added importance to us owing to its adjoining the Caucasus where both Bolsheviks and Germans were carrying on an intensive propaganda with a view to raising Persia, Afghanistan and Central Asia against us. We were already launching ventures towards the Caucasus and Central Asia.

The Volunteer Army and the Cossack Confederacies thus had a double interest for us. Our problem was to aid the local Russians to keep an Army in the field, and to see that they had some political goal to look forward to as well as the loyal desire to go on helping the Allies.[3]

The French rather than the British had greeted the Volunteer Army with most enthusiasm in its early days. However, we have seen the enthusiasm of the British leadership wax as time passed, as it became increasingly clear that it was one of the few bodies that put words into deeds and would actually fight the Germans and Bolsheviks. In conjunction with this went a growth in links and an increasing emphasis placed on its value. As the Volunteers were operating in territories surrounded by their enemies, the problem of getting effective support to them was insurmountable.

The role of the Volunteer Army in the defence of India was not one the British wished to draw attention to, especially in the United States. Indeed, the British War Cabinet recognized that the defence of their Empire in the East was not an issue that the Americans would be prepared to spend a single dollar or single life to maintain. Before the War the United States had sheltered Indian Nationalists and the general feeling of the country and its President was hostile to European Imperialism. This opposition was recognized by the British Government. In April 1918 Lord Robert Cecil had prepared a telegram that was to be sent to Lord Reading, the British Ambassador in Washington, DC, urging President Wilson to join the intended intervention in Russia. One of the arguments used to justify intervention was the need to defend India. The War Cabinet discussed the draft of the telegram:

> Lord Robert Cecil pointed out that Mr Balfour had sent instructions to Mr Lockhart to put certain definite proposals to M. Trotsky. In view of this it might perhaps be unnecessary to forward a lengthy statement of the case to America. It was also questionable whether the passage referring to India was well adapted to appeal to American opinion.[4]

The Imperial perspective stood like an ever-present ghost behind the shoulders of British statesmen and generals. Hence Field-Marshal Sir Henry Wilson, the CIGS, could write in his diary on 5 November 1918:

> Much talk with Milner this morning about our future action in Europe, in Russia, in Siberia. We are entirely agreed to keep out of Austria-Hungary, Poland, Romania, Ukraine and north of the Black Sea except in so far as is necessary to beat the Boches. But on the other hand, from the left bank of the Don to India is our interest and preserve.[5]

It was rage that led the Kaiser to unleash the greatest threat to British India since the Mutiny of 1857. The Germans had been counting on British neutrality in what was, in 1914, a European War. Both the Kaiser and his ministers preferred to see the British declaration of war in August as a profound betrayal. In response he vowed to unleash a Holy War against the British Empire in the East, ordering 'Our consuls in Turkey and India, agents, etc., must inflame the whole Mohammedan world to wild revolt against this hateful, lying, conscienceless people of hagglers; for if we are to be bled to death, at least England shall lose India.'[6]

Imperial Germany, one of the most conservative states in the Western world, was deploying the spread of revolution as an instrument of policy. Only on this occasion, instead of Ukrainians, Georgians and Russian revolutionary socialists, the Muslims under British rule were to be inflamed. This had to be a matter of the greatest concern to the British Government, for the British Empire contained a greater population of Muslims than any other political entity on earth, not excluding the Caliphate itself. This amounted to nothing short of an attack on Britain's position as a world power, with the aim of supplanting her by Germany. George Nathaniel Curzon, Marquess of Kedleston, a member of the War Cabinet and a former Viceroy of India, once remarked, 'So long as we rule India, we are the greatest power on earth.' The threat to British India was thus both real and considerable, and it entailed the gravest menace to the perception of Britain as arguably the world's leading power.

When the Ottoman Empire went to war alongside the Central Powers, it gave Germany four major advantages. By controlling the Straits she cut Russia off from the most practical route for her trade and to receive munitions and support from her Allies. She provided a base for subversive operations against the Russian Empire in south Russia. She served as the leader of the Holy War to be mounted against the British Empire, notably in India and Egypt. On top of this, she provided access to Persia and, via Persia, Afghanistan and India.

The first three years of war had seen both Germany and the Ottoman Empire seek to strike at British India by sending small parties armed with propaganda and large sums of money across Persia into Afghanistan. There they hoped to incite the Amir and the leading Afghans into launching an invasion of British India, a move they sought to combine with a massive rising within India against British rule. Until the collapse of Russia, the British and Russians between them had effectively rendered these efforts ineffective. With Russia's exit from the war, a new and far more dangerous chapter in the struggle dawned.

The Treaty of Brest-Litovsk deliberately left the frontiers in the Ukraine and south-east Russia wholly undefined and the Germans pursued a policy of continual aggression and penetration of these areas. The Ukraine itself was neither less nor more than a German puppet state. The Germans gained two advantages from this situation. They realized one of their major war aims by pushing the rump Russian state eastwards to a position where it could not be a threat to Germany. By virtue of the fluid situation in the south the Germans were able to engage in putting their dreams into practice, whereby they used the southern portions of the former Russian Empire as a direct bridge to Central Asia and thence to Afghanistan and India. In short, these territories were to be a springboard for Germany's greater aims of world power.

The British were very much alive to the danger. The Director of Military Intelligence emphasized the importance to Britain of the position in the Middle East in December 1917:

> Sir G. Macdonogh stated that he regarded the maintenance in Persia of a friendly Government as a considerable part of the defences of India, and he therefore considered the meeting of our requirements in Persia (in the form of a continuance of the moratorium, etc.) as no less essential than any other of the above-mentioned desiderata.[7]

If there is any further need to emphasize the common ground between these territories in Central Asia and the Middle East, it can be found in the fact that during the war the Indian Army established a bureau to handle precisely the problems in Persia, Afghanistan and Russia that affected the defence of India.[8] The British position in the Middle East was not only relevant to the defence of India. While the Suez Canal was endangered, a greater threat lay in the prospect of losing the Persian oilfields upon which the Royal Navy depended. It was primarily for their defence that British troops had been sent to Mesopotamia in 1914.

The War Cabinet found that its existing arrangements for handling what were overlapping problems to be in a highly confused condition with three separate government committees handling different areas of the region. As a result of a Memorandum from the CIGS on 11 March, it was decided to form a new Committee, the Eastern Committee, to coordinate information and action. Lord Curzon was instructed to draft the terms of reference for this new Committee. His draft was prepared on 13 March[9] and formed the basis of the Eastern Committee. Curzon advocated that the War Cabinet Secretary would need to be brought into intimate relations with the Foreign Office Officials at the head of the Persia Committee (Mr Oliphant) and the Middle East Committee (Sir Mark Sykes). He considered that the Russia Committee would be absorbed into the Eastern Committee, but the position of Russia in the grand scheme of British strategy was made clear:

> As regards the range of action of the Committee it is difficult to fix precise geographical limits either in the Western or on the Eastern side. But it would seem broadly speaking that what is called the Eastern front should constitute the

factor of differentiation, i.e. enemy movement or action in the Black Sea, the Caucasus, and Trans Caucasus, Armenia, Persia, the Caspian, Transcaspia, Turkestan, Afghanistan, in fact the entire western glacis of the Indian fortress should fall within its purview. South of this the sphere of the present Middle East Committee, i.e. Sinai, Palestine, Syria, the Hejaz, Arabia, Mesopotamia, the Persian Gulf, would of course be included.

So Russia, particularly southern Russia, was to be part of the defences of India. In this respect the reorganization of the Directorate of Military Intelligence reflected the new political arrangements introduced with the creation of the Eastern Committee as a response to the recognition of the political and grand strategic realities. The draft acknowledged the complexity of the situation with the words:

> The question whether the Committee should attempt to deal with the Russian situation, as it has developed in the direction of Siberia with the Siberian Railway to Vladivostock and with the intervention of Japan is more difficult. For the present the answer will probably be in the negative, the Siberia cum Japan situation being in the hands of the War Cabinet as a matter of Imperial policy of the first moment.

The contemporary uncertainty and potential danger to the British Empire were both underlined as the Report continued:

> There is another situation in which a certain and novel aspect of the Russian question may fall within the scope of the Committee. Should the Japanese not enter Siberia and should German influence or German forces establish themselves there, there might arise a new Central Asian problem, as the danger thus created began to permeate southwards and to threaten Turkestan and the regions bordering the Indian Empire on the North. In that case the whole Central Asian question would have to be treated as one, and the Eastern Committee would be responsible.

The Russia Committee continued its work, but now there was the likelihood of its tasks being swallowed by the Eastern Committee if the situation worsened. Nevertheless, there was now a degree of oversight at Cabinet level that would enable more comprehensive policy choices and avoid different Departments pulling in different directions. The need was made more urgent by the fact that the Central Powers had seized the overland telegraph lines to India via Russia. This had two strategic influences: the British Government was deprived of information from that source, and there was also a danger of leakage of information to the enemy.

Dunsterforce was an attempt to restore that situation as well as to stem the tide of Turkish and German penetration to Turkistan, Afghanistan, and so to India. Three new republics had come to life from the debris of the Russian Empire in this region: Georgia, Armenia and Azerbaijan. All were unstable, unable to defend themselves effectively, and chaos and internecine strife raged. The original strategy behind Dunsterforce had demanded only a small number of men, usually fairly eccentric officers of independent spirit and resource who operated best on their own. This was in keeping with a strong tradition where such souls had been to a great extent responsible for the creation and expansion of the British Empire.

The Young Turks planned to establish a Pan-Turanian Empire in this vast swathe of territory. This involved winning control of the Caspian Sea, which would then permit further penetration along the railway to Samarkand and Bukhara that would lead to India. The Turks would also control the Batum-Tiflis-Baku railway, and secure the valuable manganese mineral deposits of the western Caucasus and the oilfields of the East. Substantial quantities of oil, minerals, grain and cotton would fall into the hands of the Central Powers, and so undermine the naval blockade. There was real fear that the numerous German and Austrian prisoners in the POW camps in Turkistan would be organized into an army specifically for the invasion of British India.

These fears were amply justified by the events of the spring of 1918. In March Austro-German forces had seized Odessa, gaining effective control of the Black Sea. The Turks and Germans respectively occupied Batum and Tiflis. The Turks took Erzerum, Van, Trebizond, Kars, Alexandropol, and Yerevan and advanced still further by road to Jolfa. They formed a new Army, the Ninth, of approximately 12,000 men, which was to be the force to advance on Baku with its oilfields. In May Nuri Pasha, the brother of Enver, headed a military mission that went to Tabriz and established itself in the Caucasus to organize the Islamic army with which the Turks sought to crush the Armenians and Bolsheviks and then occupy Persia and Azerbaijan. Duly alarmed, the War Office informed General Marshall in Mesopotamia that as soon as the Turks entered Persia, German agents would prompt the Persian government to encourage a general rising against the British. With British forces fully stretched, there was no possibility of sending a large enough army to parry the expected blow.

The original intention had been to use Dunsterforce to form and organize the inhabitants of Transcaucasia together with such 'loyal' Russian forces as remained in the Caucasus and north-west Persia. The Russian forces in Persia had originally consisted of 10,000 men under General Bicherakov, based at Kermanshah, while a force, called (inaccurately) the Partisan Detachment, under Baratoff had been at Hamadan. British Liaison officers were with both these forces. It has been seen how this attempt, operating on the lines dictated by MIO, had been foiled. The men of Bicherakov's Army had flowed back to Russia in disorder, covered by Baratoff's Partisans. They had then largely melted away, in common with the rest of the old Russian Army. By the summer Bicherakov had a loyal following of approximately 1,000 Cossacks.

Dunsterforce had spent the intervening months at Hamadan, guarding the route from the Caspian to north-west Persia and General Marshall's right flank. It had undergone a marked transformation during that period, ceasing to be a small Intelligence-operations body, being reinforced and reconstituted to become the 39th Brigade. While still involved with Intelligence, it had effectively become a conventional part of the British Army, though too weak to fulfil any significant operational role.

British Intelligence officers had prepared the ground for Dunsterville's descent upon Baku. The British hoped to use the Armenians, who were Christians, as their linchpin in the area. The antagonism between the Turks and Armenians is well known, reaching its pinnacle in the extermination of millions of Armenians in the infamous massacres of 1915.

However, the situation was not so clear as simply arming and training a cohesive, united population within its own homeland. The population of the area comprised a medley of widely different races and religions. The pre-war Russian census had calculated that approximately 7 million souls lived in Transcaucasia. This population comprised no less than eighteen distinct races, with forty-eight different languages and dialects. For generations, the area had been swept by successive struggles for supremacy between these races. A superficial form of peace had been established with Russian rule. The underlying tensions remained.

Of the inhabitants of Transcaucasia, the Caucasian Mohammedans, called Tartars, or Tatars, by the British, were the bitterest enemies of the Armenians. The Tartars were entirely controlled by the Musavatt Party, who were Pan-Islamists, under the leadership of a man called Topshibatcheff. Because of their religion, they were inclined to favour the Turks. The relations between the two peoples might best be described as volcanic. Fighting, usually followed by barbaric massacres, continually lay below the surface and frequently exploded.

In April General De Candolle had observed:

> Tartar Mussulmans still most hostile and local Armenians are as ever needlessly aggressive to them. We are informed here that Trans-Caucasian Government proposes to carry on war with Turkey and that Bolsheviks of Baku appear willing to help though they are unable to take an active part owing to the Brest Treaty. Bolsheviks would be expected to assist in question of obtaining necessary supplies of food from Ciscaucasia which is a matter of considerable difficulty owing to the political chaos in Caucasus and am unable to consider these proposals as promising.[10]

Whatever hopes there may have been in April that the Bolsheviks at Baku might assist with supplies, they were to be rapidly disappointed. Major Goldsmith had attempted to negotiate with Topshibatcheff earlier in the year, when on his way to Tiflis. He reported that he was 'granted two lengthy interviews, which, however, confirmed that it was too late to alter the course of Mohammedan policy in TRANSCAUCASIA at the time.'[11] This effectively left the Armenians as the only people who might be open to British influence.

In 1863 the Armenians had formed a secret society, the Dashnaktsasune, or Dashnaks as they were more commonly known, to protect themselves and bring their oppression to the notice of the Great Powers. It rapidly evolved into a great secret terrorist organization. The British hoped to use this body to gain a foothold in the Caucasus and form an army strong enough to resist the Turks. This was one of the main tasks of the Caucasus Military Agency at Tiflis under Colonel Pike. Captain Edward Noel was the agent charged with making this alliance. Ranald MacDonell, who had been the British Vice-Consul at Baku and had now become a courier between Dunsterville and Pike, left a valuable memoir, in which he described Noel thus:

> Noel was a regular officer trained in political intelligence work. He was, I think, one of the bravest persons I ever met – that is, if a complete lack of any fear of consequences and the absence of any appreciation of what is known as personal safety constitutes bravery.[12]

His initial duties were to report on the situation to Baghdad, to take all measures he could to counteract German and Turkish propaganda, and to persuade such elements as he could find to remain loyal to the Allied cause. Yet Transcaucasia was rent by divisions. Early in 1918, a Transcaucasian Federation had been formed with its own Diet. It was inherently unstable, its various factions struggling to obtain supremacy and prevent each other from encroaching on what each saw as its rights.

Noel negotiated with the Dashnaks, with whom he established the basis for an alliance. MacDonell states:

> The duties of Captain Noel and others, who I was subsequently to meet, were to prepare, devise or create a situation that would enable General Dunsterville and his force to take charge. At the time anti-British feeling ran high, so the task looked pretty hopeless.[13]

Since Noel was unable to establish communications with Baghdad and Dunsterville, he set out to report in person. His route lay across territory controlled by the Bolsheviks and Jungalis. The Bolsheviks arrested him at Enzeli on 9 March, and handed him over to the Jungalis. The capture of Noel was to have an unexpected and dangerous outcome. With his capture, the Bolsheviks and Tartars discovered the Anglo-Armenian plot to overthrow the Bolsheviks at Baku. This situation was made even graver for Noel by the massacre of the Muslim Azerbaijanis by the Armenians at Baku in April 1918. Since nobody could or would do anything without money, the British had been subsidizing the Armenians. It was Noel who had been supplying the funds, and now his cheque stubs were in the hands of the Jungalis, betraying the fact. Enraged by the slaughter of their co-religionists, the Jungalis put Noel on trial for genocide and sentenced him to death.[14]

Fortunately for him, he was not executed, but was held in uncomfortable confinement in the expectation that the Jungalis could use him as a bargaining counter in any negotiations with the British. He escaped once, and remained at large in the extremely inhospitable terrain for some days until recaptured.

In the meantime, Pike instructed MacDonell to carry on in Noel's place. His memoir relates how he negotiated with various counter-revolutionary groups and individuals who all offered the prospect of rising and over-throwing the local Bolsheviks. All of them wanted money, and most of their schemes were fatuous.

One of those who contacted him he named Marie Nicholaievna (it is unlikely to have been her real name), who came to him with a message from Colonel Pike. MacDonell had to be very careful; *agents provocateurs* were numerous, and at all costs he had to avoid falling victim to them. After overcoming MacDonell's suspicions, his visitor described how he could use her and hundreds of other schoolgirls and students as couriers. She told him they were travelling all over Russia, carrying instructions and dispatches for the Tsarist organizations. They mixed with refugees or parties of peasants or even, when the Bolsheviks were moving the women from one of the town brothels, they mixed with them and so avoided suspicion. They believed they were organizing the communications that would save Russia, and their brothers in the White forces. She and her kindred spirits made a big impression on him, moving him to write:

> Marie Nicholaievna proved to be one of those wonderful Russian women who often make one feel ashamed of being a mere man. True to her promise she organised a regular service of communications, which later became of vital importance to myself and my work. These girls turned up from time to time; sometimes in the guise of beggars asking for food, sometimes peddling small wares; they carried messages in the soles of their shoes or in the leather buttons of their coats and other hiding places; some of them were hardly out of their teens – little heroines who do not appear in history books.[15]

On 10 July MacDonell received a surprise visitor. This was Captain Reginald Teague-Jones, another officer of the Indian Foreign and Political Department who was serving with the British Military Mission in Transcaspia under Major-General Malleson. However, he was actually listed as part of Lieutenant-Colonel Steel's MO5.

Teague-Jones' journal tells us very little about what was actually discussed. He wrote that MacDonell gave him at graphic description of the situation in Baku, and says that the one fact that was really important was that the Turks were making steady progress towards the town, being only 40 miles away at that time. The local forces were showing every sign of disintegration. Locally, five different regimes were competing for power: the Bolsheviks, the Centro-Caspian, the Caspian Fleet, the Armenians and the anti-Bolsheviks. Only the latter two parties were in favour of fighting. The Bolsheviks went so far as to attempt to suppress any attempts to raise forces to fight the Turks.[16]

MacDonell's account is more upbeat. He wrote that Teague-Jones told him that the policy of the British and French Governments was to support the various anti-Bolshevik forces and oust the Bolsheviks. It did not matter whether these forces were Tsarist or Social Revolutionary. He was also most interested in the Caspian Fleet, which he hoped, with the support of the Armenians and the Aviation School, would mount a coup against the Bolsheviks. Not only did Teague-Jones leave 'a couple of thugs who called themselves former Tsarist officers', he

> had come armed with the names of the principal conspirators in the counter-revolutionary movement. The first one to visit me was the Captain of one of the gunboats; he had information that a certain Colonel Oriol had arrived from Persia. Oriol hoped to persuade the Aviation School to take action against the Fleet, should the sailors refuse to toe the line. My visitor, being a sailor with real affection for his ship, was highly indignant.[17]

Clandestine meetings followed, but the planned coup never materialized. The Bolsheviks had got wind of it and the conspirators went into hiding. Nevertheless, there was one real achievement for MacDonell. He succeeded in re-establishing communications with Dunsterforce, first with the aid of a master of a vessel on the Caspian Sea. The man was a staunch royalist and reactionary and while the route proved effective enough, it was inevitably slow and subject to delay.

However, one of the people who approached MacDonell 'proved most valuable'. This was a former Tsarist Secret Service officer, who had taken service with the Bolsheviks at the local wireless station, where he was in charge of counter-espionage for the Bolsheviks. Like many of his background, he had no loyalty to the Bolsheviks. He told MacDonell that, 'for a consideration in cash, he would see that my cypher messages were in future duly transmitted and delivered.'[18]

MacDonell also managed to get across the border into Azerbaijan in the company of Shaumian, the Bolshevik Commissar who led the Baku Soviet. There he met Colonel Clutterbuck, who was attached to Bicherakov's Cossacks. Clutterbuck took a gloomy view of the situation and believed that Dunsterforce would not be able to restore the situation even if it did reach Baku.

In June Dunsterforce finally began its advance. The War Office had told Dunsterville he could move only if he kept his communications along the road from Qazvin to the Caspian Sea open. That was going to prove difficult. The province of Gilan, through which the road ran, was dominated by the Jungalis, who had been incited by Turkish and German agitators under the leadership of a German called von Passchen. Bicherakov's Cossacks opened the road to Enzeli by defeating the Jungalis at Manjil Bridge, and Dunsterville could then safely advance to Enzeli, which he occupied on 27 June.

He had left a column some 400 strong under Colonel Matthews at Resht to secure his communications. The road from Qazvin was the weak link for Dunsterforce and von Passchen and Kuchikhan attempted to exploit it. The Jungalis attacked Matthews' column, with approximately 2,500 men, at dawn on 20 July. Military Intelligence had warned Matthews of the coming attack, and after a fight that lasted all day, the Jungalis were beaten off, leaving over 100 dead and numerous prisoners. This second defeat, together with attacks from the air, contributed to a change of heart among the Jungalis, who eventually came to terms with the British. They were disarmed and Noel was finally freed.

Dunsterville still had to deal with the Bolsheviks at Enzeli. A letter from the leaders of the local Soviet to Kuchikhan and von Passchen congratulating them on the action at Resht fell into Dunsterville's hands. It showed they had been plotting with Kuchikhan. With a local superiority of force, Dunsterville was able to arrest them and send them back to Qazvin.

The door to Baku was opened to Dunsterforce on 26 July, but it had not happened as the British had hoped. Bicherakov had reached Baku, but knew he was not strong enough to take it on his own. It had been agreed between him and Dunsterville that, while the Bolsheviks were in power in Baku, he was to cooperate with them in its defence. His forces bore the brunt of the fighting but relations between his Cossacks and the Red troops became so strained that Bicherakov decided to continue the struggle on his own. The Turks were on the outskirts of the town, but advancing with disorder born of overconfidence. The Bolsheviks decided they would evacuate it, and began loading ships to make their escape. One of the leading commissars, Petrov, had collected as many of the artillery pieces with as much ammunition as he could in the church square prior to embarking them.

On the appearance of the Turks, Petrov suddenly had the guns fire on them. Encouraged by this, the formerly despondent 'Army' at Baku chose to attack the Turks. Taken by surprise by this unexpected riposte, the Turks fled back to their supports. However, the Bolshevik leaders maintained their plan to flee to Astrakhan. With the greater part of the Red Army and the contents of the arsenal, they set sail. The Caspian Fleet, which was an independent body in its own right, was having none of it. They pursued the Bolsheviks and brought them back to Baku under arrest.

Both Bicherakov and the new government in Baku, grandly calling itself the Centro-Caspian Dictatorship, sent urgent messages to Malleson and Dunsterville for help. On 3 August as the first elements of Dunsterforce set sail for Baku, a German military mission to the town arrived, convinced it was in the hands of the Turks, and sent a message ashore to inquire where the Turkish Headquarters was. A young British officer who was in Baku, Lieutenant Ward, took his revolver, boarded the vessel and arrested the Germans. A Russian boat came alongside and took the prisoners ashore. This was a startling catch, although it caused some friction with the Russians, who considered that it constituted interference in their internal affairs. Ward was ordered back to Transcaspia,[19] but the Germans remained in captivity.

The rest of the story of Dunsterforce can be rapidly told. The Turks eventually attacked the town in overwhelming numbers. Dunsterforce resisted with the greatest valour, but the local army at Baku had little stomach for the fight and many of its men fled. Dunsterforce was too small to hold the perimeter on its own and Dunsterville had no option but to withdraw. Dunsterforce slipped away by sea on the night of 14/15 September. The Turks and Tartars wreaked a terrible vengeance on the Armenians. Accurate figures do not exist, but most accounts consider that between 15,000 and 20,000 Armenians were slaughtered in cold blood.[20]

The importance of communications has already been emphasized and Dunsterforce was meant to open wireless communication between itself and the British forces in Persia and Baghdad, and thence to London by wireless. The main agency for this was to be the 1st ANZAC Wireless Signal Squadron. It was an ambitious project, since some of the sets required a 6 hp Douglas engine and an aerial consisting of two 150-foot wires carried on 50-foot masts. The regular range for communications was 150 miles, though on favourable occasions it could reach the 350 miles.[21]

In addition, Major W.T. Howe had formed a special signal company for Dunsterforce. Eleven wireless stations were initially allotted to the force, each equipped with a Poulsen arc station sent out from Britain. The ANZAC Squadron contributed two wagon and four pack stations. On top of this four lorry stations had recently arrived from home.

The movements of the ANZAC Squadron reveal how Dunsterforce was used to establish a chain of mobile wireless stations in its wake, eventually connecting Baku to Persia and Baghdad. As early as 28 May 1918, a party consisting of Lieutenant Moore and two British other ranks began to establish a permanent wireless station in the grounds of the British Consulate at Kermanshah in Persia. They completed the job by 8 June. On the 13th, three operators at Hamadan went by car to Kasvin. Number 9 Wagon Set was with the headquarters of Dunsterforce at Hamadan. Stations 18 and 19, known as Russian Stations, were at Hamadan and Kasvin respectively. Number 6 Pack Set provided the mobile communications for the force's headquarters.[22] As Dunsterforce advanced, the wireless stations were strung out at points behind it. They were the links in the chain it was hoped to establish between Baku, Persia, Baghdad and, ultimately, London.

Had Dunsterforce succeeded in its mission, the British would have had the priceless ability to transmit Intelligence rapidly from Central Asia to where it was needed. Much of it was to be based on intercepts of enemy communications, whether German, Turkish or Bolshevik. In this way Britain would have had warning of any threat to India, which would allow the threat to be countered.

Although in many ways a courageous and daring mission, Dunsterforce was a failure. In its original form and at the time it had set out there was a chance, however slim, that its aims would be achieved. In its later form it had no realistic chance of success. The force was too small to fight the new Turkish Army on its own and it arrived too late to train and organize native forces. It had effectively opened a new area of operations that the British Army could ill afford, while it had alienated both the Persians and the Muslims of the Caucasus. It may be that responsibility for that lay with the Intelligence Services that failed to arrange the desired coup and raise the local inhabitants who were pro-British. Yet they were contending with the complexity of the local political situation and the vast areas they had to cover. The responsibility really belongs to those who sent them to perform a task that was really beyond the capabilities of so few men serving under such hopeless conditions.

Those who are really responsible were in London, planning on a grand scale. Meinertzhagen claimed that whilst he was at the War Office, 'I was largely responsible for insisting on our getting a footing on the Caspian, for the first ill-fated occupation of Baku, and the removal of Dunsterville.'[23] The hand of MIO can be seen here, closely shadowed by that of MI2.

It can be argued that the danger was not as great as the Imperialists in London feared. In his study of the Mesopotamian campaign, A. J. Barker contended that the immense difficulties of terrain, climate and lack of transport meant the idea of launching a large-scale invasion of India by the armies of the Central Powers was a physical impossibility. He concluded:

> Those who spoke up for the principle of this tragic expedition talked gloomily of the German menace to India, directed from Baku. Yet, as has been stressed already, their assessment of its value was as faulty as that of those who wholeheartedly condemned the Dunsterforce activities. Dunsterforce was defeated by what Napoleon called 'the secret of war' – communications. When it came to consideration of an armed invasion of India, the Turks would have been just as impotent as a sizeable British force trying to operate from Mesopotamia in the Caucasus region.[24]

Barker mentions the danger from hostile agitators reaching India, but not that this danger would have been immensely increased had the Turks or the Germans succeeded in penetrating into Transcaspia.

Dunsterforce and the activities of British Intelligence officers and agents at Baku were not the only focus of intervention in the Caucasus. Reference has been made to the Caucasus Military Agency in Tiflis, Georgia, under Colonel G.D. Pike. The task of the Agency follows a familiar pattern, one planned by MIO: to organize Kurdish, Russian and Armenian forces to attack Turkish communications. However, we are largely reliant upon the report of Major Goldsmith for an account of its activities. Pike had decided that he would give Goldsmith orders, and in the process ignore those Goldsmith had received from the DMI and Dunsterville. He sent Goldsmith to Sarakamish, where the Russian troops were falling back on Erzerum. Captain Nash went with him as his interpreter. Goldsmith had been equipped with six incendiary bombs by MI1(c) and he was soon to have the opportunity to put these to good use. He reported:

> As a result of my work at ERZERUM, the SARAKAMISH-ERZERUM railway was running 20 trains daily from SARAKAMISH to ERZERUM within 4 days of my arrival. I evacuated 4,000 Armenian women and children with the assistance of Dr. Zavrieff. Three rubber tyre stores containing upwards of 10,000 rubber tyres were destroyed by the bombs I carried from London. ERZERUM held out 10 days longer than G.O.C. in C. had expected.[25]

Goldsmith considered that the bad spirit prevailing amongst the Russian Garrison Artillery officers meant that no stand would be made at Erzerum. This proved to be true, as on the night of 11/12 March the Turks and Kurds rushed the defences of Erzerum without a single shot from any of the guns in the surrounding forts. None of the ammunition was destroyed, so the Turks captured a very large amount and a great stock of other war material.

Goldsmith returned to Tiflis, where the surrounding countryside was in a state of anarchy, with no settled government and numerous Turkish officers and emissaries creating a strong anti-Ally feeling among the Tartars. Robbery and brigandage were rife, as was the murder of any Armenians found. Pike then sent Nash, disguised in civilian clothes, to the Volunteer Army in the north Caucasus. He carried 150,000 roubles for Kornilov and the Volunteer Army. He managed to reach Kornilov and deliver them safely.

Goldsmith found Pike beleaguered. This, he says, was due to the personal animosity shown to Pike by the American Consul, Willoughby Smith. Goldsmith considered that this undoubtedly caused great damage to Pike's prestige in Tiflis. He felt the same about the attitude of the French liaison officer Colonel Chardigné, who described himself as the Chief of the French Military Mission. Such serious friction between the representatives of the Allies was unusual. Pike then placed Goldsmith in charge of all communications. In this capacity, he secured control of the wireless station at Tiflis, which he claims enabled him to carry on conversations with Baku, 'and with the BAKU Vice Consul MacDonald'.[26] He clearly means MacDonell and it suggests that the latter was engaged in Intelligence work whilst he was still Vice-Consul, and not after he had resigned, as he claims in his memoir. Goldsmith also states that the Agency actually got into touch with Baghdad by this means, and that they intercepted all German messages, together with a few from the Turks. These were forwarded to GHQ Baghdad and the DMI in London. The means by which Goldsmith was able to do this was through the help of two operators of the Indo-European Telegraph Company, whom he smuggled into the wireless station.

This arrangement could not last for long. The Georgians were one of the peoples who had declared independence in the aftermath of the breakup of the Russian Empire. Their position was made perilous by the advance of the Turks for, as Christians, they feared massacre and despoliation at the hands of the Turks. As with all the other national groups in the Caucasus, they lacked both an army and weapons to defend themselves and consequently had to look for outside support.

Georgia's declaration of independence led Colonel Pike to decide to move the Military Agency from Tiflis. In 1915, Germany had made an agreement with the Georgian revolutionaries to recognize the independence of Georgia once Russia had been defeated. As has been noted, Georgia was fundamental to the German aim of building an overland bridge towards British India, and threatening the British there. The Turks had also been party to the negotiations and were represented by Talaat Pasha. Although he would appear to have agreed verbally to the recognition of independent Georgia, he had refused to sign the final agreement. Turkey had ambitions of her own in southern Russia and, in the aftermath of the Treaty of Brest-Litovsk, these led to considerable friction with Germany. The Germans quietly sabotaged some of the Turkish initiatives in the region.[27]

A body of German troops under General Kress von Kressenstein entered Georgia and marched on to Tiflis. They were to reach a strength of some 14,000 men. Acting on Pike's orders, Goldsmith made arrangements for the secret removal of the Agency. It left Tiflis on 29 March bound for Vladikavkaz, a town in the Terek province that was under a Soviet government controlled by the Mensheviks. These declared themselves to be anti-German and anti-Turkish and friendly to the British, provided they did not interfere in internal political arrangements. Their allegiance to the Bolshevik Government in Moscow was slight.

Pike entrusted Goldsmith with the Intelligence service to be run by the Agency, with a caution that he was not to take an interest in Russian internal affairs but devote himself solely to German and Turkish Intelligence. This would seem to be contradicted by the instruction that he was to secure secret control of the Bolshevik wireless station.[28]

Pike was awaiting definite instructions from the DMI about the further activities of the Agency. However, he had resumed contact with the Cossack leaders and exchanged messages with them, including information from General Alexeyev regarding the rising of the Cossacks in the Don, Kuban, and Terek against the Bolsheviks. Various party leaders belonging to the Cossacks, Christian Ossetines and great Garbardians also approached Pike with proposals for ousting the Bolsheviks. As was the case with MacDonell, most of these proposals were rejected because of the unreliability of the individuals involved and the large sums of money required.

Agreement was finally reached with the Cossacks to advance the large sums, provided they were prepared to raise troops to overthrow the Bolshevik government in the Terek, and afterwards link up with the Cossacks of the Don and the Kuban and wage active warfare against the Germans and Turks in the Caucasus and Transcaucasia.

A new threat appeared with the arrival in Vladikavkaz of a Bolshevik commissar for the whole of southern Russia, Orjanikidze, who was a faithful friend of Lenin and charged with bringing the area under Bolshevik rule. He arrived with full powers and 20 million roubles. His task had been made easier by the assassination of the local Menshevik President of the Soviet, Boadshidze, at a public meeting by a Cossack soldier. Orjanikidze promptly dismissed the Menshevik members of the existing government and established a local branch of the Cheka.

On 4 July Goldsmith requested Pike to move the Agency without delay to Mozdok, which was held by Bicherakov's Cossacks and from where communications with Baghdad and London would be easier to re-open. While Pike agreed, he did not consider an immediate departure necessary and instead requested Goldsmith to give him a report on all the roads leading to the Caspian Sea, and to secretly reconnoitre the exits from Vladikavkaz.

Six days later the Military Agent at Hamadan, Colonel Rowlandson, arrived at Vladikavkaz disguised as an American engineer named Robinson. He was on a secret mission to Colonel Pike from Colonel Clutterbuck, the object of which was to secure financial assistance from Pike for Bicherakov. Pike did not seem to be impressed, and replied: 'If he wants money let him come and fetch it here. There are 14,000,000 roubles in the Bolshevik Bank.'[29]

Goldsmith suspected that Rowlandson's disguise did not hide his identity and states he was 'undoubtedly' recognized by the Cheka as an Englishman connected with the Agency, and probably a British officer. It may have added to Goldsmith's unease when Colonel Pike told him that he expected some interesting developments shortly that Major Rowlandson would be able to report to Clutterbuck. He did not tell Goldsmith any more. It is abundantly clear that Pike was heavily involved in intrigues with anti-Bolshevik forces and that he expected them to attempt to seize Vladikavkaz with the cooperation of at least some members of the Military Agency. This may well explain his antagonism towards Goldsmith following the orders of the DMI, since independent action would almost certainly have disrupted his own plans. It would also explain his posting Goldsmith to Sarakamish and Erzerum after he had arrived, together with Pike's own reluctance to leave Vladikavkaz.

On 25 July the Bolsheviks declared Vladikavkaz to be in a state of siege. The general unrest in the area had been increased by the arrival in Tiflis of the Grozny oil magnate Tchermoieff, who bore the title of Pasha and elected himself President of the Hillsmen's Council and was recognized as such by the Mohammedan hill tribes of the province. He brought with him 1,000 Mohammedans dressed as Turkish Regular Infantrymen, and his object was to inspire the hill tribes with Pan-Islamic fanaticism. Goldsmith considered his real objective was a personal one, as he really desired to oust the Bolsheviks and recover his oilfields.

The day after the declaration of the state of siege a Cossack, Colonel Belikoff lunched at the Agency's mess. The reason for this soon became apparent. On the night of 4/5 August, Goldsmith was playing bridge with Pike in the Officers' Mess. At 1.15 a.m., Pike suddenly put down his cards and said to Goldsmith, 'I think you had better go home immediately and should firing occur please remain at your rooms and take no part whatever in proceedings.'[30] Goldsmith noticed intense activity by the Red Army while on his way to his quarters. At 4 a.m. heavy firing in his street awakened him. Vladikavkaz was being stormed by a force of Christian Ossetines and 1,200 Cossacks under Belikoff, with the obvious collusion of Colonel Pike.

Despite Pike's instructions, Goldsmith, Captain Gracey and a British civilian, Mr Struthers, provided Pike with all the information they could collect about the course of the fighting. The Cossacks were in dire straits from want of food and water, and both Goldsmith and Rowlandson repeatedly gave them their own spare rations. The attack was eventually beaten off as a result of the Bolsheviks sending Ingushis, a Muslim people from the north Caucasus and related to the Chechens, to attack the Cossack villages. That sufficed to draw away most of the Cossacks, who retired to defend their villages and people.

The only loss suffered by the British was Colonel Pike, who had been arrested by the Bolsheviks, along with Captain Gracey, but had then been killed by a stray bullet. The Agency, that had been so complicit in the Cossack attack, was then raided by what Goldsmith called 'a band of ruffians' who demanded, and gained, the immediate surrender of its weapons and ammunition.

The burden of command of the Agency fell upon Goldsmith's shoulders as the next senior officer. He undertook a reorganization of the Agency, which tells us a great deal about the scope of its operations. Local Intelligence was placed under Captain Durie. All Turkish and Armenian Intelligence fell to Captain Gracey, as did the provision of messengers; Gracey was assisted by

Mr Struthers, who was also charged with arranging the establishment of a chain of couriers to open communications with Baghdad and London. Lieutenant Scott was put in charge of ciphers. Lieutenant Batch was made responsible for translations and typewriting. Captain Nash took charge of stores and Bolshevik Intelligence. Mr Collins was made Chief Accountant and entrusted with all financial arrangements. Another civilian, Mr Clively, acted as Goldsmith's chief interpreter. Goldsmith was to pay tribute to all these officers and civilians, particularly Captain Gracey, whose Armenians enabled him to keep in touch with the outside world, aided by Mr Struthers' intimate knowledge of the Caucasus.[31]

Goldsmith and his team pursued an active policy. In common with Allied strategy in Russia throughout 1918, one of his main priorities was to prevent the Germans transporting foodstuffs and strategic materials, notably manganese and copper, from the area. Large quantities of foodstuffs, flour and other goods, were being sent to Tiflis from the northern Caucasus. The road along which this was transported ran through territory controlled by the Ingushis.

Goldsmith states that he

> secured the services of some of some of the most influential Ingush leaders and their most important Mullah. The Mullah assisted me in raising a force of 500 hillsmen, who effectually put a stop to the wholesale traffic in flour which was being exchanged for sugar and other products.[32]

The Germans had opened a German State Bank in Tiflis, restored the copper mines and were trading for cotton in the Elizavetopol district. They had also seized the Georgian railways and stores of food, which they were using for their own troops. Goldsmith disrupted this by producing disturbances at the Guri copper mines through the assistance of Georgian partisans. Similarly, 35,000 poods [1 pood = 36 lb] of tin lead held at the nationalized Belgian tin ore mines was immobilized by sabotaging the two back wheels of all transport wagons belonging to the mining works. No tin was ever moved from the mines. With the help of Commissar Sorokin, the Town Commissar, Goldsmith was able to influence the local Bolshevik Government to prevent food transports from leaving Vladikavkaz for Tiflis.[33]

The Germans had paid for the flour in advance, and they needed it desperately. They responded by making a demonstration on the Georgian Road and marched down to within 10 miles of Vladikavkaz. It did little good, for their Intelligence officer, Captain Meyer, had called a meeting of the Ingush leaders near the village of Balta. Goldsmith's Ingush allies turned the tables on him with an ambush, and Meyer only escaped by jumping into his fast motorcar.[34]

After the unsuccessful attack by the Cossacks on Vladikavkaz, the Bolsheviks undertook a savage and widespread suppression of all those considered counter-revolutionaries. Wholesale arrests and murders were carried out with the approval of Orjanikidze, whose inflammatory speeches provided the more murderous element in the Caucasian tribes with an easy excuse to descend on defenceless people. There was worse to come.

On the night of 5/6 October the Bolsheviks stormed the Agency. None of the British staff was killed. Major Rowlandson and Mr Clively were able to escape in disguise, assisted by a trusted Ingush and an Ossetine General. They eventually made their way to Baku. The reason for the attack on the Agency was revealed the next morning, when members of the Soviet Government arrived. Commissar Bulle said that the government demanded a search of the Agency's papers, because they had positive proof that it was connected with the Cossack rising and other counter-revolutionary movements. Goldsmith denied the accusation and demanded proof. This was immediately forthcoming in the shape of three narrow strips of paper that Bulle produced, stating they had been seized by the Cheka from a Cossack messenger who had been shot as a spy. When the strips of paper were pieced together, they contained a message from Lockhart to Pike:

Dear Colonel Pike,
The bearer will bring you important information and is to be trusted implicitly.
(Signed) Lockhart.[35]

Goldsmith reported that the message bore the official British Consulate stamp, and observed, 'There could be no doubt as to its authenticity.'[36] He was left with the alternatives of acknowledging the truth of the charges, or attempting to bluff and brazen his way out. He chose the latter, but it was essentially flannel and convinced nobody.

The Agency staff were kept as hostages and endured a harrowing journey across Russia to Moscow, which they only reached on 20 January 1919. They were imprisoned in the Butirski Prison, where they found Sub-Lieutenant MacBride of the Royal Naval Reserve, together with the sixty-three-year-old Mr Bielby who had been assistant to Captain Cromie, and Commandant Guibert, who had been commanding half of the French Military Mission.

The message from Lockhart finally puts his direct involvement in the clandestine campaign beyond the shadow of a doubt. It is the best – but by no means the only – answer to the picture of a hapless dupe, an innocent abroad, that is depicted in his *Memoirs*, a picture that has been happily copied by so many Western historians and commentators since.

What emerges from these events in Transcaucasia is a story that displays both the strengths and weaknesses of the active role the Intelligence Services were called upon to play at that time. There are a good many moments of brilliance, but there are also cases of vacillation and foolhardiness. There was a clear tendency to focus on the ends while neglecting to provide the means. The Dunsterforce expedition might have exerted some influence, had it been able to reach Tiflis early in the year. The change in its balance, together with the bolting on of new objectives, meant that it could neither fulfil its original purposes under the changed conditions, nor could it realize its new objectives. In the high summer of 1918 it could only be considered a foolhardy enterprise.

Events in Transcaucasia cannot be looked at in isolation from those that were taking place on the other, eastern, side of the Caspian Sea. Both were part of the same strategy, and both relied heavily on the work of Intelligence officers. The British initiative in Transcaspia was headed by Major-General Wilfred Malleson, a staff officer with extensive experience of Intelligence in Central Asia. He had served on the Intelligence staff of the Indian Army, on Lord Kitchener's staff and was 'thoroughly conversant with conditions in Afghanistan and Persia'.[37] He had made a complete study of communications throughout the whole of the Central Asian area. He had served as a brigade commander in the operations in East Africa, a term of service that had raised the ire of Richard Meinertzhagen, but the greater part of his military career had been spent on staff and Intelligence duties.

Ellis described him as 'a somewhat dour personality, with little interest in society or the lighter graces of an army career'.[38] Teague-Jones was unimpressed by him on their first meeting, considering him a man 'whose main quality lay in his cleverness in picking other people's brains and turning to his own advantage the work of others'.[39]

Malleson and Dunsterville might have controlled separate commands, but they were part of the same strategy and maintained communications with each other via India and Teheran. Malleson's Mission was formed in June 1918. As well as the normal collection of Staff and Intelligence officers, it had a small element of infantry and cavalry drawn from the East Persia Cordon. The Cordon had been formed in 1915 to shield the western frontiers of Afghanistan and India from German and Turkish agitators coming through Persia. It was a thinly stretched line of outposts that had done a tremendous job given the distance it had to cover and the conditions therein. The men who had been taken from the Cordon to lend weight to the Mission were from two regiments of the Indian Army, the 19th Punjabi Infantry and the 28th Lancers.

The aims of the Mission were precisely the same as that of all the other Allied missions, officers, agents, officials and organizations. It was to prevent foodstuffs and strategic materials falling into German or Turkish hands; in Transcaspia, the main 'strategic material' was cotton, which was needed to make explosives. The Mission was also to do its utmost to block the route to India and, in the absence of any real military strength of its own, the best way of doing that was to seek allies among the peoples of the area, then arm and train them for service against the enemy. If the Bolsheviks happened to be numbered among the enemy, then they were to be fought too. Officers such as Frederick Bailey, Latham Blacker, Percy Etherington, Sydney Jarvis, Reginald Teague-Jones and K. Ward were sent into Central Asia with a plentiful supply of money for these purposes, Teague-Jones tells us:

> Now I had come on this journey with a plentiful supply of money consisting of Russian paper notes of the Romanov variety, popularly known as *Nikolaevsky*. The lining of my coat was stiff with notes, but the bulk of my money was in the third *chagal* [canvas water bag, carried by horse or camel]. To anyone looking at it it appeared exactly the same as the other two, save that if you tilted it up no water came out.[40]

The accounts of Bailey and Blacker are well known, while Teague-Jones' is the most recent contemporary source to have come to light. He spoke fluent

Russian, having been brought up in St Petersburg after his father had died. MacDonell left this impression of his personality after meeting him at Baku: 'Teague Jones' energy and enthusiasm were amazing. In spite of my twinges of conscience about my relations with Shaoumian [*sic* Shaumian], he carried me with him.'[41] Like the other officers on these missions, he was evidently a man who was not only shrewd, but had the capability to inspire others and have them fall in with his plans. He was also to show himself extraordinarily versatile. He, and all the others, were going to need every one of these gifts.

Setting off from India in April, when there were still hopes that the Bolsheviks in the Caucasus would prove helpful rather than hostile, Teague-Jones encountered another British officer, Lieutenant K. Ward, who was travelling in the same direction, at Robat. He was later to be responsible for arresting the German Mission at Baku. Teague-Jones tells us that Ward was an Australian by birth, but had joined the North Staffordshire Regiment as a ranker and served with them on the North West Frontier. He further informs us:

> During the war Ward had obtained a commission in the K.R. Rifles [60th Foot, King's Royal Rifle Corps]. What his war service was I cannot remember, but I should unhesitatingly say that he had done well, for he was undoubtedly a very gallant fellow. He was very reticent about his present Mission and, noticing that he did not wish to speak, I did not press him for any explanation.
>
> He was absolutely helpless on the journey as he knew nothing of the language and could only threaten the camel men with his revolver, which he always carried about with several spare magazines in cowboy fashion.[42]

According to Teague-Jones' Journal, Ward's mission was to enter Transcaspia and destroy the Central Asian railway by blowing up a bridge thought to be between Krasnovodsk and Ashkabad in order to baulk the expected Turkish advance towards Afghanistan.[43] There is either some confusion here, or otherwise there is a question about the reliability of Teague-Jones' Journal. On 7 July 1918 Major Redl, the Military Attaché at Meshed, sent a telegram to Macdonogh that stated: 'Teague Jones was engaged at present on the very difficult task of ascertaining definite means of getting explosives across the Russian Frontier and conveying them secretly to a convenient spot.'[44] Was Ward, Teague-Jones, or both of them attempting to blow up the railway, or had Teague-Jones decided to assist Ward but omitted to record the fact in his Journal?

On several occasions Teague-Jones mentions reconnoitring those sections of the Central Asian Railway he traversed looking for suitable bridges or other locations for planting explosives.[45] It is not clear whether he was doing that for his own purposes, or whether he was trying to assist Ward. Eventually, it transpired that there was no bridge and Teague-Jones greatly enjoyed Ward's discomfiture. Of course the suspicion remains that this may be an attempt to shed the apparent naivety of the notion on to another's shoulders. It might also be the case that someone, in London or in Delhi, had been using a large-scale map to plan the enterprise.

While the officers and officials in Transcaucasia had the prospect of at least some military force, in the shape of Dunsterforce, to support their efforts, none of the officers in Transcaspia had this luxury. Rumour had inflated Malleson's Mission, with its two regiments, into an army corps or half a corps among the peoples of Transcaspia and Teague-Jones certainly encouraged this. Nevertheless, lack of effective military support, when it became known, tended to weaken the long-term influence Intelligence officers could wield. The parallel with north Russia is striking.

Most of them received assistance from individuals who favoured the British or at least feared the Turks, and it was through one of these that the only real independent success in the region was registered: the prevention of the cotton of the area falling into German hands. A German mission had entered Astrakhan to purchase all the cotton they could find and the Soviet authorities were assisting it. The German plan was to direct all the cotton they purchased to the port of Krasnovodsk on the Caspian Sea, from whence it was to travel up the River Volga to Moscow and on to Germany. One of Teague-Jones' contacts in Krasnovodsk was Dr Nikolai Nikolaevich Semov, who had a friend who remains identified only by the initial 'D', working as a technician in the Krasnovodsk Wireless Station. The wireless was unreliable, subject to frequent breakdowns.

The conspirators devised a plan that seems to have been Semov's idea, whereby a false message, contrived by Teague-Jones and 'D', purporting to come from the Soviet at Ashkabad would order the loading of the cotton onto the ships to cease. The false signal would also order the ships already loaded to be unloaded and then sent to Petrovsk to take petrol and heavy oil to Astrakhan instead. 'D' would then sabotage the wireless station, which would appear to have broken down in accordance with its usual practice, so preventing Astrakhan from finding out what had happened or sending new orders.[46]

The plot was put into action on 13 July 1918 and was completely successful. The Germans did not obtain one more bale of cotton from the region. It was a simple plan and had cost Teague-Jones only a little money that 'D' had required for some judicious bribery at the wireless station.

On the evening of 12 July, a revolution had taken place at Ashkabad. The Bolshevik regime had been overthrown and nine of their commissars had been hanged. This event did not owe anything to the Allies, but was the fruit of the brutal maltreatment of the population by the Bolsheviks. Teague-Jones brought the news in person to Meshed. The new government called itself the Turkistan Union and promptly appealed for British help. In 1918 little could be sent, but the 19th Punjabis and 28th Lancers were ordered up and they played a heroic role in defeating the initial Soviet drive to reconquer the territory. Teague-Jones was given a new posting as Political Representative to them, and in that role he became virtually the manager of a machine with very clumsy and resistant steering and gears.

What is of importance for this study is that the usual practice was followed: Intelligence agents and officers were sent ahead to assess the situation, a vital part of their activities, then to find suitable allies and make arrangements with them for using their fighting strength to resist Germans, Turks and Bolsheviks. Apart from the prevention of the cotton resources of Transcaspia from falling into German hands and disrupting the supply of food and minerals from Transcaucasia, there was little of practical value achieved. The supply of information was of diminished value because it was often too late or could not be used because there were not enough troops to use it effectively. Equally – and this was not the fault of the Intelligence officers – the bid to find allies among the native populations foundered on the divisions among those populations and their reluctance to fight. Life had been exciting – Bailey, for example, passed himself off as an officer of the Cheka and led them in a hunt for himself that was naturally a wild-goose chase. Yet enjoyment of gripping adventures was not the reason they had been sent to the area, and they had signally failed to achieve most of their main objectives.

That was not their fault. Most of the people of the old Russian Empire had had enough of the war. Others, who might have fought, such as the Armenians, were denied the military support that might have enabled them to do so because geography, local politics and the course of the greater war elsewhere prevented that support being given in time. Nevertheless, the door had been pushed ajar for British involvement in these areas after the war with Germany had finished. That was to prove to be a dubious advantage.

Although the officers themselves might not have known it, there was a fundamental misunderstanding of the Bolshevik position, and this misunderstanding may not have been entirely accidental. They were not serving as Germany's allies, whatever Allied propaganda might preach. They were seeking to establish their own dominion in the provinces in question and were not prepared to tolerate the loss of any part of the Russian Empire that they could save. In this respect, old-fashioned Russian nationalism and Russian imperialism sat on the coach box side-by-side with Bolshevism, and each had a hand on the reins.

Evidence of this is seen after the fall of Baku to the Turks in September 1918. The Turks finally captured the city on 16 September. The Bolsheviks demanded its immediate evacuation, but the Turks refused. By the 20th Moscow notified the Ottoman Empire that the Treaty of Brest-Litovsk was abrogated on its part and was no more in effect between Soviet Russia and Turkey. The Turks could not realistically have persisted with a drive towards India while there was a lengthy line of communications lying open to the Red Army and Bolshevik partisan detachments.

This aspect never features in the Western accounts of events in Central Asia. It is not as if the fact is not a matter of record. The suspicion must be that the Allies preferred to focus the attention of their peoples on a perceived threat to British India in order to justify their military presence in the area. The real reason had far more to do with an extension of British influence in an area that had been a zone of Imperial rivalry a century before, and for identical reasons.

XIV

A More Conventional Role

October–December 1918

◄○►

The Allies assiduously pursued their objective of forming a united front against the Germans and Bolsheviks. The first step had been taken in August, when several of the White governments of Siberia met at Cheliabinsk. Delegates from the government based at Omsk in western Siberia, the rump Constituent Assembly at Samara, the Ural government from Ekaterinburg, Dutov's regime at Orenburg, the Bashkirs from Ufa, and the government of Kirghizstan all sent representatives. The British and French consuls also attended.

This proved to be a false start. Squabbles, notably between the Omsk government and Dutov, and the Omsk and Samara governments, stalled the process. Unity was of paramount importance to the Allies, whose diplomats worked hard to resolve the differences. In September the representatives of the different White governments met again at Ufa. This time they agreed on a six-point plan, the first point of which was the destruction of the Bolsheviks. After that there was the restoration of the old Russia, but with unspecified differences. The Brest Peace was to be cancelled and the war with Germany was to be renewed alongside Russia's former allies. A strong politically neutral army was to be created, as was a federal Russian Republic, in which the provinces were to have considerable autonomy. Finally, the Constituent Assembly was to be reconvened.

The Allies gave their full support to this programme, but with misgivings, if German Intelligence is to be believed. The Germans commented that the programme 'would also delay the proclamation of a Tsar by the Entente which seemed to be imminent for some time.'[1] That the Allies had been negotiating with the Russian Monarchists and were competing for their favour with the Germans, together with the presence of the Grand Duke

Michael Alexandrovich in Omsk, make this plausible. Indeed, the creation of a constitutional monarchy would have made perfect sense in the context of uniting first Siberia, and then Russia against the Bolsheviks.

However, a semblance of unity was achieved with the formation of what was called the Provisional All-Russian Government, the executive authority of which was vested in a five-man team known as the Directory, modelled on the body that had governed France after the Terror. The Social Revolutionaries, who dominated the proceedings at Ufa, were fond of drawing their inspiration from the French Revolution. The members of this junta were Avksentiev, General Boldyrev, V. V. Saposhnikov, V. A. Vinogradov and Zenzinov.

Shortly after the formation of the Directory Germany, racked by revolution, was forced to capitulate. In the light of the stated objectives for Allied intervention, that ought to have led to a withdrawal from Russia. Lockhart, now safely back in London, recognized the fact that the stated reasons for intervention were a pretext in a 'Secret and Confidential' report he wrote for Arthur Balfour:

> With the defeat of Germany it is clear that our intervention in Russia has now entered upon a most dangerous phase.
>
> Our victories over Germany have removed our original pretext for intervention, and have at the same time strengthened the position of the Bolsheviks, (I) by raising their hopes for a revolution in Austria and Germany, and (II) by increasing their power in the Ukraine, Poland and the other Russian districts at present occupied by Germany.[2]

However, demands were heard about the need to combat German influence in Russia and, more persuasively, that the Allies had made a commitment to the Whites and could not now abandon them. What really underpinned those arguments was summed up admirably by the Chief of the Imperial General Staff, Sir Henry Wilson: 'Our real danger now is not the Boches but Bolshevism.'[3] In other words, the war had now become one against Bolshevism instead of Imperial Germany and the aim was the same – to overthrow the hostile government and society rather than bring it to terms. Fear was the recruiting sergeant.

Of even greater importance to events in Russia was the capitulation of the Ottoman Empire. That meant the Black Sea was at last open to Allied shipping, providing a direct route to the Volunteer Army and the Cossacks. Allied munitions and money could now flow freely to their support; there was no further need for subterfuges like the Banking Scheme to finance the White forces in southern Russia. Alexeyev never lived to see this day. He had died and command of the Volunteer Army had passed to General Denikin who had already been shouldering much of the burden for the ailing Alexeyev. British Intelligence now established direct contact with Denikin. In a report on his farewell visit to Denikin, Lieutenant-Colonel A.P. Blackwood reported:

> There is an enormous amount of intelligence material in the possession of the Headquarters, Volunteer Army, only a small sketch of which has been able to be included in the present report. The rest of the material will, however, be put together and handed to the Allied representatives on the first possible occasion when it is ready. This information is particularly valuable, as it can not be obtained elsewhere.[4]

The Directory enjoyed a brief life. An uneasy amalgam of Right Social Revolutionaries from the Committee of Members of the Constituent Assembly, or Komuch, at Samara and the more conservative Provisional Siberian Government at Omsk, it was bedevilled by personal, philosophical and institutional differences. Worst of all, it never had much real power. It was imperilled from both the left and right of the political spectrum, for it represented the policies of neither.

On to this stage stepped Admiral Alexander Vasil'evich Kolchak. His route to Siberia repays some study in light of what was to come. The Bolshevik coup had found him in the United States, from where he travelled to Japan. In Tokyo he saw the British Ambassador, Sir Conyngham Greene, to whom he volunteered to serve in the British armed forces, even as a common soldier. The British accepted and initially decided to send him to Mesopotamia. When he reached Singapore, he was handed a message from the Director of Military Intelligence that advised him that his presence in Manchuria was most desirable, so he retraced his steps.

The Japanese, who were backing Semenoff, obstructed his work there. Their Chief of Staff suggested that he might like to take a cure at a Japanese health resort. Kolchak accepted. While in Japan he met the British Military

Attaché, Brigadier-General Alfred Knox, whom he impressed enough for the latter to send a telegram to the War Office stating, 'he is the best Russian for our purpose.' It is arguable whether Knox had the Allies in mind or just the British when he used the word 'our'.

When reviewing the situation it is worth recalling the message Le Page, Cromie's deputy, had sent to the Director of Naval Intelligence in June 1918. Then he considered that Kolchak was one of three candidates to be dictator of Russia. Kolchak was now in British pay and taking orders from the Director of Military Intelligence. Many British took the view that the Russian political parties had failed, and unless a leader arose from among the masses one might have to be imposed. Added to which, General Dietrichs had been supplanted by the French Général Maurice Janin, so British influence in Siberia had been supplanted by French.

This perhaps explained what happened next. On the night of 17/18 November 1918, Cossacks under Krassilnikov mounted a coup and arrested four of the five members of the Directory. The British 25th Middlesex Regiment, under Colonel John Ward, sealed off the area with their machine guns. According to Ward, this was done to enable the Ministers of the Directory to decide what action to take. They decided to proffer Kolchak all power as the Supreme Ruler of Russia. Kolchak, with every show of reluctance, accepted.

The French were incensed. Their whole policy in Siberia and, by extension Russia, had been derailed. Janin maintained that the coup was the handiwork of Knox who, he claimed, managed it through two of his military agents, one of whom was Captain Steveni. Naturally Knox denied the allegation. Most Anglo-American historians of these events focus their attention on the role of the 25th Middlesex, but they were bit-part players in a broader game. The whole context of the views held at the time by the British lends very powerful circumstantial evidence for the coup at least being fostered by the British. However, there lies the problem. For all its weight the evidence remains circumstantial. On that ground it is impossible to state that the coup was a British ploy, but there is enough weight of evidence to suggest that the full story has not been told.

Allied Intelligence Services were also trying to rebuild their networks in central Russia. Most accounts covering the post-September 1918 period focus on the figure of Paul Dukes. He entered Russia at 3 a.m. on 25 November, crossing the river marking the border between Russia and the new state of Finland by boat.[5] Yet Dukes was not the only British agent operating there. Reports from two other agents exist for this period. All are Secret Service reports as is shown by the 'CX' identification they bear. The earliest, dated 1 December, is a translated Russian report on naval affairs that was described as 'Information received by a reliable channel from H.Q. on the *Kretchet*'.

It deals with the capture of the town of Narva by the Bolsheviks and the part played by the cruiser *Oleg*. It includes a subsidiary report dated 28 November on the attitude of the Kronstadt sailors, the 'glory of the Revolution' according to Trotsky:

> Tonight, the sailors residing in Petrograd, but attached to Kronstadt, are compelled to present themselves in Kronstadt. Such orders were issued on the previous day but not carried out by the majority. Many are inclined to mutiny. Unwillingness to fight is openly expressed. Undoubtedly the feelings have changed for the better for us.[6]

There is every probability that the informant was a Russian Naval Officer who was forced to serve the Bolsheviks.

The second report, by agent ST.18, dated 10 December, was of a meeting of the Petrograd Commissars in the aftermath of the revolution in Germany. The meeting criticized several senior naval officers, including Admiral Altvater who had been supplying Cromie with information about the negotiations at Brest-Litovsk earlier in the year. The effects of the October Revolution on the morale of the officers were also reported: they were 'indifferent to everything'. It was not a recipe for an efficient and effective navy. Then there was the arrival in Helsingfors of General Yudenitch, whom local Russian military men regarded as the future commander of the Northern Army.[7] That was intended to be a replica of the Volunteer Army in southern Russia, only with a wholly anti-Bolshevik purpose.

The first report from Dukes was made on 20 December. It took the form of a secret report from Admiral Altvater to Trotsky on the future of the Russian Baltic Fleet. It is probable that Altvater had himself given the report to Dukes or one of his associates. Due to a chronic shortage of coal, not least because the Soviet had requisitioned 3 million poods from the naval stores for 'other purposes', it was seriously proposed to place the ships in permanent reserve. The officers were adamant that this would be impractical. If that were done it would be impossible to get the Fleet to sea in fighting trim for several months. It was finally resolved to put only part of the Fleet into reserve, because of a more imminent threat.

That was the possibility of an attack by the Royal Navy and the Allies. The British lost no time in establishing a naval presence in the Baltic, sending the 6th Light Cruiser Squadron there within ten days of the signing of the Armistice on the Western front. It was acting with Mr Bosanquet, the British Consul at Reval and Colonel Wade, the newly appointed Military Attaché to Poland. The Squadron suffered an early loss when HMS *Cassandra* sank after striking one of the many wartime mines that still littered the sea. However, major reinforcements joined it in December under the command of a fighting Admiral, Sir Walter Cowan. It was a move indicative of the British Government's intentions towards Russia.[8]

Liaison with the Estonians started uncertainly. There were considerable doubts whether they and the Northern Army were anti-Bolshevik pure and simple or tools of the Germans, intending to overthrow the Bolsheviks and restoring a pro-German monarchy. The British distrusted the Northern Army but the plight of the Estonians attracted increasing sympathy, as German forces retired homewards and the Red Army swept into the newly emerging Baltic States. There seemed only one way to stop it and that was to land an effective Allied army in the region, but this was impossible in the aftermath of the terrific struggle the Allies had just been through. The Light Cruiser Squadron and a small group of military advisers would have to suffice. Fortunately for the Estonians, a chain of lakes protected their eastern frontier and the Red Army chose to pass south of this and marched into Latvia instead.

The Squadron arrived on 12 December and landed supplies in Estonia, together with several thousand volunteers from Denmark and Sweden. There were also almost two thousand Latvians who had been cut off from their homeland and had retreated into Estonia. The British arranged to supply and arm them on condition they fought alongside the Estonians. With this small force, the Estonians were able to take the offensive and push back such Russian units as had entered Estonia and stabilize their frontier.

Sydney Reilly had returned to Britain after his escape from the wreckage of the plot to overthrow the Bolsheviks. His escape gave rise to suspicion that he may have been a double agent. It was the United States' Consul-General, De Witt C. Poole, who voiced these concerns to Sir Mansfeldt Findlay at Christiania, who in turn sent them to Arthur Balfour in a document marked 'Most Secret':

> United States Consul-General Moscow has suggested to me that a warning should be conveyed to Allied authorities in Northern Russia against an agent lately in the employment of Mr. Lockhart by name of Riley [sic Reilly].
> Riley officially known as S-T was used by Mr. Lockhart for propaganda work amongst the Letts, object being to prevent them resisting the Allied forces. He was instructed to restrict himself to this object but there is good reason to suspect either that he has ignored stringent instructions and sought to cause an anti-Bolshevik revolution or that he has even betrayed Mr. Lockhart. It is known that he was in favour of promoting such a revolt. Mr. Lockhart has now been arrested; but neither Riley nor a certain Russian believed to be an agent provocator [sic provocateur] with whom he was in touch and who knew the address where he still lived a short time ago has been touched.[9]

The fact that Reilly had managed to escape is, at best, too circumstantial a hook to hang a case for treachery on. Certainly British Intelligence gave the allegation short shrift. It was this smear that gave rise to Lieutenant-Colonel French's exposition that has already been a subject of comment.

We can perceive a switch in emphasis in the nature of Intelligence activity now. Instead of acting more or less independently in a political role – in short the undermining and eventual overthrow of the Bolshevik regime – Intelligence was reduced to being what it had been in 1914, an accessory to military operations. The point is well made by General Ironside who, after taking over command from Poole at Archangel, informed the Director of Military Operations at the War Office:

> I found the Intelligence Office here very well run as regards information from the centre of Russia but the organisation of agents, spies, scouts, guides and general tactical intelligence had hardly been touched. This is now being organised with the help of the Russians but it is extremely hard to know whom to employ as Head Russian Agent because, as soon as I have chosen someone, the

secret service come and tell me that he is a German spy. The real reason is that everyone distrusts everyone else and denouncements are taking place every day.[10]

Allied efforts were now bent on supporting conventional White armies that, it was confidently expected, would overthrow the Bolsheviks at bayonet point and Intelligence came to take a back seat in the civil war that gripped Russia. This was mirrored in the changes that took place in the organization of British Intelligence at this point. Major Kisch's sub-section, MI2(d), was overwhelmed by the sheer volume of work involved in covering twenty countries spread over four continents. A new section, designated MIR, was created specifically to deal with Russia, the Caucasus, Central Asia, Persia and the Far East. It was also charged with liaising with the General Staff in India. Kisch was appointed as its head, but he now had the staff and organization to handle the workload.[11]

McGrath was recalled to London where, promoted to Major, he worked in the War Office with MI6(e) until December 1918, when he was transferred to use his expertise with Lieutenant-Colonel Steel in MO5(a).

On the Western front GHQ had run two branches of its own secret service, one of which had been led by Major Cecil Aylmer Cameron. The author of the official manuscript dealing with the history of Intelligence (B) with the BEF, Colonel R.J. Drake, recorded that he resigned and applied to join the army in the field because his secret service had declined to the point where it was 'practically non-existent'. His health was also supposed to have been suffering after the strain of more than three years' continuous work in that field.[12] Drake was being economical with the truth. In fact Cameron had been recalled to serve with MI2(c) at the War Office in order to groom him for service in Russia. On 20 August 1918 Knox was informed that Cameron would be sent out to take charge of his Intelligence Service.[13] He arrived to take charge of the Military Secret Service at the end of September, a move sharply illustrating the change of emphasis from the political sphere to the more narrowly military one.

There was one more incident that needs to be recorded in December 1918. On the 14th of the month Douglas Young, now back in London and serving with the Department of Overseas Trade, published an article in the

Daily Herald strongly critical of the policy of intervention in Russia. His motive was 'to attract official attention to the dangers which, to my own knowledge, were more than a matter of individual opinion and of which H.M.G. had not been forewarned owing to a stoppage in the Foreign Office.'[14]

The day before, an article with the title 'The Allies in North Russia – a Defence of Intervention' by Rear Admiral Kemp had appeared in *The Times*. The article was designed to influence the British public to support the government's policy of intervention as the General Election of December 1918 (the so-called 'Coupon Election') was looming. It was highly misleading, containing misstatements of facts and making several key omissions.

Young replied,[15] writing to *The Times* to draw attention to these errors and further correspondence on each side ensued. The government took no immediate steps, but they were to come.

XV

Confidence Tricks

1919

◄○►

The Bolsheviks had made several approaches to the Allies and the United States towards the end of 1918. In a note to President Wilson of 24 October 1918, they had asked precisely how they could buy off the attacks on them by the Entente Powers. Using the good offices of the neutral representatives in Moscow, on 3 November they proposed opening peace negotiations with the Allies. On 23 December Litvinov, who was in Sweden, sent a circular note to the Allied representatives there proposing preliminary negotiations to remove all the causes of conflict. Finally, on 12 January, after hearing the Chairman of the US Senate Foreign Relations Committee speaking on the causes of intervention in Russia, the Bolsheviks sent a wireless message to the American Government stating that all the motives he had mentioned, regardless of any validity they might once have had, were no longer applicable and requesting that a place and date be set for the opening of negotiations.[1]

Most Allied leaders, meeting at Versailles to formulate the peace treaty, recognized that it was essential for Russia to be represented at the peace conference. Lloyd George, who had always been reluctant to intervene in Russia, felt that genuine world peace was unobtainable without Russia's participation. However, their different ambitions meant there was often a considerable distance between the leaders' views on how this was to be achieved. Lloyd George and Woodrow Wilson suggested bringing the warring parties in Russia to meet in Paris where, they hoped, they could be brought to compromise. French antagonism, backed by the Italians, was strong. They refused to countenance the Bolsheviks in Paris at any price. Clemenceau even threatened to resign over the issue.

The British and Americans then suggested a variation to the plan. This time they proposed that a conference between the Russian belligerents

284

should be held on the island of Prinkipo in the Sea of Marmara. The name of the island translates into English as Princes Island, and was so named because it had been used as a place of exile for unsuccessful contenders to the Byzantine throne. The British dominated European Turkey, including the Sea of Marmara, as a fruit of the Armistice with Turkey. The Allies accepted the proposal, and at the end of January a message was broadcast by wireless to all the parties in the Russian Civil War, inviting them to a conference there on 15 February. This was a novel way of conducting diplomacy, and at first the signs looked promising. While the White regimes rejected the proposal, the Bolsheviks signified their assent though, as the Whites were utterly dependent upon the Allies, they could have been rapidly brought to heel. However, as always, the situation was more complex than that. Francis Lindley reported:

> Petrograd paper 4th February reports Mr. Zinoviev's speech to Petrograd Soviet on the subject of Prince's Island invitation. He stated that offers of concessions etc were made by Bolsheviks on account of bad food situation and in order to gain time to train army and agitate abroad. There was no more intention of keeping faith with Allies than there had been with Germans at Brest-Litovsk.[2]

The information was repeated at greater length and in more depth on 28 February.[3] The Bolsheviks showed themselves here to be the equals of the Allies in duplicity. Unsurprisingly the Prinkipo proposal fizzled out.

The manoeuvres over the Prinkipo proposal had a bearing on the fate of Douglas Young. On 25 January, the Foreign Office sent him a letter demanding an explanation for his article in the *Daily Herald* and his letters in *The Times*. They pointed out that officials employed by His Majesty's Government were not permitted to publish any views they might hold or opinions they might have formed in the course of their duties while carrying out their instructions. Young replied that an explanation would be forthcoming in due course, but pointed out that he had not been exercising any Consular functions since 17 August 1918. On 7 February the Foreign Office informed him that Lord Curzon had directed that he should be suspended without pay until he had furnished the required explanation and Lord Curzon had accepted it.[4]

Now came news that Young's Russian mother-in-law had died but, due to the Revolution, his wife would not receive the property she would have inherited in the normal course of events. In Young's words:

> I accordingly seemed to be faced by the choice, in the matter of my trouble with the F.O., of going through with what I conceived to be my public duty or submitting to force of circumstances in the hope of completing the family disasters by losing the employment which constituted my livelihood.[5]

However, the Prinkipo proposal appeared to Young to indicate a speedy liquidation of the intervention, so rendering any further action on his part superfluous. He duly submitted his explanation to the Foreign Office and was asked to see Sir Ronald Graham, the head of the Northern Department. He suggested that Young might make a formal expression of regret, not for his opinions, but for the technical offence of having expressed them publicly without the permission of Lord Curzon. Young followed this advice.

Lord Curzon accepted his explanation, but added a threat of dismissal if there was any repetition of the offence. On 9 May Young was instructed to report to the Department of Overseas Trade, which was headed by Sir Arthur Steel-Maitland. The Department intended to send him to Novorossisk in south Russia in support of General Denikin's White Army. This was to send Young back to participate in a movement that he believed was doomed to failure and which would compromise his honour and integrity.

Consequently Young requested to be put on the unemployed list, without pay, for six months. In order to avoid further controversy, he asked for this period of unemployment on the grounds of health alone. His request was granted. In the summer of 1919 the Allied plan to join forces with Kolchak had clearly failed and the withdrawal of British troops from north Russia had been decided. As he was no longer employed by the Foreign Office, Young wrote privately to the Primer Minister, offering his services to secure the peaceful withdrawal of British troops. He only received a formal acknowledgement from the Prime Minister's office, but three months later the Foreign Office stepped in. They chose to treat his private letter as a technical repetition of his previous offence and sacked him. It was not until 1923, under Ramsay MacDonald's Labour Government, that this wrong was righted and Young restored to his post.

Any hopes that the British were entertaining that they could restore their secret networks in Bolshevik Russia were rapidly unravelling. Okerlund and members of his ring were arrested. They were incarcerated in the Butirski Prison where they met Major Goldsmith, who left an account of Okerlund's fate.

The wife of F.F. Raskolnikov, the Commissar of the Red Navy, had accused Okerlund and his colleagues of being British counter-revolutionary agents. Raskolnikov was already a prisoner of the British, having been captured aboard the destroyer *Avtroil* that, with her sister ship *Spartak*, had been captured in an engagement with Cowan's forces on 26 December 1918. He had been found hidden under twelve sacks of potatoes.

The accusation was perfectly true. However, according to Goldsmith, I.K. Peters made indecent proposals to Okerlund's 'very beautiful companion described as his wife, the sister of a well-known Petrograd dancer'.[6] Peters' advances were rebuffed, and he allegedly swore revenge on Okerlund and directed the judge, Galkin, who was to preside over his trial, to sentence him to death. According to Goldsmith, Galkin publicly stated afterwards that he was against the death sentence, but had been forced to yield to the majority of the members of the tribunal who desired it.[7]

Goldsmith sought to help Okerlund through the good offices of Sister Hansen of the British Red Cross. She enlisted the help of a Dr Martini, who approached Karachan and secured a guarantee for Okerlund and Captain Ivanoff, who was imprisoned with him. Goldsmith felt the guarantee was insufficient and events proved him correct. Okerlund and Ivanoff were tried, and at midnight they were sentenced to death. Shortly after sentence had been passed, the two men were taken down to the cellars underneath the tribunal building and shot. Ivanoff, who was ill with appendicitis, was killed with one bullet. Okerlund evidently made a fight of it, for there were seven large bullet wounds on his body.[8] It was a tragic end for a gallant officer.

Dunin Barkovski and Colonel Abramovitch, other members of the OK ring were also shot. They, too, were accused of spying for the British Admiralty. While it may be a matter for sorrow that these men were executed, it must be borne in mind that they had foreknowledge of the possible consequences when they embarked on their venture and they had willingly accepted the risk. In that sense their loss was neither more nor less tragic than that of any of the men who had volunteered for military service in the World War and paid the price.

Yet this did not mean that being a prisoner of the Bolsheviks meant an end to all hope. Maria Spiridonova, the Left Social Revolutionary, who had been a prisoner in the Kremlin whilst Lockhart was there, managed to escape at the beginning of 1919 with the aid of four Red Army officers. The Red Army, like its White opponents, was forced to recruit from all strata of Russian society. It would be useless to pretend that all who were conscripted would prove loyal. Without knowing the background of the officers involved in her escape, it is impossible to be certain, but the probability is that they had been officers in the old Russian Army, or were Cadets, or Social Revolutionaries.

The British and French swung their weight behind Denikin's forces and military supplies aplenty began to arrive at the ports of south Russia. Contingents of French troops were also sent. The support the Allies gave the different White leaders was consistently undermined by the perception that most of the Russian people had of them. Colonel Tallents, one of the British officers who had been sent to advise the Baltic States, reported:

> In general States disliking both alternatives, would prefer already modified Bolsheviks to a Denikin Government but conference were impressed by reputed remarks of Lenin, that Bolsheviks would not last out the winter without peace.[9]

Tallents was far from alone in this view. Terence Keyes, arguably a more informed observer, who had been appointed as Political Officer to the Volunteer Army in the Caucasus, drew

> attention to the probable tendency of the present anti-Bolshevik movement to culminate in the restoration of the monarchy, with the implied assistance towards this end of the Allied Powers; (4), points out that the recrudescence of Bolshevism, for example, in Siberia, is directly related to fear of such a *dénouement* on the part of large elements of the population.[10]

An unidentified British official signalled the Foreign Office from Archangel on the prospects of the Allied troops in north Russia linking up with Kolchak:

it would not do at all to have British troops acting in close contact with forces, which even fairly moderate papers like the 'New Statesman' already call reactionary monarchists, if there were legitimate grounds for accusing them of excesses.[11]

Yet many of the members of the British Government were determined to back the White leaders. This raises the question of why the Allies remained in Russia. Their original stated motives, the restoration of the Eastern front and the protection of the stores were no longer viable; indeed, Lockhart, as has been observed, described them as pretexts. There was legitimate concern for the safety of their Russian allies, but it has to be acknowledged that Great Powers do not normally undertake expensive military campaigns solely in order to save friends in trouble. This may be part of the answer, but it is insufficient on its own. A more powerful reason is to be found in a hatred of Bolshevism, a motive that turns the intervention into a form of crusade, as some Allied leaders wanted. Milner, for example, informed the British Ambassador to Peking: 'We have not changed our policy of active opposition to Bolshevism.'[12] That indicates that it was the theory and ideals that were the enemy, not the Bolsheviks themselves. It was a mistaken course to follow. Bullets cannot kill ideas. Military victory might have led to a suppression of the Bolsheviks, but they would have reverted to the underground life that had flourished before March 1917 and their ideas would have lived on.

Milner was at least straightforward and open about British policy, not so Winston Churchill, who was now Secretary of State for War. He and Sir Henry Wilson, the Chief of the Imperial General Staff, were both eager advocates of intervention. Both men recognized that the existing British contingent in north Russia could exert no influence on the situation. To remedy this would require reinforcements, but with the British public having experienced four gruelling years of war, there was no appetite for Imperial adventures in Russia. As Lord Esher informed Hankey, 'The British people were "thoroughly tired of the war" [and] were determined not "to embark again on extensive military operations in Russia".'[13]

Indeed, there were many in Britain who sympathized with the aims and ideals of the Bolsheviks. If reinforcements were to be sent, then subterfuge had to be involved. The solution was to plead that the troops already in north

Russia were so under strength that they were in mortal danger and needed reinforcements to save them. A minute by Wilson appears at the end of the document that outlines this ploy. It displays both awareness of the domestic opposition, and how public opinion is manipulated and thus deserves quotation in full:

> I consider that in the present temper of the troops & country, it would be very risky to order any drafts to Russia. Policy has been gravely attacked by a considerable portion of the Press, & before any troops are sent out it seems necessary that an atmosphere should be created, which will lead the public to suppose that reinforcements were needed in order to save those men who are already in that theatre. A statement to this effect by the S of S or Prime Minister would greatly assist.
>
> I consulted C in C Gt Britain who replied: 'With regard to Russia I can express no definite opinion, but ?reviewed? here is most unpopular, &, from what I have gathered, the men are, rightly or wrongly, under the impression that it has been authoritatively stated that no more troops will be sent to Russia, which they interpret as no more drafts.'[14]

The cynical ploy did not deceive the press or all of the British public. The *Daily Express* went so far as to label the campaign in Russia 'Churchill's own little war'. In the event Churchill and Wilson could only manage to send two infantry brigades consisting entirely of volunteers, hardly a significant contribution towards the overthrow of the Bolsheviks, and far short of the army of a million conscripts that Churchill desired to send to Russia.[15] The history of this episode shows quite clearly why people like Douglas Young had their carefully considered views smothered.

The Intelligence war continued, but in a much lower gear than in mid-1918. Agent N.63 reported that the Baltic Fleet was in full fighting order. The ships that mattered, because they outgunned any under Admiral Cowan's command, were the cruiser *Oleg* and the battleship *Andrej Perbovanny*. The battleship *Petropavlovsk* was in dry dock, but would soon be fit for service. More hopefully, food intended for Petrograd was being detained in Moscow and only brought into the city in small quantities, since Petrograd was not considered safe. A caveat was added. 'If the Allies should decide to occupy Petrograd, they must bring food along not only for their troops but also for the civilian population.'[16] The report continued that the sailors at

Kronstadt were not part of the Bolshevik organization, but were independent anarchists who were allied to the Bolsheviks.

In December 1918 Sydney Reilly and George Hill reappeared in south Russia. Leaving London on 12 December, they had arrived in Sevastopol on Christmas Eve. They had been sent to assess the situation there for 'C' and make their recommendations upon which of the White factions in south Russia should receive British aid. Most of Reilly's despatches are available in the National Archives.[17] They can be readily summarized as recommending the Volunteer Army as 'the only concrete dependable force and living symbol of Russian unity', then describing its shortage of arms and equipment, together with his assessment of what it needed to continue the struggle. He recorded that the National Centre and Denikin were in harmony in their political views. He finally met Denikin on 10 January whose views he forwarded in his fourth despatch:

> People think that in order to pacify Russia, all one has to do is to take Moscow. To hear again the sound of the Kremlin bells would, of course, be pleasant, but we cannot save Russia through Moscow. Russia has to be reconquered as a whole, and to do this we have to carry out a very wide-sweeping movement from the south, moving right across Russia. We cannot do this alone. We must have the assistance of the Allies. Equipment and armament alone are not sufficient; we must have Allied troops which will move behind us, holding territories which we will reconquer, by garrisoning the towns, policing the country and protecting our lines of communication.[18]

This was the last thing the British Government wanted to hear. The French and Greeks had committed troops to south Russia, but given the unrest at home where the Government feared subversion and particularly, Bolshevism, the British chose to be more cautious. Their fears had been inflamed by the Police strike of August 1918, which led many in government to fear that the Police could not be relied upon to effectively combat Bolshevism. The opening months of 1919 saw considerable industrial unrest and the Government created a Secret Service Committee that recommended the formation of a Directorate of Intelligence under Sir Basil Thomson, the head of the Special Branch. He took office in the new Directorate in May, and every week sent a report on revolutionary tendencies to the War Cabinet. When numbers of troops mutinied over the unfairness and slow pace of demobilization, fuel was added to the alarmist fire. The British were not going to risk increasing the instability by committing the country to a new and vicious war. In the end, Britain supplied money and munitions, together with small numbers of specialists and instructors: precisely the sort of tactics that had been favoured by MIO, but which Lockhart had specifically warned London against and which Denikin had said would not be sufficient.

Reilly's high opinion of Denikin and the Volunteer Army contrasted with his pessimistic view of the Cossacks and their Ataman, General Krasnov. He characterized Krasnov's regime as reactionary and doubted whether his recent alliance with Denikin could be relied upon, questioning whether Krasnov would respect Denikin's authority. However, he considered the formation of Denikin's government to be in the experimental stages, while Krasnov's reactionary regime had 'a fully organised apparatus to take charge not only of the military but also of the economical tasks'.[19]

Reilly encountered Keyes at this time. He took a dislike to him, apparently on the grounds that, when Reilly bought everyone champagne on hearing that he and Hill had been awarded the Military Cross, Keyes refused to drink with them. He described him in his diary as 'a cad and a fool'.[20] The whole episode appears petty and unworthy. Keyes' views remain unknown.

On 21 February, Reilly requested that he should be ordered to return home. He considered that prolonging his stay in south Russia was a waste of time, and wanted to report verbally on the intricate situation. He returned to London only to be ordered to Paris, where the Peace Conference was meeting.

However, he did not go there until September, if his Service File is a reliable guide. On 5 September 1919 it states: 'This is to certify that Lieutenant S.G. Reilly, R. A. F., is proceeding to Paris and back on special duty for M.I.1.c.'[21] He remained there for the greater part of a year, involving himself in intrigues with Savinkov and the White Russians. At the time, the British Government was fearful of alliances between German militarists and Russian Bolsheviks on the one hand, and German Spartacists and the Russian Bolsheviks on the other. Reilly was dismissive of the prospect of any meaningful alliance between the German militarists and Russian Bolsheviks, and proceeded to forge the links with Savinkov that were ultimately to lead to his capture and death.

That leaves the question of what Reilly had been doing until September. The answer lies in the resurrection of the Banking Scheme. The main proponent of this resurrection seems to have been John Picton Bagge, to whom Reilly had been formally attached while in south Russia. On 27 August 1919, Bagge wrote to Sir Arthur Steel-Maitland, informing him:

> I am sounding Yaroshinsky on its form, namely, strong in personnel, but with a small capital, and for this purpose ran up to town on Monday, and arranged with Reilly to go over to Paris today or tomorrow for a day. Yaroshinsky went there last Saturday for a short business visit. Reilly takes with him a translation of Draft 'D', & will endeavour to put Yaroshinsky's amendments in detail. In principle he has stated both to Reilly & myself during the past fortnight that he concurs.[22]

The predominant interest of Yaroshinsky, the banker most deeply involved in the original version of the Banking Scheme was, as always, political, but it was being disguised as a scheme for 'strengthening Anglo-Russian commercial relations'.[23] Behind that lay the intention of finding 'ways and means for financing General Yudenitch,'[24] whose White army was attacking Bolshevik Petrograd from the west.

The whole plan, which was first mooted in July, was based on the expectation of imminent White victory in the Civil War, a prospect that appeared realistic at that time. It was felt to be vital to create a powerful business organization that would take the lead in a systematic economic reconstruction of Russia, employing Yaroshinsky's financial influence and British finance, while supplanting German influence.

The means were to be the re-establishment of those Russian banks that would be controlled by the proposed organization and the bringing of other Russian banks within its influence. This banking conglomerate would then finance and develop the various commercial and industrial enterprises that fell within its extensive orbit. Finally, it was planned 'to coordinate the numerous activities of the organisation in such a way as to make it a permanent and powerful factor in the political and economic life of Russia'.[25] This amounted to control of the entire Russian economy, with the clear implication that control of Russia's political life would follow. The controlling company, called Yaroshinsky Limited, was to be formed by Yaroshinsky and a group of British financiers. This was no mere scheme to finance the Cossacks, but economic imperialism on a grand scale. Elements of that had existed in the original schemes; this time the intention was naked.

The scheme was dependent upon Lord Curzon giving it his approval, but this was delayed until the British Government could see that White victory was certain. After Kolchak's forces were heavily defeated in the summer of 1919, the approval was withheld indefinitely. The final collapse of the White armies meant it would never be put into practice.

The Red Army had counter-attacked Kolchak's forces in May 1919 with dramatic effect. Kolchak's armies were tumbled back in headlong flight that proved unstoppable. The Czechoslovaks were by now demoralized, having done most of the fighting through 1918 and appearing no nearer to reaching their newly established homeland than they had been a year previously. There were also tensions with Kolchak, who was relieved to see them fall back to garrison the Trans-Siberian Railway. Ultimately they were to surrender Kolchak and the former Imperial Russian gold reserves to the Bolsheviks at Irkutsk, in return for their departure to Vladivostock and then home.

On 7 July 1919 Hankey accompanied Lloyd George to the Prime Minister's country home at Criccieth for a rest. After a week the two main advocates of intervention, Winston Churchill and Sir Henry Wilson, arrived. Hankey's records provided the basis for his biographer to provide an account of what followed:

> Then Churchill and Henry Wilson joined the party, both of them depressed – Hankey thought by the collapse of Admiral Kolchak's anti-Bolshevik movement in Siberia. Lloyd George, who had always been opposed to the war of intervention, 'twitted Winston a good deal' about the failure of his pet project.[26]

In the meantime French influence in the south Ukraine and the Crimea had suffered a serious reverse. A Red Army counterattack had surprised the French, Greeks and White Russians and driven them back with losses. Part of the French Expeditionary Force mutinied, as did a significant number of men on their ships in the Black Sea. It was, understandably, enough to persuade the French to withdraw from major military adventures in the region.

In the Baltic Paul Dukes continued to report on the Russian Baltic Fleet, including one on a meeting summoned by the Petrograd Bolsheviks on

17 January to consider the Fleet's morale, and another in February on the steps Trotsky had taken to stir the fighting spirit and effectiveness of the Fleet. A further report outlined the steps the Bolsheviks were preparing to take to defend themselves against a British amphibious assault.

Dukes' sources repay attention. Much of the more sensitive information probably came from a Russian Naval Officer who was employed at the Russian Admiralty and who Dukes mentions in his account of his work.[27] Another was an Army Officer named Melnikov, whose uncle, a doctor, provided Dukes with valuable assistance and was to save his life. Dukes says another informant was a former General, 'who furnished me with information about the Red army.'[28] Another was a commander of a unit in the Red Army.[29] All belonged to that stratum of society that the Bolsheviks had declared 'class enemies'.

The other major task Dukes faced was to reopen contact with the National Centre. He provides no details about how he did it or whom he contacted, since when his book was first published members of the National Centre were still alive in Russia and he was not going to be the instrument to betray them. Although the National Centre had played only a small part in the military events of 1918, its importance was augmented by the strategic situation facing the Bolsheviks in 1919. They were beset from four directions – Kolchak to the east, Denikin to the south, the Allies and their hodgepodge of Russian allies to the north, and General Yudenitch to the west. Dukes had a role in supplying Yudenitch with Military Intelligence to assist his advance on Petrograd.

Not only did the National Centre provide the White forces with information on the movements, strength and deployment of the Red Army, but they returned to the old plan of preparing risings in Petrograd and Moscow as the White armies approached those cities. They did more than that, if Lenin and Dzerzhinsky are to be believed. As Yudenitch marched on Petrograd in May 1919, Stalin was sent to the city to try and stabilize the situation there as panic was beginning to spread through Bolshevik ranks. Lenin sent him a telegram that warned of widespread treachery behind the front and possibly in the front line itself. A more dramatic development was the appearance of a proclamation, bearing the signatures of Lenin and Dzerzhinsky, with the title 'Beware of Spies'. It claimed:

Death to spies! The White-Guard advance on Petrograd has clearly demonstrated that along the whole frontal zone, and in each sizeable town, the Whites
possess an extensive organisation which is effecting espionage, treason, blowing
up of bridges, insurrection in the rear, killing of Communists and of prominent
members of workers' organisations.[30]

These are far-reaching claims. If the National Centre had achieved so formidable a measure of success then the reasons for the reverses suffered by the
Red Army are readily discernible. However, it is necessary to be very wary of
Bolshevik propaganda. The information may have been deliberately exaggerated to inspire greater efforts on the part of the Bolsheviks among the
population. Unfortunately we lack any independent record of the instances
of 'espionage, treason, blowing up of bridges, killing of Communists and
prominent members of workers' organisations' to be entirely sure of either
the scale or effectiveness of the National Centre's activities in these respects.
They do not appear to have been sufficient to have seriously dislocated the
Red Army's deployment.

One signal failure was the lack of any effective stroke against the railway
line that brought reinforcements to the Petrograd front from Moscow and
central Russia. It ought to have been possible to disrupt this line somewhere
along its length, and the effects would have been considerable.

Assassination and terrorism were not the exclusive preserve of the
National Centre and the Whites. There was at least one Bolshevik plot to
assassinate Admiral Kolchak. Despite French resentment of him, it was
French and Czechoslovak counter-espionage that thwarted it. In March
1919, the French Military Mission in Siberia sent a report to Commandant
Bolifraud from a secret agent with the codename 'JOHN' [English 'John' is
used in original, not French 'Jean'] and Lieutenant Zemand of the
Czechoslovak counter-espionage section. It reported that one of the
Bolshevik circles at Tomsk had organized an assassination attempt on
Kolchak during his stay at Ekaterinburg, but they had prevented it.[31]

As well as obtaining information and coordinating activities, one of
Dukes' missions was to provide the National Centre with funds. That was not
an easy task. With the nationalization of the banks and the flight or impris-
onment of most of the bankers, there could be no replay of the original
Banking Scheme in central Russia. Trading promissory notes against roubles

was equally unthinkable. To do that without the shelter of diplomatic cover in the conditions of 1919 would simply have drawn much unwelcome attention to Dukes.

The alternative was for courageous couriers to smuggle them in. This was done, but the results were not always happy. One of his couriers, identified as Peter Petrovich, brought him a large sum of money. Opening the parcel in the Smolensk Cemetery, his initial satisfaction turned to dismay: '*Bad money? Or spoilt?...In transit?...No, more likely in printing...*' Dukes explained:

> The notes sent to me had the correct design and wording, but the paper was thin, its dye was not good, and the inscription on some of them was smudged. The sheets were not of uniform thickness or colour. They had the appearance of being trial sheets, those run off while the dye and type were getting set. 'Some of Kolchak's or Yudenitch's half-baked stuff,' I thought to myself as I fingered it. Good enough, perhaps, for use outside Russia, but quite useless within.[32]

There was nothing for it but to bury the forgeries, suitably enough, in the cemetery. It is noteworthy that Dukes blames either Kolchak's or Yudenitch's service for the debacle, but Christopher Andrew states the forgeries came 'from Cumming'.[33] It is perfectly possible that Dukes was trying to divert attention for the error away from his employer, and that Andrew may well be right. Dukes tells us that Peter Petrovich was given the forgeries by Augustus Agar of the Royal Navy, who had been specially selected by 'C' for this sort of operation. With two high-speed, shallow-draft CMBs based in Finland, Agar was the key link with Dukes. He received and despatched couriers, often at great personal risk. He was to become famous, winning the VC, when he not only torpedoed and sank the *Oleg*, but once reinforced had the audacity to raid the Soviet naval base at Kronstadt, sinking the submarine depot ship *Pamyat Azova* and crippling the two battleships.

The Bolsheviks responded to the perceived threat from the National Centre by carrying out a widespread search of church property and bourgeois households in Petrograd on 14 June. To find the manpower to carry out this sweep, 20,000 workers were drafted in for the search. No doubt a significant proportion of them joined in with an eye to loot and other bonuses. Reputedly a large quantity of arms was found. This did not break the National Centre, but its days were numbered. Two couriers attempting to cross into Finland were arrested on 14 July. This led to the unravelling of Yudenitch's Intelligence organization, of which Dukes had no high opinion, commenting after meeting an officer from it who was one of his contacts: 'Yudenitch's organisation for which he worked was run on hopeless lines. It was discovered and hundreds were executed.'[34] One of those arrested was V.I. Shteininger, the National Centre's chief link with Yudenitch.[35]

On the night of 18/19 September the Cheka struck in Moscow. They knew the National Centre was planning a rising to take place there in mid-October, timed to assist Denikin's advance on the city, having been alerted by a denunciation made by one of the plotters in August. The capture of a courier from Admiral Kolchak to the National Centre had then put another important card into the Cheka's hands. The courier had been on his way to N.N. Shchepkin, the Chairman of the National Centre, bearing a large subsidy for him. The Cheka pounced on Shchepkin on the night of 28/29 August while he was 'in the very act of receiving a courier from General Denikin'. Worse still, Shchepkin kept a list of the members of the National Centre, together with reports on the Red Army's dispositions and strength on the front facing Denikin. These reports were awaiting despatch to Denikin and the outcome of the Russian Civil War might have been very different had they reached him.[36]

According to Leggett:

> The conspirators, who disposed of many motor vehicles, some armoured cars, and even artillery, and who could count on the support of three officer-cadet schools and certain military units, intended to capture Moscow's railway stations and telegraph offices, and to storm the Kremlin; they expected the peasantry in the countryside around Moscow to come to their assistance.[37]

Claims vary as to the number of its adherents who were arrested, from over 1,000 to the slightly more modest 700. Perhaps the sixty-seven seized after the Shchepkin disaster need to be added to the total. All of these latter, including Shchepkin, were executed.

Subsequently, the National Centre's organizations in Petrograd were crushed, largely as a consequence of the arrest of a Colonel Liundekvist, who had until recently been the Chief of Staff to the Seventh Red Army. He had put together a plan by which Yudenitch might capture Petrograd and succeeded in getting the plan to him. He had also planned a rising within the city that was to take place when Yudenitch approached.[38] Knowledge of this assisted the Bolsheviks to mount a successful defence of Petrograd and to scotch the internal rising before it took place. It effectively sounded the death knell for the National Centre.

At times the issue had hung very much in the balance. Gordon Brook-Shepherd has pointed out that the Bolshevik leadership were ready to flee in the ominous summer of 1919, just as they had been in the perilous summer of 1918. Yet the Bolsheviks survived and went on to rule over the territories of most of the Russian Empire by 1920. One of the reasons for this was that the Allies decided to withdraw from Russia and leave the Whites they had encouraged to their fate. There were sound reasons for this. A more virile policy would have meant commitments in terms of men and money that the Allies could not make, not least because of domestic opposition to any extension of the war to Russia.

The British decided to leave Russia in March 1919, but they continued to support the White cause with money, munitions and small teams of specialists into 1920. Their final offensive in north Russia in the summer of 1919, a highly successful tactical operation, was no more than a cover for the intended withdrawal. Intelligence had increasingly taken a back seat since the disaster of August 1918 and its priority now was to try to stem Communist agitators and ideas from subverting Britain and the Empire.

Some remnants clung on for a time. For instance, the Anglo-Russian Motor Company was established at Baku as a cover for the Secret Service, but it had to scuttle away when the Red Army conquered Caucasia in 1920. A new scheme to undermine the Bolsheviks financially was hatched by Reilly and Yaroshinsky in 1920. It initially attracted some attention in both the Foreign Office and the Department of Overseas Trade. However, it failed to inspire any enthusiasm in either Sir Ronald Graham or Lord Curzon so the proposal never went any further.

British successes against Soviet codes continued for some years, enabling them to partially frustrate many of the initiatives the Soviet Union mounted against Britain and her Empire. In this they were aided by the establishment of a decoding section from MI1(B) that was based at Constantinople from 1918 to 1922. After Turkey's reformation under Kemal Ataturk, the wireless station and the decoding team were transplanted to Sarafand in Palestine,[39] where they continued to render sterling service. It was little enough to show for the struggle to secure dominance over the communications routes to India.

XVI

Epilogue

◄◉►

Examining the Intelligence intervention in Russia is revealing. With that perspective, much about the political background to both the intervention and the Russian Civil War becomes clear. The Intelligence Services were the initial spearhead of the intervention. That had been dictated by the peculiar conditions – action in a state that had been a vital part of the Entente war effort, and upon which the Entente Powers' hopes of victory had rested. A major German offensive was anticipated on the Western front, and this anticipation was realized in shocking fashion in March 1918.

There was also a genuine fear that Russia's immense wealth of minerals and foodstuffs would be made available to the Central Powers, thus destroying the naval blockade that was one of the Allies' most powerful weapons. Words such as 'treason' and 'betrayal' were heard levelled at the Russians in the capitals of the Allies.

The situation appeared to be made worse for the Allies by the attitude of the President of the United States. At the beginning of 1918, the United States was the only state in the Western world with the manpower and the money to make a difference. The stance taken by Woodrow Wilson towards Russia gave no comfort at all to America's increasingly desperate associated Powers. Deprived of the hope of reopening the Eastern front through the deployment of American troops in Russia to rally those who were still prepared to fight the Germans, the Allies increasingly turned to their Intelligence Services to perform the miracles of denying Russia's resources to the enemy and restoring the Eastern front.

There is a common and very human thread that binds these influences together. That is fear. It was fear born from anticipation, but that does not mean it was any less real. The pressure was on the Allied Governments to do something, one might say anything, to remove that fear. Yet their options, as has been seen, were severely limited. Their position smacked of desperation, as did their response. So an imaginative campaign was born. The Intelligence Services were sent to pluck if not victory then a new Eastern front out of defeat. The Allies might have thought there was every good reason for at least some chance of success in this strategy. They had before them the towering success of the German subversive campaign in Russia, run in conjunction with the Bolsheviks. That had knocked Russia out of the war, so delivering to Germany her dream of a war on one front.

The British created a new organization, MIO, to try and effect this in Russia. No study of the intervention or Russian Civil War appears to refer to this body, probably because it was never openly in the front line, but also because its documentary history has largely disappeared. Nevertheless, it exerted a profound influence, bearing a considerable part of the responsibility for the unsettled state of Russia in the first six months of 1918. One of the main methods employed to achieve its ends was money. It was money that appeared persistently to pave the road to the attainment of the goals of all the Great Powers. This study has shown the influence of money, but also its limitations. There is no doubt that in the Russia of 1918 many Russians would promise the world in return for healthy subsidy, but would then do nothing. Therefore careful choices had to be made. The various existing national and cultural groups within the Russian Empire were the first targets. Hence Armenians, Georgians, Cossacks, Czechoslovaks, Poles and Ukrainians were offered blandishments to help them secure what were perceived to be their particular ends.

This was not a novel policy; money, subsidy, has long been a strategic weapon, as have the employment of spies, *agents provocateurs*, the disbursement of bribes, blackmail and the encouragement of treason. There exists a diplomatic underworld where these transactions are carried out. Formal diplomacy helps to conceal this underworld, indeed it may be said to be part of its purpose to so do. However, shafts of light occasionally penetrate and there are increasing numbers of them from the middle of 1918, when the Allies began to turn their attention increasingly towards forming covert alliances with the anti-Bolshevik political parties in Russia.

Foreign ambassadors and missions usually took the decisions to act, but then turned the action over to political officers, Intelligence officers, Secret Service officers and special representatives. They then averted their eyes from what these operatives did, so the operations remained deniable, and the diplomatic underworld remained an underworld with little of its activities ever coming to light.

The strategy was simple enough: identify those parties or political groupings that have a grievance against the existing government or state of society, and are ready to use every means to overthrow the government or society. The political parties involved were then promised every assistance and support to achieve their goals; yet that inevitably entailed the Allies becoming bound to those goals. In that context the parties with which the Allies made common cause were no different from the Bolsheviks when they collaborated with the Germans. There was one significant difference that contains no small amount of irony – whereas the Bolsheviks sought to over-throw the existing social structure, their opponents were to a considerable extent intent upon restoring it.

It might be argued that the Bolsheviks could claim no legitimacy, having seized power in a *coup d'état*, and thus were justifiable targets for any and every attempt to overthrow them. Such an argument neglects the fact that many of the Russian people, as embodied in the army, had already voted with their feet to end the war and it cannot be legitimate for foreign governments to contradict that will. It is equally valid to ask whether a government supported by the money and bayonets of the Allies would have had any more legitimacy. The Allies initially sought to install a dictatorship with Alexeyev at its head. Later they toyed with the idea of imposing a monarchy. Only after the war with Germany was over did they address the issue of restoring the Constituent Assembly, and that was only in response to the need to reassure their own peoples and the requirement to retain the United States as party to the intervention.

The histories of British agents such as Sydney Reilly, Frederick Bailey and Paul Dukes are well known, even if their real or alleged deeds have been subjected to much exaggeration and mythmaking over the years. Since their identities have been disclosed they have been very handy decoys for the British authorities. While attention has been focused on these men, others like Bell, Cromie, Hall, Keyes, Litch, McGrath, Steveni and Teague-Jones have been able to remain in the background. The same could be said of French and American operatives. It is vital also to realize that operatives such as Dukes and Reilly were simply cogs in a much larger machine. In the statement Reilly wrote for his OGPU captors in 1925, he reputedly said of his operations in 1918:

> The money was allocated from the funds I had received; I had in my possession considerable amounts of money, which, in view of my special status (total financial independence and exclusive confidence due to my ties with highly placed persons) were provided me unaccountably. These very funds I spent on my fight against Soviet power.[1]

While this needs to be read with caution, for it must be remembered that Reilly is not a reliable witness and was telling his captors what he thought they wanted to hear, it does indicate that he was not the famed lone swordsman of myth. It also raises the issues of from whom the money came and who the 'highly placed persons' were that placed such confidence in him. Despite all the claims of 'accountability' made on behalf of Western democracies, both remain unaccountable.

It has been seen that the Allied stores at the Russian ports were used as a pretext to justify intervention to the British, French and American peoples. Poole and Lockhart both described the reason given for intervening in Russia as a pretext. They were intimately involved with the intervention and thus were in a position to know. Two officers – the Director of Military Intelligence and Lieutenant-Colonel Richard Steel – were also in a position to know. As the war with Germany drew to its close, Steel wrote a paper on future Allied policy in Russia. It opened with the words:

> With the anticipated disappearance of the German menace, our original pretext for intervention in Russia, i.e., the encouragement of continued military resistance to the Central Powers, vanishes. From the purely military point of view, there is no longer any immediate object to be gained by the retention of forces in Russia.[2]

The paper developed its theme by maintaining that if intervention was to continue, it had to be directed either against Bolshevism or towards eliminating every trace of German influence in Russia. Steel went on to argue that no great help could be expected from effective action in the north, since communications were 'too exiguous' and the population was both scanty, and had shown no marked response to the Allied call to them to rise against Bolshevik oppression. Not only that, 'It is in the North that Bolshevism has its stronghold, and where, according to Mr Lockhart, it is growing stronger every day.'[3]

Steel proceeded to torpedo his case with his next point, which tried to present a case for continuing the intervention in the north: 'One factor stands out – we cannot desert and hand over to the vengeance of the Bolshevists the population which we have taken under our protection.' Here was a fine contradiction. The population of the region was on the one hand largely hostile, but it was still worthy of British protection against the vengeance of the very people it supported.

The reason for Steel's confusion is apparent. He wanted the Allies to stay in Russia; the whole policy of intervention had owed a lot to him over the preceding year, but now he was fishing for justification for it. The real reason behind his support for intervention is found in the third paragraph of his paper: 'From the military point of view we have to consider this point in connection with the defence of India and our position in the East.'[4]

The problems posed by British rule in India and by her position in the Middle East have been touched upon several times. At their roots lay two factors: the possession of a global empire and the real reason for the war, which was the struggle for world supremacy between Britain and Germany. The British Empire lent considerable prestige to the country, and while in many respects it was a source of strength, the World War had also shown it to be a potential weakness. The latter point was driven home most strongly in the Second World War. It was the danger to the Empire in the East that conditioned much of British thinking towards Russia, Bolshevism and intervention.

Certainly the Bolsheviks had not made themselves any friends among the higher British political echelons with their attempts to foment risings in the East against the colonial overlords. In turn, this meant not just the Bolsheviks, but Bolshevism and then Communism were enemies to be destroyed in the eyes of those echelons. The great struggle between the capitalist powers of the West and the Soviet Union was initially drawn in great part from this perspective. Western propaganda endeavoured to portray the Bolsheviks as allies of the Germans, and all sorts of nonsense about German troops fighting alongside the Bolsheviks in Siberia was pedalled to the publics of the capitalist world.

Writing in 1920, Keyes had this to say about the accusations that Denikin's White Army was no better than the Bolsheviks in humanitarian terms:

> Over three hundred British officers have been in South Russia during Denikin's campaign, and, though many may have been disillusioned by the corruption and incompetence which nullified the gallantry and devotion of the original volunteer army, most have been able to see beneath this and to realise, that, with all their failings, these people have been fighting in defence of Christian civilisation against the most damnable evil the world has ever seen, and, incidentally, have been acting as an outpost of the British Empire in the East.[5]

That the Bolsheviks were regarded as a threat to Western civilization, as the British elite understood 'civilisation', is beyond doubt. This theme was harped upon with increasing frequency throughout 1918. This served as an additional justification for intervening in Russia. It was pressed by Poole as early as 13 February in a letter to Colonel Byrne and more strongly in his *Report on Visit of British Military Mission to the Volunteer Army*: 'The successful movement in South Russia is the only spontaneous Russian effort to maintain the principles of order and civilisation against the menace of Bolshevism.'[6]

It was a view shared across Intelligence circles. When the Director of Naval Intelligence retired in November 1918, he addressed a short farewell speech to the members of Room 40. According to his biographer, its last words were:

> Above all we must thank God for our victory over the German nation; and now I want to give you all a word of warning. Hard and bitter as the battle has been, we have now to face a far, far more ruthless foe, a foe that is hydra-headed, and whose evil power will spread over the whole world, and that foe is Russia.[7]

These facts did not incline the British authorities to regard the new regime in Russia with any degree of friendliness. The destruction of the Eastern front, regarded as essential for victory in the war with Germany, occasioned understandable feelings of betrayal. What practical courses were left open to the Allies?

They could have recognized the Bolshevik Government, which undoubtedly would have been a constructive step that might have opened the doors to a potentially widespread collaboration on a cushion of goodwill. Such a step might well have strengthened Bolshevik inclinations to resist German aggression and inclined them to accept military support to this end. The Bolsheviks had actively sought such aid in the first months of 1918. There was no telling where such a course might have led, but it was arguably more constructive than the intervention that was ultimately undertaken, which signally failed to cause a single German division to be withdrawn from the Western front and instead committed Allied troops and resources to an additional front.

Restoring the Eastern front and defending the British Empire in India might be considered compelling reasons for intervention in Russia, although Steel has been seen to have dismissed restoring the Eastern front as a pretext. Yet did intervention offer any realistic prospect of renewing the war in the east when many of the Russian people had no will to fight the Germans? Did the intervention draw a single German division from the Western front? Germany continued to maintain thirty-five-and-a-half divisions in the east irrespective of the Allied intervention, and they never required a single company of reinforcements from the Western front. To argue that the Eastern front was a necessity when the Allies could look forward to the prospect of millions of fresh American troops on the Western front simply neglects the conditions faced by the Central Powers in 1918. In these terms the intervention can be seen as an enormous gamble; it was one that failed.

Alternatively they could have gently encouraged the Bolsheviks in their passive resistance to Germany, a form of resistance that led in part to the German divisions being tied down in the east, as Lenin had informed them would happen. However, they would have been able to exert little control over this and to do nothing if the strategy misfired. Moreover, the Allied military experts looked askance at the idea, conditioned as they were to dealing with formed armies of massed divisions and artillery.

The military experts were part of the problem, as much as the politicians. The soldiers required political leadership, but the political leadership of the

Allies, and notably the British, was divided and uncertain. After the decision of 3 December 1917 the military experts, especially the Intelligence officers, had been given their head and they committed their countries to a greater extent than the political leadership calculated.

The Allies founded their hopes on the domestic opposition to the Bolsheviks uniting to overthrow Lenin and his colleagues, but for that they found that the opposition parties demanded direct Allied support, military support, not merely advisers and money. It was expected that the Russian opposition parties would join the intervention with a large-scale rising against the Bolsheviks, and it would be an understatement to describe the prospect as beguiling. Civil war was an inevitable part of this scheme, though it is more than probable that the Allies did not consider that it would last long, descend to the depths it did, or cost so many lives. Allied to this was the poor performance of the then embryonic Red Army against the Germans when the Brest-Litovsk negotiations had broken down. This helped to create the illusion that military success in Russia would be swift and easy, and would not require large forces that the Allies could not spare.

In this the Allies and the Russian opponents of Bolshevism made a mistake. They thought it a perfectly safe course of action, underestimating as they did both the resilience of the Bolsheviks, the expertise of the Cheka and the strength of the Red Army. Their judgement was based on wishful thinking rather than a sound and reasoned calculation of probabilities. As with most people, when they set their hearts on a goal they will trust to hope, believing it will happen because they want it to. Reason only features when its full force is deployed to reject ideas that are unpalatable to the hope.

Yet if the restoration of the Eastern front and the removal of Allied stores are called into question, we must ask what was the hidden agenda behind the intervention? This is answered, at least in part, by the history of the Banking Scheme. This was repeatedly reborn throughout the period and there can be little doubt that its economic and political goals were to reduce the former Russian Empire to the position of a satellite of the British Empire. The economic fruits of the success of this strategy would have meant any Russian government would have been rendered open to British influence at every turn. It would have been indirect empire on a grand scale. The fact that this outcome was ever present in each of the reincarnations of the Scheme leaves little room for denying it.

What we are left with on the eve of armed intervention are politicians, senior civil servants and officers of the armed services pursuing an essentially Imperialist policy. The restoration of the Eastern front might be deemed a legitimate aim, but there seems to have been little inclination to explore other options. The Allied stores at the Russian ports, supposedly in danger of falling into German hands, had but a small basis in reality. The true value of the stores to the Allied Governments lay in the fact that they could be used as a gigantic bluff to justify intervention to their citizens. One further theme that has evolved during the writing of this book has been the ambiguous nature of loyalty. Many, particularly those in positions of power, seem inclined to regard unconditional loyalty as a given fact. In fact loyalty is far more complicated, frequently conditional and is invariably founded upon mutuality. The First World War shows this repeatedly. When loyalty is put under the greatest stress – by imminent danger, starvation, cold or disease – it frays in many people.

By making 'class enemies' of many Russian specialists, the Bolsheviks lost any loyalty they might have won from them. Equally, the Allies and Whites sometimes found themselves having to trust people who had something to gain from the Bolsheviks, or were ideologically committed to them. Questions of time and scale inhibited either party from thoroughly vetting all who presented themselves, which meant both were frequently obliged to build upon foundations of sand. The Bolsheviks were almost defeated by the officers and specialists who turned to the Allies, while the Letts who presented themselves as erstwhile allies and kingmakers crippled the Allied Intelligence Services.

The Cheka had been a formidable opponent. To an extent they had been assisted by the amateurish conduct of some of their opponents. The Bolsheviks were in many respects poachers turned gamekeeper. They had long experience of an underground, conspiratorial existence and they could turn that experience to account when faced with similar opposition.

The clandestine war reveals significant changes in the role of the Intelligence Services of all the Great Powers. From being accessories to military operations in 1914, they had become major players in the survival and destruction of states. While this had always been true to some extent in the case of secret services, the whole Intelligence apparatus of every major state was now involved and on a much greater scale than ever before. What is also apparent is the paradox of deeply Imperialist states turning to the spread of revolution and subversion to achieve their aims. It became the task of the Intelligence Services to foment and nourish this in hostile states. Since the end of the First World War this has been the common practice of every Great Power and both the Super Powers.

The British Intelligence Services can be seen to have influenced and sometimes even led the government. That reflects a dubious development in the modern state: the influence of the expert and specialist on leaders who are often well out of their depth when facing foreign policy and military problems.

Intelligence was the spearhead of the Allied attempt to restore the situation in Russia in their favour. Ultimately it failed. The cost in human terms was born by the peoples of what had been the Russian Empire. Millions perished by war, starvation and disease brought about by the machinations of these services. The basic fact that the Russians were not interested in fighting the Germans anymore seems to have been disastrously not acknowledged in the Western capitals, thus heaping the odds against the aims of the Allies from the beginning.

The Whites were impotent without the support of the Allies. Had the Allies refrained from taking counsel of their fears and interfering in Russia, the suspicion is that local opposition, much of it inspired by the Bolsheviks, would have kept many German troops in the east, as would Germany's dreams of imperial expansion in south Russia and Central Asia. The Allies were frightened to the point of desperation through viewing the situation in narrowly military terms. That made the difference in what was to be a shabby and inglorious venture that was paid for in the lives of millions of Russians.

Notes

Abbreviations Used in Notes

BL	British Library, London
CCC	Churchill College Archives Centre, Cambridge University
HLRO	House of Lords Record Office, London
IWM	Imperial War Museum, London
LHCMA	Liddell Hart Centre for Military Archives, Kings College, London
NA	National Archives (formerly the Public Record Office), Kew, Surrey
NAS	National Archives of Scotland, Edinburgh
RNSM	Royal Naval Submarine Museum, Gosport
SHAT	Service Historique de l'Armée de Terre, Château de Vincennes, Vincennes

Chapter I: Insidious and Effective

1 Member of State Duma Vasily Shulgin in Protocol of talks between deputies of the State Duma Aleksandr Guchkov and Vasily Shulgin and Nicholas II in Pskov concerning the signing of an act of abdication from the throne, 2 March 1917, in *The Fall of the Romanovs*, Mark D. Steinberg & Vladimir M. Khrustalev, p.98.

2 Z.A.B. Zeman (ed.), *Germany and the Revolution in Russia 1915–1918. Documents from the Archives of the German Foreign Ministry*, p. vii.

3 The best source in English for an account of Parvus' life and activities is Z.A.B. Zeman & W.B. Scharlau, *Merchant of Revolution: The Life of Alexander Israel Helphand (Parvus) 1867–1924.*

4 Thucydides, *The Peloponnesian War*, p. 242.

5 Zeman & Scharlau, *op. cit.*, p. 185.

6 R.P. Browder & A.F. Kerensky (eds), *The Russian Provisional Government 1917 Documents*, Vol. II, pp. 848–9.

7 *Ibid.*, pp. 846–8.

8 No. 25, Minister in Berne to the Foreign Ministry, Tel. No. 601, 3–4 April 1917, AS 1288, Zeman, *op. cit.*, p. 34.

9 The Minister in Berne to the Chancellor, Report No. 1273, 30 April 1917, A14332, *in* Zeman, *ibid.*, p. 52.

10 W. Gerhardie, *Memoirs of a Polyglot*, p. 155.

11 Sir John Wheeler-Bennett, *Brest-Litovsk: The Forgotten Peace March 1918*, p. 45.

12 The State Secretary to the Foreign Ministry Liaison Officer at General Headquarters, Tel. No. 1610, 29 September 1917, AS 3640, *in* Zeman, *op. cit.*, p. 70.

13 Browder & Kerensky, *op. cit.*, Vol. III, p. 1365.

14 For more on these financial dealings, see R. Pipes, *The Russian Revolution*, Zeman, *op. cit.*, and Antony C. Sutton, *Wall Street and the Bolshevik Revolution*.

15 Browder & Kerensky, *op. cit.*, Vol. III, p. 1375.

16 *Ibid.*, Vol. III, p. 1367.

17 O. Figes, *A People's Tragedy: The Russian Revolution 1891–1924*, p. 432.

18 Colonel B.V. Nikitine, *The Fatal Years: Fresh Revelations on a Chapter of Underground History*, p. 110.

19 *Ibid.*, pp. 117–27.

20 Full details can be found in Zeman, *op. cit.*, pp. 6–8.

Chapter II: 'Support Any Responsible body...'

1 Browder & Kerensky, *op. cit.*, Vol. II, pp. 592/3. An *uezd* was a local government district.

2 The State Secretary to the Foreign Ministry Liaison Officer at General Headquarters, Telegram 1610, AS 3640, in Z.A.B. Zeman, *Germany and the Revolution in Russia 1915–1918: Documents from the Archives of the German Foreign Ministry*, p. 70, Document 71.

3 Browder & Kerensky, *op. cit.*, Vol. II, p. 593.

4 S. Constant, *Foxy Ferdinand:Tsar of Bulgaria*, p. 308.

5 NA, FO371/2881, p. 408, 13 February, 1917.

6 NA, *ibid.*, 36933, p. 412, 16 February, 1917.

7 For more about the efforts to subvert the German Empire, see my *Armour Against Fate: British Military Intelligence in the First World War*.

8 Secret Service officer (unnamed), Montreux to Foreign Office, NA FO371/2885, No. 32, p. 84, 16 July 1917.

9 *Ibid.*, p. 83, 2 August 1917. The underlining is Cecil's.

10 Secret Service officer (unnamed), *ibid.*, p. 87.

11 *Ibid.*, p. 125, C/322, 21 August 1917.

12 *Ibid.*, No. 173441, 26 August 1917.

13 *Ibid.*, 20 September 1917.

14 NA FO371/2863, No. 80030, 16 April 1917.

15 *Ibid.*, Sir George Buchanan to Foreign Office, No. 941, 22 June 1917.

16 NA FO371/2884, Arthur Balfour to Sir George Buchanan, 22 April 1917.

17 A.F. Kerensky, *The Catastrophe*, p. 323.

18 Nikitine, *op. cit.*, p. 279.

19 NA FO800/376, Nicolson Papers, letter from A.J. Balfour, 28 December 1914.

20 V.I. Lenin, *SelectedWorks*, Vol. VI, pp. 243–4. The italics are Lenin's.

21 NA FO371/3018, No. 229611.

22 NA CAB23/4, 280th meeting of the War Cabinet, 22 November 1917.

23 John W. Wheeler-Bennett, *Brest-Litovsk:The Forgotten Peace*, p. 136.

24 NA CAB23/4, 286th meeting of the War Cabinet, 29 November 1917.

25 Wheeler-Bennett, *op. cit.*, pp. 136–7.

26 NA CAB23/4, 289th meeting of the War Cabinet, 3 December 1917.

27 *Ibid.* The 'Maximalists' was another contemporary term used by the British Cabinet for the Bolsheviks.

Chapter III: Forging an Instrument

1 NA FO371/3018, No. 242595, p. 38, G.T. 3068, *Organisation of Military Forces in South Russia on the Persian Frontier (Memorandum by Director of Military Intelligence as asked for in War Cabinet 303, Minute 11).*

2   NA CAB23/4, 295th meeting of the War Cabinet, 10 December 1917, Appendix G.T. 2932, *Notes on the Present Russian Situation.*

3   NA CAB23/4, 295th meeting of the War Cabinet, 10 December 1917.

4   R.B. Lockhart, *Memoirs of a British Agent*, pp. 158–9.

5   *Ibid.*, 302nd meeting of the War Cabinet, 19 December 1917.

6   *Ibid.*, 304th meeting of the War Cabinet, 21 December 1917.

7   D. Lloyd George, *War Memoirs*, Vol. I, p. 942.

8   P. Guinn, *British Strategy and Politics 1914 to 1918*, pp. 192–3.

9   Lord Beaverbrook, *Men and Power*, facing p. 276.

10 Lockhart, *op. cit.*, p. 136.

11 BL, Cecil Papers Correspondence of Lord Robert Cecil with David Lloyd George, Cecil to Lloyd George, 7 June 1918, Add Mss 51076.

12 NA CAB23/4, 306th meeting of the War Cabinet, 26 December 1917.

13 NA CAB23/5, 319th meeting of the War Cabinet, 19 January 1918.

14 *Ibid.*, 340th meeting of the War Cabinet, 7 February 1918.

15 Richard K. Debo, 'Lockhart Plot or Dzerzhinskii Plot?' in *Journal of Modern History*, Vol. XLIII, 1971, p. 421.

16 NA CAB23/4, 289th meeting of the War Cabinet, Paper G.174.

17 NA FO371/3018, no. 228823.

18 NA WO106/1150, no. 396, Lindley to Foreign Office, 9 February 1918.

19 NA CAB27/189/20, 8 February 1918.

20 NA WO32/10776.

21 NA FO371/3313, pp. 216–220.

22 NA WO95/4960, *South Russia Report from Major G.M. Goldsmith, British Military Agent Army of Caucasus*, p. 78. Goldsmith was in Butirski Prison with Weinberg, who gave him this information.

23 NA G.T. 3068, *loc. cit.*

24 NA FO371/3018, p. 389.

25 NA FO371/3283, *Political Russia File 2 (TO P.P. 3927)*, No. 7723, Consul (Odessa) to Foreign Office, 12 January 1918.

26 NA CAB23/4, 298th meeting of the War Cabinet, 14 December 1917.

27 BL Keyes Collection, Mss Eur F131/11, p.62.

28 NA FO371/3283, Sir C. Marling (Tehran) to Foreign Office, No. 7725, 12 January 1918.

29 NA WO95/4960, *loc. cit.*

30 *Ibid.*

31 NA CAB23/5, 342nd meeting of the War Cabinet, 11 February 1918.

32 BL L/PS/11/137 1918 P.2951–3350, Political and Secret Department, no. 3026.

33 NA CAB23/6, 417th meeting of the War Cabinet, 24 May 1918.

34 NA CAB27/189/4, Poole to Byrne, 13 February 1918.

35 NA FO371/3018, no. 2629, 26 November 1917.

36 NA FO371/3019, Buchanan to Foreign Office, no. 243030, p. 192, 24 December 1917.

37 NA CAB23/5, 316th meeting of the War Cabinet, 7 January 1918.

38 *Ibid.*, 341st meeting of the War Cabinet, 8 February 1918.

39 *Ibid.*, 350th meeting of the War Cabinet, 4 March 1918.

40 NA FO371/3018, Military Attaché for CIGS, no. 226952, 26 November 1917.

Chapter IV: '…what must develop into a civil war'

1 NA FO371/3018, Buchanan to Foreign Office, no. 224839, 23 November 1917.

2 *Ibid.,* Foreign Office to Buchanan, no. 2349, 26 November 1917.

3 NA CAB23/5, 327th meeting of the War Cabinet, 21 January 1918.

4 BL Keyes Collection, Add Mss Eur F131/12(a), Untitled, p. 62.

5 SHAT, 7N 796, Dossier 3, 2ème Bureau, Général de la Panouse à M. le Président du Conseil, Ministère de la Guerre, Paris, 11 November 1917.

6 R. Luckett, *The White Generals*, p. 97.

7 BL Keyes Collection, *loc. cit.*

8 NA FO371/3283, no. 2428, 3 January 1918, p. 45.

9 NA FO371/3019, no. 243216, Buchanan to Foreign Office, 25 December 1917.

10 NA FO371/3283, no. 2143, p. 165, Buchanan to Foreign Office, 28 December, 1917.

11 BL Keyes Collection, *loc. cit.*

12 NA FO371/3283, *1918 Russia File II*, Cecil to Crosby, 2 January 1918, p. 11. Oscar T. Crosby was with the US Embassy in Paris.

13 BL Keyes Collection, *loc. cit.*, p. 65.

14 BL Keyes Collection, Add Mss Eur F131/21 *Loans to Russian Banks*, p. 73.

15 *Ibid.*, *Russian Bank Scheme (I)*, p. 12. *n.b.* Keyes prepared two memoranda, both with the title *Russian Bank Scheme* for the inquiries into the scheme by the Foreign Office and Treasury on his return to London. I have numbered them *(I)* and *(II)* in the order in which they appear in his Collection at the British Library.

16 NA FO175/16, *British Economic Mission to Russia. Report No. III, Report on the Banking Schemes Negotiated by Colonel Keyes*, pp. 2–3.

17 *Ibid.*, p. 1.

18 NAS, Papers of Sir Arthur Steel-Maitland, GD193/328, Appendix *MR. KAROL IAROSHINSKI*, p. 39.

19 *Ibid.*, p. 40.

20 BL Keyes Collection, *Russian Bank Scheme (I)*, *loc. cit.*

21 BL Keyes Collection, *Loans to Russian Banks*, pp. 77–8, *loc. cit.*

22 E. Radzinsky, *The Last Tsar: The Life and Death of Nicholas II*, p. 224.

23 BL Keyes Collection, *Russian Bank Scheme (I)*, *loc. cit.*, p. 16. See also NA FO371/3283, Buchanan to Foreign Office, 28 December 1918.

24 NA FO371/3283, no. 12745, p. 251, 17 January 1918, 'Most Secret', Keyes to Foreign Office.

25 BL Keyes Collection, *Russian Bank Scheme (II)*, *loc. cit.*, p. 18. However, in a letter dated 11 April 1918 the Treasury stated it was the Russian Commercial and Industrial Bank that was the target.

26 NA FO371/3283, no. 7867, p. 192.

27 NA FO175/16, *loc. cit.*

28 BL Keyes Collection, Add Mss F131/21, *Office of the Political Agent Russian Banks*, Letter from Robert Chalmers of the Treasury, 11 April 1918. The majority of the material dealing with the confusion caused by Yaroshinsky's offer to Lindley relies on this source.

29 *Ibid.*

30 *Ibid.*

31 BL Keyes Collection, *Russian Bank Scheme (II)*, *loc. cit.*

32 NA FO371/3283, no. 118, p. 257, 'Very secret Very Urgent'.

33 *Ibid.*, no. 25763, p. 419, Lindley to Foreign Office, 'Most Secret'.

34 NA FO175/16, *Memorandum based on the original documents relative to the Banking Schemes negotiated by Colonel Keyes*, p. 6.

35 NA FO175/16, *loc. cit.*, p. 12. See also p. 10.

36 NA FO95/802, Minutes of proceedings of meeting of the Russia Committee, 15 February 1918.

37 BL Keyes Collection, *Loans to Russian Banks, loc. cit.*

38 Lockhart, *op. cit.*, pp. 164–6.

39 BL Keyes Collection, Untitled, *loc. cit.*, pp. 65–6.

40 S. Roskill, *Hankey: Man of Secrets*, Vol. I, p. 501.

41 NA F0371/3283, p. 107, Foreign Office minutes on South East Russia, G.R. Clerk, 4 January 1918.

Chapter V: Where there is No Peace

1 C. Sheridan, *Russian Portraits*, p. 85.

2 K. Young (ed.), *The Diaries of Sir Robert Bruce Lockhart 1915–1938*, p. 35.

3 Cromie to Commodore Hall, 19 February 1918, *Letters On Russian Affairs From Captain F.N.A. Cromie, C.B., D.S.O., R.N.*, no. 33, p. 105, Cromie Papers, A1990/73, Royal Navy Submarine Museum, Gosport.

4 CCC, Hankey Papers, HNKY 8/5, Letter to the Prime Minister, 8 February 1918.

5 NA CAB27/189/4, Colonel Byrne to Poole, 10 October 1917.

6 *Ibid.*, 7 November 1917.

7 This material is drawn from NA FO371/3350, No. 203967, Events in Russia Captain G.A. Hill's report on his work in Russia for D.M.I., 11 December 1918.

8 NA CAB23/5, 354th meeting of the War Cabinet, 26 February 1918.

9 *Ibid.*, 356th meeting of the War Cabinet, 28 February 1918.

10 NA CAB24/48, G.T. 4211, *Memorandum on the Russian Situation*, Political Intelligence Department, Foreign Office Russia/004, 8 April 1918.

11 Wheeler-Bennett, *op. cit.*, p. 254.

12 Lockhart, *op. cit.*, p. 180.

13 HLRO, Diaries of Sir Robert Bruce Lockhart, Hist. Coll. 313 R. Bruce Lockhart 1–13 LOC, 1918 3, entry for 11 March 1918.

14 NA FO1093/75, Permanent Under-Secretary's Department, M Files, C.X. 02769/M.12997, Petrograd, 7 April 1918.

15 *Ibid.*, minutes.

16 NA CAB23/5, 330th meeting of the War Cabinet, 24 January 1918. See also CAB24/40, G.T. 3421 & G.T. 3422 of the same date.

17 NA CAB23/6, 420th meeting of the War Cabinet, 29 May 1918.

18 Lockhart, *op. cit.*, p. 170.

19 HLRO, Diaries of Sir Robert Bruce Lockhart, *loc. cit.*, entry for 7 May 1918.

20 NA CAB23/5, 359th meeting of the War Cabinet, 5 March 1918.

21 G. Chicherin, *Two Years of Foreign Policy*, p. 10.

22 Young (ed.), *op. cit.*, entry for Wednesday, 13 March 1918, p. 34.

23 NA CAB24/45, G.T.3927, *The Present Situation in Russia*, Colonel A.W.F. Knox, 13 March 1918.

24 For the documentary evidence demonstrating Bolshevik complicity in the Allied landing at Murmansk, see R. Pipes, *The Unknown Lenin: From the Secret Archive*, pp. 42–5.

25 NA ADM223/743, Telegrams received from worldwide sources, No. 55.

26 CCC, Denniston Papers, DENN1/4.

27 Briefing from Cabinet Office on Sydney Reilly personal file, CXM 1590, 29 March 1918.

Chapter VI: Fleets and Duplicity

1 NA CAB23/5, 369th meeting of the War Cabinet, 21 March 1918.

2 Roskill, Vol. I, *op. cit.*, p. 462, diary entry for 23 November 1917.

3 NA ADM137/4644, Telegrams to and from Russia and Admiralty, No. 1618.

4 *Ibid.*, No. 1620.

5 HLRO, Lockhart Diary, *loc. cit.*, entry for 15 May 1918.

6 NA FO371/3286, No. 92955, Lockhart to Foreign Office, 18 May 1918.

7 NA CAB26/6, 395th meeting of the War Cabinet, 19 April 1918.

8 Roskill, Vol. I, *op. cit.*, p. 525, diary entry for 12 April 1918.

9 *Ibid.*, p. 529, diary entry for 19 April 1918.

10 NA ADM223/743, Telegrams received from worldwide sources, 9.) Russia, 5 May 1918.

11 NA FO371/3286, No. 94955, pp. 45–6, Lockhart to Foreign Office, 23 May 1918.

12 R. Pipes, *The Russian Revolution*, p. 616.

13 NA FO371/3286, No. 90741, From Mr. Wardrop Moscow, 22 May 1918.

14 Zeman, *op. cit.*, 122, Telegram No. 1047, A 19596, 8 May 1918, p. 123.

15 *Ibid.*, 123, 10 May 1918, pp. 123–4.

16 HLRO, Lockhart Diary, *loc. cit.*, entry for 25 April 1918.

17 NA CAB23/6, 395th meeting of the War Cabinet, 19 April 1918.

18 Zeman, *op. cit.*, 121, Telegram No. 1034, from the Liaison Officer at General Headquarters to the Foreign Ministry, 6 May 1918.

19 NA WO32/21671, covering letter from Ballard to the Director of Military Intelligence, 11 April 1919.

20 *Ibid.*, Report of Colonel J.W. Boyle.

21 *Ibid.*, Ballard, 12 November 1918.

22 NA GFM6/140, A 33969, *Schluss zum Berichte ueber die Innere Politische Lage Russlands Anfang Juli 1918.*

23 Ballard, *loc. cit.*

24 NA WO106/1150, *loc. cit.*, No. 68, 3 April 1918.

25 Hill, *loc. cit.*

26 *Ibid.*

27 *Ibid.*

28 HLRO, Lockhart Diary, *loc. cit.*, entry for 13 April 1918.

29 Hill, *loc. cit.*

30 *Ibid.*

31 *Ibid.*

32 *Ibid.*

33 *Ibid.*

34 Briefing from Cabinet Office on Sydney Reilly personal file, CX 027753, 16 April 1918.

35 *Ibid.*, CXM 236, 20 April 1918; the underlining is handwritten in the original, in blue ink.

36 NA WO32/5669, CX 03592 M/14 383, Moscow, 12 May 1918.

37 *Ibid.*, CX 035176 M/14636, Moscow, 3 June 1918, S.T. Report No. 10, Interview with General Bonch.

38 NA FO371/3313, P.B. 1751, p. 6, from the British Military Equipment Section in Russia to Lord Milner's Committee, 8 December 1917.

39 NA CAB27/189/7, Miscellaneous letter from Russia, Lieutenant Garstin to Colonel Byrne, 14 January 1918.

40 NA CAB27/189/18, From BRITSUP, Archangel to RUSPLYCOM, Charles, Received 27 March 1918.

41 NA FO371/3329, Letter from Brigadier-General Alfred Knox to Sir Eric Drummond, 25 April 1918.

42 *Ibid.*, Paper by Captain Alexander Proctor.

43 BL, Papers of Douglas Young, Add Mss 61846, Vol. III, p. 8.

44 BL, Papers of Douglas Young, Add Mss 61850, Vol. VII, p. 202.

45 NA CAB27/189/18, *Telegrams from 'Britsup' Petrograd to 'Rusplycom' Charles*, McAlpine to Captain Dunlop, Vladivostock & repeated to Rusplycom, 7 May 1918.

46 NA FO371/3313, Foreign Office to Lockhart, No. 87, 18 April 1918.

47 HLRO, Lockhart Diary, *loc. cit.*, entry for 5 May 1918.

48 NA CAB24/46, G.T. 4033, *Proposals for Future Policy in Russia*, 15 March 1918.

49 NA CAB24/46, G.T. 4046, *The Russian Situation Memorandum by Lord Curzon*, 26 March 1918.

50 NA CAB27.189/16, *Proposals for Future Policy in Russia*, 15 March 1918.

51 NA CAB27/189/18, Britsup, Petrograd to Rusplycom, Charles, c. 9 May 1918.

52 NA GFM6/140, *loc. cit.*

53 Pipes, *op. cit.*, p. 631.

54 NA CAB23/6, 393rd meeting of the War Cabinet, 17 April 1918.

55 *Foreign Relations of the United Sates,* 1918, Russia Vol. II, p.476.

56 Zeman*, op. cit.*, Telegram No. 122, A 20991, Mirbach to Foreign Ministry, 16 May 1918.

57 *Ibid.*, Telegram No. 121, A 20991, Kuhlmann to Mirbach, 18 May 1918.

58 *Ibid.*, pp. 130 & 137.

Chapter VII: '...up to the last moment'

1 Zeman, *op. cit.*, 124, Telegram No. 96, A 20377, Mirbach to the Foreign Ministry, 13 May 1918, p. 124.

2 *Ibid.*, 125, *Protocol of a Meeting at Spa,* 13 May 1918, AS 2230, p. 125.

3 See NA FO371/3286, Nos. 94955, 95626, 95630, 96656, 99204 & 102870.
4 NA FO371/3286, No. 94955, Lockhart to Foreign Office, 23 May 1918.
5 *Ibid.*
6 Both statements are in BL, Keyes Collection, Untitled, Mss Eur F131/12(a).
7 NA FO371/3286, No. 99204, Lockhart to Foreign Office, 28 May 1918.
8 NA CAB23/6, Appendix to the 417th meeting of the War Cabinet, 24 May 1918. Also G.T. 4617.
9 NA FO371/3313, No. 249, Lockhart to Foreign Office, 1 June 1918.
10 *Ibid.*, p. 241.
11 NA FO371/3286, No. 95628, Lockhart to Foreign Office, 26 May 1918.
12 NA FO371/3286, No. 100267, Lockhart to Foreign Office, 28 May 1918.
13 *Ibid.*
14 *Ibid.*
15 Zeman, *op. cit.*, 133, AS 2562, Enclosure: Memorandum for the State Secretary, for discussion with Count Rödern, 5 June 1918, p. 133.
16 Lockhart, *op. cit.*, p. 212.
17 H. Baerlein, *The March of the Seventy Thousand*, pp. 85–6.
18 HLRO, Lockhart Diary, *loc. cit.*, entry for 31 May 1918.
19 Lockhart, *op. cit.*, p. 209.
20 NA CAB23/6, Appendix to the 410th meeting of the War Cabinet, 13 May 1918. Also G.T.1519.
21 *Ibid.*
22 NA CAB23/6, 413th meeting of the War Cabinet, 17 May 1918.
23 *Ibid.*
24 *Ibid.*
25 NA CAB23/6, 415th meeting of the War Cabinet, 23 May 1918.
26 Chicherin, *op. cit.*, p. 12.
27 Lockhart, *op. cit.*, p. 211.
28 *The Army List*, June 1918, p. 2681g.
29 HLRO, Lockhart Diary, *loc. cit.*, entry for 3 June 1918.

30 NA FO371/3286, No. 116763, Prime Minister to Lockhart, Circulated to the King and War Cabinet, 2 July 1918.

31 Chicherin, *op. cit.*, p. 12.

32 Z.A.B. Zeman, *A Diplomatic History of the First World War*, p. 314.

33 Richard B. Spence, *Boris Savinkov: Renegade on the Left*, p. 2.

34 NA FO371/3332, No. 92708.

35 *Ibid.*, No. 95780, Lockhart to Foreign Office. The underlining is either by Lockhart or, more probably, the Foreign Office.

36 Spence, *op. cit.*, p. 190.

37 *Ibid.*, p. 191.

38 *Ibid.*, pp. 192 & 435, f/n.169.

39 *Ibid.*, p. 202.

40 Brook-Shepherd, *Iron Maze*, pp. 257–8.

41 HLRO, Lockhart Diary, *loc. cit.*, entry for the 31 March 1918.

42 NA FO371/3332, Decypher Mr. Lockhart Moscow.

43 Hill, *loc. cit.*

44 LHCMA, *Papers of General Sir Frederick Poole: Report of Work Done in Russia to the end of 1917*, George Hill.

45 Hill, *loc. cit.*

46 NA FO371/3329, 14 May 1918.

47 *Ibid.*

48 RNSM, A1990/73, *Letters on Russian Affairs From F.N.A. Cromie, C.B., D.S.O., R.N.*, No. 40, Letter to Admiral Hall, 17 May 1918, p. 126.

49 NA FO371/3286, No. 96630, 25 May 1918.

Chapter VIII: The Horns of a Dilemma

1 NA ADM223/758, No. 503, D.N.I's Secret Telegrams, 7 June 1918.

2 R. Pipes, *The Unknown Lenin: From the Secret Archive*, pp. 93–4.

3 Briefing from Cabinet Office on Major Stephen Alley personal file, 'C' to Thornhill, 27 June 1918.

4 C. Nabokoff, *The Ordeal of a Diplomat*, p.189. This is confirmed in NA FO371/3340, Nos. 150440–157211.

5 HLRO, Lockhart Diaries, *loc. cit.*, entry for 24 October 1918.

6 Nabokoff, *op. cit.*, pp. 215–18.

7   BL L/PS/11/138, 64th meeting of the Russia Committee, 2 October 1918.

8   NA ADM223/759, *loc. cit.*, No. 367, from Commodore, Paris to D.N.I., 9 October 1918.

9   NA ADM223/758, *loc. cit.*, D.N.I. to R.A. Murmansk, 6 August 1918.

10 NA WO95/4960, *loc. cit.*, p.79.

11 A. Judd, *The Quest for C: Mansfield Cumming and the Founding of the Secret Service*, p.436.

12 NA ADM137/963, Director of Naval Intelligence to S.N.O. Archangel, 5 September 1918.

13 NA ADM223/758, *loc. cit.*, No. 80, 20 June 1918.

14 *Ibid.*, No. 552, 16 July 1918.

15 *Ibid.*, No. 514, 8 June 1918.

16 BL Cecil Papers, *loc. cit.*

17 F. Fischer, *Germany's Aims in the First World War*, pp. 570–1.

18 Wheeler-Bennett, *op. cit.*, pp. 325–6, f/n 2.

19 W. Baumgart, *Von Brest-Litovsk Zur Deutschen Novemberrevolution Auf den Aufzeichnungen von Alfons Pacquet, Wilhelm Groener, Albert Hopman*, (Wilhelm Groener), p. 422.

20 NA ADM137/883, No. 551, Naval Attaché, Petrograd to Admiralty; *see also* ADM223/758, *loc. cit.*

21 For a more detailed examination of this, see my book *The Romanov Conspiracies*, pp. 77–88.

22 Zeman, *op. cit.*, 134, The First Quartermaster General to the State Secretary, A 29471, 9 June 1918, p. 136.

23 NA GFM6/139, Armin von Reyher to HRH Prince Henry of Prussia, A 29471, 15 June 1918.

24 NA ADM137/1714, No. 662, 10 August 1918, p. 138.

25 NA FO371/3286, No. 108179, 11 June 1918.

26 HLRO, Lockhart Diaries, *loc. cit.*, entry for the 6 June 1918.

27 BL, Keyes Papers, Untitled, *loc. cit.*

28 NA FO175/6, Report By 'S.T.', 14 June 1918.

29 NA FO371/3315, No. 121517, CX 038307 P/C 383, Affairs in Russia: The following from S.T.1, 22 June 1918, p. 302.

30 NA FO371/3286, No. 227, Lockhart to Foreign Office, 12 June 1918.

31 *Ibid.*, No. 260, Mr. Woodhouse, Petrograd, to Foreign Office, 15 June 1918.

32 *Ibid.*, No. 102633, *Russia Military* Mr. Young (Archangel), 6 June 1918, pp. 161–2.

33 *Ibid.*, No. 120496, Lockhart to Foreign Office, 26 June 1918, p. 560.

34 IWM, Department of Sound Records, Interview with Lieutenant E.J. Furlong, 015/08/04, Reel 05.

35 NA ADM223/758, *loc. cit.*, No. 705, 11 July 1918.

Chapter IX: Vicissitudes of Assassination

1 Leggett, *op. cit.*, p. 73.

2 Zeman, *op. cit.*, 134, The First Quartermaster General to the State Secretary, A 252028, 9 June 1918, pp. 134–7.

3 NA GFM6/139, Riezler to Foreign Ministry, A 30727, 20 July 1918.

4 Luckett, *op. cit.*, pp. 158–60.

5 *Ibid.*, p. 159.

6 NA FO337/87, Lockhart, Moscow, to Foreign Office, 7 July 1918, p. 40.

7 E. Mawdsley, *The Russian Civil War*, p. 41.

8 Young (ed.), *op. cit.*, entry for Sunday 7 July 1918, p. 38.

9 Lockhart, *op. cit.*, p. 231.

10 Baumgart, *op. cit.* [Pacquet], p. 59.

11 Wheeler-Bennett, *op. cit.*, p. 342. See also Chicherin, *op. cit.*, p. 16.

12 NA FO371/3287, No. 2295 (R), Sir E. Howard, Stockholm, to Foreign Office, 15 August 1918, p. 574.

13 SHAT, 5N 180 Renseignements Sur Messages Téléphones et Télégrammes Russie juillet 1918–novembre 1918, No. 965, 23rd July 1918.

14 Baumgart, *op. cit.*, p. 84.

15 *Ibid.*

16 NA FO337/87, Report from the British Consulate-General, Moscow, dated 5 August 1918.

17 Spence, *op. cit.*, p. 201.

18 Chicherin, *op. cit.*, p. 17.

19 Baumgart, *op. cit.* [Groener], p. 407.

20 *Ibid.*, [Pacquet], p. 61.

21 *Ibid.*, p. 77.

22 NA FO337/87, *loc. cit.*

23 NA FO371/3286, No. 122866, Lockhart via Lord Derby (Paris), 12 July 1918, p. 579.

24 NA FO371/3286, No. 119820, Lockhart via Lord Derby (Paris), 9 July 1918, p. 550.

25 NA WO33/962, Telegrams, European War: Russia 1918–1919, No. 120, from General Officer Commanding, Archangel, to Director of Military Intelligence, 13 August 1918.

26 NA FO175/1, Archangel Consulate, Lockhart to Balfour, No. 31, 13 July 1918.

27 NA FO371/3287, No. 130221, 13 July 1918.

28 Spence, *op. cit.*, p. 211.

29 NA FO371/3287, No. 130221, *loc. cit.*

30 NA FO337/87, *loc. cit.*

31 NA FO371/3287, Lockhart to Foreign Office, 6 July 1918. A mutilated version of the message appears in FO337/87, *loc. cit.*, 8 August 1918, p. 58.

32 *Ibid.*

33 *Ibid.*

34 Lockhart, *op. cit.*, p. 216.

35 Richard K. Debo, 'Lockhart Plot or Dzerzhinsky Plot', in *Journal of Modern History*, Vol. XLIII, 1971.

36 Brook-Shepherd, *op. cit.*, pp. 114–15.

37 NA FO371/3348, Enclosure No. I in Mr. Lockhart's despatch of 5 November 1918. Secret and Confidential Memorandum on the alleged 'Allied Conspiracy' in Russia.

38 *Ibid.*

39 NA FO371/3287, Mr. Grahame (Paris), Mr. Lockhart to Foreign Office, 13 July 1918, pp. 106–7.

40 NA FO371/3287, Mr. Lockhart (Moscow) via Paris, 16 July 1918, pp. 260–1. An official has appended a Note: 'Telegram arrived very corrupt and mutilated'.

41 NA FO371/3287, Foreign Office to Mr. Lockhart (Moscow), 30 July 1918, p. 109.

42 Lockhart, *op. cit.*, p. 227.

43 Young (ed.), *op. cit.*, p. 52.

44 NA WO157/1215.

45 SHAT, 5N 180, No. 520, R.Q.517/2, 28 July 1918.

46 Spence, *op. cit.*, p. 206.

47 BL, Papers of Douglas Young, Vol. VIII, Add. Mss/61851, p. 200 (4).

48 NA FO371/3287, Mr. Grahame (Paris), 25 July 1918, *loc. cit.*

Chapter X: Not So Secret

1 SHAT, 5N 180, 17 July 1918, *loc. cit.*

2 NA FO337/87, Cromie, Petrograd to S.N.O. Murmansk and General Poole, 8 August 1918.

3 R. Bainton, *Honoured By Strangers: The life of Captain Francis Cromie CB DSO RN*, p. 297, f/n. 7.

4 Judd, *op. cit.*, p. 439.

5 NA FO175/1, 63, Mr. Balfour, Telegram No. 32, 12 July 1918.

6 NA FO371/3350, No. 203967, Events in Russia Captain G.A. Hill's report on his work in Russia for D.M.I., 11 December 1918.

7 *Ibid.*

8 NA FO337/87, R.H. Clive, Stockholm, to Foreign Office, No. 353, 5 September 1918.

9 NA FO371/3348, Enclosure No. I, *loc. cit.*

10 *Ibid.*

11 NA WO157/1215, *Reports from Murmansk M.I. / 1 / 26*, No. 77 Murmansk, 3 August 1918.

12 Young (ed.), *op. cit.*, entry for Sunday 2 June 1918, p. 37.

13 RNSM, A1990/73, *loc. cit.*, letter to Admiral Hall, 26 July 1918, p. 128.

14 *Ibid.*

15 NA GFM6/140, *loc. cit.*

16 Zeman, *op. cit.*, 132, A23614, The Counsellor of Legation in Moscow to Minister Bergen, 4 June 1918.

17 BL Papers of Douglas Young, Add. Mss 61846, Vol. III.

18 Judd, *op. cit.*, p. 436.

19 NA FO371/3287, No. 138589, From Mr Lockhart (via Paris), pp. 401–2.

20 NA FO371/3287, No. 125131, Mr Young, Archangel, to Foreign Office, 12 July 1918.
21 Chicherin, *op. cit.*, p. 14.
22 Lockhart Diary, *loc. cit.*, entry for Saturday 13 July 1918.
23 NA WO33/962, No. 83, From Captain Steveni, Vladivostock, to Director of Military Intelligence, 4 August 1918.
24 NA FO371/3286, No. 116763, 3 July 1918, p. 485.
25 NA FO371/3319, 17 June 1918, p. 247.
26 Brook-Shepherd, *op. cit.*, pp. 52–3.
27 Lockhart Diary, *loc. cit.*, entries for 14, 15 and 16 July 1918.
28 NA FO337/87, No. 323, from Lockhart, Moscow, by hand 8 August 1918.
29 NA WO33/962, No. 120, *loc. cit.*
30 *Ibid.*
31 Lockhart, *op. cit.*, p. 228.
32 Hill, *loc. cit.*
33 Hill, *loc. cit.*
34 SHAT 5N 180, No. 986, 25 July 1918.
35 Cook, *op. cit.*, p. 246.
36 Chicherin, *op. cit.*, p. 21.
37 NA WO33/962, No. 120, *loc. cit.*
38 NA FO371/3286, No. 120496, Mr. Lockhart (Moscow), dispatched 26 June 1918, received 9 July 1918, pp. 559–60.
39 NA WO157/1215, *Précis of intercepted telegrams*, Petrograd 22 July 1918.
40 Lockhart Diary, *loc. cit.*, entry for 23 July 1918.
41 BL Papers of Douglas Young, *loc. cit.*, Vol. III, Add. Mss 61846, pp. 72–3.
42 NA WO33/962, No. 51, From the War Office to Brigadier-General Poole, Murmansk, 12 July 1918. Poole's request for reinforcements can be found in the same file, No. 47.
43 BL Papers of Douglas Young, *loc. cit.*, Memorandum on attached correspondence between the Foreign Office & Mr. Douglas Young regarding an alleged breach of discipline in 'criticising' the Russian policy of His Majesty's Government in 1918–19, Vol. V, Add. Mss 61848.
44 NA WO106/1151, Nominal Roll of Officers 'Syren' and 'Elope'.

Chapter XI: The Grand Unravelling

1 Lockhart, *op. cit.*, p. 211.
2 For details of the Headquarters Staff of 'Elope', see NA WO106/1151.
3 NA FO337/87, Report from British Consulate General, Moscow, dated 5 August 1918.
4 *Ibid.*
5 RNSM, *Letters on Russian Affairs*, letter from Cromie to Admiral Hall, 14 August 1918.
6 *Ibid.*
7 NA FO337/87, British Legation at Christiania, No. 372, 20 August 1918.
8 Hill, *loc. cit.*
9 NA FO337/87, Wardrop to Foreign Office.
10 Wheeler-Bennett, *op. cit.*, pp. 342–3.
11 NA FO337/87, British Legation at Christiania, 20 August 1918.
12 Cromie to Admiral Hall, 14 August 1918, *loc. cit.*
13 *Ibid.*
14 *Ibid.*
15 NA WO33/962, No. 175A, from Director of Military Intelligence to G.O.C. Archangel, *No. 65256 cipher M.I.*, 28 August 1918.
16 Hill, *loc. cit.*
17 NA FO337/87, Report from the British Consulate General, *loc. cit.*
18 British Legation Christiania, 20 August 1918, *loc. cit.*
19 Hill, *loc. cit.*
20 *Ibid.*
21 *Ibid.*
22 *Ibid.*
23 NA FO337/87, p. 35.
24 SHAT, 5N 180, No. 878, 6 July 1918.
25 Hill, *loc. cit.*
26 BL Papers of Douglas Young, Vol. I, Add. Mss/61844.
27 BL Papers of Douglas Young, Vol. V, Add. Mss/61848.
28 Hill, *loc. cit.*
29 NA ADM223/637, C.X. 059344, From Stockholm, 19 November 1918, Report from H.T. Hall.

30 *Ibid.*

31 *Ibid.*

32 *Ibid.*

33 NA FO371/3368, No. 190442, *loc. cit.*

34 Brook-Shepherd, *op. cit.*, p. 103.

35 Cook, *op. cit.*, p. 167.

36 Hill, *loc. cit.*

37 Cook, *op. cit.*, p. 167.

38 Brook-Shepherd, *op. cit.*, p. 104.

39 *Ibid.*, p. 107.

40 NA FO371/3319, Colonel French to Mr Campbell, 10 October 1918, p. 450.

41 Hill, *loc. cit.*

42 Brook-Shepherd, *op. cit.*, pp. 49–51.

43 *Ibid.*, p. 108.

44 See NA FO337/87, *Copy of a statement made before Consul Bosanquet at Petrograd, September 1st 1918*, by Mrs. Nathalie Bucknall.

45 NA FO371/3342, No. 159609, 20 September 1918.

46 Hill, *loc. cit.*

47 Cromie to Admiral Hall, 14 August 1918, *loc. cit.* The bold text is as the original.

48 Hill, *loc. cit.*

49 SHAT, 17N 622, *French Military Mission. Ekaterinburg Group.* Official Telegram Cipher, 14 August 1918, Nos. 176–180.

50 NA WO106/1220, No. 98, Mr. Hodgson, 20 July 1918.

51 NA WO106/1318.

52 NA WO106/1233, 67072 cipher, D.M.I. to General Knox, 24 September 1918.

Chapter XII: Terror and Instability

1 NA CAB23/5, 328th meeting of the War Cabinet, 22 January 1918.

2 *The Times*, 7 September 1918.

3 NA ADM137/1613, p. 366, Letter from D.N.I. to C-in-C, Grand Fleet, V.A.O & S. & S.N.O. Aberdeen.

4 *The Navy List*, October 1918, Vol. 4, 1089, No. 1281.

5 See NA ADM53/45508, Log of HMS *Jupiter II*, 20–6–18 – 17–9–18.

6 NA ADM137/1613, p. 366, D.N.I. to D.C.N.S., 12 September 1918.

7 *Ibid.*, pp. 364–5.

8 *Ibid.*, p. 365.

9 Brook-Shepherd, *op. cit.*, pp. 231–4.

10 *Ibid.*, pp. 104/5. Brook-Shepherd's source is Orlov.

11 Hill, *loc. cit.*

12 Cook, *op. cit.*, pp. 169–70.

13 Chicherin, *op. cit.*, p. 23.

14 Hill, *loc. cit.*

15 NA FO371/3288, No. 153298, 7 September 1918, p. 46.

16 Hill, *loc. cit.*

17 NA ADM137/963, From Rear Admiral Archangel to Admiralty, unnumbered, 31 August 1918.

18 *Ibid.*, No. 931, From S.N.O. White Sea, Archangel, 10 September 1918.

19 NA ADM223/759, No. 952, S.N.O. White Sea at Archangel to Admiralty, 14 September 1918.

20 NA ADM223/759, Admiralty D.N.I. to S.N.O. White Sea Archangel, 21 September 1918.

21 NA ADM223/759, Admiralty D.N.I. to S.N.O. White Sea Archangel, 17 September 1918.

22 C. von Clausewitz, *On War*, Book I, Chapter Seven, p. 119.

23 NA FO175/1, Lord Reading to Mr. Balfour, 12 September 1918, p. 518.

24 *Ibid.*, From General Poole, Archangel To:- Chief, London, E498.

Chapter XIII: '…a double interest for us'

1 NA CAB24/45, G.T. 3927, *loc. cit.*

2 NA CAB23/5, 369th meeting of the War Cabinet, 21 March 1918.

3 BL Keyes Papers, *Loans to Russian Banks (II)*, *loc. cit.*

4 NA CAB23/6, 391st meeting of the War Cabinet, 15 April 1918.

5 C.E. Callwell, *Field-Marshal Sir Henry Wilson Bart.*, *G.C.B., D.S.O. His Life and Diaries*, Vol. II, diary entry for 5 November 1918, p. 148.

6 Fischer, *op. cit.*, p. 121.

7 NA FO371/3283, Interdepartmental Committee at the Foreign Office on 19 December 1917.

8 CCC, Denniston Papers, DENN 1/4.

9 NA CAB24/45, G.T. 3905.

10 BL, L/PS/11/135, 1918 P.1501–2250 Political and Secret Department, Telegram No. 42, 14 April 1918, De Candolle to CIGS, sent via Mr. Wardrop, Moscow.

11 Goldsmith, *loc. cit.*, p. 8.

12 Ranald MacDonell, *And Nothing Long*, p. 187.

13 *Ibid.*, p. 205.

14 P. Hopkirk, *On Secret Service East of Constantinople*, p. 282.

15 MacDonell, *op. cit.*, p. 219.

16 Reginald Teague-Jones [Ronald Sinclair O.B.E., M.B.E. (Mil.)], *The Spy Who Disappeared: Diary of a Secret Mission to Russian Central Asia in 1918*, pp. 60–1, ed. by Peter Hopkirk.

17 MacDonell, *op. cit.*, p. 224.

18 *Ibid.*, pp. 222–3.

19 Teague-Jones, *op. cit.*, p. 94.

20 Sources for the account of Dunsterforce are: Major-General L.C. Dunsterville, *The Adventures of Dunsterforce*; A.J. Barker, *The Neglected War: Mesopotamia 1914–1918*; C.H. Ellis, *The Transcaspian Episode 1918–1919*; NA WO106/916, Mesopotamia Expeditionary Force: Despatch on operations by Lt-Gen. Sir W.R. Marshall; NA WO32/5215, Diary of Operations of Mesopotamia Expeditionary Force 1914–1919.

21 Major-General R.F.H. Nalder, CB, OBE, *The Royal Corps of Signals: A History of its Antecedents and Development*, p. 193.

22 NA WO95/5001, Mesopotamia Army Troops ANZAC Wireless Signal Squadron, July 1916–July 1919.

23 R. Meinertzhagen, *Army Diary 1899–1926*, p. 242.

24 A.J. Barker, *op. cit.*, p. 453.

25 Goldsmith, *loc. cit.*, p. 10.

26 *Ibid.*, p. 15.

27 F. Fischer, *op. cit.*

28 Goldsmith, *loc. cit.*, p. 24.

29 *Ibid.*, p. 27.

30 *Ibid.*, p. 29.
31 *Ibid.*, pp. 36–7.
32 *Ibid.*, p. 37.
33 *Ibid.*, p. 38.
34 *Ibid.*
35 *Ibid.*, p. 47.
36 *Ibid.*
37 Ellis, *op. cit.*, p. 25.
38 *Ibid.*
39 Teague-Jones, *op. cit.*, p. 78.
40 *Ibid.*, p. 49.
41 MacDonell, *op. cit.*, p. 224.
42 Teague-Jones, *op. cit.*, p. 27.
43 *Ibid.*, p. 35.
44 NA WO106/60, Telegram No. M.D. 163, 7 July 1918.
45 See Teague-Jones, *op. cit.*, pp. 49, 52, 57, 58 & 69.
46 *Ibid.*, pp. 62–8.

Chapter XIV: A More Conventional Role

1 NA GFM6/128, A40950, Chief of the General Staff of the Army in the Field. Foreign Armies Section, 1 October 1918.
2 Young (ed.), *op. cit.*, p. 49.
3 Callwell, Vol. II, *op. cit.*, diary entry for 10 November 1918, p. 148.
4 LHCMA, Papers of General Sir Frederick Poole, Diary of Mission to Volunteer Army, 18 November 1918 to 15 December 1918. [Lieutenant-Colonel A.P. Blackwood.]
5 Sir Paul Dukes KBE, *Secret Agent 'ST25':Adventure and Romance in the Secret Intelligence Service in Red Russia 1917–1920*, pp. 38–49.
6 NA ADM223/637, Agents' Reports, CX 062394, Stockholm, 14 December 1918, S/N 51.
7 *Ibid.*, CX061350, Nos. 84 & 13, 10 December 1918, S/N39.
8 For the early British involvement in the Baltic, see NA ADM137/1663, Baltic Proceedings 1918 to 1919 January.
9 NA FO175/6, No. 205, 5 October 1918, p. 815. An almost identical report, but with some differences of no great significance, appears in

FO371/3319 dated 30 September 1918. It is quoted by Cook, *op. cit.*, pp. 175–6.

10 NA WO158/714, G.S. No. PE/G/22/20, G.H.Q. Northern Russia Expeditionary Force to Director of Military Operations, War Office, London, 9 December 1918.

11 NA WO32/10776, *loc. cit.*

12 NA WO106/45, History of Intelligence (B), British Expeditionary Force, France. From January 1917 to April 1919, by Colonel R.J. Drake, p. 10.

13 See NA WO33/977A, WO106/1318 and WO33/962, No. 162. Note that in the latter two sources Cameron's initials are incorrectly given as 'A.D'.

14 BL, Papers of Douglas Young, Vol. V, Add. Mss 61848.

15 *The Times*, 13 and 19 December 1918.

Chapter XV: Confidence Tricks

1 Chicherin, *op. cit.*, pp. 29–30.

2 NA FO175/1, Lindley to Prodrome, No. 03402, p. 886.

3 *Ibid.*, p. 750.

4 BL, Papers of Douglas Young, Vol. I, Add. Mss 61844.

5 BL, Papers of Douglas Young, *Memorandum*, Vol. V, Add. Mss 61848.

6 Goldsmith, *loc. cit.*, p. 79.

7 *Ibid.*, p. 79.

8 *Ibid.*, pp. 79–80.

9 NA PRO30/30/15, No. 273, Colonel Tallents (Reval), 2 October 1919. The underlining is as appears in the original document.

10 BL, Keyes Collection, F131/12(a), Memorandum on Russia in View of Peace: A Prospectus with Conclusions, 1 May 1919, Political Intelligence Department, Foreign Office, Russia/024.

11 NA FO175/1, Politico-military situation & future policy, Archangel, 20 May 1919, p. 686.

12 NA PRO30/30/15, Cypher telegram to Sir J. Jordan (Peking), No. 392, 1 September 1919.

13 Esher to Hankey, 7 April 1919, Esher, *Journals*, Vol. IV, pp. 228–30, cited in Roskill, *op. cit.*, Vol. II, p. 77.

14 NA WO32/5677, Reinforcements for Northern Russia, 8 February 1919.
15 Roskill, *op. cit.*, Vol. II, p. 47.
16 NA ADM223/637, CX 063671, 8651, Christiania, From N.63, No. 01746, 10 January 1919.
17 NA FO371/3962.
18 *Ibid.*, 11 January 1919.
19 *Ibid.*, Despatch No. 5, 17 January 1919.
20 Briefing from Cabinet Office on Sydney Reilly personal file, CX 2616, Diary of Sydney Reilly, entry for 22 January 1919.
21 Briefing from Cabinet Office on Sydney Reilly personal file, CX 2616.
22 NLS, Steel-Maitland Papers, GD193/328, (6) Yaroshinsky (1919).
23 *Ibid.*
24 *Ibid.*
25 *Ibid.*
26 Roskill, *op. cit.*, p. 110.
27 Brook-Shepherd, *op. cit.*, pp. 136–8.
28 Dukes, *op. cit.*, p. 193.
29 *Ibid.*, p. 181.
30 G. Leggett, *The Cheka: Lenin's Political Police*, p. 285.
31 SHAT, 17N 622, French Military Mission Ekaterinburg Group, No. 1529, 27 March 1919.
32 Dukes, *op. cit.*, pp. 231–2.
33 C. Andrew, *Secret Service: The Making of the British Intelligence Community*, p. 321.
34 Dukes, *op. cit.*, p. 253.
35 Leggett, *op. cit.*, p. 285.
36 *Ibid.*, p. 286.
37 *Ibid.*, pp. 285–6.
38 *Ibid.*, p. 286.
39 CCC, Denniston Papers, DENN 1/4.

Chapter XVI: Epilogue

1 Cook, *op. cit.*, pp. 246–7.
2 NA FO1093/61 Foreign Secret Service Accounts 1916–1920: pensions, Missions and Consulates, Espionage Bureau and special allowances and grants.
3 NA WO106/1166, Allied policy in Russia consequent on the German collapse with special reference to the dispositions of the Allied Forces in the North, 13 October 1918.
4 *Ibid.*
5 BL Keyes Papers, *loc. cit.*, Mss Eur F131/12(a), Memorandum by General Keyes to Earl [*sic* Marquess] Curzon, 26 April 1920.
6 For the letter to Byrne see NA CAB27/189/4; for the *Report on Visit of the British Military Mission to the Volunteer Army under General Denikin in South Russia. November–December, 1918*, see LHCMA, Papers of General Sir Frederick Poole.
7 Admiral Sir William James, *The Eyes of the Navy*, p. 177. NA FO371/3283, p. 107, Foreign Office Minutes on S.E. Russia, G.R. Clerk, 4 January 1918.

Source List

◄o►

Primary Sources

British Library

Balfour Papers Correspondence with David Lloyd George Add. Mss 49692
Cecil Papers Add. Mss 51076
Keyes Collection Mss Eur F131
Papers of Douglas Young Add. Mss 61844 – 61855
Political and Secret Department, L/PS/11/135–141

Churchill College Archives Centre, University of Cambridge

William F. Clarke's Papers
Denniston Papers
Hankey Papers
Papers of Admiral Hall

House of Lords Record Office

Diary of Sir Robert Bruce Lockhart

Imperial War Museum

Department of Documents
Diary of Lieutenant-Colonel A.G. Burn
Papers of Major Ambrose E. Sturdy
Papers of A.E. Thompson
Diaries of Field-Marshal Sir Henry Wilson

Department of Sound Records
Interview with E.J. Furlong 015/08/04

Intelligence Corps Museum, Ashford*

*This museum has since been combined into the Defence Intelligence Museum, Chicksands. However, when I studied the papers they were still at Ashford.
Papers of Lieutenant M.R.K. Burge

Liddell Hart Centre for Military Archives, King's College, London

Papers of General Sir Frederick Poole

National Archives, Kew, Surrey

Many of the collections in the National Archives hold hundreds, sometimes thousands of pieces. The Class Marks only are given here except where certain files are of particular importance or, more rarely, when only one file needed to be consulted.
ADM53/45508
ADM196/47 (Captain F.N.A. Cromie's Personal Service Record.
ADM137/482, 883, 963, 1613, 1642, 1663, 1707, 1708, 1714–1716, 1719, 4466, 4467, 4471, 4640, 4641, 4642–4647, 4476, 4832, 7290
ADM223/637, 669, 735, 743, 758, 759, 773
Pieces 758 & 759 contain the Director of Naval Intelligence's Secret & Special Telegrams respectively.
ADM233/1
BT61/3/10
CAB1/25
CAB21/96
CAB23/4–7
CAB24/40, 45–8, 52
CAB27/189/2–20.
CAB45/201
FO95/802
FO175/1–29 Papers of the British Consulate, Archangel.
FO176/1
FO262/1324, 1331

FO263/26
FO337/87, 88
FO366/787
FO369/1017
FO371/2863, 2881–2885, 2942–3365, 3368, 3962
FO395/184
FO566/1196–1199
FO800/25, 196–198
FO1093/26, 54, 55, 56, 57, 66, 75, 76, 104
GFM6/128, 139, 140
GFM33/2212, 2655, 3378
HO45
HO144/1667/300707
HW3/1, 8
HW6
HW7/3, 18, 22
HW7/3 contains Volume II of Birch & Clarke's *A Contribution to the History of German Naval Warfare 1914–1918*
HW12/1, 2
PRO30/30 Milner Papers
WO32/5215, 5643, 5669, 5677, 10776, 21671
WO33/962, 977A
WO73/108, 109
WO95/4960, 5001
WO106/45, 60, 315, 606, 679–684, 916, 1098, 1147–1159, 1166, 1190, 1218, 1219, 1220, 1232, 1232, 1233, 1318, 1510, 1512, 1513,
WO157/1212–1218
WO158/712–715, 748, 965
WO160/14, 16, 17
WO339/136290
WO374/19738

National Archives of Scotland, Edinburgh

Papers of Sir Arthur Steel-Maitland

Naval Historical Section, Portsmouth Dockyard

Volume III of Birch & Clarke's *A Contribution to the History of German Naval Warfare 1914–1918 in 3 Volumes*
(At the time of writing this was due to be transferred to the National Archives and has probably reached there since.)

Royal Naval Submarine Museum, Gosport, Hampshire

Letters on Russian Affairs from Captain F.N.A. Cromie A1990/73

Service Historique De L'Armée De Terre, Château de Vincennes, France

The French Military Archives are arranged by person, subject and place. The arrangement of the files below reflects this, thus particular groupings remain together, irrespective of numerical order.
5N 174, 175, 176, 177, 178, 179, 180, 181
6N 53
6N 146, 230
7N 628
7N 679
7N 828
7N 1448
16N 1200
16N 2960, 2961, 2962, 2963
16N 3008
16N 3030
17N 573, 574
17N 679
17N 796
17N 828

Select Bibliography

—◄o►—

Agar, A. *Baltic Episode: a classic of secret service in Russian waters*, London, 1983.
—— *Footprints in the Sea*, London, 1959.
Andrew, C. *Secret Service: The Making of the British Intelligence Community*, London, 1986.
Baerlein, H. *The March of the Seventy Thousand*, London, 1926.
Bailey, F.M. *Mission to Tashkent*, London, 1946.
Bainton, R. *Honoured by Strangers: the life of Captain Francis Cromie CB, DSO, RN*, Shrewsbury, 2002.
Balfour, Earl of, *Chapters of Autobiography*, London, 1930.
—— *Essays: Speculative and Political*, London, 1920.
Barker, A.J. *The Neglected War: Mesopotamia 1914–1918*, London, 1967.
Baumgart, W. *Von Brest-Litovsk Zur Deutschen Novemberrevolution Auf den Aufzeichnungen von Alfons Pacquet, Wilhelm Groener, Albert Hopman*, Göttingen, 1971.
Beaverbrook, Lord, *Men and Power 1917–1918*, London, 1956.
Beesly, P. *Room 40: British Naval Intelligence 1914–1918*, London, 1982.
Birse, A.H. *Memoirs of an Interpreter*, London, 1967.
Blacker, L.V.S. *On Secret Patrol in High Asia*, London, 1922.
Brook-Shepherd, G. *The Iron Maze*, London, 1999.
—— *The Last Empress: The Life and Times of Zita of Austria-Hungary 1892–1989*, London, 1991.
—— *The Last Habsburg*, London, 1968.
Browder, & Kerensky, A.F. *The Russian Provisional Government 1917 Documents*, 3 Vols., Stanford, Ca., 1961.
Buchan, J. *Memory Hold The Door*, London, 1984.

Callwell, Maj.-Gen. C. E. *Field-Marshal Sir Henry Wilson Bart., GCB, DSO. His Life and Diaries*, 2 vols, London, 1927.

Carr, E.H. *History of Soviet Russia: The Bolshevik Revolution 1917–1923*, 3 vols, London, 1950–3.

Chambers, F.P. *The War Behind The War 1914–1918*, London, 1939.

Chicherin, G.V. *Two Years of Foreign Policy*, New York, 1920.

Connaughton, R.M. *The Republic of the Ushakovka: Admiral Kolchak and the Allied Intervention in Siberia 1918–1920*, London, 1990.

Constant, S. *Foxy Ferdinand: Tsar of Bulgaria*, London, 1979.

Cook, A. *Ace of Spies: The True Story of Sydney Reilly*, Stroud, 2004.

Dallas, G. & Gill, D. *The Unknown Army: Mutinies in the British Army in World War I*, London, 1985.

Deacon, R. *A History of the British Secret Service*, London, 1969.

——— *A History of the Russian Secret Service*, London, 1972.

Debo, R.K. *Revolution and Survival: The Foreign Policy of Soviet Russia 1917–1918*, Liverpool, 1979.

——— 'Lockhart Plot or Dzerzhinsky Plot', in *Journal of Modern History*, Vol. XLIII, pp.413–39, 1971.

Dobson, C. & Miller, J. *The Day We Almost Bombed Moscow: The Allied War in Russia 1918–1920*, London, 1986.

Dunsterville, L.C. *The Adventures of Dunsterforce (British mission to Tiflis), etc.*, London, 1920.

Dukes, Sir Paul, *Secret Agent 'ST25': Adventure and Romance in the Secret Intelligence Service in Red Russia 1917–1920*, London, 1938.

Ellis, C.H. *The Transcaspian Episode 1918–1919*, London, 1963.

Figes, O. *A People's Tragedy: The Russian Revolution 1891–1924*, London, 1996.

Fischer, F. *Germany's Aims in the First World War*, London, 1967.

——— *World Power or Decline: The Controversy Over Germany's Aims in the First World War*, London, 1975.

Fleming, P. *The Fate of Admiral Kolchak*, London, 1963.

Freund, G. *Unholy Alliance: Russian-German Relations from the Treaty of Brest-Litovsk to the Treaty of Berlin*, London, 1957.

Gankin, O.H. & Fisher, H. H. *The Bolsheviks and the World War*, Stanford, 1940.

Gerhardie, W. *Memoirs of a Polyglot*, London, 1973.

Guinn, P. *British Strategy and Politics 1914 to 1918*, London, 1965.

Gardo, L. *Cossack Fury: The Experiences of a Woman Soldier* with the White Russians, London, 1938.

Hankey, Lord, *The Supreme Command 1914–1918*, 2 vols, London, 1961.

Helfferich, Staatsminister Dr. *Die Friedennsbemuhungen im Weltkrieg*, Berlin, 1919.

Hill, G. *Go Spy The Land: Being the adventures of I.K.8 of the British Secret Service*, London, 1932.

Hoffmann, Maj.-Gen. M. *War Diaries & Other Papers*, London, 1929.

Hopkirk, P. *On Secret Service East of Constantinople*, London, 1994.

—— *Setting the East Ablaze*, London, 1984.

—— *The Great Game: On Secret Service in High Asia*, London, 1990.

Jackson, R. *At War with the Bolsheviks: The Allied Intervention into Russia*, London, 1972.

James, Admiral Sir William, *The Eyes of the Navy: A Biographical Study of Admiral Sir Reginald Hall*, London, 1956.

Jones, G. & Trebilcock, C. 'Russian Industry and British Business 1910–1930', in *Journal of European Economic History*, Vol. XI, 1982.

Judd, A. *The Quest For C: Mansfield Cumming and the Founding of the Secret Service*, London, 1999.

Kerensky, A.F. *The Catastrophe: Kerensky's own story of the Russian Revolution*, New York, 1927.

Leggett, G. *The Cheka: Lenin's Political Police*, Oxford, 1981.

Lenin, V.I. *Selected Works*, 12 vols., London, 1936–8.

Lettow-Vorbeck, Generalmajor von (ed.), *Die Weltkriegspionage (Original SpionageWerk)*, Munich, 1931.

Lloyd George, D. *War Memoirs*, 2 vols, London, n.d. (c.1938).

Lockhart, R.B. *Comes The Reckoning*, London, 1947.

—— *Memoirs of a British Agent*, London, 2003.

Loukomsky, General, *Memoirs of the Russian Revolution*, Westport, CT, 1975.

Luckett, R. *The White Generals*, London, 1971.

Ludendorff, E. *My War Memories, 1914–1918*, London, n.d.

MacDonell, R. *And Nothing Long*, London, 1938.

Manderstam, Major L.H. (with Heron, R.) *From the Red Army to SOE*, London, 1985.

Masaryk, T.G. *The Making of a State: Memories and Observations 1914–1918*, London, 1927.

Mawdsley, E. *The Russian Civil War*, Winchester, MA, 1987.

Meinertzhagen, R. *Army Diary 1899–1926*, Edinburgh & London, 1960.

Milner, Lord, *The Nation and The Empire*, London, 1998.

Nabokoff, C. *The Ordeal of a Diplomat*, London, 1921.

Nalder, Maj.-Gen. R.F.H. *The Royal Corps of Signals: A History of its Antecedents and Development*, London, 1958.

Nazaroff, P. *Hunted Through Central Asia*, Oxford, 1993.

Neilson, K. '"Joy Rides"?: British Intelligence and Propaganda in Russia, 1914–1917', in *Historical Journal*, Vol. XXIV, 1981, pp. 885–906.

—— *Strategy and Supply: The Anglo-Russian Alliance 1914–1917*, London, 1984.

Niessel, Général, *Le Triomphe Des Bolcheviks et la Paix De Brest-Litovsk: Souvenirs 1917–1918*, Paris, 1940.

Nikitine, B.V. *The Fatal Years: Revelations on a Chapter of Underground History*, London, 1938.

Occleshaw, M. *Armour Against Fate: British Military Intelligence in The First World War*, London, 1989.

—— *The Romanov Conspiracies: The Romanovs and the House of Windsor*, London, 1993.

Official

—— *The Official History of the War: Operations in Persia 1914–1919* – F.J. Moberley, London, 1929.

—— *The Official History of the War: Naval Operations*, Vol. V – Sir Henry Newbolt, London, 1931.

—— *The Army List*, various edns.

—— *The Foreign Office List*, various edns.

—— *The Indian Army List*, various edns.

—— *The Navy List*, various edns.

—— *The War Office List*, various edns.

—— *The War Office List and Administrative Directory for the British Army 1919*.

—— *Papers Relating to the Foreign Relations of the United States, 1918, Russia* Vol. I, II, III, Washington, DC, 1931, 1932.

Pipes, R. *The Russian Revolution*, New York, 1990.

—— (ed.) *The Unknown Lenin: From the Secret Archive*, New Haven & London, 1996.

Radkey, O.H. *The Election to the Russian Constituent Assembly of 1917*, Harvard, 1950.

Radzinsky, E. *The Last Tsar: The Life and Death of Nicholas II*, London, 1992.

Rhodes, C.J. *The Last Will and Testament of Cecil Rhodes* (ed. W.T. Stead), 1902.

Riezler, K. *Tagebucher – Aufsatze – Dokumente. Eingeleiter und herausgaben von Karl Dietrich Erdmann*, Göttingen, 1972.

Roberts, B. *Cecil Rhodes: Flawed Colossus*, London, 1987.

Rotberg, R.I. *Cecil Rhodes and the Pursuit of Power*, New York, 1988.

Rodzyanko, P. *Tattered Banners*, London, 1939.

Roskill, S. *Hankey: Man of Secrets*, 3 vols, London, 1970–4.

Sadoul, J. *Notes sur la Révolution bolchevique, octobre 1917–janvier 1919*, Paris, 1971.

Seymour, C. (arranged by), *The Intimate Papers of Colonel House*, 4 vols, Boston & New York, 1926–8.

Sheridan, C. *Russian Portraits*, London, 1921.

Spence, R.B. *Boris Savinkov: Renegade on the Left*, New York, 1991.

Steinberg, M.D & Khrustalev, V.M. *The Fall of the Romanovs*, London, 1995.

Stone, N. *The Eastern Front 1914–1917*, London, 1975.

Sutton, A.C. *Wall Street and the Bolshevik Revolution*, New York, 1974.

Swinson, A.H. *Beyond the Frontiers: The biography of Colonel F.M. Bailey, explorer and special agent*, London, 1971.

Teague-Jones, R. alias Ronald Sinclair, *The Spy Who Disappeared: Diary of a Secret Mission to Russian Central Asia in 1918* (ed. P. Hopkirk), London, 1990.

The Times (various edns).

Ullman, R.H. *Anglo-Soviet Relations 1917–1921*, 3 vols, London, 1961–72.

Voigt, B. *Cecil Rhodes Der Lebenstraum eines Briten*, Potsdam, 1939.

Weber, F. *Eagles on the Crescent: Germany, Austria and the Diplomacy of the Turkish Alliance, 1914–1918*, New York, 1970.

Wheeler-Bennett, Sir John, *Brest-Litovsk: The Forgotten Peace March 1918*, London, 1938.

Who Was Who (various edns).

Wildman, A.K. *The End of the Russian Imperial Army*, 2 vols, Princeton, NJ, 1980 & 1987.

Wilson, Lieutenant-Colonel Sir Arnold T. *Loyalties Mesopotamia 1914–1917: a personal and historical record*, London, 1930.

Winstone, H.V.F. *The Illicit Adventure: the story of political and military Intelligence in the Middle East from 1898 to 1926*, London, 1982.

Woodruff, P. *The Men Who Ruled India – The Guardians*, London, 1954.

—— *The Men Who Ruled India – The Founders*, London, 1953.

Wrench, J.E. *Geoffrey Dawson and our Times*, London, 1955.

Yeats-Brown, Major F.C.C. *The Star and Crescent: The Story of the 17th Cavalry*, printed privately by the Pioneer Press, Allahabad, n.d.

Young, K. (ed.), *The Diaries of Sir Robert Bruce Lockhart 1915–1938*, London, 1973.

Zeman, Z.A.B. *A Diplomatic History of the First World War*, London, 1971.

—— (ed.) *Germany and the Revolution in Russia 1915–1918: Documents from the Archives of the German Foreign Ministry*, London, 1958.

Zeman, Z.A.B. & Scharlau, W.B. *The Merchant of Revolution: The Life of Alexander Israel Helphand (Parvus) 1867–1924*, London, 1965.

Index

—◀◦▶—